A Student Handbook to the Plays of Tennessee Williams

The Glass Menagerie
A Streetcar Named Desire
Cat on a Hot Tin Roof
Sweet Bird of Youth

STEPHEN J. BOTTOMS

PATRICIA HERN AND MICHAEL HOOPER

PHILIP C. KOLIN

KATHERINE WEISS

Edited by
KATHERINE WEISS

B L O O M S B U R Y
LONDON · NEW DELHI · NEW YORK · SYDNEY

Bloomsbury Methuen Drama

An imprint of Bloomsbury Publishing Plc

50 Bedford Square	1385 Broadway
London	New York
WC1B 3DP	NY 10018
UK	USA

www.bloomsbury.com

Bloomsbury is a registered trade mark of Bloomsbury Publishing Plc

© Bloomsbury Methuen Drama, 2014

Material from the present edition was previously published in the Methuen Drama
Student Edition series as follows: Plot, Commentary, Notes, Further Reading,
Questions for Further Study previously published in *The Glass Menagerie*,
A Streetcar Named Desire, *Cat on a Hot Tin Roof* and *Sweet Bird of Youth*.
Commentary and notes copyright *The Glass Menagerie* © 2010 by Bloomsbury
Methuen Drama, Commentary and notes copyright *A Streetcar Named Desire*
© 2009 by Bloomsbury Methuen Drama, Commentary and notes copyright
Cat on a Hot Tin Roof © 2010 by Bloomsbury Methuen Drama, Commentary and
notes copyright *Sweet Bird of Youth* © 2010 by Bloomsbury Methuen Drama.

British Library Cataloguing-in-Publication Data
A catalogue record for this book is available from the British Library.

ISBN: HB: 978-1-4725-2182-8
PB: 978-1-4725-2186-6
ePDF: 978-1-4081-5179-2
ePub: 978-1-4725-3244-2

Library of Congress Cataloging-in-Publication Data
A catalog record for this book is available from the Library of Congress.

Typeset by Newgen Knowledge Works (P) Ltd., Chennai, India
Printed and bound in India

A Student Handbook to the
Plays of Tennessee Williams

Contents

Introduction

Speaking in a slow southern drawl, an aged Tennessee Williams eloquently told interviewer Bill Boggs, 'I have never cared whether I shocked people. People who are shocked by the truth are not deserving of the truth. And the truth is something you need to deserve.' This carefully crafted statement by a man whose plays so often shocked and intrigued audiences for his representation of taboo subjects seems to fly in the face of the imaginary worlds so many of his characters create. It is tempting to align the illusions that the Wingfields of *The Glass Menagerie*, Blanche DuBois of *A Streetcar Named Desire*, Margaret and Brick Pollitt of *Cat on a Hot Tin Roof* and Chance Wayne and Alexandra Del Lago of *Sweet Bird of Youth* create with lies. Although they create fantasies to survive their brutal realities and the past disappointments haunting them, his characters are not liars. It is Laura, Amanda and Tom (not Jim), Blanche (not Stanley), Maggie (not Sister Woman), and Chance and Del Lago (not Tom Junior), whom audiences empathise with, perhaps even living with them in those make-believe worlds. Williams, himself, has more in common with his frail characters than, for example, Stanley or Mitch in *Streetcar*, who tear down the Chinese lanterns to bring ugly realities to light. He is, as C. W. Bigsby argues, 'the protagonist of all his plays',[1] fleeing his own guilt and trauma, and in doing so, is a truer, more vulnerable creature. In his magical dramatic works, Williams gives voice to the weak by having them create imaginary worlds that are not untruthful. The illusions belonging to his characters, after all, do not offer the escape they desire. Their pasts, as did Williams's, haunt their imagination.

As children, Williams and his sister Rose lived on their imagination. Williams recalled that their fantasies were a form of escape, especially after having moved with his family to St Louis, Missouri, where Williams and Rose felt like fugitives.[2] The twelve-year-old Williams began to channel his imagination into writing essays, short stories and poetry. At the age of 16, still called Tom, he won his first prize placing third in a literary contest for his essay, 'Can a Wife Be a Good Sport?'; the prize was the publication of the work. In these early years, his essays, stories and plays, although the flawed work of an adolescent writer, were already unique and poetic. But the early successes he had did not smooth the way for Williams to become a professional writer. The journey entailed changing his name to Tennessee, leaving college prematurely (years later he resumed his education at another university), working in a shoe warehouse, failing to be admitted into the Work Progress Administration (WPA) and being fired from the Metro-Goldwyn-Mayer (MGM) movie studio, before Williams became America's leading playwright, shocking his critics and drawing large crowds to his plays.

Despite some success with writing leftist plays for a St Louis theatre company called the Mummers and winning literary awards including the National Institute for Arts and Letters Award for his play *Battle of Angels*, it was not until the success of *The Glass Menagerie* in 1945 that Williams's talent was confirmed, opening stage doors for him. On Broadway, *Menagerie* ran for 561 performances and won several accolades, including the New York Critics' Circle Award. The years 1945 to 1963 were productive and successful for Williams. Two years after the success of *Menagerie*, Williams's *A Streetcar Named Desire* opened, running for an incredible 855 performances and winning Williams more awards, including the Pulitzer Prize for drama. With *Streetcar*, Williams dared to break more taboos than any other serious playwright of his time, and in doing so, he created Blanche DuBois, one of the most memorable female protagonists in American drama. Blanche is a figure that to this day inspires directors. Woody Allen's 2013 film, *Blue Jasmine*, starring Cate Blanchett, who played Blanche in the 2009 Sydney Theatre Company and Brooklyn Academy of Music production of *Streetcar*, is a less violent rewriting of Williams's masterpiece. In 1955, Williams's *Cat on a Hot Tin Roof* drew the praise of critics and audiences, alike, running for 694 performances. This remarkable play won Williams his second Pulitzer Prize. Breaking social barriers, the curtain rises, revealing a bedroom occupied by Maggie and Brick. During this opening act, the audience learns of their troubled marriage. In a daring move, Williams also incorporates another off-stage homosexual couple, but unlike the condemnation Blanche's husband, Allan Grey, receives, Big Daddy accepts the love that Jack Straw and Peter Ochello shared. Like *Cat*, *Sweet Bird of Youth* confronts the audience with their desire to look into the bedrooms of others. The voyeuristic pleasure gained in *Cat* and *Sweet Bird* resembles that of the pleasure one gains from watching Alfred Hitchcock's 1954 classic film, *Rear Window*. Wanting to gawk at the dirty laundry of others, crowds flocked to the play when it debuted in 1959 even though New York theatre critics received the play coolly. *Sweet Bird* ran for 375 performances.

Williams's plays reveal his preoccupation with the South of his early childhood. Although Tennessee loved the South and admired much about the gentility he associated with it, the South he portrays in his plays is far from idyllic. It is a place where the outsider, whether a man of colour, a homosexual, a sex worker or a promiscuous woman can lose his or her life through cruelty, violence or neglect. In *A Streetcar*

Named Desire, Stella tells her husband Stanley that Blanche has been destroyed by her marriage to a 'degenerate' who, when caught with a lover, committed suicide. Later, Blanche suffers a mental breakdown after losing Mitch and being raped by Stanley. In *Sweet Bird of Youth*, the fate of Chance Wayne, a gigolo, is paralleled to that of a black man who, before the play begins, has been castrated for allegedly being with a white woman. The Southern small towns in Williams's plays are bigoted, dangerous spaces. The Mississippi of Williams's youth was wrought with racism. When not set in the Deep South, Williams's plays include traces of his family's move to St Louis, Missouri, where the young Tom felt overwhelmed by feelings of being uprooted. The move, for Williams, was more than a disorienting relocation. It meant living in a small cramped space, cut off from his extended family. While the small Southern towns in Williams's plays represent danger, the Midwest urban spaces in his plays, as seen in *Menagerie*, are suffocating while simultaneously being isolating.

Other biographical elements that appear in Williams's plays are his attempts to cope with his overbearing mother, his distant and often cruel father, his homosexuality and his sister's mental illness, which eventually led to her lobotomy. Being taunted by his father as a 'sissy' was a life event that became symbolic for Williams. He utilises memories of his family to explore the weak when faced with the dominant and often unjust masses. In *Cat*'s conclusion, Maggie says it best when she finds a way to entice her husband to sleep with her, 'Oh, you weak people, you weak, beautiful people!'[3] This statement is present in all Williams's plays. Those who the dominant in society see as weak, frail and sick are to him beautiful people. Those who are considered strong in his plays are often violent and crude. They lack the beauty of those who are fragile like Laura with her glass unicorn. But what we see repeatedly in his plays is also the destruction of beauty. The weak, beautiful people of his plays are abandoned (as is Laura), raped (as is Blanche), crippled (as are Laura and Brick), and castrated (as is Chance). The weak, too, are always alone even when accompanied by others. They are lonely, as was Williams. Having been in a committed relationship with Frank Merlo from 1947 to 1963, Williams suffered greatly when Merlo died, turning once again to alcohol and drugs to fight off his loneliness. Ultimately, however, he died alone in a prestigious New York hotel room.

The events that cast the longest shadow on Williams were the institutionalisation and lobotomy of his sister, Rose. While studying playwriting at the University of Iowa in 1937, Williams learned that his sister's mental illness had worsened and that his parents had her sent away. Six years later, they agreed to the procedure which transformed Rose into a shadow of what she once was. Williams and his sister were very close; the sister, who was just three years older than Williams, shared her thoughts and imagination with him. The figure of a crippled or mentally disturbed woman who would shatter the world of another appears in many of Williams's plays. His first Broadway success, *The Glass Menagerie*, is a ground-breaking memory play, in which Tom Wingfield, a thinly disguised Tennessee, remembers his life in a cramped St Louis apartment with his sister Laura and overbearing mother Amanda. Throughout the work, as Stephen Bottoms reveals in his commentary, it becomes apparent that Williams has drawn heavily on his life. Regardless of the biographical material that arises in his drama, Williams's plays nonetheless do not function solely on an autobiographical level as the commentators of this book assert. Bottoms reminds us that 'if it is true that all of his work is in some way autobiographical, it is equally true that none of it is'. Although Laura Wingfield in *Menagerie* and Blanche DuBois in *Streetcar* are images of Rose, Williams does not give us mere autobiography. He is writing about the South, loneliness, the enemy called time, the falsehood called the American dream or Cinderella Story and the difficulty of flight, among other topics.

The chapters that follow provide a thorough commentary on four of Williams's most successful plays, *The Glass Menagerie*, *A Streetcar Named Desire*, *Cat on a Hot Tin Roof* and *Sweet Bird of Youth*. Stephen Bottoms discusses Williams's delicate balance between fact and fiction in *The Glass Menagerie*. Bottoms makes a case for reading and seeing *Menagerie* beyond Williams's private guilt, arguing that Williams's 'theatrical magic' lies in his ability to change the time of the events that deeply affected him in order to incorporate a political dimension to his work. Like Matthew Roudané who argues that 'For Williams, the personal insight and private doubts . . . outline the political concerns and moral anxieties of a nation whose faith in the future, though ever present, seems as indeterminate as the troubled heroes of Williams'[s] theatre',[4] Bottoms invites us to see the play as a reflection of 1930s America and its relation to the global world. Bottoms points out by drawing on his own production of the play at the University of Glasgow in Scotland, in which he executed Williams's stage directions (dropped in its debut production) for screens projecting images and legends, that Williams 'avoids the usual mundane trappings of conventional stage realism . . . and instead arrives at a kind of heightened, intensified emotional reality through the play's use of tight focus and "sculptural" stillness'. Using these poetic techniques, Williams takes the play out of the realm of realism and thereby elevates the play beyond his own personal trauma.

Like Bottoms, Patricia Hern and Michael Hooper recognise the importance of following the traces of biographical material in *A Streetcar Named Desire*, and like Bottoms, they do so to explore Williams's exploitation of the biographical to reveal deeper concerns with America. In their commentary, Hern and Hooper argue that *Streetcar* weaves together many people Williams knew and in doing so he presents his audience with a truly American context. Blanche and Stanley both represent 1940s America. Blanche, the fading Southern belle, is found in American classics, including the immensely popular novel, turned film, *Gone with the Wind*. Indeed, Williams repeatedly draws on Margaret Mitchell's iconic novel and film. In *Menagerie*, Amanda tries to sell magazine subscriptions, claiming that the new serial in it is a '*Gone with the Wind* of the post-World-War generation!'[5] And, Chance Wayne greets Miss Lucy of *Sweet Bird* by comparing her to Scarlett O'Hara, the protagonist of *Gone with the Wind*. While Blanche represents the old South, Stanley represents the 'new America, an immigrant, a man of the city'. For Hern and Hooper, then, the tension in the play goes beyond the biographical; its tension comes from the clashes between an old, dying, but beautiful dream of the South (Belle Reve) and a new urban brutality of New Orleans. Throughout Williams's work these dichotomies are represented not merely in his characters, but also in his detail to space. The old, dying dream of America as a place of ample space, acres of land and large porches to receive gentlemen callers is often remembered, whereas the present reality is represented in the cramped apartments and crowded streets of an urban landscape. Interestingly, when Stanley discovers that Blanche prostituted herself after her beautiful dream slipped out of reach, he has no sympathy for her. Instead, he rapes her, perhaps as an attempt to conquer more territory in the new world.

In his commentary, Philip Kolin excavates *Cat on a Hot Tin Roof* to examine American history, the South and the politics of the 1950s. Undoing audience expectations of the romantic icons of Southern plantation literature (most notably Mitchell's *Gone with the Wind*), Williams peoples his Mississippi Delta plantation with, what Kolin's calls, a 'crass, menacing new South'. Kolin reminds us that the Pollitts swear, tell dirty jokes, wish each other dead and fight over the future ownership of the plantation. The vulgarity the Pollitts display is also found in Blanche at times albeit not as openly. While she attempts to present herself as refined, she reveals that it was 'epic fornications'[6] that lost Belle Reve, and her bigotry when referring to Stanley as a Pollock is painfully evident.

Cat, Kolin continues, also displays the fears and anxieties of the 1950s. On the one hand, Brick's fear of being associated with homosexuality is just one example of 1950s repression. Brick's dread of being labelled a homosexual goes beyond the fact that homosexuality was illegal in America, in 1955. Being identified as gay, for Kolin, symbolises 'a crisis in national identity politics'. Kolin points out that although some famous American political figures were secretly in loving homosexual relationships, the image projected outward was that of a hetero masculinity. The injured Brick, then, attempts to stave off rumours of being gay, as his buddy Skipper proved to be, by resorting to homophobic slurs, calling Peter Ochello and Jack Straw an 'ole pair of sisters'.[7] Ironically, despite crudely asserting his hetero masculinity with his obscene sexual suggestions and humour, it is Big Daddy, on the verge of losing his empire due to cancer, who speaks with understanding about the love between Straw and Ochello and homosexual desires. He understands the love that the two men had for one another – itself an echo of Williams and Frank Merlo's secret marriage of 16 years. On the other hand, Kolin shows how *Cat*'s motif of repression recalls the Red Scare. Gooper and Mae's whispering, eavesdropping and spying are reminiscent to the techniques used by the House on Un-American Activities Committee (HUAC). While not as outwardly political as his contemporary Arthur Miller, Tennessee Williams's concerns with political wars and witch-hunts are present in all of the plays included here: Tom in *Menagerie* references the devastation that occurred in the First World War and the Spanish Civil War; Stanley in *Streetcar* mentions the racist Louisiana governor and US State Senator, Huey Long; and *Sweet Bird*'s Boss Finely is one such corrupt and racist political figure. Williams's plays use the family structure, as Roudané and Bigsby note, to examine (albeit not solve) America's ugly politics.[8]

The last chapter examines the ways in which *Sweet Bird of Youth* reflects 1950s America. In his 1959 play which he struggled with and rewrote throughout the 1950s, Williams reveals the destruction of preaching hate. Hate is explicitly sermonised by Boss Finley's racist propaganda; he is a politician who claims to have been called upon by God to protect white women from non-whites. The preaching of hate is more subtly approached in this play in its reference to the Korean War, an event that has destroyed Chance. Although Chance and Del Lago call each other monster, the audience recognises them as being less monstrous than Boss Finley, his son Tom Junior or the war rhetoric that swayed men into battle. Chance's actions are desperate attempts to be someone.

In *Sweet Bird*, Williams also attacks the Cinderella story, a dream represented in many American realist novels of the nineteenth century and in the Hollywood dream. Chance ultimately is a dreamer, a man who desperately wants to be someone in an America full of monsters. In the process, he too has become a monster, resorting to blackmail and contributing to the corruption and rot of his ideal love, Heavenly. In his attack on Hollywood, Williams reveals that time is the enemy that threatens the success and livelihood of all the characters on stage: Boss lashes out at Miss Lucy because she reveals that he is growing too old to be a lover; Del Lago is in flight after her comeback which confirmed to her that she is growing too old to be a glamorous star; Heavenly is dried up, old before her time, because of her inability to bear children; and Chance is losing his golden hair which ultimately will limit his Hollywood possibilities as well as number his gigolo days. The ticking of the clock at the play's conclusion reminds the audience that they, too, will fall victim to time.

In the years that followed, Williams's plays failed to dazzle theatre critics and audiences. Most of his plays no longer were staged on Broadway and many of them received dismal reviews. What are missing from his plays of the late 1960s onwards are the tension and the need to express topics that were considered taboos. Homosexuality, promiscuity, racism and hate were not shocking anymore. The more open America became the less convincing writing about fugitives was. Despite this, his plays from 1945 to 1961 are still immensely popular, as is evident in the production histories and reviews commented on here. They have been labelled American classics. The topics that still scream out to us are that of ageing, loneliness and time's devastation. As such, the plays work best, ultimately, when the costumes and sets are not updated but instead reflect the time when the plays were written, and when they emphasise the eternal anxieties of growing old and being alone.

Regardless of the waning success of his later plays, Williams continued to write. In *Where I Live*, he provides insight as to why he did so. Quoting Williams, Christine Day writes that he kept writing 'not with any hope of making a living at it, but because I found no other means of expressing things that seemed to demand expression'.[9] Williams, though not always successful, was and remains an American stage artist. And, like another creature of loneliness, Samuel Beckett, he finds himself 'obligated to express'[10] that which may have seemed inexpressible and shocking. Like Beckett, Williams struggles to create out of the bareness of the Second World War, focusing on the weak and impotent. He, however, gives the weak a beauty Beckett does not and Eugene O'Neill cannot. Tennessee Williams's personal lyricism, while having lost some of its potency in the years after the death of his lover and with the increasing acceptance of the other in American society, keeps the ugly and brutal forces at bay.

Katherine Weiss

Notes

1 C. W. Bigsby, *A Critical Introduction to Twentieth-Century American Drama: Volume Two: Williams, Miller, Albee,* Cambridge: Cambridge University Press, 1984, 19.
2 Bigsby, *A Critical Introduction,* 21.
3 Tennessee Williams, *Cat on a Hot Tin Roof,* with commentary and notes by Philip C. Kolin, London: Methuen Drama, 2010, 115.
4 Matthew Roudané (ed.), *The Cambridge Companion to Tennessee Williams,* Cambridge: Cambridge University Press, 1997, 6.
5 *The Glass Menagerie* (with 'The Catastrophe of Success'), with commentary and notes by Stephen J. Bottoms, London: Methuen Drama, 2000, 20.
6 Tennessee Williams, *A Streetcar Named Desire,* with commentary and notes by Patricia Hern and Michael Hooper, London: Methuen Drama, 1984 reissued 2009, 22.
7 Williams, *Cat on a Hot Tin Roof,* 83.
8 See C. W. Bigsby, 'Entering *The Glass Menagerie*', in Roudané, *The Cambridge Companion,* 29–44 and Roudané (ed.), 'Introduction', in *The Cambridge Companion,* 6.
9 Tennessee Williams, *Where I Live: Selected Essays,* ed. Christine Day and Bob Woods, New York: New Directions, 1978, x.
10 Samuel Beckett, *Disjecta: Miscellaneous Writings and a Dramatic Fragment,* ed. Ruby Cohn, New York: Grove Press, 1984, 139.

Chronology of Tennessee Williams

Tennessee Williams: 1911–83

1908   Williams's sister, Rose Isabelle, is born on 19 November in Columbus, Mississippi.

1911   Thomas Lanier Williams III is born on 26 March in Columbus, Mississippi.

1911–18 Rose, Tom and their mother, Edwina Dakin Williams, live with Edwina's parents, the Reverend Walter Dakin, an Episcopal priest, and his wife Rosina Otte Dakin, chiefly in Clarksdale, Mississippi, while father Cornelius Coffin Williams works as a travelling salesman.

1918   Williams's younger brother, Walter Dakin, is born on 21 February; the Williams family moves to St Louis, Missouri, where father becomes a branch manager at the International Shoe Company.

1926   Owing to financial pressure, Williams's family moves to cramped apartment at 6554 Enright Avenue, in downmarket University City area of St Louis. After only one semester at Soldan High School, Williams transfers to University City High School.

1927   First publication, an essay, 'Can a Good Wife Be a Good Sport?', was published in *Smart Set*.

1928   Publishes the first story for which he is paid – 'The Vengeance of Nitrosis' – in *Weird Tales*. Goes on a European trip with his maternal grandfather.

1929   In September, Williams enters the University of Missouri and joins Alpha Tau Omega fraternity. In October the stock market crashes resulting in the Great Depression.

1932   Williams's father withdraws him from the University of Missouri. There are conflicting accounts as to whether Williams leaves university because of his family's financial difficulties or because he failed ROTC (Reserve Officers Training Course). Williams's father starts him as a clerk at the International Shoe Company, a job that Williams loathes.

1935   First production of Williams's one-act play, *Cairo! Shanghai! Bombay!*, by Memphis Garden Players, a group of amateur actors. Williams's family finally moves out of Enright Avenue apartment to a two-storey house on Pershing Avenue, thanks to improvements in economic climate.

1936   In January, Williams enrols at Washington University in St Louis and writes the one-act play *Twenty-Seven Wagons Full of Cotton.*

1937   Writes a full-length, leftist play, *Candles to the Sun*, about a coal-mine strike, staged by the Mummers, amateur group of actors, in St Louis. Rose is committed to Farmington (Missouri) State Mental Hospital; Williams is heartbroken and feels tremendous guilt.

1937–9   Studies playwriting at the University of Iowa with Edward Charles Mabie, nicknamed 'the Boss'; Mummers stage *Fugitive Kind*. Graduates from Iowa with a BA in English. Writes another leftist play, *Not about Nightingales*, about a prison riot in Pennsylvania. Becomes a vagabond, travelling to New Orleans where he possibly has his first homosexual experience in the French Quarter.

1939   Meets Audrey Wood, his agent for over 30 years. Signs his name Tennessee Williams for the first time in a short story 'Field of Blue Children' in *Story Magazine*. Receives a $100 prize in a competition organised by the Group Theatre (where Elia Kazan's wife, Molly Day Thatcher, is one of the readers) for his collection of one-act plays *American Blues*. Wins a grant of $1,000 from the Rockefeller Foundation.

1940   Studies playwriting with John Gassner and Erwin Piscator at the New School for Social Research. His first professional production of the play, *The Battle of Angels*, has a disastrous Boston tryout on 30 December and closes on 11 January 1941 after the City Council protests about its sexual content.

1941–2   Travels around the country, writing one-act plays, stories and poems; visits Key West for the first time; has the first of his four cataract operations. Collaborates on *You Touched Me!* with Donald Windham. Works on short stories, including 'Portrait of a Girl in Glass', later developed into *The Glass Menagerie*. Meets Jordan Massee, Sr, a model for Big Daddy.

1943   Works for Metro-Goldwyn-Mayer (MGM) on a screenplay *The Gentleman Caller* (later becomes *The Glass Menagerie*) but is fired after only six months. Rose has a prefrontal lobotomy, leaving her mentally challenged for life; the operation is referenced in *Suddenly Last Summer*.

1944   National Institute for Arts and Letters awards Williams $1,000 for *Battle of Angels*. Margo Jones, theatre founder and long-time friend, directs the one-act play *The Purification* at the Pasadena Playhouse in California. *The Glass Menagerie* premieres in Chicago on 26 December.

1945	After a successful run in Chicago, *The Glass Menagerie*, Williams's first big success, runs for 561 performances on Broadway, winning the New York Drama Critics' Circle Award, the Donaldson Award and the Sidney Howard Memorial Award. *You Touched Me!*, by Williams and Donald Windham, adapted from D. H. Lawrence's short story, opens on Broadway in September to tepid responses. He publishes 13 one-act plays in *Twenty-Seven Wagons Full of Cotton*.
1947	*A Streetcar Named Desire*, directed by Elia Kazan, opens on 3 December at the Barrymore Theatre on Broadway and runs for 855 performances, spawning 2 road companies. The play makes history by winning the Pulitzer Prize for Drama, Donaldson Award and New York Drama Critics' Circle Award (first play ever to win all three). Williams meets his long-time companion and lover Frank Merlo (1929–63), a US Navy veteran.
1948–9	British premiere of *Streetcar* directed by Laurence Olivier, starring wife Vivien Leigh. *One Arm and Other Stories*, a collection of sexually explicit stories, is published. *Summer and Smoke* opens on Broadway. British premiere of *The Glass Menagerie*, directed by John Gielgud, with Helen Hayes as Amanda.
1950	First (and worst according to Williams) film adaptation of *The Glass Menagerie* released by Warner Brothers. The novel *The Roman Spring of Mrs Stone* is published.
1951	*The Rose Tattoo* opens in New York for 306 performances. Warner Brothers releases film of *Streetcar*, also directed by Kazan and designed by Jo Mielziner; produced by Irene Selznick, former wife of David O. Selznik, producer of *Gone with the Wind*. *I Rise in Flames, Cried the Phoenix* published.
1952	*Streetcar* wins National Film Critics' Circle Award. Williams is elected to the National Institute of Arts and Letters. Publishes the story 'Three Players of a Summer Game', the genesis of *Cat on a Hot Tin Roof*.
1953	*Camino Real*, with gay characters and themes, opens on Broadway.
1954	*Hard Candy* (another collection of explicit fiction) is published. Works on drafts of *Cat on a Hot Tin Roof*. Kazan insists on major revisions.
1955	*Cat on a Hot Tin Roof* premieres on 24 March on Broadway and runs for 649 performances, winning Williams his second Pulitzer Prize and third New York Drama Critics' Circle Award; film of *The Rose Tattoo* released. Reverend Walter Dakin dies at the age of 97.

1956	*Baby Doll* screenplay condemned for sexual content by the Catholic Church. *Cat on a Hot Tin Roof* opens in Paris (16 December); it is banned in Ireland. First book of poetry, *In the Winter of Cities*, is published.
1957	*Orpheus Descending* (revision of *Battle of Angels*) closes in New York after 68 performances. Cornelius Coffin Williams dies.
1958	Film version of *Cat on a Hot Tin Roof* is released by MGM, directed and co-written by Richard Brooks; it is Williams's biggest box-office hit. *Suddenly Last Summer* opens Off-Broadway. British premiere of *Cat on a Hot Tin Roof* using Williams's original third act is staged at a private club because of ban by Lord Chamberlain.
1959	*Sweet Bird of Youth*, with antagonist Boss Finley, opens for 375 performances on Broadway. Screen version of *Suddenly Last Summer* is released.
1960	Williams's comedy *Period of Adjustment* opens in New York for 132 performances. Film of *Orpheus Descending*, set in a hellish Delta, is released under the title of *Fugitive Kind*.
1961	Williams's last Broadway success, *The Night of the Iguana*, wins the New York Drama Critics' Circle Award and runs for 316 performances. Film versions of *Summer and Smoke* and *The Roman Spring of Mrs Stone* come out.
1962	The first film version of *Sweet Bird of Youth*, directed by Richard Brooks and starring Paul Newman as Chance Wayne and Geraldine Page as Alexandra Del Lago, is released. The film version of *Period of Adjustment*, starring Jane Fonda, is released. *The Milk Train Doesn't Stop Here Anymore* opens at Spoleto Festival, Italy.
1963	*The Milk Train Doesn't Stop Here Anymore* opens on Broadway. Frank Merlo, Williams's long-term lover, dies of lung cancer.
1964	Film of *The Night of the Iguana* is released, starring Richard Burton as a drunken clergyman.
1965	First major revivals of *The Glass Menagerie* open in both New York and London. American production at Brooks Atkinson Theatre is highly acclaimed and runs for 175 performances with Maureen Stapleton as Amanda, George Grizzard as Tom, Piper Laurie as Laura. London revival at Theatre Royal, Haymarket.
1966	*Slapstick Tragedy* (*The Mutilated* and *The Gnadiges Fraulein*) closes after only seven performances. CBS television production of *The Glass Menagerie* airs.

1967   First version of *The Two-Character Play*, about a brother and sister, opens in London.

1968   *The Kingdom of Earth* opens in New York. Film version of *Milk Train*, retitled *Boom!*, is released. *The Seven Descents of Myrtle* (later titled *Kingdom of Earth*) opens on Broadway for 27 performances; the play contains graphic sex scene.

1969   *In the Bar of a Tokyo Hotel* premieres in New York for 23 performances. Williams is awarded the Gold Medal for Drama by American Academy of Arts and Letters. Williams is committed to psychiatric unit of Barnes Hospital, St Louis, 27–28 June. Stonewall (named after the gay bar) Riots erupt in New York City, marking the start of the Gay Liberation movement. Williams is baptised a Roman Catholic in Key West.

1970   *Dragon Country: A Book of Plays* is published. Williams appears on the *David Frost Show* and for the first time publicly admits his homosexuality.

1971   *Out Cry* (rewritten version of *The Two-Character Play*) opens in Chicago. Williams splits with his agent, Audrey Wood.

1972   *Small Craft Warnings* moves to Broadway for 200 performances; Williams plays the role of Doc, a drunken, disbarred physician – the only time he acts in a professional production of his plays. Williams wins National Theatre Conference Award.

1973   ABC television version of *The Glass Menagerie*, with Katharine Hepburn as Amanda, Sam Waterston as Tom, airs.

1974   *Eight Mortal Ladies: A Book of Stories* is published. *Cat on a Hot Tin Roof* opens at the American Shakespeare Festival Theatre, Stratford, CT, with Williams's final, new third act.

1975   Williams is given the Medal of Honor for Literature by the National Arts Club. *Memoirs* published, as well as a novel, *Moise and the World of Reason*. *Red Devil Battery Sign*, occasioned by Watergate, is staged in Boston and New York. First Broadway revival of *Cat on a Hot Tin Roof*. The Broadway revival of *Sweet Bird of Youth*, starring Irene Worth, opens at the Harkness Theatre.

1976   *Eccentricities of a Nightingale* (revision of *Summer and Smoke*) premieres in New York. *This is (An Entertainment)* premieres in San Francisco. Williams is president of the jury at the Cannes Film Festival.

1977   *Demolition Downtown* opens in London. *Vieux Carré* opens in New York, only to close after a mere 11 performances. Second book of poetry, *Androgyne, Mon Amour*, published. First televised *Cat on a Hot Tin Roof* airs.

1978   *A Lovely Sunday for Crève Coeur* opens in New York for 36 performances.

1979   Receives Presidential Arts Achievement Award.

1980   President Jimmy Carter presents Williams with Medal of Freedom. Edwina Dakin Williams dies at the age of 95. The poorly received *Clothes for a Summer Hotel*, about Zelda Fitzgerald's madness, opens on Broadway. Julie Haydon, *Menagerie*'s original Laura, plays Amanda in short-lived New York revival.

1981   *Something Cloudy, Something Clear* opens Off-Broadway; last of Williams's plays to be professionally produced while he was alive.

1983   Williams dies on 24 February in New York at the Hotel Elysée (Elysian Fields, the 'Land of the Happy Dead' in *Streetcar*) after choking on a medicine-bottle cap. Broadway revival of *The Glass Menagerie* opens with Jessica Tandy as Amanda. Runs 92 performances.

1984   Showtime (cable television) airs *Cat on a Hot Tin Roof*, reshown on PBS television in 1985.

1985   *Collected Stories* is published. London revival of *Menagerie* at Greenwich Theatre, with Constance Cummings as Amanda. Also on stage in London is the premiere of *Sweet Bird of Youth* at the Haymarket Theatre, directed by Harold Pinter and starring Lauren Bacall.

1987   Cineplex Odeon releases film version of *The Glass Menagerie*, directed by Paul Newman with Joanne Woodward as Amanda and John Malkovich as Tom.

1988   British revival of *Cat on a Hot Tin Roof*, directed by Howard Davies, uses Williams's original 1955 script, the first production of the play in Britain in 30 years.

1989   London revival of *Menagerie* at Young Vic, with Susannah York as Amanda.

1990   Davies directs *Cat on a Hot Tin Roof* for its Broadway revival.

1994   The London revival of *Sweet Bird of Youth* opens at the National Theatre. Roundabout Theatre mounts New York revival of *Menagerie*, with Julie Harris as Amanda and Calista Flockhart as Laura.

1995   Donmar Warehouse mounts acclaimed London revival of *Menagerie*, directed by Sam Mendes with Zoë Wanamaker as Amanda and Claire Skinner as Laura. Transfers to West End's Comedy Theatre after initial run.

1996   Rose Williams dies on 5 September at the age of 88.

1998   *Not about Nightingales* premieres at London's Royal National Theatre. Written in 1938, the play was rediscovered in the 1980s by Vanessa Redgrave. Corin Redgrave stars as warden Boss Whalen.

2004   Festival of Tennessee Williams Plays at the Kennedy Center.

2005   *Mister Paradise and Other One-Act Plays*, including 13 previously unpublished one-acts, is released.

2008   Dakin Williams dies on 20 May. *The Traveling Companion and Other Plays* (12 previously uncollected experimental plays) is published. First professional production of *Cat on a Hot Tin Roof* with a black cast on Broadway (to London, 2009).

A Note on Quotations from the Plays

Unless stated otherwise, all quotations from the four plays that follow are taken from the Student Editions published by Bloomsbury Methuen Drama, with page numbers from those editions given in parentheses.

The Glass Menagerie

commentary and notes by
STEPHEN J. BOTTOMS

Plot

The Glass Menagerie is divided into seven scenes. These are of uneven length: in production, the interval follows Scene Five, since Scenes Six and Seven are easily the longest in the play. The scenes are written in episodic form, which means that, rather than each scene simply leading directly on to the next in a single narrative trajectory, each scene (or 'episode') has its own internal narrative, largely self-contained in its action and themes. Of course, each also contributes to the development of an overarching plot, yet in several instances we are led to understand that long periods of time have elapsed between scenes: taken as a whole, the play's narrative is spread out across a large part of 1938, from winter to summer. Perhaps it is useful to think of the play as operating like a series of inter-related paintings, each one of which presents a key component in a much bigger narrative, and which together build up to create an impression – but perhaps not a conclusive understanding – of that 'whole story'. Williams shows us enough to give us a strong sense of the way that the Wingfield family operates (and indeed disintegrates), but also leaves much that is mysterious or uncertain. The reason for this approach is clear: could the 'whole story' of *any* family be told on stage in two hours?

Scene One (Opening Narration)

The play opens with a scene-setting narration from the storyteller character, Tom. He addresses the audience as if he knows he is standing in a theatre, in the same time and place as the audience, and asks us to imagine ourselves into the past, the 1930s of his youth. (When the play was first produced, in 1944, it was easy for audiences to imagine Tom as a real person talking about his own family history. More than fifty years later, Tom would have to be a very old man to exist in the audience's 'present time', so instead today he seems more like a mysterious chorus figure, standing outside of time itself.) Tom briefly sketches in 'the social background of the play', referring to the Great Depression and the economic problems then facing America, and also to the Civil War taking place in Spain (1936–9). His reference to Guernica, which alludes to the merciless aerial bombing of the Spanish town of that name in April 1937, implicitly locates the action of the play after that event. His reference to St Louis, on the end of a brief list of American cities (and with a slight pause after he has mentioned it), obliquely indicates the setting for the action which is to follow.

Having alluded to the real time and real place of the story, Tom then goes on to complicate matters by stressing that what we are about to see is *not* actually 'realistic' at all. We are not going to see a photographic reproduction of his life in the 1930s, but his life as he *remembers* it. We will view the action through the lens of Tom's self-confessed nostalgia, and this is going to affect everything from the lighting of the stage to the music we hear. By stressing the way that memory can play tricks on us, Tom is implicitly warning us that we should not necessarily take everything we see at face value. We have to understand that the events we are about to see are being depicted the way Tom remembers them, rather than as some straightforward, objective reality. For example, Tom's description of the 'larger-than-life-size photograph' of his absent father, which looms over the living-room setting, seems to suggest that the size of the image has grown artificially large in his memory – thereby reflecting the length of the shadow which the father's memory still casts over the characters in the play. Tom also lets it be known that he might at times wilfully distort or manipulate the facts (as he remembers them) for the sake of dramatic or poetic effect. Referring to the gentleman caller, he tells us unashamedly that 'I am using this character . . .'. The overall effect of this opening speech is double-edged: the audience is simultaneously drawn into Tom's memory-world and – thanks to such comments – set at something of a critical distance, left to puzzle over what might be 'real' and what might be distortion or invention.

Scene One (Amanda)

Having described his father's abrupt departure 'a long time ago', Tom ends his own narration rather abruptly and we move straight into a scene from his past. His mother, Amanda, calls him in for dinner. Seconds later, though, we seem to have jumped forward into the middle of the meal, and Amanda is berating Tom for eating too hastily. This stitch in time, coming after only three lines of regular dialogue, further underlines the point that what we are seeing is conditioned by Tom's memory of what is significant. This first episode in the play is, in effect, a portrait of Amanda, but we are seeing first the way Tom remembers Amanda – calling for him to hurry to the table, nagging him about the way he eats, telling him he smokes too much. Instantly she appears as a pressure and a burden *on* Tom.

As the scene develops, however, Amanda begins to talk about her own memories of *her* youth (or rather, Tom remembers her remembering). Now she begins to be fleshed out as a character in her own right. In some ways she seems quite comic, recalling a golden age of gentility in the Deep South which must surely be her own romanticisation of the past: do we really believe, for instance, that she once had seventeen gentlemen callers, or is that a statistic that is exaggerated a little further each time the story is told? Has she, likewise, romanticised the fates of her various old boyfriends (a drowning, a shooting, etc.) so that they now sound like events from some old melodrama? Amanda's memories further emphasise the theme of the past being unstable, and subject to reinvention, which Tom himself has already introduced. Towards the end of her monologue, though, we come to recognise the emotional truth underlying Amanda's romanticism: she feels that the glory of her youth was lost because of her decision to marry Tom's and Laura's father, a choice which took her away from the old Southern ways of Blue Mountain and into this cramped, modern, urban apartment. Nostalgia and regret dominate Amanda's life – or at least her life as Tom presents it in this first scene.

We are also given the impression that this scene is one which took place, with slight variations, many times over: the tale Amanda tells is apparently one that her children have heard time and again. The scene ends, however, with the focus of attention shifting slightly toward Laura: Amanda apparently wants to be able to live vicariously through her daughter, to see her receive the kind of attention from gentlemen callers which she herself claims she received in her long-ago youth. Laura, however, is not the kind of girl to attract male admirers, and in the scene's final lines we glimpse briefly both her loneliness and the source of her alienation from her uncomprehending mother.

Scene Two (Laura)

The conclusion of Scene One thus sets us up for a fluid progression into Scene Two. Here, our attention is focused on Laura herself, although since she is a much quieter figure than her mother, she does not present herself through monologue as Amanda has. Laura's story is instead told more through her interaction with her mother, and we are shown a particular incident – during the winter months – in which Amanda returns home to confront Laura. Amanda has just discovered that Laura has only been pretending to attend a secretarial course at a business college each day, and that in fact she has been absent from the college for the last six weeks. Laura has to face the anger and indignation of her mother, and to try to explain why she dropped out, and why she could not bring herself to tell Amanda about this earlier. She is clearly terrified by the memory of the typing course, which made her feel physically sick because she could not cope with its pressures, but she is perhaps even more afraid of her mother's disappointment in her, which is why she has been pretending that she was still taking the course.

What we see in this scene, then, are two different kinds of 'acting'. Laura attempts, rather pathetically, to keep up the illusion that she is studying: she rushes to hide her glass animals when Amanda returns home and pretends to be quietly studying her typewriter chart. Her mother, by contrast, decides to play out her revelations as full-blown melodrama: the stage directions specify '*a bit of acting*' after Amanda's first line – suggesting that she is *putting on* an air of bitter disappointment so as to emphasise her daughter's humiliation. She then goes on to play out the story of her trip to Rubicam's Business College as a blow-by-blow account in which she even mimics the voice of the woman she spoke to, so that we can imagine the whole dialogue that took place (as Amanda tells it, this was a rather terse, or even bitchy exchange). Amanda uses the story as a weapon against Laura, missing no opportunity to twist the knife by pointing out that, if Laura is not going to learn a job skill, then she has no future ('what is going to become of us?'). Laura, meanwhile, cannot stand up to her mother and responds only with inarticulate sounds of helplessness ('Oh'), and by taking refuge in trying to wind up her Victrola, an action which only infuriates her mother further.

It becomes clear during this scene that Laura has been hiding not only from her mother but also from life outside the apartment. She has created an imaginary world for herself, into which she retreats whenever she can, and especially when she is placed under pressure. This imaginary world revolves around three of her personal possessions. First, there is the collection of tiny glass animals (the menagerie of the play's title) which we see her cleaning lovingly at the scene's opening. Second, there is the old Victrola record player left behind by her father, which is the ostensible source for the nostalgic, faraway music which accompanies the whole play (and which is described so carefully by Williams in his production notes). Laura's third precious possession is her high school yearbook, which she treasures chiefly because of the pictures it holds of Jim, the unrequited love of her life. In this scene, Laura plucks up courage to show her mother the yearbook, after Amanda has finally stopped ranting at her and has asked, with apparent pity, whether or not she ever 'liked some boy'. Invited to speak about something she really cares about, Laura finally finds a voice and begins to enthuse about Jim and all his exploits as 'high school hero'. It becomes clear from her comments that he barely knew her, but that she particularly treasures the few moments when she spoke with him, and the fact that he even had a nickname for her. (Jim would 'holler, "Hello, Blue

Roses!"' whenever he saw her, she tells us: the hollering indicates that she only really saw him in passing at a distance.)

Laura also preserves a six-year-old newspaper clipping, presumably tucked inside the yearbook, which details Jim's engagement to Emily Meisenbach ('It says in the Personal Section', rather than 'it said', indicates that she still has the clipping with her). She seems to see his having married as marking the end of her one and only hope of ever having a happy relationship with a man, but that hope had clearly only ever been based on a dream, a longing, rather than anything more solid. Here we see the depths of Laura's isolation and lack of faith in herself, and Amanda too, seeing as if for the first time that Laura does (or at least did) dream of loving a man, resolves to help her find one to marry. This, in her view, is the only realistic alternative to the secretarial career which Laura has thrown away. Ironically then, we see that it is Laura's mention of Jim which prompts Amanda to find a 'gentleman caller' for her – a caller who, when he later appears, is in fact that same Jim.

If that seems rather too convenient a plot twist, we must remember a further underlying factor in this scene; namely, that Tom does not actually appear in it. If he was not there, how could he 'remember' these events? Perhaps what we see here is only the way Tom *imagines* that it must have taken place, based on what he learned about it afterwards, or even what Tom *wants* to have taken place, for the sake of neatness in his plot. He does not draw our attention to this point, of course, and it is not vitally important that we notice it, but if we are aware of it, this adds further to our sense that what we are seeing is a fabrication of memory and imagination.

Scene Three (Opening Monologues)

Tom reappears to assert his presence as narrator at the opening of Scene Three, explaining how – as winter moved into spring – Amanda's campaign to find a gentleman caller for Laura began to bring added emotional pressure to the already tense relations among the Wingfields. Amanda's preoccupation with this idea, we are told, only added further to Laura's chronic nervousness and to Tom's discomfort at home. It also apparently prompted Amanda herself to take up a telesales position to earn extra money 'to plume the bird and feather the nest' (i.e. to put toward making Laura's appearance and possible dowry more appealing to prospective suitors). We next see Amanda at work making one of her telephone sales pitches, and here again her talent as a performer becomes apparent. She first gushes with sympathy for one of her friends from the

D.A.R. (Daughters of the American Revolution: a respected women's organisation), and then tries to talk up the latest pulp fiction story in the *Homemaker's Companion*. Her hard-sell approach is underlined by the absurdly exaggerated claims she makes for the story as a successor to Margaret Mitchell's classic Civil War novel, *Gone With the Wind*. Comically though (and perhaps Tom's sense of irony is again apparent here), her friend finds an excuse to hang up on her in mid-sentence.

Scene Three (Tom)

Scene Three proper finally brings the focus back to Tom himself, and his sense of being trapped in his home and his job (as a clerk at a shoe factory), unable to find the time or privacy in which he can pursue his interest in literature. He dreams of becoming a writer, but Amanda even attempts to censor what he can read, banning D. H. Lawrence's novels from the house. Tom resents this, not least because he himself pays for the upkeep of the house out of his wages. Yet Amanda is still in charge of the home through sheer force of will. Tom is frustrated, powerless and penniless, and in this scene, prevented by his enraged mother from simply leaving the house as usual, he erupts into a blazing row with her. As each grows angrier, they become more hurtful towards each other, Amanda eventually accusing Tom of lying about his nocturnal habit of going to movies, and suggesting that he is really spending his nights getting drunk. Tom reacts to this with an impassioned monologue in which he desperately tries to make her understand how unhappy he is and how much he is sacrificing for her and Laura, yet she seems unwilling to listen. He therefore gives up and instead becomes blisteringly sarcastic: he too now proves himself a gifted 'actor' as he launches into a parody of what he believes she is waiting to hear, confessing to all kinds of bizarre, exaggerated nocturnal sins. Losing his head completely, he concludes by openly mocking Amanda, calling her a witch, and attempting once again to storm out of the door. In the process, he accidentally flings his coat in the direction of Laura's treasured glass menagerie, breaking something as a result. Laura, who has witnessed this whole scene, is understandably horrified, but so too is Tom himself, who stops dead in his tracks when he realises what he has done to Laura's treasures. Amanda, preoccupied with Tom's insults and oblivious to Laura, declares that she will not speak to Tom until he apologises to her, and storms out leaving her children to clean up the damage.

Although this scene seems to revolve around Tom and his struggles with his mother, it is important to note that Laura is present throughout, suffering through their fighting. Indeed, Williams specifies that she is to be lit differently and more clearly than either of the other characters: he thus creates a kind of split focus on stage, so that the audience remains strongly aware of Laura throughout the scene, again noticing her isolation even within the family. Yet it also becomes clear in this scene that there is more to Laura than helpless shyness, since the one occasion when she plucks up courage to intervene in Tom and Amanda's argument is when Tom is on the verge of swearing at his mother. This moment, echoing a similar such intervention during Scene One, demonstrates that Laura is very much aware of the need to maintain a careful emotional balance in the house in order for the family to function. She will try to intervene in the situation if Tom and Amanda are in danger of doing something they will regret. Sadly for her, though, in this scene she remains powerless to stop Tom building himself into a rage, or his consequent damage of her treasured glass collection.

Scene Four (5 a.m.)

Scene Four depicts events in the Wingfield household early one morning in spring. In practice, though, it is really two separate scenes. The first, shorter scene takes place at 5 a.m. (the time chimed by a nearby church clock), when Tom returns home very drunk from one of his nocturnal sprees. The second begins, according to Laura, at 'nearly seven'. In between these scenes we also hear the clock striking six, Amanda's consequent calls of 'Rise and Shine!', and Tom's sleepy protests. Apparently he sleeps on for nearly an hour longer than he is supposed to. That missing hour is marked only by a few moments on stage during which the lighting increases slightly in intensity. In effect, what we as the audience witness are the moments in which Tom himself is awake (or semi-awake), which are – of course – the way he would remember these events.

    The short scene at five in the morning is intriguing for the audience because it confirms for us Amanda's suspicions that Tom does not merely go to the movies at night (we can assume that no movie-theatre opens that late). Yet the mystery of what has occurred during Tom's lost hours remains unanswered: when Laura – awakened by his drunken fumbling for his doorkey – asks him where he has been, he simply explains that the movies had 'a very long program', and goes on to describe the magician's stage show which he also saw as part of the same bill. There is, of course, no particularly good reason why we should believe this story. He says the magician gave him whisky, but that could be just an embroidered cover story. Likewise, he could have found the rainbow-coloured scarf which he gives to Laura at some open-all-hours backstreet jumble shop. We might legitimately choose to believe that he did get it from 'Malvolio the Magnificent', as he claims, but the point is that neither we nor Laura have any way of knowing for sure (and since Malvolio is a character in Shakespeare's *Twelfth Night*, even that name could be a private literary joke of Tom's). What is clear, however, is the underlying emotional truth of this scene: Tom's desperation to escape the suffocating, 'nailed up coffin' of his home life has caused him to stay out all night and to lose himself in alcohol. As a result, he can catch only a couple of hours' sleep before having to go back to work. There is the unmistakable sense, as Tom climbs into bed, that something will have to give soon in this situation.

Scene Four (7 a.m.)

The later part of this scene opens with Laura pressing Tom to wake up, and to apologise to Amanda for what he said in Scene Three, as she is not speaking to him. We might conclude that this is the morning after that row took place, although it is by no means certain (perhaps there has been frosty silence in the house for days!). Moreover, Amanda's mention later in this scene of Tom having come home drunk one night, in a 'terrifying condition', seems to overlap with what we have just seen, and yet presumably refers to another, earlier occasion. These touches leave us with the impression that the situations depicted in these scenes are by no means one-off occurrences.

After waking Tom, Laura is sent out for groceries, leaving her brother to confront Amanda. A lengthy series of stage directions indicates a sort of comic, silent-movie sequence taking place between them – all averted eye contact and awkward clearing of throats – before Tom finally plucks up the courage to apologise for calling her a witch. This acts as a kind of trigger, releasing the torrents of Amanda's pent-up emotion. If she has appeared rather falsely melodramatic at times in previous scenes, we now begin to get a deeper and more sympathetic impression of her. Although she cannot quite find it in herself to apologise for her sometimes cruel behaviour, it is clear from her explanation how much she really loves and cares for her children, and that it is *circumstances* which have made her as hard and embittered as she is. We realise here that Amanda's struggle to bring her children up and provide for them, in very difficult economic times, without the support of a husband, has made her who she is. And now it becomes clear that her continual nagging at Tom (over drinking his coffee too fast, eating a proper breakfast, staying out at night drinking, etc.) is born out of genuine, and not entirely misplaced concern for his welfare. Likewise, Amanda's insistence on discussing Laura's situation with Tom is driven by her awareness that something needs to be done for her; whereas Tom himself – however much he loves his sister – has seemed too preoccupied with his own unhappiness to think clearly about helping her. Amanda confronts him directly with this point towards the end of the scene, accusing him of thinking only about himself. This is a moment which in a way sums up the tensions between mother and son, for she is at once quite right in her criticism and overly harsh, failing to understand things from his point of view. This scene summarises, perhaps better than any other in the play, Williams's deeply humane awareness that, while an individual's behaviour might seem cruel or selfish from the outside, it may well become understandable or even sympathetic when one tries to appreciate circumstances from that individual's point of view. On several occasions in this scene, both Amanda and Tom seem simultaneously 'right' and 'wrong' in their words and actions.

A further complicating factor is that it seems Amanda and Tom are never very likely to appreciate each other's points of view fully, because they are fundamentally unable to communicate. Amanda admits that she does not know how to express to him what she feels in her heart, and the irony is that it is in this moment of helpless inarticulacy that mother and son actually seem closest: he understands her because he has had exactly the same difficulties in expressing himself. Elsewhere in the scene, though, Tom is conspicuous for his failure even to attempt to help Amanda understand him, despite her unusual openness to him. He continues in this scene to evade her questions about where he goes at night, and offers only facetious, one-line retorts to her attempts to talk about his job. Perhaps he knows that telling her where he really goes, what he really thinks, would only hurt and upset his mother more, and this is why he sidesteps her pestering. (Sure enough, in the one moment when he does speak freely, she instantly responds with a lecture on bourgeois, 'Christian' ethics.) Yet Tom, by failing to respond fully to his mother's fumbling attempts at communication, only adds further to the gulf of understanding between them. Their situation seems intractable.

Yet another subtext in the scene is, quite simply, Amanda's obvious fear for her own future. She finally confronts Tom with her knowledge that he has been in touch with the Merchant Marine, and must be thinking of running away to sea. This would deprive the family of his warehouse wage and plunge them into poverty. Amanda insists that she is not concerned for her own future, only for Laura's, but in this she is clearly being disingenuous ('I'm old and don't matter!'). Her insistence that Tom help find a potential husband for Laura is clearly motivated as much by her own concern to be provided for in old age as it is by love for Laura. Again we are aware of how the understandable instinct for self-preservation can become mixed up with the more noble motive of concern for others. For Williams, there are no easy, unambiguous explanations for people's behaviour. Similarly, when Tom finally agrees to find a gentleman caller for Laura, it seems to be driven as much by the guilt which Amanda has stirred up, and by his own desire for her to stop pestering him, as by any sense of brotherly love for his sister. Tom seems to remain justifiably sceptical that a husband is what Laura really needs, or indeed that she could attract one (a point he makes explicitly in the next scene). Yet Amanda, the bit between her teeth, plunges ahead with her campaign; after Tom has left for work, his promise made, she returns to her fundraising telesales campaign. The repetition of her sales pitch here seems like a sadly ironic touch: she disappears again behind the brittle façade of the performer, after a scene in which she has allowed herself to appear more vulnerable than at any previous point in the play.

Scene Five (Annunciation)

This scene takes place some time later, on a spring evening warm enough for Tom to sit outside smoking on the fire escape after dinner. He is driven outside, once again, by Amanda's pestering, although on this occasion (perhaps learning from their conversation before) she seems to be making more of an effort to be constructive rather than simply nag him. She suggests that if he gave up smoking, he could afford to improve himself with a nightschool course, but Tom, dreaming of escape, is not interested in learning to be an accountant.

On the terrace, he steps out of the scene itself to address the audience as narrator once again. Accompanied by the sound of dance music, he wistfully describes his fascination with watching the goings-on in the dance hall across the alley, and – more seriously – his sense that its sensuous pleasures provided a kind of welcome distraction from the impending sense of doom which was felt that spring of 1938 by anyone paying attention to the news from Europe. Tom's newspaper headline notes that General Franco, the fascist leader, has scored another victory in the Spanish Civil War, while in his narration Tom alludes to the misguided attempts of Western leaders, like the British Prime Minister Neville Chamberlain, to appease Nazi Germany's Adolf Hitler by signing a deal in Munich which would allow Germany to annex large parts of Czechoslovakia. As Tom's last line here makes clear ('all the world was waiting for bombardments'), a second world war seemed imminent, despite Chamberlain's belief that he had secured 'peace in our time'.

The appearance of such a speech, at this juncture in the play, functions to bring an added sense of ominousness to what follows: Tom announces to Amanda, who has followed him out onto the terrace, that Laura is finally to have a gentleman caller. Although this news is delivered in one of the most playfully light-hearted exchanges between mother and son in the entire play, its location after Tom's rumours-of-war speech provides a dark counterpoint to their good humour, a sense that the news of Jim's imminent arrival might itself herald a disaster of smaller scale but of similar irreversibility.

Tom's announcement that Jim will come for dinner tomorrow night sends Amanda into a whirl of panicked preparations. Tom insists that no fuss is necessary, although he also finds amusement in his mother's predictable reaction to his news (which is perhaps partly why he drops it in so casually and at such short notice). He then responds with a kind of wry disbelief as Amanda begins to grill him with questions about every detail of Jim's background, career and appearance. She also does not let slip the chance to do a little reminiscing about her own days of receiving gentlemen callers in Blue Mountain. Amanda has very fixed ideas about what to look for in a potential suitor, and it eventually emerges that the ambitious Jim is indeed eminently suitable (if with a few regrettable foibles). Tom attempts gently to remind his mother that Jim has not even met Laura yet, let alone asked for her hand in marriage, but Amanda is not to be deterred. Once again, an ironic reversal takes place here as Tom – faced with a mother so intent on pursuing her quarry that she will not admit to the problems on her doorstep – forcibly reminds her of Laura's acutely shy and withdrawn personality, which will be an obstacle to any attempt at engineering a romance for her. Tom finds himself saying to his mother almost exactly the same lines as she said to him at the end of the previous scene, when trying to remind him of his responsibility to his sister. Williams thus subtly points out the way that we can all lose sight of the obvious when blinded by our own preoccupations. Unlike his mother in the previous scene, though, Tom gives up trying to press his point home, and simply takes the familiar option of walking out. His wearily evasive explanation that he is going to the movies predictably infuriates his mother, but even this will not deter her from her path now that a gentleman caller is imminent: the scene concludes with Amanda dragging Laura out of the kitchen and onto the fire escape so that she can make a wish on the moon for happiness. It is a poignant climax to the first half of the play: Amanda is willing to draw even on the fragile sense of hope provided by the softly glowing heavens, as if this alone might provide her family with a way out of its current, self-destroying stasis.

Scene Six (Opening Narration)

The audience is welcomed back from the interval by Tom, who begins a lengthy narration about Jim O'Connor, the imminent gentleman caller. Jim, it emerges, not only works in the shoe warehouse with Tom, but was also at the same high school. Tom speaks wryly but also a little enviously of Jim's near-legendary status as all-round high school star, a career which contrasted sharply with his own insignificance. Yet he also notes how Jim's ambitions after high school were thwarted, apparently by the economic realities of the Depression, which have placed him on the same plane of apparent mediocrity as Tom himself. Now, they seem almost to rely on each other. Jim, Tom tells us, finds reassurance in knowing that Tom, at least, remembers his former glories and thus, perhaps, his future potential. Yet it is also clear that Tom finds reassurance in knowing that Jim understands at least a little about him: Jim is the one person in Tom's life who seems to acknowledge and even encourage (if only lightheartedly) his ambition to be a poet.

Tom concludes his narration, however, by shifting our attention to the fact that Jim and Laura had known each other slightly at high school. He tells us that, when he invited Jim to dinner, he did not know whether or not Jim would even remember Laura when he met her. Tom also indicates that, at this time, he was unaware quite how much Jim's memory meant to Laura (he only remembers her speaking 'admiringly of his voice'). The older Tom who is narrating, knowing the results of this meeting with hindsight, does not give anything of his plot away, but clearly suggests to us – through the sense of portent in this last paragraph – that the play is now beginning to move toward events of life-changing significance.

Scene Six (Preparations)

The lights come up across the stage to show us an apartment which looks far neater and more 'presentable' than it has been in the first half of the play. Amanda has 'worked like a Turk' to get it ready for the visit, and is now doing the same for Laura herself, who stands sheepishly in a new dress as Amanda fixes its hem. It is clear, however, that Laura is being made to feel very uneasy and pressurised by all the fuss her mother is making –

especially when Amanda insists on artificially enlarging her bosom using powder puffs. Laura does not feel pretty or alluring, and being forced to put on a show like this only makes her still more self-conscious than usual. By stark contrast, though, the opportunity to dress up prettily is one which fills Amanda with excitement, a point which becomes very clear when she reappears, after a brief absence, in her old cotillion dress. She proceeds to 'sashay' around the room while reminiscing at length about her days as a debutante in Blue Mountain. She seems to have rediscovered her youthful vigour, and although we might suspect that her memories of those days are somewhat rose-tinted, her excitement is nonetheless entertaining and even infectious for an audience: her story about her obsession with jonquils is one of the most straightforwardly entertaining moments in the play. The fun ends quite suddenly, however, when Amanda recalls how those golden days abruptly came to a halt when she met Laura's father.

Bringing herself back to the present, Amanda notes that it is about to rain: this is an unfortunate omen for the evening which renews the sense of foreboding that Tom established earlier. That foreboding deepens further as Laura asks her mother to repeat the name of the man who is coming to dinner. She then hesitatingly reveals to her mother what we have already guessed; that this is the same Jim she knew and loved in high school. This is the last straw for her: she cannot face the pressure any longer and tells Amanda that she will not be able to meet their visitor. Amanda tells her not to be so foolish, and almost immediately the doorbell announces Tom and Jim's arrival. Ordered by her mother to answer it, Laura grows almost hysterical with terror, pleading not to be made to go, until finally Amanda commands her with such force that she meekly goes to the door (as Amanda disappears into the kitchen). Yet having opened the door and been introduced to Jim by Tom, Laura instantly turns tail and retreats to the security of her Victrola, leaving Tom and Jim to entertain themselves.

Scene Six (Jim and Tom)

Feeling very awkward with the situation in the apartment, Tom too takes his usual way out and steps out onto the fire escape to smoke. Jim opts to follow him almost immediately, rather than be left alone with only the newspaper for company, and begins goodnaturedly to lecture Tom on the self-improving benefits of taking a public speaking course – no doubt responding to Tom's obvious discomfort with 'company'. Tom, though, rejects the advice and ignores Jim's attempts to suggest that he needs to improve his performance at work. Tom finally reveals that he no longer cares how he fares at the warehouse, because he is on the point of running away to sea. In an impassioned speech, Tom explains that he is sick of watching movies, of watching life happen to other people, and that he is now determined to seize a new life for himself. Jim dismisses Tom's dreams as empty fantasy, but his uncharacteristic harshness here (he calls Tom 'you drip') perhaps suggests that the contempt he feels is really for himself, a disgust at his own failure to rise above mediocrity. Here is Tom, a nobody at high school, apparently showing more guts than he in dreaming of escape. Tom is plainly thinking of pursuing a dream wherever it takes him, no matter what the risks, whereas Jim's life – by contrast – is a model of playing safe and seeking to work one's way gradually up the career ladder.

The men's discussion is interrupted by Amanda's rather startling arrival on the terrace – all girlish vivacity and swinging cotillion dress. Without giving the men a chance to draw breath, she launches into a chattering monologue, flirtatiously addressing Jim as if he were a gentleman caller come to call on *her*. Once again she quickly finds a way into talking about her own youth in the Deep South; once again she ends up dwelling on her own choice of husband. We begin to see a certain circularity in Amanda's train of thought here (this is the second time in the scene that a speech has ended on this subject), but more important than what she says here is our awareness of her apparently incessant need to *talk*. It seems as if this is her way of dealing with nervousness and excitement. In this respect her behaviour stands in marked contrast to that of Laura, whose crippling shyness means she cannot even bring herself to face Jim. When Amanda finally calls her in from the kitchen, where she has taken refuge, she collapses in a faint from sheer nervous exhaustion. With the strange appropriateness of a dream (or perhaps of doctored memory), a thunderstorm breaks out outside at the same instant. Tom picks his sister up and lays her down on the sofa before taking his place at the dinner table with Jim and Amanda. The scene closes with grace being said for the meal, as rain comes down outside and as the audience watches not only the diners, but Laura too, alone and terrified.

Scene Seven (Jim and Laura)

Time has passed and the meal is now finishing. Laura remains where she was. However, almost as soon as the lights have come up to reveal this tableau, they are cut out again, simulating a power blackout in the apartment. Amanda, still flirting shamelessly with Jim, lights candles and persuades him to come into the kitchen with her to look at the fuse box.

We hear their voices from offstage and watch Tom and Laura wait silently on the darkened stage, until Amanda returns having concluded that the electricity has been cut off because Tom forgot to pay the power bill. Jim knows that Tom deliberately did not pay it, in order to use the money to join the Merchant Marine (as he explained in the previous scene), but Jim opts to cover for Tom by joking about his forgetfulness. Amanda now steps back from her flirtatious hostess role (although she cannot resist one last little anecdote about her candelabrum), and none-too-subtly drags Tom to the kitchen to help wash the dishes. She thus leaves Jim alone with Laura – as she clearly had always intended to do.

Clutching the candelabrum and a glass of dandelion wine, Jim hesitantly approaches the sofa where Laura is still hiding. The simple words 'Hello there, Laura' initiate what is by far the longest dialogue sequence in the play: the encounter between Jim and Laura lasts for a full half-hour of playing time on stage. This intimate, physically static scene (i.e. the stage picture remains much the same throughout, neither character moving very much) needs to be especially carefully handled in production so as not to lose the audience's attention, but when well performed it is compulsive viewing, for what we see developing during Jim and Laura's conversation is – in effect – the entire cycle of an evolving relationship. The scene goes from very nervous first contact, through a gradual building-up of Laura's confidence thanks to Jim's gently insistent attention towards her, and arrives at real mutual enjoyment of each other's company. Unfortunately for Laura, though, things then begin to fall apart, as Jim brings about unintentional damage to her most treasured glass animal – the unicorn. When he then belatedly realises that she is in love with him, he grows nervously awkward before finding a way to confess to her that he already has a steady girlfriend, Betty, to whom he is engaged to be married. Within the space of half an hour, Laura is brought out of her shell, has her most fantastic hopes built up, and then watches them vanish into nothing.

One of the most noticeable things about this scene is how genuinely decent and well-intentioned Jim seems to be. We actually know very little about him prior to their dialogue, other than what Tom has told us, and what we do know has been mostly to do with his ambitiousness and popularity. It becomes clear, though, that he has not been spoiled by his successes – or perhaps that, as he himself suggests, his humbling experiences at the warehouse have helped make him more mature and down-to-earth. He still has high hopes for himself, but his concern in this scene is not to talk about himself (as might be expected). Despite Laura's terrible shyness and initial lack of responsiveness to him, he works very hard to draw her into a real, two-way conversation. First, he invites her to sit with him, then to move closer into the light, and then – after talking casually to help put her at her ease a little – he questions her directly about her obvious shyness. Laura responds to his apparently genuine concern for her by plucking up the courage to ask him about his singing career, and from here it is a short step to Jim realising where he has seen her before. They begin to reminisce laughingly about high school, and although Laura's mention of her crippled foot brings about a few moments of awkward embarrassment for both of them, Jim nevertheless tries to overcome this setback and continue the conversation by attempting to persuade her that she has no need to be so self-conscious about herself.

When the conversation turns towards memories of *The Pirates of Penzance*, the high school operetta in which Jim starred, Laura produces first her yearbook and then a copy of the show's programme. She confesses that she saw him perform 'all three times'. It would be easy for Jim to be embarrassed as he begins to realise the extent of Laura's adulation of him, but he playfully offers to sign the programme for her, six years too late, and jokes about the diminished value of his autograph. Shortly after that, Laura learns that Jim did not in fact marry – nor ever intended to marry – the girl who had announced their engagement in the personal column of the newspaper. The news that he is free of other ties, combined with the fact that Jim clearly likes her and wants to encourage her to have more confidence in herself, allows Laura to begin to fantasise that her dreams about loving Jim might just come true. (Obviously, this is not stated explicitly in the text itself, but the implication is there subtextually.) The extent of Laura's newfound willingness to open up to Jim, to allow him into her private world, is now demonstrated as she shows him her glass collection, and particularly her most loved piece – a tiny, fragile unicorn that she refers to not as 'it' but as 'he'. Despite Jim's protestations, she trusts him to hold this treasure in his hand – just as if she were trusting him to hold her heart. They joke gently about the unicorn as if it had a personality, Laura now showing a sense of wit and humour which has previously remained hidden, and which Jim has brought to the surface.

After putting the unicorn down, there is a momentary lull in the conversation, suggesting a certain awkwardness about what they could discuss next after such an intimate exchange. Jim tries to cover his unease by commenting first on the size of his shadow, then on the weather, then on the music from the Paradise Dance Hall. He leaps on the idea of having Laura dance with him, and, despite her protests, sweeps her up and helps her to dance a waltz. Here we see, in miniature, an echo of the course of their whole encounter, as she moves stiffly at first but gradually gains in confidence and enjoyment. This makes the result of their dance all the more tragic: accidentally bumping into the table where Jim had placed the unicorn, they knock it off onto the floor. Picking it up, Laura discovers that its horn has been broken off. She tries to assure Jim, who is shocked at the damage he has done, that it really does not matter that much to her, but it is clear from what we know of Laura that this is a desperately sad moment for her. Her most loved possession has been irreparably damaged. We might also speculate that this breakage is symbolic of Laura herself being irreparably hurt, either by this moment or by what follows shortly afterwards. Yet, equally, we can see an admirable strength and dignity emerge in her at this moment, as she struggles against her own grief to put Jim at ease through her gentle humour. It is almost as if she is repaying the kindness he has shown, throughout the scene, in trying to put *her* at ease.

Touched by this moment, Jim attempts to express to Laura just how special she appears to be to him. She is lost for words, but he too is unable to articulate fully, almost as if what he is feeling is inexplicable even to himself. He tries to suggest that he feels for her just what he would feel for a much-loved sister, and that he wants to aid and encourage her as he would his own sister, but seconds later the pair of them have stumbled into a passionate kiss. This is a crucial turning point, just as was the breaking of the unicorn. Jim pulls away from the kiss, cursing himself for losing control, but Laura seems simply stunned. Reduced once again to silence, she offers no response to his various attempts to return to casual conversation as if nothing had happened, and so Jim finds himself explaining, haltingly and awkwardly, that he should not have kissed her, and cannot be a boyfriend to her, because he is already engaged to be married. There are two possible readings of his actions here. One is that he really had been just foolishly lost in the moment, that the kiss meant nothing, and that he looks on Laura as he would a fragile younger sister. The second and still sadder interpretation would be that he has seen something in Laura which he loves deeply, but that – because he is already engaged – he feels he must stay faithful to Betty, despite the fact that all he can really say in praise of her is that 'in a great many ways we – get along fine'. Jim is a responsible, respectable young man who feels he must 'do the right thing' by his fiancée. Yet, according to this reading of events, that means depriving both Laura and himself of possible happiness. Fate and social custom have conspired against them both.

Still more striking than Jim's obvious awkwardness and conflicting feelings is the way in which Laura responds to this outpouring of excuses. After quietly absorbing the fact that her dream of being with him is over not only for tonight but for ever, she finds the strength and presence of mind to offer him the broken unicorn as a gift. This, she tells him, is a souvenir.

The words hang in the air, conjuring an extraordinary mixture of emotional possibilities. Is she giving him a gift out of love? Is she asking him to take a small part of her with him? Is she even quietly accusing him of an act of destruction? (Is she saying, in effect, 'keep this to remember how easy it is to hurt people'?) It is impossible to tell, and Jim has no chance to ask, because the moment is shattered by Amanda's loudly unsubtle entrance bearing lemonade. Jim, Laura and the audience alike are jarred rudely out of a deeply intimate moment, and Amanda's chatter resumes as if it had never left off, except that now it seems horribly, painfully invasive and inappropriate. Amanda, of course, has no idea what she has interrupted, and when Jim tries to make his excuses and leave, she pressures him to arrange a date to come again. He explains quietly about his obligations to Betty, and now it is Amanda's turn to have her hopes reduced to dust. There is nothing left to say but the conventional pleasantries, and Jim exits as hastily as decency will permit.

Amanda, unlike Laura, is not the kind of person to accept humiliation quietly, and she calls Tom in from the kitchen to accuse him of playing a cruel joke on them all. When he realises what has happened, Tom protests his innocence, insisting he had no knowledge of Jim's engagement (a fact which Jim himself has already confirmed), but Amanda does not want to listen to him. She needs someone to blame, and Tom is the most convenient target for her final, furious outburst. She also, however, unthinkingly rubs salt into Laura's wounds by describing her as a jobless, unmarried cripple: her own previous attempts to reassure Laura that she is not crippled now seem shockingly hollow. Laura, however, has retreated to her usual silence and does not react. Tom, likewise, resorts to his usual tactics and storms out of the apartment. The family seems to be right back where it started, except that this time, Tom claims, he is not going to the movies. And, as he tells us moments later in his closing narration, he ran away for ever shortly after this fateful night. For him, Jim's visit was the straw which finally broke the camel's back.

Closing Narration

Significantly, though, Tom's final speech to the audience makes no attempt to justify his leaving. He knows full well, in retrospect, that his departure – however necessary it was for his own sanity and his own hopes for future happiness – was a betrayal of his family and, most particularly, of his sister. Indeed, as he makes tragically clear to us, his escape did not mean freedom for him at all, because he is still helplessly imprisoned by a sense of guilt at having left Laura alone when she must have most needed his love and support. The bleakly poetic tone of this final narration reminds us, again, that everything we have been watching is memory, or perhaps even – in the case of Jim and Laura's scene – simply an imaginary construction of what might have happened between them. Tom's description of being haunted by memories of his sister suggests that he has spent many long, painful hours dwelling on the events of that night and on what must, or might, have occurred while he was in the kitchen with Amanda. The entire play, it seems to us now, has been an attempt on Tom's part to exorcise the ghosts of that night, and now that the play is over, there is nothing further to say. But as Laura blows out her candles for the last time, there is no guarantee that Tom has succeeded in his exorcism. Perhaps he will have to come back and perform it all over again, night after night. Perhaps he is doomed to repeat this story forever – trapped by his guilt, by his memories, and by simply not knowing what became of his mother and his sister after he deserted them.

Commentary

The Glass Menagerie is often thought of as Tennessee Williams's first major play, because it was this piece that first brought serious critical and public attention to his work when, in 1945, its premiere production became the hit of the theatrical season – initially in Chicago and then in New York.[1] Two years later, the arrival of *A Streetcar Named Desire* confirmed Williams as a world-class playwright with a distinctive, poetic voice. It is often forgotten, however, that Williams had already written a great many plays before his success with *Menagerie*, and indeed that other, far less acclaimed works appeared on Broadway in the wake of each of his first two hits (*You Touched Me* later in 1945, and *Summer and Smoke* in 1948). Williams wrote prodigiously, and in a wide range of styles, always following his own creative instincts rather than any preconceived notion of what would make a commercial or critical success.

As a result, there was (and indeed still is) debate over the artistic merit of much of his output, some of which was misunderstood or simply dismissed during his own lifetime. This is true, particularly, of the work he produced in the last two decades of his life: after a string of successes during the 1950s, his last Broadway hit, *Night of the Iguana* (1961), was followed by flop after flop until his death in 1983. Yet, Williams kept writing, determined that he had something to express regardless of whether or not the commercial theatre wanted to hear it. In the 1990s, a serious reassessment of his work began in the subsidised theatre sector, with many directors believing that much of his work – and particularly his later work – had been unjustly neglected. Along with the many revivals and reassessments which resulted from this interest, an early, previously unproduced work from the late 1930s, *Not About Nightingales*, was unearthed and produced at Britain's Royal National Theatre in 1998, before finding its way to acclaim on Broadway.

All of this is relevant here because it helps us to understand the pivotal significance of *The Glass Menagerie* in Tennessee Williams's career. It was this play which plucked Williams out of the penniless obscurity in which he had lived for most of his adult life (he had just turned thirty-four when the Broadway production opened). If *Menagerie* had not proved successful for him at that time, it is possible – or even probable –

---

1 The production opened in a try-out version at Chicago's Civic Theatre on 26 December 1944, and gradually gathered press and public attention. It transferred to the Playhouse Theatre, on Broadway, in March 1945, and ran there for 561 performances.

that he would never have achieved widespread recognition. With this piece, Williams finally succeeded in finding a dramatic mix which made his own avowedly experimental instincts accessible to a large, popular audience – an audience which understood that this was a play quite different from what was then considered 'normal' Broadway fare, and yet was drawn in by its humour, subtlety and emotional complexity. Williams, who always remained ambivalent about the seductive nature of success, had stumbled upon this winning combination of experiment and accessibility almost by accident, and it was a fine balance which he found great difficulty in striking again. To this day, *The Glass Menagerie* remains the most frequently produced of his plays, and arguably the most popular with audiences. Although *A Streetcar Named Desire* and *Cat on a Hot Tin Roof* (1955) – which both achieved a similarly fine balance of conventional and innovative elements – tend to be cited by critics as Williams's greatest achievements, *Menagerie* retains a unique appeal all its own. Moreover, when discussed, it often provokes the most intensely personal responses from Williams enthusiasts.

What, then, makes this play so peculiarly appealing? A large part of the answer to this question seems to depend, quite simply, on the fact that this is a play about a family. There are, of course, many plays about families, but few of them really take the whole family as their central focus: Arthur Miller's *Death of a Salesman* (1949), for example, is mostly concerned with the relationship between a father and elder son, with the mother and other son portrayed as little more than props to this action. *Salesman*, moreover, clearly attempts to deliver a message about the insubstantiality of the American dream of material success. Williams, by contrast, has no governing agenda in *Menagerie* other than to write as truthfully as he can about his four characters – their strengths, their weaknesses, their hopes and fears – and how they function together in the claustrophobic proximity within which he places them. 'If anyone ever wrote more shrewdly and feelingly about family politics than Williams does here', the critic Benedict Nightingale has commented, 'I don't know him.'[2] That assessment pinpoints the fact that, while Williams has no 'message' to peddle, the very act of writing as honestly and even-handedly as this about the shifting power struggles and tortured love within a family situation is in itself revelatory. Partly thanks to the episodic structure of the play, which allows Williams to shift the focus of

---

2 From Nightingale's *Times* review of the 1995 London production of *Menagerie*. Reprinted in the *London Theatre Record*, 1995 volume, 1283. Subsequent reviews from the same source are annotated parenthetically using the abbreviation *LTR*.

his attention slightly for each scene, we are given the opportunity to see all four characters express themselves and their individual perspectives. We are also, very importantly, given the chance to make up our own minds about these characters: Williams does not try to tell us what to think about them, or tell us that any one of them is more right or wrong, good or bad, than the others. Audience members are thus allowed the space to reflect quite personally on those aspects of the family's story which connect most closely with their own experiences. 'No one among critics or audiences could understand why this ostensibly slight play affected them so deeply', Lyle Leverich writes of the premiere production, before pointing out that the play's concerns – though very specific in time and place – are also to some extent universal: 'What they witnessed was the tragic failure of three family members to understand one another in their intertwined love' (Leverich, 563).

Nowhere is the play's openness to personal interpretation and response more apparent than in relation to the character of Laura. If one had to say that the play is more 'about' any one of its characters than the others, it would probably be fair to argue that this is, ultimately, Laura's play. It is, after all, Tom's guilt over leaving his sister which eventually turns out to be the main motive for him telling the story of the play. And yet Laura has far fewer lines than any of the other characters (including Jim, who only appears in the last two scenes). She spends long periods sitting silently on stage watching the others talk, fight and laugh, and when she does speak, it is often simply in direct response to what others have said. We have largely to *guess* at what is going on inside Laura's head, and yet it is precisely because of this that she is a figure who commands such intensely personal responses from audiences. All we really know about her is that she is very fragile and shy, and in the absence of further reliable information, we tend to see her as a mirror for our own inner shyness and fragility (or that of someone we know). Many people will claim to feel something in common with Laura, which is to say that they fill in the blanks of the character's silence with some of their own most private, sheltered emotions. Laura comes to embody the vulnerability that we all hide and suppress in order to be able to function in 'a world lit by lightning' – a world of relentless noise, competition and pressure. She also embodies, more particularly, the experience of unrequited love, of having your heart broken – even unintentionally – by someone you adored but who did not adore you back. Most of us can identify directly with that, and Williams's play succeeds in tapping right into our memories of those experiences. Perhaps, just as Tom's telling of his story seems to act as a kind of exorcism for his own tortured memories, so the play itself can facilitate a kind of emotional healing for the audience members themselves, as deeply personal feelings are brought to the surface and confronted through identification with Laura's plight.

Autobiography or Fiction?

The Glass Menagerie was also, of course, very personal for Tennessee Williams himself. His real name was Thomas Lanier Williams, and in his youth he was always known as Tom, until he chose for himself his literary alias. An awareness of that fact instantly alerts us to the possibility that, on some level, the Tom of the play is a depiction of Tennessee himself, and that his memories and his need to exorcise them are more than merely fictional. Indeed, *Menagerie* is Williams's most blatantly autobiographical play – and this from a writer whose every work was to some degree a reflection of his own history. However, as Williams himself once remarked, if it is true that all of his work is in some way autobiographical, it is equally true that none of it is. *Menagerie* is a fiction which draws heavily on Williams's own experiences of young adulthood in St Louis, Missouri (the city in which the play itself is set), but the details of the story are also fictionalised, enhanced and rearranged in numerous ways. The events of the play are not revelations of a personal history but the component parts of a distinct, poetic vision dealing with themes of memory and loss, isolation and interdependence, to name but the most obvious. Williams clearly drew heavily on personal experiences in constructing his narrative, but was in no way limited or bound by them.

Even a cursory examination of the various biographical accounts of Tennessee Williams's life show us just how much the play owes to his own background. From the late 1920s to the mid-1930s, a period which encompassed the worst years of America's Great Depression, the Williams family lived in a small St Louis apartment (at 6544 Enright Avenue) almost identical to the one in which the play is set. In this ugly, cramped building – remembered with such lyrical disgust in Williams's opening stage directions – he learned first hand about the pettiness and degradation of lower-middle-class existence. It was also from this apartment that he could often hear the strains of music from a nearby ballroom, imaginatively recreated in the play as the Paradise Dance Hall.

Like Tom, Williams also had to listen frequently to his mother – Edwina Dakin Williams – reminisce longingly about the Deep South. The daughter of an Episcopalian minister who had had a series of parishes, she had spent most of the formative years of her youth in Tennessee, before moving even further south to Mississippi, after graduating from high school shortly after the turn of the century. Here she was able to play to the full the part of the Southern belle, as a member of one of the last generations to attempt to keep alive the traditions of the antebellum (or pre-Civil War) South.[3] Indeed, family accounts suggest that Edwina was known on occasion to receive thirty gentlemen callers in a single day, a figure which makes Amanda Wingfield's seventeen seem quite modest in comparison. However, like Amanda, Edwina made the 'mistake' of falling in love with a travelling representative of the Cumberland Telephone and Telegraph Company, Cornelius Coffin Williams. After they were married, Edwina at first remained at home in Clarksdale, Mississippi, while Cornelius continued to travel about, and their two elder children, Rose and Thomas, were born there. (Clarksdale reappears in many works by Tennessee Williams – *The Glass Menagerie* included – under the alias 'Blue Mountain'.) Eventually, however, Cornelius's company required him to settle in St Louis, Missouri, and he moved his young family there. Neither northern nor southern, Missouri had been a free state during the Civil War. Edwina always felt like a fish out of water there, and idealised her past in the South just as does Amanda in the play.

If Amanda is clearly based on Edwina, Laura is equally clearly based on Tennessee's sister Rose. Like Laura, Rose loved to play old Victrola records, and would even teach her brother the steps to dances she knew. Like Laura, Rose once enrolled after school at Rubicam's Business College (the name in the play is unchanged) in order to learn typing and shorthand, but could not handle the pressure of the coursework. She stopped going to the classes without telling her mother, and would wander about the city until it was time to go home; events which are recreated in every detail in Scene Two of the play. Amanda's subsequent decision to have Tom find a gentleman caller for Laura from among the employees of the shoe warehouse is also based on actual events. Tennessee himself worked for a period in the soul-deadening 'celotex interior' of the Continental Shoe Company for the princely sum of sixty-five

---

3 The American Civil War had taken place between 1861 and 1865, with the Southern states fighting for the right to break away from the United States and form their own Confederacy. The heavy defeat suffered by the Confederacy, and the South's enforced acceptance of the Union, meant that southern traditionalists shifted the battle to the field of culture instead, striving to keep alive the traditional, pre-war social customs in the face of the rapid industrialisation brought in by Northern capitalists after the war. These customs, of course, included a sharp divide between classes and races; hence Amanda Wingfield's casually unthinking references to the 'nigger' servants of her youth.

dollars a month (exactly Tom's wage in the play). His workmates there included Stanley Kowalski, whose name he was to immortalise in *A Streetcar Named Desire*. However, the boy whom he apparently did once bring home to meet Rose – Jim Connor – was actually known to him through the college fraternity of which he had been a member. In the event, it turned out that Connor already had 'strings attached' – just as Jim O'Connor has in the play.

Although much of the play's action is based on real-life events, it is also clear that Williams adapted and manipulated these details for his own purposes. For example, the episode at Rubicam's Business College and Edwina's campaign to find callers for Rose actually took place several years apart, in 1930 and 1934 respectively, rather than a few months apart. In 1930, aged twenty, Rose had in fact had no trouble attracting male visitors (whereas Laura has apparently never had any), but by twenty-four she was in danger of being 'left on the shelf'; hence her mother's campaign. This is typical of Williams's tendency carefully to rearrange actual experiences into new dramatic contexts. Thus, in the play, both Laura and Tom are said to have attended Soldan High School right up to graduation (or failure to graduate), but though Rose and Thomas did attend the actual St Louis school of that name, neither was there for more than a term, after which each moved elsewhere. Williams created a past in which both siblings attended the same school at the same time in order to lend greater emotional weight to the story of Jim's visit. Furthermore, to help give Jim and Laura's relationship a 'history' (which the real-life Jim and Rose never had), Williams borrowed the story of the word 'pleurosis' being misheard as 'blue roses' from the family anecdotes of a childhood friend whose father was a surgeon with German-speaking patients who misunderstood his English (see Leverich, 87–8). Williams found a way to take what had been a private joke and give it poetic resonance, 'Blue Roses' becoming the treasured pet name Jim had for Laura.

Other appropriated stories include Jim's account of taking his fiancée on a boat-trip upriver to Alton – which came directly from Williams's own memory of doing just that with an old girlfriend (see Leverich, 82). However, perhaps the most significant such 'borrowing' is the image of the glass menagerie itself, which – in real life – seems to have belonged not to Rose but to Mrs Maggie Wingfield, a resident of Clarksdale during Tennessee's childhood years. Mrs Wingfield, who was obviously the source for the name of the family in *Menagerie*, used to keep her collection of glass animals on display in her front window. This fact, discovered by Williams's authorised biographer Lyle Leverich, contradicts Williams's own story – sometimes told in interviews – that Rose had indeed kept glass animals, and that he had helped add to her collection. As Leverich points out, Williams was a notorious fabricator of such personal stories – 'the dramatist dramatizing himself' (Leverich, xxiv). According to Rose and Thomas's younger brother, Dakin (who has no equivalent in *Menagerie*), Rose had some glass ornaments, but 'just two or three pieces . . . very cheap little things, probably purchased at Woolworth's'.[4] Williams seems to have extrapolated from this small detail, marrying it with the memory of Mrs Wingfield's window, to create a symbolic representation of (as he himself put it) 'the fragile, delicate ties that must be broken, that you inevitably break, when you try to fulfil yourself' (quoted Devlin, 10).

The danger of causing damage in the process of trying to fulfil yourself is further emphasised in the play's narrative by virtue of another notable deviation from Williams's own family history. In *Menagerie*, Tom's father – the 'telephone man who fell in love with long distance' – has long since abandoned his family, leaving them to the untender mercy of fate in order to follow his own dreams. In real life, however, Cornelius Williams traded his telephone job for one with a shoe company (which is why young Thomas was able to find work with them), and stayed for the rest of his life in St Louis. He never did leave his family, even though he and his wife were constantly fighting – at considerable cost to the emotional stability of their children. Williams, by effectively rewriting his family's history as if his father had left them, achieves several dramatic purposes. For one thing, he is able to concentrate more tightly on depicting the remaining three members of the Wingfield family, who are each haunted in different ways by the absence of the father-figure. For another, he is able to render the father as a mysteriously romantic figure, a roamer of the world, rather than the stuffily unimaginative working man that Cornelius seems to have been. Tom thus has a father-figure whom he can aspire to emulate – and yet at the same time, the father's selfish desertion of his family has entrapped Tom more tightly than Williams himself ever was. Tom has to be the main breadwinner for the family, and his own struggle over whether or not to leave thus has far greater consequences than it actually did for Williams. His mother and sister will be deprived of an income by his departure, and Tom himself will thus inevitably be haunted by guilt at leaving them.

Of all the play's rearrangements of historical fact, arguably the most telling is Williams's decision to locate the dramatic action very specifically around 1937 and 1938. These years are clearly alluded to by

4   Quoted on xi of Robert Bray's Introduction to *The Glass Menagerie*, published by New Directions 1999.

Tom's various oblique narratorial references to the bombing of Guernica, the Spanish Civil War, and Neville Chamberlain's attempts to appease Hitler. However, the period of Williams family history which the play draws on was actually much earlier in the decade (around 1932–4). By 1938, the Williamses had moved out of Enright Avenue into a better home, Tennessee was at university in Iowa, and Rose had been committed to a sanatorium for the mentally unstable. The decision to locate the play in this year suggests two motives on Williams's part, the one obvious and the other far more private. Clearly, there is a wish to relate the events of the play to the broader historical realities of 1938, with the sense of foreboding and the threat of war which seemed to be in the air at that time: Williams wanted to parallel the domestic crisis of the play with far greater crises in the world at large, creating an interwoven narrative of public and private calamity. Moreover, as Christopher Bigsby has pointed out, the allusion to Chamberlain – the British Prime Minister who thought he had secured 'peace in our time' by dealing with Hitler – 'is an invitation to read the events of the play ironically'. With historical hindsight and distance, we see that, in their own ways, each of Williams's characters is as guilty as Chamberlain of blinding himself or herself to the stark realities of their situation, and of indulging 'the desire to live with comforting fictions, rather than confront brutal truths, a doomed and ultimately deadly strategy' (Bigsby, 1997, 35).

On a still more personal level, the choice of 1937–8 also perhaps implies that Williams is attempting to deal, in his own allusive way, with the greatest tragedy of his family life – Rose's descent into schizophrenia. It was this event, more than any other, which troubled Williams for the rest of his life, not only because of his own helplessness to do anything about it, but also because of a sense of guilt: he himself had been too preoccupied at this period – in trying to complete his stop-start university career and to find publishers for his writing – to be of much assistance to Rose at the time when she most needed his love and help. In subsequent years, Williams repeatedly attempted to exorcise the memory of his sister's decline through his writing, and it can be no mere coincidence that Tom Wingfield's abandoning of his helpless, shy sister to face the future alone shares exactly the same historical timetable as Tennessee Williams's failure to prevent his schizophrenic sister being committed to a sanatorium. (Rose was to remain institutionalised for the rest of her long life.)

The Glass Menagerie, then, can be read on one level as an attempt to find a way of dramatising the undramatisable. Not wishing to humiliate his beloved sister further by depicting Laura as insane, Williams imaginatively translated the memories of Rose's decline into a different, quieter kind of tragedy. The depiction of Laura's shyness and vulnerability – of the shattering of her tiny unicorn and of her fragile hopes for love – stands in as a kind of personal metaphor for the still more delicate state of Rose's mind. (Laura's crippled leg is also, of course, indicative of her fundamental difference and isolation from the rest of the world.) Crucially, though, Laura's situation is also far more comprehensible to an audience than is actual madness: we can sympathise with her as a person with acute emotional difficulties, whereas a schizophrenic character on stage would inevitably be viewed as something frighteningly alien to most people's experience. By hitting on the story of the gentleman caller, Williams found a way not only to face his own family's demons but also to translate them into terms which seem universally accessible and applicable. That, surely, is a hallmark of great writing.

Earlier Versions

An examination of Williams's various writings in the years preceding the appearance of *The Glass Menagerie* demonstrates that he struggled long and hard to find a satisfactory way of translating his sister's story into fictional terms. An early, unpublished one-act play titled *If You Breathe, It Breaks* tells the story of Mrs Wingfield and her *three* children (a girl and two boys), and focuses on the daughter's love for her glass menagerie and her mother's attempts to find her a gentleman caller. Similarly, a short story titled 'Portrait of a Girl in Glass' tells a tale almost identical to the one in *Menagerie*: many lines which eventually appeared in the play were first used here, and the closing paragraphs were adapted with little alteration to become Tom's closing speech. One noticeable difference between these early treatments of the story and *Menagerie* itself, however, is that the sketches actually give us more information about 'Laura' – her personality and character – than does the play. In *If You Breathe, It Breaks*, for instance, the daughter rejects her mother's attempts to find her a caller, saying that she prefers to be a 'front porch girl' and watch boys go by without them coming to see her. In 'Portrait of a Girl in Glass', Jim comes to call and Laura is let down just as in the play, but she seems eerily calm and unaffected by his revelation about his fiancée Betty, commenting simply that 'People in love take everything for granted' (Williams, 1967, 111). This and other moments in the story suggest that this Laura is rather otherworldly, or perhaps even a little simple. She asks at one point, for example, whether real stars actually have five points like the ones on Christmas trees. The narration also describes her fascination with a romantic novel called *Freckles*, which she reads parts of over and over again, apparently because she is strangely in love with the story's hero.

(This is the equivalent of *Menagerie*'s focus on Laura's yearbook and on the pictures of Jim it contains. In the last scene of *Menagerie*, Laura even refers to Jim as 'Freckles', a hangover from the earlier story.) Such touches, however endearing, also make the Laura of the story version seem more than a little odd. Perhaps they were quite faithful to Williams's experience of his sister's own oddness, but he seems to have realised that, by having Laura say less – thus making her less odd and more mysteriously shy – the play would be more profoundly affective for an audience.

Biographical accounts indicate that Rose herself was in fact anything *but* quiet and restrained. Though undoubtedly very vulnerable, she apparently 'looked and talked' very much like her mother – that is, she would chatter away incessantly just as Amanda does in the play (Leverich, 77). As a young woman, she had no shortage of young men wishing to date her, and she recorded lists of them in her journal, but none seems to have shown sustained interest – partly, it seems, because of her nervous chattering. By age twenty-four, an unmarried virgin, she was growing desperate enough that she even sexually propositioned one of her dates (a colleague of Thomas's from the shoe company, in fact). At the time, this was an unforgiveable breach of social customs: according to their brother Dakin, Thomas was sufficiently shocked by Rose's actions to corner her at home and tell her, loudly, that she disgusted him (see Leverich, 142). Given this information, it is perhaps not surprising to discover that, in the years prior to writing *The Glass Menagerie*, Williams created several short pieces which seem to allude to the more unsettling, sexually provocative or taboo-breaking side of Rose's behaviour and incipient schizophrenia. A short story entitled *The Dark Room* (1940), for example, depicts an Italian mother explaining to a social worker that her 'crazy' daughter never comes out of her permanently darkened bedroom. Eventually she reveals that the girl is regularly visited in the dark by an ex-boyfriend, and that as a result she is pregnant. This is a bizarre, grotesquely funny little piece haunted by the implications of madness.

Two other short plays deal more seriously with sexually provocative young women perceived from their brother's point of view. *The Long Goodbye* (1940) depicts a young man sitting in the same apartment as *Menagerie* is set in, watching removal men take away the furniture and reminiscing about his sister, whom he sees as if in a dream. Some unnamed fate seems to have befallen her, as a result of which she has lost all self-control: 'I used to have high hopes for you, Myra. But not any more. You're goin' down the toboggan like a greased pig. Take a look at yourself in the mirror. [You look] like a whore, a cheap one' (Williams, 1945, 176). *The Purification* (1940) – a strangely poetic one-act fable which seems heavily influenced by Lorca's *Blood Wedding* – also depicts a young man conjuring up his now vanished sister from memory, but here the girl's loss is lamented in poetry. The language strongly suggests that Williams was thinking of Rose's madness when he wrote this piece: 'For nothing contains you now, / no, nothing contains you, / lost little girl, my sister, / not even those – little – blue veins / that carried the light to your temples' (Williams, 1945, 59–60). The twist in this play is that the young man seems to have had an incestuous affair with his sister, a crime for which he finally decides to take his own life. Williams was to comment in later years that his relationship with Rose had indeed bordered on a kind of sexless incest – that their attachment to each other was the deepest one in either's life, and 'perhaps very pertinent to our withdrawal from extrafamiliar attachments' (quoted Leverich, 142).

For many, the most touching of these early one-act plays is *This Property Is Condemned*, in which a young boy named (again) Tom encounters a girl named Willie on a deserted railway embankment. Willie, Williams tells us in his stage directions, 'is a remarkable apparition . . . dressed in outrageous cast-off finery. . . . There is something ineluctably childlike and innocent in her appearance despite the make-up. She laughs frequently and wildly with a sort of ferocious, tragic abandon' (Williams, 1945, 197). This seems to be his most direct attempt to dramatise, in metaphoric terms, his sister's schizophrenic condition, and the result is an eerily affectionate portrait of someone who exists completely outside the normal human world. Willie talks wildly about how she is now homeless, cast out of the house in which she grew up, which now bears a sign, 'This Property is Condemned'. The label seems to apply as much to the character as to the building.

An analysis of these various short plays leads to the necessary conclusion that the character of Laura in *The Glass Menagerie* is not, as some commentators have suggested, simply an attempt to dramatise Rose straightforwardly, as Williams remembered her. Rather, Laura is just one manifestation of Williams's many, varied attempts to exorcise his sister's memory. Still other, later variations on the same theme include Cathy in *Suddenly Last Summer* (1958), who is held in a mental hospital and is in danger of being lobotomised – as was Rose – if she does not stop 'babbling'. Laura is in fact one of the quietest and most seemingly sane of Williams's many troubled young women, and the one with whom – as has been noted – audiences seem most able to empathise. One might even argue that Williams himself seems to understand more about Laura than he does about some of his other young female characters. If that is the case, it might well be because he – like many audience members after him – was able to project something of his *own* vulnerability and shyness onto this strangely quiet character.

Indeed, the available evidence suggests that Laura is based as much on the young Tennessee as she is on Rose. Most notably, the entire scenario of her tragically unrequited love for Jim is one which draws directly on Williams's adoration of Hazel Kramer, rather than on any infatuation of Rose's. Williams and Hazel were inseparable friends throughout most of their teenage years, and he was apparently convinced that the two of them would eventually marry and start a family. This, obviously, was before he had come to terms with his homosexuality, but even in later years Williams would describe Hazel as 'the great extra-familial love of my life' (quoted Leverich, 72). Hazel did not, however, feel the same way about him. Instead she met and fell in love with Ed Meisenbach, who was taller and much better looking than young Thomas, and the two of them eventually married. According to his biographers, it took Williams years to come to terms with Hazel's 'betrayal', years during which he was perceived by many as acutely shy and withdrawn. Understandably then, in *The Glass Menagerie*, Williams seems to be attempting an exorcism of these events too, at the same time as exploring his sense of guilt and responsibility in regard to Rose. With the sexes reversed, the character Jim O'Connor is as much Hazel Kramer as he is Jim Connor the fraternity man, and Ed Meisenbach is even worked mischievously into the play as 'Emily Meisenbach', the 'kraut-head' whom Jim was supposedly due to marry after high school. Given such information, one might speculate that the closeness of the relationship between Tom and Laura can be interpreted as reflecting the interdependence shared by two parts of the same psyche – with Tom as the controlled, ironic, public voice of the poet, and Laura as his private loneliness and vulnerability (a contrast of the 'masculine' and 'feminine' sides of one self?). But perhaps that would be to venture too far into the realms of psychoanalysis. The real interest of the play, after all, lies not in any window it opens to the writer's mind, but in the way that an *audience* can connect these characters with feelings and experiences of their own.

Theatrical Magic

The deft touch with which Williams rewrote and restructured his private family history to create a more universally accessible narrative was mirrored, very importantly, by the similarly free-handed approach he took in rewriting the rulebook of theatrical convention. Considered in relation to the staid, naturalistic fare which was standard in the American theatre in the 1940s, *The Glass Menagerie* constituted a minor revolution of stylistic innovation, and the play's originality in that time helps to explain why, in many ways, it still seems so fresh today, more than half a century later. 'In this play', the *New York Times* critic Clive Barnes commented when reviewing the 1975 Broadway revival, 'there was once a new dawn for the American theatre. And, naturally, dawns always survive' (quoted Arnott, 22–3).

That new dawn, it should be noted, had been preceded by a false dawn or two. Williams, always the experimentalist, had pushed his instinct for theatricality rather too far in writing what became his first full-length, professionally produced play, *Battle of Angels*. This complex allegory of good, evil and the struggles of the creative spirit proved too bewildering for audiences when first mounted in Boston in 1940, and the production was cancelled before its intended move to Broadway. Part of the problem had been the play's over-reliance on elaborate stage effects which created a minefield of possible technical hitches (the cue sheet reportedly called for 'endless sound effects, drums, guns, lightning and thunder, offstage pinball machines, wind, rain, guitars, songs, "hound-dawgs" and musical noises': quoted Leverich, 391). Indeed, on one night of the short-lived run, a pyrotechnic device almost torched the audience. Williams had to wait a full four years before *The Glass Menagerie* gave him a second chance at mainstream recognition, and in this play he applied the painful lessons of *Battle of Angels* by creating a far subtler, less bombastic piece which would stand or fall on the quality of the writing and acting rather than on the efficiency of the stage management.

The primary innovation of *Menagerie* lay in its very simplicity. Williams's notebooks for the period leading up to his writing of the play include an important meditation on his struggle to find a new working method. Most conventionally realistic theatre, he believed, was dull and prosaic, and his concern was to create a kind of stage poetry, which had accounted for the overreaching ambition of *Battle of Angels*. He had concluded, however, that he needed to seek 'apocalypse without delirium', by exploring muted understatement rather than elaborate spectacle: 'I have evolved a new method which in my own particular case may turn out to be a solution. I call it the "sculptural drama". . . . I visualize it as a reduced mobility on stage, the forming of statuesque attitudes or tableaux, something resembling a restrained type of dance, with motions honed down to only the essential or significant' (quoted Leverich, 446). It was from this principle that Williams derived the episodic structure for *The Glass Menagerie*: rather than adhering to the then-conventional practice of presenting a play's action in two or three extended acts, he broke his narrative down into seven scenes, each of which could serve to depict a distilled, 'sculptural' image of a situation, a relational dynamic between characters. These scenes rarely call for much physical action, and to prevent them becoming merely dully static, great precision is required from directors in creating on stage the kind of moving portraiture which Williams calls for, so as to encapsulate visually the emotional circumstances of each scene. Some of his stage directions help to emphasise this point explicitly. At the beginning of Scene Five, for example, he writes of Amanda and Laura 'removing dishes from the table in the dining room . . . their movements formalized almost as a dance or ritual, their moving forms as pale and silent as moths' (38). At the end of Scene Seven, Amanda is described as sitting with Laura in a silent tableau in which the only movements are her 'slow and graceful, almost dancelike [gestures], as she comforts her daughter' (96).

The charged stillness and deliberate understatement of the play helps to focus the audience's attention on the subtleties of the immediate moment. The forward narrative thrust of most conventional, realistic drama is thus suspended – at least partially – and we are enabled to find a heightened awareness of both the visual presence and emotional undercurrents of the scene at hand. When *Menagerie* first appeared, this technique caused some bewilderment among critics, who were unable to account for the strange power of a play whose plot seemed so simple and even uneventful: 'The lack of action in *The Glass Menagerie* is a bit baffling at first', noted the *New York Herald Tribune*, 'but it becomes of no consequence as one gets to know the family'.[5] The process of 'getting to know' the family is assisted greatly by the peculiar intimacy created by the play's relative stillness. 'Be prepared to listen and not cough', *New York Daily News* critic John Chapman warned his readers in 1945, 'else everybody but [Jim, played by Anthony] Ross will be almost inaudible in the back of the house. But I would not have it otherwise. A higher key might dispel the enchantment.' As Chapman implies, the quietness was not a result of flawed performances, but of the play itself, which needs to be played so delicately. The extended tableau of Scene Seven, in particular, in which Jim and Laura barely move from their seats on the floor around the candelabrum, has to create the illusion of being a deeply private conversation between two people sitting only inches away from each other. The scene is still frequently described by reviewers as both the highlight of the play and the point at which audiences are held in a kind of rapt silence, as they strain to hear a conversation which must necessarily be pitched in as hushed a tone as the theatre's physical size will permit.

In short, then, Williams's concern in writing *The Glass Menagerie* was to avoid the usual, mundane trappings of conventional stage realism (a

5 This quotation – along with all subsequent quotations from reviews of the 1945 New York premiere – is taken from material held in *The Glass Menagerie* press clippings folder at New York Public Library's Billy Rose Theatre Collection. Clippings are unpaginated.

manner in which, unfortunately, it is often presented), and instead arrive at a kind of heightened, intensified emotional reality through the play's use of tight focus and 'sculptural' stillness. As he says in the production notes preceding the published text, his concern is not with creating the 'photographic likeness' of a family's life, in a 'straight realistic play with its genuine Frigidaire and authentic ice-cubes', but with achieving 'a more penetrating and vivid expression of things as they are'. As if to trumpet this point from the very start, Tom declares in his opening monologue that the play 'is not realistic': rather, it attempts to evoke the hazy atmosphere of memory, and to achieve this, Tom explains, it uses dim, 'sentimental' lighting and background music to underscore scenes (common in cinema but not theatre). Technical stage devices are thus employed in a far subtler but no less significant way than they were in *Battle of Angels*. As Williams stresses in his production notes, the lighting and music are no mere appendages to the play but an integral part of his concern to create 'a new, plastic theatre' – by which he means a theatre that provides a three-dimensional sensory experience, as opposed to being primarily verbal or literary.

In America in the mid-1940s, Williams's staging ideas were highly unusual, but their successful employment in a play which proved so popular meant that *Menagerie* became extremely influential. The use of evocative music, atmospheric lighting and semi-transparent sets to create a heightened, even dream-like, new form of stage realism – which became known internationally, for a time, as 'the American Style' – was first seen in *Menagerie*, and then subsequently developed in other Williams plays such as *A Streetcar Named Desire*, and by other playwrights like Arthur Miller, who freely acknowledges the profound influence of Williams's work on the development of his own ideas for *Death of a Salesman*. One of the key staging devices in all these works was the use of gauze scenery, which when lit from the front can create the illusion of a solid wall, but which can then vanish almost completely when lit from behind. Williams made explicit use of this device in writing the stage directions for *Menagerie*, so that scenes behind the gauze could appear or dissolve magically, as they might in one's memory. Jo Mielziner, the legendary American set and lighting designer who worked on the premiere productions of all Williams's and Miller's most famous plays, once stated that, if Williams 'had written plays in the days before the technical development of translucent and transparent scenery, I believe he would have invented it.' Such devices, Mielziner stressed, 'were not just another stage trick' when used by Williams, but 'a true reflection of the contemporary playwright's interest in – and at times obsession with – the exploration of the inner man' (quoted Bigsby, 1984, 49–50).

That phrase 'the inner man' was a familiar one among artists of the first half of the twentieth century, not least because of the emergence – first in Germany and then, in different forms, elsewhere – of 'expressionism'. This was an aesthetic approach used in theatre, film and painting, which involved a rejection of the everyday surfaces of realism in favour of nightmarish imagery suggesting an outward 'expression' of the 'inner life' of either the artist or of the drama's protagonist. Typically, expressionist works were characterised by the use of heavily symbolic settings, stark black and white lighting, looming shadows, and so forth, to evoke a sense of inner, psychic turmoil (or *angst*, to use the German word). Williams was exposed to such ideas early on in his artistic formation (it is known, for example, that his high school mounted a production of Eugene O'Neill's expressionist play *The Hairy Ape* in 1931), and they seem to have been very important to him: in his production notes for *Menagerie* he refers to 'expressionism and all other unconventional techniques in drama' as helping inspire his concern to create a 'new plastic theatre'. *Menagerie* itself can be seen as expressionist insofar that it explores Tom's inner turmoil by depicting his memories – obviously an 'expression' of his inner mind – with the help of appropriately 'dreamlike' lighting and sound.

However, this is not an expressionist play *per se*, any more than it is a straightforwardly realistic one. For while expressionism would normally assume a tight, central focus on the struggles of the central character (as is the case, for instance, with *The Hairy Ape*), Tom is in many ways the character *least* central to the play's narrative action (which focuses on Amanda's attempts to find a gentleman caller for Laura, and the results of the caller's visit). Moreover, in Scene Three, at the point when Tom is having his most impassioned row with his mother, Williams specifies that Laura is to be lit more clearly than either of them, as if her reactions to the fight should be the real centre of attention. This is a good example of Williams's repeated use in the play of a kind of split focus effect, whereby the audience's attention is drawn in two directions at once, allowing a choice of what to look at. This strategy, as the critic David Savran has astutely pointed out, is antithetical to expressionism, and seems to have more in common with surrealism (see Savran, 94–6). This was another school of modernist aesthetics which was concerned less with the idea of expressing a central, governing consciousness than with the way that the workings of the subconscious mind – experienced through dreams and the spontaneous connections of memory – can seem both entirely irrational and strangely appropriate, producing images that are laterally linked by some hidden, subliminal logic. One need only look at the paintings of René Magritte or Salvador Dali to see how multiple images or contradictory ideas can co-exist in the same pictorial space, so as to create not a centrally focused image but a kind of dream landscape.

The clearest indication of *The Glass Menagerie*'s 'surrealist' side is Williams's directions for the use of magic lantern slides during the performance of the play; he suggests various captions and images which are to be projected onto a section of the stage set's (semi-transparent) walls. Clearly this device extends his use of split focus, as the audience's attention will sometimes be drawn away from the actors to the projections, but for this very reason Williams's suggestions for projections are almost always ignored by producers. Eddie Dowling, directing the premiere production, dispensed with them because he believed they were too strange and unwieldy, and although Williams still insisted on having them included in the published script, it has often been assumed that Dowling was correct, and that the author had not really thought his ideas through properly. Some critics have even suggested that Williams's interest in this device represented a misguided attempt to borrow from the German political theatre of Erwin Piscator and Bertolt Brecht. Williams had had personal experience, in the early 1940s, of working with Piscator at New York's New School for Social Research, but he came to despise Piscator and his methods. Although he was perhaps inspired by the German director's use of film sequences and titles in his plays, his own interest in such devices had very little in common with Piscator's attempts to drum a political message into his audiences by using, for instance, documentary film footage. Rather, Williams's suggestions for his magic lantern slides indicate an extension of his concern for the creation of a highly atmospheric theatrical experience.

Magic lanterns are an early form of slide projection which produce quite hazy, unfixed images. Playing on this quality, Williams outlines a series of titles and images which suggest an attempt to evoke something of the evocative, illogical logic of dreams, rather than the political didacticism of Piscator. For example, the very first projection, in Scene One, is 'Ou sont les neiges', which is part of a famous line by the French poet Villon: 'Ou sont les neiges d'antan?' The phrase translates as 'Where are the snows of yesteryear?', and for those familiar with it, it would automatically conjure a certain sense of nostalgia, as it does in its original context. Even for those unfamiliar with the source (or even with French), there is an oddly evocative feel to the phrase. Williams is using it as a kind of shorthand to generate in his audience the kind of wistful emotions which are associated with nostalgic remembrance. And yet at the same time, his fragmenting of the quote, and its repetition later in the same scene, in its entirety, creates a strange sense of disjuncture: the phrase seems oddly broken, but recurs insistently, just as – in dreams – words sometimes nag at us which seem both obscure and eerily significant.

A similar use of repetition occurs in Scene Two. At the start of the scene, an image of blue roses is projected on the screen. Blue roses do not, of course, exist in real life, and the projection of the image is bound to provoke questions for audiences because it precedes any mention of blue roses in the dialogue itself (Laura explains later in the scene that this was Jim's nickname for her in high school). However, when the words are eventually mentioned, the spectator's mind is likely to connect back to the floating, poetic image of blue roses seen previously. Williams thus creates a strange, elliptical link between present and past moments, looping backwards in time rather than obeying the usual, logical linearity of dramatic narrative.

Throughout the play, the use of projections operates in suggestive ways like this, opening up strange connections and resonances rather than making specific, definable points. Titles are also used to provide a kind of ironic commentary on the dramatic action – as for instance when Jim informs Amanda that he already has a steady girlfriend. A caption reading 'the sky falls' accompanies Amanda's stunned pause, underlining just how much this means to her in a manner which is both mischievously witty and oddly moving. It should be noted that not all of Williams's projection ideas are as telling as this, partly because he never had the chance to see them 'road-tested' in production and so amend the text appropriately. He does, however, specify that productions should experiment with and extrapolate from his suggestions. The common decision to dismiss the projections as an inappropriate appendage to the action is unfortunate, because a whole dimension of Williams's conception for the play is thus lost. Even audiences of the acclaimed London production of 1995 (which experimented with staging in various innovative ways) only saw a watered-down version of the projection idea: the director Sam Mendes opted to use title captions at the beginning of each scene (some of them different from those in the script), but not to try out any of the other phrases or images suggested by Williams.

It is sometimes possible, however, in smaller-scale productions, to see all Williams's ideas put into practice. In the interests of seeing what might happen if the projection device were given a chance, I myself chose to direct a production in 1999 in which the projections were an integral part of the show. Instead of a magic lantern, we used modern video technology to create fluid, dream-like image sequences inspired by Williams's suggestions. Audience reactions to the production made it clear that we had successfully disproved the conventional assumption that the projections would distract from, rather than enhance, the actors' performance of the dialogue. The critic for Glasgow's *Herald* newspaper commented that the production had brought 'yet another layer to an already multi-faceted play, without detracting from the vital fragility that is the drama's core'. For me, that judgement demonstrates that Williams knew exactly what he was doing in his suggestions for the play's staging. *Menagerie* draws on and hybridises elements of realism, expressionism and surrealism to create what is still – more than fifty years on – a highly original theatrical experience.

Playing the Roles

As should by now be clear, *The Glass Menagerie* has to be seen in production in order for one to gain a full impression of Williams's vision. The play as written is simply the blueprint for a visual, sculptural, musical event, a fully conceived example of 'a new plastic theatre'. Simply to read the words on the page is akin to reading the score of a concerto without actually hearing it. That said, it should also be stressed that the successful presentation of *The Glass Menagerie*'s 'vital fragility' on stage depends, above all, on the work of the actors. No amount of inventiveness in direction or design will help a production if the characters are not presented persuasively.

To an extent, of course, that is true of any play, but it is especially true of a piece requiring such restrained understatement in its performance. *Menagerie* calls for a uniformly strong, ensemble cast (as opposed to a cast dominated by one or two stars), in which each actor is able to make apparent the many different sides of his or her character. Williams's notion of a 'sculptural' drama is useful in underlining the fact that this play operates to present each character from a number of different perspectives – almost as if the audience were moving around a three-dimensional sculpture to gain a complete picture of it. Viewed from one angle, for example, Amanda might appear to be an oppressive, selfish monster of a mother, yet from another she seems deeply caring. The key to any production of this play lies in the actors' ability to create the kind of heart-rendingly human portraits which allow us to understand and even sympathise with each character, as well as seeing clearly his or her flaws and mistakes. Ultimately, what makes *The Glass Menagerie* so moving is that it presents neither villains nor victims, but four characters who are all seeking, in their own ways, to 'do the right thing'. The desperate irony of the situation is that their seeking – so often at cross-purposes – leads them inexorably to create their own small tragedy.

Amanda

Amanda is the most obviously complex and multifaceted of these characters, and Williams acknowledges as much in his initial character notes. His description of 'a little woman of great but confused vitality' immediately indicates some of her contradictions, as does his note that 'there is much to admire in Amanda, and as much to love and pity as to laugh at'. In Amanda, Williams presents us, unapologetically, with a detailed portrait of his own mother, Edwina Dakin Williams. His own conflicted feelings toward a woman he both adored and resented are readily apparent here. Whereas all the other characters in *Menagerie* are – as has been noted – creatively adapted from their real-life counterparts, the biographical evidence suggests that Amanda's characterisation represents a fairly direct attempt on Williams's part to portray Edwina as he saw her, in all her complexity. Edwina herself often denied any connection to the character, but at other times would reportedly play up the link for her own benefit – a pattern of contradiction which would be plausible coming from Amanda herself. Certainly almost every detail of the characterisation is consistent with Amanda's real-life model – from her incessant chattering to her moments of desolation, from her romantic attachment to the old South to her discomfort in St Louis, from her loudly voiced dissatisfaction with her husband to her reminiscences about her one true lost love (Duncan J. Fitzhugh in the play; John Singleton in real life: see Leverich, 31). According to his brother Dakin, Williams's depiction of Amanda was so true to life that Edwina could have sued him for plagiarism: he claims that not only turns of phrase but also entire speeches (such as Amanda's opening monologue about not eating too fast) were lifted almost verbatim from Edwina's repertoire (see Leverich, 567).

Williams's sheer attention to detail in creating this portrait meant that the character of Amanda was at the very heart of the play as originally conceived. After Williams submitted an early treatment to his agent, Audrey Wood, she encouraged him to concentrate his attention on Amanda, and Williams replied that 'yes, the central and most interesting character is certainly Amanda and in the writing the focus would be on her mainly' (quoted Leverich, 509). Sure enough, Amanda dominates the stage for large portions of the play, with her chattering monologues and her forceful arguments with her children. And yet she is not, in the final analysis, 'the central character': a play's protagonist needs to be seen to go on an emotional journey and, finally, to be somehow changed by it, but Amanda, of all the characters in *Menagerie*, is the one who changes least. Her final, screaming rage at Tom simply reiterates all the qualities and flaws we have seen throughout the play, as her passionate concern for her daughter's well-being becomes mixed up with selfishness and unthinking cruelty (in a particularly harsh blow, she even refers to Laura as 'a cripple', despite insisting throughout the play that she does not see her as one). Williams, it seems, had to present Amanda as he saw his mother – as an unchangeable force rather than as a dramatic subject capable of emotional evolution. The play is written in such a way that, however much we may come to sympathise with her – understanding that her over-protectiveness, for example, is a result of years of having to hold the family together by sheer force of will – we nevertheless always view Amanda from the outside rather than as a character to identify with directly. We see her, in short, through Tom's eyes.

The challenge for any actor playing Amanda, therefore, is to find her way 'inside' a character that the play itself seems to view from the 'outside' – to inhabit the part in such a way that its external pyrotechnics seem supported by a plausible inner emotional life. For while Amanda is certainly the 'flashiest' part in the play, she is also the hardest for an actor to flesh out convincingly. She is, as one critic observes, 'the play's dominating force. Her asphyxiating, over-protective concern for her grown-up offspring combined with an irritating manner, a genteel dottiness and a tendency to live in the past, requires an actress with a larger than life persona and a formidable technique' (*LTR*, 1995, 1279). The play's original production succeeded in large part thanks to the fact that just such a person was found to play Amanda: Laurette Taylor, one of the great stars of the American theatre, who had been out of favour with producers for some years because of her unreliability due to alcoholism, was persuaded to make a final, glorious 'comeback' to play this part. She herself came to see her performance in *Menagerie* as the crowning achievement of her career, and certainly the critics saw that first production as being very much Taylor's show. 'Miss Taylor's performance is one of the most superb that I have ever seen in the theatre', commented the reviewer in New York's *Morning Telegraph*, while the *World Telegram*'s Burton Roscoe noted simply that 'I can't say anything adequate' to describe her: 'You can't describe a sunset. . . . I never hope to see again, in the theatre, anything as perfect.'

In subsequent years, the part of Amanda has been played by a string of star actresses. As one of the few truly complex, challenging roles for middle-aged women in the contemporary repertoire, it has attracted the likes of Helen Hayes (who played Amanda in the London premiere in 1948, and then again in New York in 1956), Maureen Stapleton (who appeared in New York productions in both 1965 and 1975), Jessica Tandy (New York, 1983), Susannah York (London, 1989), Julie Harris

(New York, 1994) and Zoë Wanamaker (London, 1995). The part has also been played on screen by Gertrude Lawrence (1950 film version), Katharine Hepburn (1973 television version) and Joanne Woodward (1987 film version). In the hands of such performers, the role of Amanda has been successfully played as the *tour de force* that it is, although Laurette Taylor's performance remains the most celebrated of all.

Today, the part of Amanda is considered the definitive depiction of the 'ageing Southern belle', a female type who appears in many other plays and movies, always lamenting the loss of the old, pre-Civil War days of debutante balls and gentlemen callers. This is so much the case that in 1994, the American playwright Christopher Durang even wrote an affectionate parody of *The Glass Menagerie* entitled *For Whom the Southern Belle Tolls* (in which 'Lawrence' receives a 'feminine caller' who breaks the most treasured swizzle stick in his collection). The portrait of the mother in this play is a satirical pastiche of the stereotypical Southern belle, but one cannot help feeling that Durang has somewhat missed the point of Williams's portrait of Amanda, which is already highly satirical and ironic. Amanda, after all, must have been born in the last decades of the nineteenth century (Edwina was born in 1884), and so is far too young to remember the pre-War days herself (the Civil War lasted from 1861 to 1865). Even assuming that all her romantic memories of her youth are true, they must necessarily be memories of a Southern culture which was, even then, looking backwards to idealised, bygone days. Moreover, Williams makes very clear that Amanda's memories are themselves an inextricable mix of fact and rose-tinted fiction. His decision to portray her attempting to peddle cheap romantic fiction over the telephone is a further, wryly ironic touch: Amanda's picture of herself as a Southern belle seems to owe as much to reading pulp novels like *Gone With the Wind* as it does to her actual youth. Williams, through his portrait of Amanda, cuttingly satirises the tendency of many Southerners of his day to romanticise a golden age that never was. He may also have been thinking of his mother's tendency to 'perform' her own constructed idea of Southernness: the daughter of mid-Westerners from Ohio, Edwina chose to cultivate and maintain a genteel Deep South accent throughout her life, despite living the majority of it in urban St Louis. Clearly, any actor playing Amanda should be careful to explore the emotional complexities lying behind her adoption of stereotypical Southern belle behaviour, rather than simply playing her as a comic old woman. As Williams stresses in his character notes, she must not be played as a type, but as a distinct individual with unique assets and flaws.

Notably, however, one aspect of Amanda's 'Southernness' which Williams does not explore in any detail in the play is her racism. Race issues are dealt with more fully in other Williams works, but in *Menagerie*, Amanda's casual references to 'darkies' and 'niggers' pass without comment. When the play was first written, this would simply have been accepted as a standard (if regrettable) part of the vocabulary of a person like Amanda: for her, blacks are simply the social inferiors she was brought up to regard them as. Yet today – words such as 'nigger' are particularly inflammatory and controversial – many people are likely to find the play's failure to query Amanda's racism problematic. One option, of course, is simply to cut or change the offending words. In 1989, Washington DC's Arena Stage chose this option when mounting a revival of the play with an all-black cast. Ruby Dee, who played Amanda in that production, rejected criticisms of the casting choice by insisting that the play's story could plausibly apply to a black family as well as a white one, and that even Amanda's memories were believable because there were, in fact, property-owning blacks in the old South. Few reviewers found either the production or Dee's explanation convincing, but it is intriguing to note that two years later, when San Francisco's Lorraine Hansberry Theater also presented an all-black production, the notices were much more favourable. In this instance, not a word of the script had been cut, so a black Amanda was heard to refer to 'the darky'. An unsettling double focus effect was thus created, with the play's language appearing to be contradicted by the visual sign of skin colour: this production did not pretend the Wingfields were a black family, but presented a white family played by black actors. This approach allowed for an implicit critique of Amanda's racism to be apparent in the very staging of the play. It was the kind of overtly theatrical strategy which one suspects Williams himself might have approved of.

Tom

Another controversial issue, which would never have occurred to audiences when the play was first staged, is raised by the unanswered question of exactly where Tom goes at night. He repeatedly insists that he simply goes to the movies, but his story is never entirely convincing, especially as he periodically returns to the apartment in the small hours of the morning, blind drunk. Various critics have suggested in recent years that Tom – like Tennessee Williams himself – might be gay, and that *The Glass Menagerie* can be seen as an example of a 'closet drama' in which homosexuality is never mentioned, but into which those 'in the know' can read a hidden gay subtext. According to this theory, Tom's nocturnal activities might include attending gay bars, which would certainly help explain why he feels unable to discuss his whereabouts with his mother.

There is, however, nothing to support this reading besides speculation, and there are many legitimate objections to it. For one thing, Williams himself did not begin to experiment with homosexuality until after he had left St Louis: during the period of his life fictionalised in *Menagerie*, he was still lusting hopelessly after Hazel Kramer. Accordingly, the character Tom sometimes seems very lonely and unloved – as is most clearly indicated by his reference in Scene Five to his voyeuristic watching of the couples making out in the dark alleyway beside the apartment: 'this was the compensation for lives which passed like mine, without change or adventure' (39). Even so, the debate over where Tom goes at night is indicative of the shadowy uncertainties which seem to shroud this character: despite his being the play's narrator and moving force, he seems to be the one about whose motives and behaviour we can be least sure. It could be argued that Williams, in portraying Tom as a version of his younger self, chose to surround him with ambiguity precisely because he himself felt very uncertain and ambiguous about his own identity at that time. In that sense, the question of Williams's sexual orientation – which was clearly part and parcel of his youthful confusion and anxiety – does perhaps have a significant, subtextual role in the play.

The critic David Savran, who has written very shrewdly on the gay dimensions of Williams's work in his book *Communists, Cowboys and Queers*, could be summing Tom up when he refers to 'the never-quite-whole subject that commandeers Williams's work', who is 'unable to claim the position of "hero" or even "protagonist". Instead, [he] is constantly decentered and dispossessed, stumbling through a dramatic structure that is similarly decentered and unstable' (Savran, 98). Whereas Amanda is an intricately drawn, fully filled-out portrait of a woman seen from the outside, Tom is at once a character to whom we have more direct emotional access (as the play's narrator) and of whom we know less. His mysteriousness is underlined, in particular, by the fact that he operates on a hazy borderline between the past events he is describing and the unspecified 'present' from which he narrates to us. In playing the role, an actor must decide whether he is presenting two clearly distinct Toms – older and younger – or whether in fact the older Tom is *reliving* the events himself. The latter possibility would make his behaviour in the scenes themselves even more uncertain (did he 'really' say this 'back then', or is he rewriting his words in retrospect?), and it should be noted that it is this latter possibility that Williams himself seems to call for in specifying that Tom appears at the start 'dressed as a merchant sailor'. Since the actor playing Tom has no opportunity to change into clothes more appropriate to his warehouse-working days (at least during the first scene), we thus see the character enacting the events of his past while wearing the uniform of the future career into which he will escape at the end of the play. Again, it is a shame that this costume specification is a stage direction so often ignored in production, because it underlines vividly the ambiguous doubleness (or even the double vision) which seems to surround Tom throughout the play. The younger Tom needs urgently to leave his family and St Louis, but he also needs to stay, for Laura's sake; the older Tom looks back with fond nostalgia, but also with haunted guilt. As his final speech makes particularly clear, Tom is constantly reliving the past in his present, and the collision of those two worlds seems to be steadily driving him to distraction.

It is interesting to note that Williams himself remained extremely ambivalent about his portrayal of Tom in the play, agreeing with a number of his critics that 'the narrations are not up to the play' (quoted Arnott, 23). That judgement is, to say the least, a questionable one, given that Tom's narrations do so much to contextualise, comment on, and ironise the events depicted in the scenes. The play would be much the poorer (and more sentimental) without the frame of critical perspective which the narrations place around the action. Moreover, without the narrations, we would know still less about Tom, who remains so peripheral to so many of the scenes – watching from the dark like the movie-viewers he describes to Jim in Scene Six, rather than participating directly. The opening of Scene Four, in which Tom comes home drunk at 5 a.m., is one of the few moments in the play when our attention is focused exclusively on Tom's personal conflicts, and even this was a late addition to the text. It was written by Williams to prevent the play's first director Eddie Dowling, who was also playing Tom, from inserting his own drunk scene to give himself a 'star turn' moment. Williams later conceded that the scene he was required to add 'does little harm to the play', but Lyle Leverich is more accurate in his assessment that it is positively beneficial – that Dowling's instincts about what the play needed were right, even if his methods were questionable (see Leverich, 552–3). Williams had written Tom from such a personal, ambivalent perspective that he needed an objective eye to point out where the character needed fleshing out a little. In the final script, Williams strikes just the right balance between mystery and clarity in his characterisation of Tom.

Jim

By comparison with Tom, the role of Jim seems quite straightforward. He is, as Williams specifies in the shortest of his character notes, 'a nice, ordinary young man', and that is indeed, on one level, all that needs to be said about him. Although Tom admits, in his opening narration, to using this character as a symbol more than a person, his comment applies more to the *idea* of the gentleman caller as it is deployed through the first half of the play than it does to Jim himself. In my own 1999 production, we extended our non-naturalistic approach to the play by having the caller visible through most of the first act, as a ghost-like figure standing at the window of the apartment, and occasionally moving through the living space. This idea, which was very effective visually, was inspired by Tom's description of the caller as a 'specter' who 'haunted our small apartment' (19). However, once he was on stage as Jim in Scene Six, the actor playing Jim (Jack Fortescue) found that he had to shed all sense of ghostliness and become very ordinary and human.

Unlike the three Wingfields, Jim is in touch with the realities of the outside world, and seems happy to function according to social conventions such as climbing the career ladder and marrying a nice girl from the same religious background. Indeed he seems, by some distance, to be the most well-adjusted character in the play. He has apparently experienced his fair share of disappointments, which makes him able to sympathise with Laura, and he has dreams and ambitions for himself just as does Tom, but he has managed not to let these haunt him. There is no reason not to suppose that, when he leaves at the end of the play, he will go off to lead a happy, ordinary life with Betty and find a solid (if unspectacular) career in radio or television.

Some have argued that Jim's ordinariness is intended by Williams to be seen as dully oppressive, and certainly the forces of conformity are seen as dangerously destructive in other Williams plays. It might be possible to play Jim as a crass, rather oafish character whose jolly exclamations such as 'comfortable as a cow!' and 'Hey there Mr Light Bulb!' seem grating, and whose dreams of '*Knowledge* – Zzzzp! *Money* – Zzzzzzp! – *Power!*' seem hollow and greedy (82). Yet to do so would be to miss not only the playfulness of these lines ('I guess you think I think a lot of myself!'), but also to remove the emotional depth from Jim's entire encounter with Laura. If he were played as a blundering corporation man, Laura's adoration of him would seem merely foolish, and the aftermath of the kiss between them would lack dramatic tension. An audience has to be convinced that Jim is fundamentally a good person, and to want – for Laura's sake – to see a relationship between the two of them begin to flower. The tragic irony of the situation is only apparent if we are convinced that he is trying to 'do the right thing' – first, in trying to encourage Laura and bring her out of herself (which leads him, unwittingly, into a romantic entanglement with her), and secondly in deciding to tell her about his fiancée Betty. He himself seems trapped by convention at that point, having to return to his 'steady girl' even though he seems to see something more indefinably radiant in the crippled Laura: both of them thus suffer *because* of his basic decency.

Reviewers of the 1995 London production made a particular point of praising Mark Dexter for his performance as Jim. According to *What's On*'s Graham Hassell, Dexter had 'the personable ebullience of a young James Stewart, a good-intentioned young old fogey' (*LTR*, 1995, 1685). The *Financial Times* critic Ian Shuttleworth concurred that 'Jim's smug self-satisfaction [is] offset by a genuine warmth and sympathy', and that Dexter 'is visibly "doing" Jimmy Stewart: there could be no finer model for such a figure' (ibid.). In the original 1945 production, Anthony Ross was also singled out by critics – almost as often as Laurette Taylor herself – for his remarkably sympathetic performance as Jim. According to the *Wall Street Journal*, Ross 'did the most perfect job of all'. Interestingly, praise such as this is rarely if ever accorded to actors playing the part of Tom, even though that role might seem, on first inspection, to be the more significant. For where Tom always remains in the margins of the play, a facilitator more than a star player in his own drama, Jim controls the ebb and flow of events in the final, climactic scene between himself and Laura – an encounter described, even as early as 1945, as 'one of the most amazing love scenes ever written' (*New York Journal-American*).

Laura

One of the most notable things about that crucial scene is that Jim and Laura's conversation is somewhat one-sided. Jim, who aspires to social improvement through acquiring skills in public speaking, tends to talk a lot even when he is most nervous (this much he shares with Amanda), whereas Laura rarely speaks in anything other than short, hesitant sentences, and several times retreats into complete silence. The great difficulty for an actor playing Laura, throughout the play, is that the part is primarily *reactive* rather than active: Laura almost always responds to the words and actions of others rather than initiating anything herself. Her responses, moreover, frequently come in the form of loaded silence. Somehow, given very little to work with in terms of dialogue, the actor has to convey an almost unearthly delicacy – to embody the most fragile and vulnerable feelings imaginable by an audience. In this regard, playing Laura is perhaps an even bigger challenge for an actor than playing Amanda.

Tellingly, Williams's intentions for the way Laura is to be perceived are made most apparent not in his character notes (though these are well detailed) but in his lighting suggestions. 'The light upon Laura should be distinct from the others, having a peculiar pristine clarity such as light used in early religious portraits of female saints or madonnas . . . where the figures are radiant in atmosphere that is relatively dusky.' Clearly, while Williams saw Jim as the most bluntly realistic character in the play, Laura – by contrast – is intended to be iridescent, representing the most sheltered and treasured of our inner hopes. How, exactly, is an actor to carry this off? To begin with, there are practical issues to consider, such as not overplaying Laura's limp. If she seems too awkward in her movements (or even grotesquely comic, as I have seen in one misguided instance), the audience may look *at* her with a pity, but will be unlikely to identify *with* her directly. Williams's insistence that Laura's limp 'need not be more than suggested on the stage' is important because it focuses attention not on an actual physical handicap, but on an inner vulnerability: Laura *feels* that her 'clumping' is more obvious than it is because, as Jim astutely observes, she is suffering from an 'inferiority complex' – feeling herself to be worthless in the eyes of the world.

Yet while these considerations can be discussed between director and actor, a successful portrayal of Laura is dependent, ultimately, on casting. An actor has to be found who can project a kind of ethereal yet vivid presence, and this is not something which can be learnt or acquired. Notably, in most major productions, casting directors have opted for quite slender actresses – presumably because they can more readily appear fragile. This was certainly true of the original Laura, Julie Haydon, in the 1945 production (Haydon eventually went on to play Amanda in a 1980 New York revival), and more recent Lauras have included waif-like figures such as Amanda Plummer (New York, 1973), Martha Plimpton (Chicago, 1999), and Calista Flockhart – best known as the alarmingly thin star of television's *Ally McBeal* (New York, 1994). Perhaps the most celebrated performance of Laura to date, however, was that in Sam Mendes's 1995 London production at the Donmar Warehouse: 'Claire Skinner delivers a luminous performance, arousing a magnificent pity without ever becoming simply pitiful', commented Ian Shuttleworth (*LTR*, 1995, 1685). 'The pale, tremulous centre of this production is Claire Skinner's Laura', concurred *Time Out*'s Jane Edwardes: 'even when her brother and mother are having one of their frequent rows, one's main concern is with what effect it will have on her' (ibid.). Such comments suggest that Skinner's award-winning performance was directly in line with Williams's intentions for the part.

Crucially, though, Skinner also demonstrated that the part requires far more than an emphasis on either physical or mental fragility. Critics were quick to point out the underlying strengths of the character as she played it. Robert Butler, in the *Independent on Sunday*, wrote of Skinner's urgency and freshness, counterbalancing the usual hesitancy and dreaminess, and stressed that, 'above all, she has an exceptional quality of stillness' (*LTR*, 1995, 1280). It is important for any production to find such qualities in Laura, so that she does not become merely a victim – and so that the narrative in general does not become merely 'sentimental' or 'mawkish'. This 'tough, delicate masterpiece' of a play (Jeremy Kingston in *The Times*) is made all the more moving because 'the playwright knew, as so many of the subsequent directors have not, to leaven the torment with darts of grim humour; nowhere is this more touching than when Skinner's Laura strives to alleviate Jim's guilt at having accidentally broken the horn off her favourite glass unicorn whilst dancing with her' (Shuttleworth). The moment described here is central to the play, as Laura forces back her desperate disappointment at the damage to her most treasured possession, and tries to assure Jim that 'It doesn't matter. Maybe it's a blessing in disguise' (86). She even jokes about the unicorn being happier now that he can blend in with the other horses and appear 'less freakish', and in so doing she succeeds in putting Jim at ease again despite her own pain. This is a key example of the hidden emotional strength which Laura demonstrates at pivotal moments throughout the play (another one comes minutes later as she gives Jim the unicorn as 'a souvenir'). In performances such as Claire Skinner's, one realises that Laura is, paradoxically, the most resilient of the characters in the play, as well as the most delicate.

And yet if this is the case, we must ask whether Tom's despairing guilt at the end of the play is justified or not. The closing narrative suggests that, in leaving St Louis, Tom has abandoned Laura to some terrible fate of loneliness and isolation, yet Tom can be wrong – as the play makes very clear. Desperate regret may indeed have been Williams's legitimate feelings about his own sister's committal to a mental institution, but there is nothing in the play besides Tom's narrative to suggest that Laura has been consigned to a similarly hopeless fate. Indeed, if anything, the unexpected strength she finds with which to comfort Jim for his blundering suggests that she might be able to find it in herself to recover from the blows she receives. Perhaps the damage Jim causes really is 'a blessing in disguise'. In my own 1999 production, Elly Reid – playing Laura – found that one of the most crucial moments in deciding her character's fate was the 'Yes!' which Laura utters after Amanda asks her whether or not she wishes the best for Jim in the future (94). This is also Laura's final line in the play, and if it is delivered in a downbeat or tearful way, Laura is left appearing broken and empty. Yet if, as Elly chose to do, Laura looks up with a smile, fighting back her own sadness in order to bless Jim, to thank him for his goodness to her, then a quite different possibility is registered. Perhaps, we speculate, she can now find it in herself to 'get over' Jim, and move on. In our production, at the moment in Tom's final speech when he speaks of feeling his sister touch his shoulder, Laura actually did step up to him, place a hand on his shoulder, and look longingly at him as if to say – across time and space – 'Tom, please don't torture yourself, I'm doing fine!' Tom, of course, remained lost in his own torments, but many audience members commented how unexpectedly hopeful they found the play's ending, as a result of the way Elly played it.

Our approach to the play was partially inspired by Paula Killen's one-woman show, *Still Life with Blue Roses* (Chicago, 1997) – one of a growing number of creative responses to *The Glass Menagerie* (others include Durang's *For Whom the Southern Belle Tolls* and a 1993 dance adaptation by New York's Classic Stage Company, intriguingly entitled *Faith Healing*). Killen, clearly a great admirer of the play, took as her starting point the fact that Laura, although central to *Menagerie*, never really has the chance to speak for herself. In the first part of *Still Life with Blue Roses*, she sits on a couch in a candlelit set reminiscent of that in *Menagerie*, and – as Laura – explains to the audience that, while she appreciates Tom's efforts to write about her, she wishes that he had made the effort to find out how she really felt about things. Killen's wryly amusing commentary is, implicitly, a feminist critique of the tendency of male authors to place their female characters in silenced positions where they seem powerless to help themselves, and are dependent on or subjected to the actions of men (in this case, Jim and Tom, who both leave Laura abandoned). Turning this situation on its head, Killen has her Laura leave St Louis. Part two of *Still Life* is in the form of a public lecture, as Laura presents a sequence of film clips to her audience, documenting her attempts to move to Hollywood and make a movie of her life. Again the presentation is both very funny (especially her attempts to get the casting right) and very poignant, making full use of imagery and titles from Williams's neglected ideas for projections to form a new narrative in which Laura takes control of her life as a modern, media-conscious woman. The irony is – probably quite deliberately on Killen's part – that one is left by the end with a real sense of loss, a feeling that Laura's fragile uniqueness has somehow been mislaid amid the rough and tumble of modern life, and that she (like her unicorn before her) has become 'just like all the others'.

Responding to *Still Life with Blue Roses*, I wanted to see if it was possible to present *Menagerie* in such a way as to bring out a sense that Laura, though largely silent, is still in some way the author of her own narrative, rather than the helpless puppet of Tom's. We discovered, interestingly, that there are numerous points in the play which lend themselves to this idea. Even moments as simple as when she accidentally calls Jim 'Freckles' can be rendered in such a way as to suggest that such a slip betrays a whole world of private passions which remain hidden within her, but which might one day begin to find their way out into the world. Still more telling, in our production, was the point in Scene Four when Tom falls asleep, as Laura watches over him. At this point, a simple glance from Laura up to the audience was enough to suggest that, just maybe, she is quietly presenting us with a kind of alternative narrative to Tom's own story. He believes himself to be in control of the memories he is presenting, but in moments such as those when he 'sleeps' or is absent from the stage, we can perhaps glimpse another possibility.

Experiments such as this one demonstrate clearly that there are many different ways to approach *The Glass Menagerie*, and many possible readings to be found. Far from being the mawkishly sentimental piece it is sometimes thought to be by those who have not properly explored its many layers of emotion, wit, irony and theatrical inventiveness, *Menagerie* remains a rich source of material to be tapped afresh by each new generation of actors, directors and designers. Yet while it is demonstrably a play which constantly lends itself to new interpretations and adaptations, it also remains, at base, a very simple and moving narrative about a family, which has the power to speak to us all about memory and loss, love and hope.

Production History since 2000 (by Katherine Weiss)

Since its successful debut, *The Glass Menagerie* has become a favourite for audience members across the world and an American staple in introductory drama courses and anthologies. Williams's 1945 memory play remains relevant to twenty-first-century audiences despite its references to Guernica, the Spanish Civil War, the Great Depression and the film *Gone with the Wind*. Its popularity lies in both its economic realities, as twenty-first-century Americans face a recession, and in its memorable characters – a family of three struggling with their own financial hardships. For these reasons, the play continues to be performed on major and small stages in America, the United Kingdom and Europe. This well-crafted play with strong characters is perfect for seasoned actors, university students and amateurs.

Gregory Mosher's 2004 revival of *The Glass Menagerie* at the Kennedy Center in Washington DC was named a 'fresh interpretation of a familiar' classic by Brett Ashley Crawford. What Mosher brought out, according to Crawford, was 'the social and economic realities of the family'. While on the surface, the production looked traditional, the focus on more than just Tom's subjected memory, for Crawford, made this production stand out. The cast was also praised. Sally Field portrayed Amanda as 'a hard-working, frustrated woman and mother whose actions emerge from a maternal desire for happiness for both her children and security for her daughter'. Peter Marks of the *Washington Post* calls Field's Amanda a 'woman of southern refinement worn down by poverty and worry'. He also commends Jennifer Dundas as Laura and Jason Butler as Tom, calling them 'marvelous foils for Field's Amanda, pushing back when Amanda's will of granite threatens to crush them, yielding when the mother herself appears ready to crumble'. Mosher's direction was lauded by Dolores Gregory of *Curtain Up* for being even-handed, 'mining the comedy organically from small moments – the incongruity of Amanda's plantation-era wardrobe in the drab apartment, the look on Tom's face when he inspects his mother's attempt at redecorating'. The only criticism reviewers such as Gregory found was in the oversized photograph of the father hanging on the wall. She, like many reviewers, felt as though Mosher was taking Williams's set description too literally.

Despite much promise, David Leveaux's 2005 production at the Ethel Barrymore Theatre in New York City was not well received. For Ben Brantley of the *New York Times*, the production was miscast and misdirected. Jessica Lange's Amanda Wingfield was much more reminiscent of Blanche DuBois; Christian Slater's Tom was a 'red-hot roughneck' rather than Williams's poetic narrator and son; and Sarah Paulson's Laura was flat, registering 'the single sustained note of an anguished, terrified 2-year-old'. Such a Laura could hardly enchant Jim. Matthew Murray of *Talkin' Broadway* agrees with Bentley. He points out that the production was flawed, and noted that Slater's performance was stiff and stolid. Murray, unlike Bentley, recollected one salvageable moment in the production, 'the climatic encounter between Jim and Laura' which he felt was 'truly on track'. This moment was saved by Josh Lucas (Jim) who subtly suggested Jim 'too is trapped in the past'.

In 2007, Lange again was cast as Amanda, this time in Rupert Goold's production at London's Apollo Theatre. Michael Billington of the *Guardian*, too, found Lange a less than convincing Amanda, stating that Lange 'never persuaded [him] that she inhabited a world of fantasy'. Likewise, other reviewers found fault with Lange, but more generally enjoyed the production as a whole. Philip Fisher of *British Theatre Guide* reminds his readers that a Hollywood star does not always make the show. Although he was dissatisfied with Lange's performance, he called the show a 'brilliant, dreamy production' largely as a result of Paul Pyant's lighting design and Matthew Wright's set design.

In 2010, the Salisbury Playhouse toured its production of *The Glass Menagerie*, visiting London, Oxford, Liverpool and Glasgow, among other major cities in the United Kingdom. According to the *Guardian*'s Lyn Gardner, the production tried too hard to be experimental, adding film footage of Amanda as a young woman awaiting her gentlemen callers. The film images, Gardner argues, made the play seem 'too blowsy and way too melodramatic'. While other reviewers agreed that the film footage was a mistake, Dominic Cavendish of the *Telegraph* applauded the acting, stating that although Imogen Stubbs looked a bit young for the role, her Amanda was splendid; she 'catches [Amanda's] spirit of fretful, neurotic devotion'. Tom (Patrick Kennedy), Laura (Emma Lawndes) and Jim (Kyle Soller) were equally well cast. All in all, this production was well received by London theatre critics.

In spite of the success of the Salisbury Playhouse, London's Young Vic Theatre, only months thereafter, went on to stage their own production of Williams's classic. London theatre critics unanimously applauded Joe Hill-Gibbins's production. Among the attributes of the production was its fidelity to the author's intentions. Even Michael Billington of the *Guardian*, perhaps the only critic not wholly satisfied, acknowledged that he could 'forgive the production's dutiful obeisance towards the gratuitous expressionist trappings' because '[a]ll this is exactly what Williams wanted'. The acting, too, was admired. Paul Taylor of the *Independent*, for example, noted that 'Sinéad Matthews and Kyle Soller [who had just completed the role in the Salisbury Playhouse production] are beyond praise in the climatic, candle-lit scene in which the fragile romantic hopes of Laura are raised and then dashed by the gentleman caller's well-meaning but ill-considered attention'. Charles Spenser of the *Telegraph* like Taylor, expressed his gratitude for a 'terrific cast' which does 'this beautiful play proud'.[6] Sarah Hemming of the *Financial Times*, among other reviewers, praised Deborah Findlay's Amanda, noting that she 'makes Amanda a complex composition of delusion and pragmatism, beadily busy and then unbearably sad'. Reviewers also commended Leo Bill's Tom for, as Paul Taylor noted, capturing 'the character's cabin fever and frantic frustration'. Spencer applauded Bill's decision to base Tom Wingfield on Williams, 'the artist as a young man, with nervy intensity and moments of raw pain and anger, capturing both the aching love of the brother for his sister and the frustration of the writer who longs to escape this claustrophobic home for wider horizons beyond'.

In 2009 to 2010, the Long Wharf Theatre Company in New Haven took their production of the play to Off-Broadway's Roundabout Theatre

---

6   Note that Stephen Bottoms in his commentary argues that a crucial element to the play's success was an all around strong cast rather than casting one star to carry the play (56).

and Los Angeles's Mark Taper Forum Theatre. Charles McNulty, writing for the *Los Angeles Times*, praised Judith Ivey, as did most reviewers, for stealing the show; her Amanda was so natural it was 'almost Darwinian'. Equally pleased with her performance, Charles Isherwood of the *New York Times*, wrote of Ivey's performance: 'The lively allure of the flirt Amanda once was still shines in her girlish smiles, piping laughter and ebullient lapses into reveries on the golden days of her youth.' In addition to Ivey's performance, many reviewers noted the director Gordon Edelstein's changes to the script. McNulty posited that Patch Darragh embodiment of Tom as a 'gay man who has yet to fully acknowledge his secret to himself' was an effective new interpretation. Finding this and other changes refreshing, Charles Isherwood, Paul Hodgins and Charles McNulty favoured Edelstein's transformation of Tom as a writer creating the characters for us while he types away in his New Orleans residence. However, Carol Jean Delmar of *Opera Theater Ink* argued that the rewriting of the older Tom 'diminishes the impact of the climax found in the original version'. Tom has succeeded in becoming a writer in Edelstein's version whereas in Williams's original, Tom may still be struggling.

Chicago's renowned Steppenwolf Company worked with Northwestern University graduate directing and design students for their 2012 production of *The Glass Menagerie*. Other than some grumbling over Aaron Roman Weiner's Tom who was 'a bit monotonous, and doesn't feel as natural in the space as the others' according to Paul Kubicki of *Stage and Cinema* and that Weiner and Kathy Scambiatterra (Amanda) 'occasionally confuse[d] Williams'[s] poetry for complicated southern pastoralism' according to Johnny Oleksinski of *New City Stage*, the production received positive reviews. Oleksinski recommended the production, stating that not only is the Steppenwolf Garage a 'terrifically appropriate space', but also the 'classic Gentleman Caller scene . . . is gloriously realized in director Laley Lippard's claustrophobic production'.

Shortly after the Steppenwolf's run ended, Chicagoans could once again see Williams's fragile family play. The Mary-Arrchie Theatre production of Williams's classic is a different beast altogether. This experimental production, featuring the older Tom Wingfield as a bearded, grizzly homeless man haunted by the past, was highly recommended by reviewers and loved by audiences. Mary Shen Barnidge of the *Windy City Times* poignantly wrote, 'You won't find a single classroom cliché anywhere in Mary-Arrchie Theatre Company's astonishing production, which restores the expressionistic motifs incorporated into the text by the author.' Hedy Weiss, in her review for the *Chicago Sun Times*, noted that unlike the portrayal of Tom in most productions, Hans Fleischmann (who also directed the production) depicts him as a 'homeless alcoholic, still poetic, but living in an alleyway where he has amassed an enormous collection of glass bottles – a powerful "reflection" of his crippled sister's delicate "glass menagerie"'. Along with praising Fleischmann's Tom, Justin Hayford of the *Chicago Reader* commended the production for its ghostly quality, noting that 'Joanne Dubach's Laura and Maggie Cain's Amanda inhabit that environment like specters emerging from Tom's tortured brain'. Through its experimentation, this production appears to have accomplished returning the focus to Tom Wingfield's struggle. While Amanda has stood out in productions of the recent past, predominately because of casting choices, Fleischmann's production casts Tom as our protagonist.

The most recent revival of *The Glass Menagerie* is the American Repertory Theatre's 2013 Broadway production at the Booth Theatre, starring Cherry Jones as Amanda, Zachary Quinto as Tom, Celia Keenan-Bolger as Laura and Brian Smith as Jim. The production was also staged at Harvard University, Massachusetts. The director John Tiffany and creative team worked together on the Tony Award winning *Once*. Together again, they put on a beautiful production of Williams's classic. *New York Times* reviewer Ben Brantley lauded praise on the production, stating that it was 'such a thorough rejuvenation of Tennessee Williams's 1944 drama that [he] hesitates to call it a revival'. Brantley continues his praise; Jones, he told his readers, was 'perhaps the greatest stage actress of her generation' to play Amanda Wingfield. Jeffrey Gantz of the *Boston Globe* agrees with Brantley, writing that 'This Amanda dominates the stage, as if she were still the belle of the ball, and she dominates her children, leaning into Tom right from the start.' Despite Cherry Jones's domineering presence on stage, the strength of Zachary Quinto as an 'irritating, exasperating, and selfish' Tom was, for Gantz, also memorable. Worth noting, too, are the applause Celia Keenan-Bolger (Laura) and Brian J. Smith (Jim) received by reviewers. *Metrowest Daily News*'s David Brooks Andrews described Keenan-Bolger's Laura as 'completely lovable, beautiful, and heartbreaking'. Brantley noted that Smith was simply excellent. With revivals like John Tiffany's as well as experiments like Hans Fleischmann's, Williams's *The Glass Menagerie* will surely continue to dazzle audiences.

Notes

The notes below explain words and phrases from the play, with page numbers referencing the Student Editions published by Bloomsbury Methuen Drama. They are intended for use by foreign-language students as well as by English-speaking readers.

page

3   *hive-like conglomerations . . .*: compares the cramped identical units of an apartment block to the cells of a beehive.

3   *interfused mass of automatism . . .*: suggests that the American lower-middle class has been trained to behave like robots, without individuality, and continues the idea of worker bees.

3   *poetic license*: the freedom to use poetic imagination.

3   *garbage cans*: dustbins.

4   *proscenium*: arch which surrounds stage in some theatres.

4   *portieres*: a curtain over door.

4   *whatnot*: a stand with shelves for knick-knacks.

4   *doughboy*: American infantryman.

4   *Gregg shorthand diagram*: chart indicating conventions for secretarial note-taking.

5   *Braille alphabet*: alphabet for the blind; system of raised dots which can be 'read' by the fingertips.

5   *In Spain there was revolution . . .*: refers to the revolt against the Republican government by the Fascist leader General Franco in 1936, which sparked the three-year-long Spanish Civil War.

5   *Guernica*: refers to the ruthless aerial bombardment of the town in April 1937 by German bombers fighting for Franco.

5   *emissary*: messenger.

5   *mantel*: shelf over fireplace.

5   *skipped the light fantastic*: danced.

6   *'Ou sont les neiges'*: 'Where are the snows?' (French). Part of a well-known quotation *'Ou sont les neiges d'antan?'* ('Where are the snows of yesteryear?') from a poem by François Villon; an expression of nostalgia.

6   *drop-leaf table*: a table with a hinged flap which can be used to make it larger or dropped to take up less space.

6   *scrim*: gauze screen which becomes transparent when lit from behind.

6   *mastication*: chewing.

7	*Metropolitan star*: singer at the Metropolitan Opera.
7	*blancmange*: gelatine-based dessert.
7	*darky*: offensive term for African-American.
7	*gentleman caller*: term for suitor visiting a young lady in the Old South.
8	*nigger*: offensive term for African-American.
8	*Parish house*: church hall.
8	*planters*: owners of large cotton farms (plantations).
8	*Mississippi Delta*: region of the Deep South in which the Mississippi river broadens before flowing into the Gulf of Mexico.
9	*elegiac*: an elegy is a song of lamentation; Amanda looks nostalgically to the past.
9	*Government bonds*: investment certificates guaranteed by US government.
9	*beaux*: boyfriends.
9	*Memphis*: biggest city in the state of Tennessee.
9	*Wall Street*: New York City's financial district.
9	*Midas touch*: refers to the mythical King Midas, whose touch would turn objects to gold.
10	*in a fugitive manner*: as if running away.
10	*old maid*: spinster.
11	*cloche hats*: bell-shaped hats.
11	*pocketbook*: handbag.
11	*D.A.R.*: Daughters of the American Revolution: an organisation of respectable middle-class women.
13	*a swarm of typewriters*: a disorientating image of many typewriters; the phrase suggests them buzzing like bees.
13	*Rubicam's Business College*: further education college in St Louis, Missouri.
14	*Famous-Barr*: department store.
14	*up the spout*: disappearing like steam from a kettle.
14	*Victrola*: brand name of an early record player.
14	*courting pneumonia*: risking catching severe illness from the cold.
15	*The Crust of Humility*: phrase suggesting the scraps of dried bread given to beggars.
16	*phonograph*: early form of record player.
16	*nervous indigestion*: stomach pains resulting from stress.
16	*occupy a position*: take up a wage-earning occupation.
16	*yearbook*: annual high school publication detailing the achievements of that year's class members.

16	*'The Pirates of Penzance'*: comic operetta by Gilbert and Sullivan.
17	*the Aud.*: high-school auditorium.
17	*debating*: competition in public speaking and rhetoric.
17	*jolly disposition*: a happy temperament.
17	*pleurosis*: disease involving inflammation of membrane covering lungs.
17	*Soldan*: name of a high school in St Louis, Missouri.
17	*Personal Section*: part of newspaper dedicated to readers' announcements.
17	*not cut out for*: not designed for.
19	*fiasco*: ludicrous or humiliating failure.
19	*archetype of the universal unconscious*: refers to the psychological theories of C. G. Jung, who believed that the same basic character types recur in the dreams and mythologies of all human cultures, and represent aspects of underlying psychological needs.
19	*specter*: ghost.
19	*feather the nest and plume the bird*: provide money and beautiful clothing to make a daughter more attractive to potential suitors.
19	*roping in subscribers*: attracting regular customers for a journal.
19	*matrons*: mature married women.
19	*serialized sublimations*: refers to episodic magazine stories; 'sublimation' is a concept of psychologist Sigmund Freud, who believed that the human being's animal instincts for sex and pleasure are suppressed and so rechannelled (sublimated) into more 'respectable' forms by societal convention.
19	*delicate cuplike breasts* . . . (etc.): satirises politely restrained manner in which women's magazines of the period alluded to sex.
19	*Etruscan sculpture*: sculpture from early pre-Roman Italy.
19	*glamor magazine*: fashion magazine.
20	*sinus condition*: inflammation of the air passages between skull and nose.
20	*Christian martyr*: one who suffers for the faith.
20	*'Gone with the Wind'*: episodic romantic novel of the American Civil War by Margaret Mitchell; made into blockbuster movie in 1939.
20	*Scarlett O'Hara*: heroine of *Gone with the Wind*.
20	*post-World-War generation*: those who came of age in the years directly after the First World War (1914–18).

20	*hold the wire*: stay on the telephone line.
20	*hung up*: cut off telephone communication.
21	*that insane Mr Lawrence*: refers to poet and novelist D. H. Lawrence, whose controversial books (such as *Lady Chatterley's Lover*) treated sex with unusual frankness and explicitness.
22	*gesticulating shadows*: suggests wild hand gestures and pointing from Amanda and Tom, being cast in shadow form on ceiling.
23	*moping, doping*: suggests Tom behaving as if miserable and exhausted.
23	*celotex interior with fluorescent tubes*: suggests claustrophobic working environment, with industrial wall cladding and no natural light.
24	*opium dens, dens of vice*, etc.: secret locations for illegal activities such as drug-taking.
24	*tommy gun*: light machine gun (invented by J. T. Thompson).
24	*cat houses*: brothels.
24	*czar of the underworld*: leader of organised crime ring.
24	*whiskers*: beard.
24	*El Diablo*: the Devil (Spanish).
26	*Garbo picture*: film starring Greta Garbo.
26	*travelogue*: documentary film about exotic journey.
26	*newsreel*: before the days of television news was shown in the cinema.
26	*organ solo*: many cinemas were still equipped with the organs which had accompanied silent films and these sometimes provided musical interludes.
26	*Milk Fund*: charitable organisation.
27	*pitchers*: jugs.
27	*Kentucky Straight Bourbon*: type of whisky.
27	*two-by-four*: standard size of strips of wood.
29	*Sticks and stones . . .* (etc.): Amanda's variation of the old proverb, 'Sticks and stones may break our bones, but words can never hurt us.'
29	*gloomy gray vault of the areaway*: dark, narrow passage between tall apartment buildings.
29	*satirical as a Daumier print*: refers to nineteenth-century French artist, Honoré Daumier, famed for satirical caricatures.
30	*Ave Maria*: Roman Catholic prayer to the Virgin Mary, often sung.
30	*right-hand bower*: 'a right bower' is the knave of trumps, a useful card in card games, possibly with connotations of being a bit of a rogue. Here the phrase also suggests a right-hand man or trusted deputy.

31   *natural endowments*: talents and abilities.

31   *Purina; Shredded wheat*: breakfast cereals.

32   *Spartan endurance*: ability to endure great difficulties or deprivation. In ancient Greece, the citizens of Sparta were famous for living lives of austere simplicity, without luxuries or comforts.

33   *inquisition*: intense questioning; interrogation.

33   *Jolly Roger*: flag of pirate ship, with image of skull and crossed bones.

34   *to punch in red*: to arrive late for work.

35   *handwriting on the wall*: a prophecy of future doom (Biblical reference).

35   *Merchant Marine*: Merchant Navy.

35   *Young People's League*: church-based social group.

36   *wool muffler*: scarf; neck-warmer.

37   *horsey set*: rich people who own horses.

37   *Long Island*: affluent suburb of New York City.

38   *Annunciation*: announcement (usually refers to the story of the Angel Gabriel telling the Virgin Mary of her pregnancy).

38   *Franco*: General Franco, leader of the Fascists in the Spanish Civil War.

39   *ash pits*: where ash from home fires was disposed of.

39   *Berchtesgaden*: country retreat of German dictator Adolf Hitler.

39   *Chamberlain*: British Prime Minister Neville Chamberlain; responsible for discredited policy of 'appeasing' Hitler by allowing him limited territorial expansion in Europe.

39   *hot swing music*: type of upbeat jazz.

40   *sphinx*: inscrutable creature of ancient Egypt; lion with a woman's head; spoke in riddles.

42   *putting on*: teasing.

43   *work like a Turk!*: work very hard.

43   *chintz*: cotton printed with coloured design.

43   *Durkee's dressing*: type of spiced dressing for fish.

44   *cowlick*: tuft of hair sticking up from head.

44   *get-up*: energy and initiative ('get-up-and-go').

46   *homely*: plain-looking, or perhaps rather ugly.

47   *eloquent as an oyster*: ironic epithet referring to Tom's frequent silences (i.e. his mouth is shut as tight as an oyster shell).

50   *senior class*: final-year high school students (17–18 years old).

50   *glee club*: singing group specialising in merry songs.

50   *White House*: official home of the President of the United States.

51   *folks*: family.

52   *Gay Deceivers*: padding for brassière.
53   *Possess your soul in patience*: wait patiently.
53   *voile*: thin, semi-transparent material.
53   *jonquils*: flowers of narcissus family; similar to daffodils.
53   *cotillion*: in America, a formal coming-out ball for debutantes.
53   *cakewalk*: energetic dance competition from the Deep South
          (developed from African-American slaves or servants dancing
          wildly for a prize of a cake).
53   *sashay*: ostentatious, gliding walk aided by big skirts.
53   *quinine*: bitter medicine used for malaria.
54   *dogwood*: small tree with white flowers and purple berries.
57   *goings on*: activities; occurrences.
57   *'Dardanella'*: popular tune.
58   *'Post Dispatch'*: *St Louis Post Dispatch*; local newspaper.
59   *Dizzy Dean*: famous baseball player.
59   *sell you a bill of goods*: Jim is saying he will try to persuade
          Tom to 'buy into' an idea he is 'selling'.
59   *executive positions*: jobs with managerial status within
          corporations.
59   *helluva lot*: 'hell of a lot'; a very great deal.
60   *incandescent marquees and signs*: the brightly-lit advertising
          hoardings above and outside theatres, etc.
60   *first-run movie houses*: cinemas where films appear first before
          general release.
61   *gassing*: talking emptily ('hot air').
61   *hogging it all*: selfishly holding on to everything.
61   *dark room*: interior of cinema.
61   *Gable*: Clark Gable, the movie star.
62   *Union of Merchant Seamen*: trade union for sailors.
63   *stand-offish*: distant; unfriendly.
64   *angel-food cake*: simple cake made of flour, sugar and egg-
          whites.
68   *howdy-do*: bothersome business.
68   *Benjamin Franklin*: American statesman (1706–90), also famous
          for his scientific experiments and the invention of the lightning
          conductor referred to here.
69   *Mr Edison*: Thomas Edison, inventor of the electric light bulb.
69   *Mazda lamp*: brand of electric lamp.
70   *Gypsy Jones*: famous evangelist.
72   *Wrigley Building*: headquarters of Wrigley's chewing-gum
          corporation.

72   *Century of Progress*: large exposition in Chicago celebrating American achievements of nineteenth and twentieth centuries.

75   *clumping*: suggests the dull, hollow sound made by a braced or wooden leg when it makes contact with floor.

76   *'The Torch'*: title of Soldan High School's yearbook.

78   *beleaguered*: constantly pestered by; weighed down by.

79   *kraut-head*: derogatory term for person of German descent.

80   *inferiority complex*: psychoanalytic term for person who thinks of him- or herself as insignificant, inferior to others.

82   *electro-dynamics*: study of electricity in motion, or of the interaction of electric currents.

83   *unicorn*: mythical, horse-like creature with single horn on its forehead.

84   *cutting the rug*: dancing.

84   *is your program filled?*: at a ball a gentleman would book a dance with a lady in advance and his name would be written on her dance-card or programme.

88   *Stumblejohn*: clumsy, awkward person.

89   *Life Savers*: brand of American peppermints.

89   *drugstore*: chemist's shop, usually selling a variety of goods including refreshments.

90   *Alton*: town in Illinois just up the Mississippi from St Louis.

90   *Centralia*: Missouri town over 100 miles west of St Louis.

91   *macaroons*: sweet biscuits made of almonds.

92   *maraschino cherries*: cherries preserved in liqueur, used for decorating cocktails.

92   *outdone with him*: peeved or miffed.

92   *it's only the shank of the evening*: the night is young.

93   *go steady with*: have longstanding relationship with.

93   *cat's not out of the bag*: secret has not been revealed.

94   *Wabash depot*: train station on Wabash Avenue.

94   *jalopy*: dilapidated motor car.

95   *I'll be jiggered!*: expression of astonishment.

97   *the world is lit by lightning*: refers poetically to the brash modern era of bright lights and noise, in which Laura's extreme delicacy is helplessly out of place.

Questions for Further Study

1 Whom do you regard as the central character in this play, and why? In developing your argument, make sure you consider possible reasons why other characters might or might not also be seen as central.

2 In what ways do Amanda's rose-tinted memories of her past impact on her hopes for her family's future? And do those hopes impact positively or negatively on her children's present well-being?

3 Choose a scene in which Laura's silences seem to you particularly acute. Provide an analysis of the scene's 'subtext' by explaining what you think she is thinking and feeling in her quietness. How might this subtext best be brought out in a performance of the scene?

4 In what ways do we see Tom struggling with his conscience during the play, and to what extent are we encouraged to sympathise with him in his struggle? Does the presence in the play of the 'older' Tom, as narrator, mean that we see the younger Tom's anxieties in a different light than we might otherwise?

5 Why do you think Tom describes Jim as 'the most realistic character in the play'? To what extent does Jim's 'realism' suggest a contrast to the 'idealism' or 'romanticism' of the other characters?

6 Consider the significance of the absent father-figure to the action of the play. In what ways does Williams succeed in rendering this absence as a kind of ghostly presence?

7 *The Glass Menagerie* is presented by Tom as a 'memory play' about his own past. How important is this framing of the play's events as memory to our understanding of the action? (Would it matter if Tom's monologues were cut?)

8 Consider how differently the play's events would be presented if we were to see them from the point of view of one of the other characters, instead of Tom. You should consider whether the play's key dramatic moments might be 'remembered' differently, but make sure you also think about such elements as scene structure, and the choice of which events are significant to show on stage in the first place (rather than just describe in narration).

9 Why do you think Williams divided the play into seven 'scenes' of such irregular lengths, rather than using longer 'acts' (two, three or four) of more even length, as was the convention at the time? (It might help to contrast the play with a more conventional piece of the same period, such as Arthur Miller's *All My Sons*.)

10   What does an awareness of Tennessee Williams's personal family history add to an understanding of *The Glass Menagerie*? What are the possible advantages or drawbacks of viewing the play in this light?

11   What role does the idea of 'the South' play in *The Glass Menagerie*, given that it is set in St Louis Missouri (which is a Southern state, but not in 'the deep South')? How might an understanding of the history of America's north/south divide aid an understanding of the play?

12   Williams carefully sets the play's action in 1938, during the Spanish Civil War, and on the verge of the Second World War. How significant is this historical location to an understanding of the play's action?

13   Williams insisted that *The Glass Menagerie* is not 'a straight realistic play with its genuine Frigidaire and authentic ice-cubes', and in the opening monologue, Tom also stresses that 'it is not realistic'. What is meant by the term 'realism' in drama, and to what extent do you think this play resists or questions the 'rules' of realism?

14   How is Williams's notion of 'sculptural drama' (see commentary, 50) realised through his stage directions for the play? Consider some of the ways in which this sculptural quality is made apparent in particular scenes or moments in the play, and discuss the ways in which you think it relates to or enhances the play's narrative.

15   If you were to direct a production of *The Glass Menagerie*, would you seek to follow or to disregard Williams's suggestions for the projection of images and titles to accompany the stage action? Give reasons for your choice, using specific examples to support it.

16   Analyse Williams's decision to set the whole play in a single, cramped apartment. What 'role' does this setting play in the action of the play, and in the light of your analysis, what are the most important considerations for a set designer working on the play?

17   Choose two characters in the play, and discuss the moment(s) in the action when you think they display the most tenderness towards each other. Contrast this with discussion of moments in which there is particular tension or hostility between them. What do these contrasts tell us about the characters' relationship?

18   Choose one or two of the play's characters, and analyse the ways in which they can be seen, on occasion, to be 'play-acting' or 'performing a role' for the benefit of other characters. Consider some of the contrasting motives (conscious or unconscious) underlying such role play, and the degrees of deception (or self-deception) involved.

19 Consider the extent to which any one or two of the play's characters can be seen to be avoiding or hiding from the truth of their situation(s). To what extent are we encouraged to sympathise with, or to criticise, this self-deception?

20 Look in detail at the long dialogue between Jim and Laura in Scene Seven. Analyse the emotional journeys on which both characters go during the course of this almost static scene, considering the (possibly differing) ways in which each understands the significance of particular moments. In the light of your analysis, what would be the key advice you would give to actors performing the scene?

21 Do you see the play, ultimately, as a tragedy or a kind of bittersweet comedy? Be sure to research the meaning of these terms, and to explain your reasoning carefully.

22 Williams is often credited with initiating what became known as 'the American style' of post-war drama, thanks to the way that plays like *The Glass Menagerie* and *A Streetcar Named Desire* blend aspects of domestic realism with more fluid states suggesting dream or memory. Consider some of the ways in which Williams established this 'style' in *Menagerie*, and compare and contrast his approach to that of Arthur Miller in *Death of a Salesman* (another prime case of 'the American style').

A Streetcar Named Desire

commentary and notes by
PATRICIA HERN and MICHAEL HOOPER

Plot

Scene One

On an evening in early May, Blanche DuBois arrives at Elysian Fields in New Orleans to find her younger sister, Stella, with whom she hopes to stay. She is disconcerted to discover that Stella, who is married to Stanley Kowalski, the son of Polish immigrants, has a small apartment in a shabby house in the French Quarter (Vieux Carré). Blanche is evidently nervous and helps herself to a drink of whisky. When Stella returns, Blanche greets her excitedly but cannot conceal her shock at Stella's way of life. Stella, however, is happy, fulfilled by her relationship with Stanley. Blanche defensively confesses to the loss of Belle Reve, their family home in Mississippi, to pay off debts accumulated, she claims, through the dissipations and deaths of older generations of the DuBois family. Stanley returns with two friends: Steve lives upstairs with his assertive wife, Eunice; Mitch lives with his invalid mother. Stanley accepts Blanche's presence with good humour but little ceremony. She is ruffled by his lack of refinement. She reveals that she was married when very young and that her husband died.

Scene Two

The following evening, while Blanche is in the bath, Stella tells Stanley about the loss of Belle Reve. She is unconcerned, but he suspects Blanche of keeping to herself the profits from the sale of the estate – profits which he believes he has a legal claim to as Stella's husband. When Blanche appears, he demands to see the documents concerning Belle Reve. Blanche is distressed when he snatches a bundle of papers, poems written by her young husband, then she hands him a box full of legal documents. He justifies his attitude on the grounds of his legal rights and his concern for the future of the baby Stella is expecting. Blanche and Stella go out for an evening together, leaving the apartment free for Stanley's poker game.

Scene Three

Stanley, Steve, Mitch and Pablo are still playing when Stella and Blanche return. It is nearly 2.30 in the morning. Blanche is struck by the relative gentleness and politeness of Mitch. Stanley grows more belligerently drunk; finally he hurls a radio out of the window and then hits Stella, who is immediately shepherded upstairs by Blanche. Sobered by a cold shower, Stanley calls in anguish for Stella to come back to him. Slowly she descends the stairs. They embrace, then Stanley carries her into their flat. Blanche is appalled by Stella's reconciliation with Stanley, but is soothed by Mitch.

Scene Four

Next morning Stella tries to explain to Blanche the way her relationship with Stanley works. She accepts his sporadic violence as inseparable from the passion they share. Blanche hopes to persuade Stella to leave Stanley, planning a future for herself and her sister, to be financed by an old admirer who is now apparently a millionaire. Stanley overhears part of this, but, when he appears, Stella's fierce embrace demonstrates that her loyalties remain with him.

Scene Five

Upstairs Steve and Eunice are brawling. On his return from bowling, Stanley frightens Blanche by asking her about a man called Shaw and a disreputable hotel called the Flamingo in Laurel, the town where Blanche was an English teacher. When he leaves, Blanche anxiously seeks reassurance from Stella that nothing unpleasant is known about her. She is expecting Mitch for a date and is desperate for him to provide her with a secure future. Between Stella's departure and Mitch's arrival, Blanche flirts with and kisses a young man who calls to collect subscriptions for a newspaper.

Scene Six

Blanche and Mitch return from an unsuccessful evening out. Blanche is coquettish but appears offended when he tries to kiss her. She complains of Stanley's hostility. Mitch talks about his mother. Blanche then speaks of her youthful and very short-lived marriage, which was destroyed when she discovered her young husband in bed with another man: she had later voiced her disgust, and her husband had rushed out and shot himself. Mitch puts his arms around her and kisses her.

Scene Seven

It is 15th September, Blanche's birthday. Blanche is singing in the bath; Stella is decorating a cake. Stanley enters, armed with the destructive truth about Blanche's recent past: she has been promiscuous, slipping out at night to answer the calls of soldiers who were returning, drunk, to their barracks near Belle Reve, then, after leaving Belle Reve, she has lived like a prostitute in a cheap hotel while also teaching in the local school. Finally she lost her teaching post for trying to seduce a seventeen-year-old pupil and was, effectively, driven out of Laurel. Stella tries to defend her sister, talking of the unhappiness of Blanche's early life and of her short-lived marriage. She is horrified to hear that Stanley has told Mitch all he knows. Blanche emerges happily from the bathroom but is frightened as she senses that something threatening has happened.

Scene Eight

As the birthday meal ends, in an atmosphere made tense by Mitch's non-appearance, Stanley erupts into fury when Stella criticises his manners. He presents Blanche with a bus ticket back to Laurel. She rushes out to be sick. Stella turns angrily on Stanley but suddenly feels the first movements of childbirth and asks him to take her to the hospital, leaving Blanche alone.

Scene Nine

Mitch arrives, unshaven and a little drunk. He is hurt and angry at having been deceived. Blanche no longer denies but tries to excuse her disreputable past as being a refuge from her grief and guilt at the death of her husband. She asks for Mitch's protection, but he clumsily tries to rape her. He retreats in confusion when she calls out 'Fire!'

Scene Ten

Stanley returns from the hospital, to find Blanche dressed up in a crumpled evening dress and wearing a cheap tiara. She claims to have received a cable from the oil millionaire inviting her on a Caribbean cruise. Stanley becomes aggressive when Blanche starts to lie about Mitch's attitude to her. She tries to ward off Stanley's sexual advances with a broken bottle, but he disarms her easily and carries her off to the bed to rape her.

Scene Eleven

Some weeks later, Stanley and his friends are again playing poker. Stella is packing Blanche's trunk while Blanche is in the bathroom. Unbeknown to Blanche, they are awaiting the arrival of a doctor and a nurse from a State-run institution for the mentally sick, to which Stella has reluctantly agreed to have her sister committed. Stella has decided that she cannot believe Blanche's account of Stanley's assault upon her; for her own sake and that of her new baby, she must reject her sister and align herself with her husband. Blanche imagines that she is going on holiday with an admirer, but is frightened by the appearance of the nurse. However, when the doctor addresses her courteously, she goes willingly with him, leaving Stella in distress, holding her baby. Stanley tries to comfort her and starts to make love to her.

Commentary

Williams's Writing: Repressed Self-knowledge?

In the introduction to a collection of letters from Tennessee Williams, Donald Windham wrote: 'his art sprang from his repressed self-knowledge'.[1] Windham went on to infer that Williams used his plays and stories as a way of translating himself into an acceptable fiction. Tennessee Williams himself often emphasised the close connection between his writing and the circumstances of his own life; he, however, did not describe the process as being an evasion of the truth nor an attempt to glamorise his own image. In interviews and articles written in his middle years, he was able to stand back from earlier experiences and observe the foundations of his work being laid down in his childhood and adolescence. Certain elements are clearly visible in both life and art; for example, the distress and guilt he felt at the lobotomy of his sister Rose (which was carried out when he was away at college) feature in *Suddenly Last Summer* where Catharine fights to remain intact in the face of Mrs Venable's determination to destroy her memories and her mind. In his short story *The Resemblance between a Violin Case and a Coffin*, Williams describes the shock of seeing a loved sister grow into a disturbingly separate young woman:

> I saw that it was all over, put away in a box like a doll no longer
> cared for, the magical intimacy of our childhood together.
> [. . .] And it was then, about that time, that I began to find life
> unsatisfactory as an explanation of itself and was forced to
> adopt the method of the artist of not explaining but putting the
> blocks together in some way that seems more significant to him.
> Which is a rather fancy way of saying that I started writing. (See
> *Remember Me to Tom*, 79)

The relationship between the aspiring writer and his shy, emotionally vulnerable young sister is also explored in *The Glass Menagerie*. In that play, too, the spirit of Miss Edwina, Williams's mother, finds a body and voice (although she herself denied the relationship). Williams was a sickly child, so his early years were spent close to his mother, an intimacy heightened by Miss Edwina's dissatisfaction with her husband. As the daughter of a Southern preacher – a man respected in his own community – she was never wealthy, but enjoyed a degree of social prestige when growing up, protected from poverty, insecurity or harshness. As the

1 *Tennessee Williams's Letters to Donald Windham*, London, Rinehart and Winston, 1972, vi.

disillusionment of marriage closed in on her, so her youth glowed more rosily in retrospect, as she herself wrote:

> Life is as unpredictable as a dream. Once I was young and gay and danced night after night with beau after beau, the belle of the ball. Then a handsome young man from a fine family came along, fell in love the first time he saw me and asked my hand in marriage. How was I to know this charming youth would turn into a man of wrath and that I and my children would live by his side consumed by terror. (*Remember Me to Tom*, 88)

This insistent nostalgia and puzzled, defensive self-pity echo, too, through the words of Amanda, the mother, in the first scene of *The Glass Menagerie*:

> **AMANDA:**   My callers were gentlemen – all! Among my callers were some of the most prominent young planters of the Mississippi Delta – planters and sons of planters! [. . .] There were the Cutrere brothers, Wesley and Bates. Bates was one of my bright particular beaux! He got in a quarrel with that wild Wainwright boy. They shot it out on the floor of Moon Lake Casino. Bates was shot through the stomach. Died in the ambulance on his way to Memphis. [. . .] And I could have been Mrs J. Fitzhugh, mind you! But – I picked your *father*!

It is interesting to note the reference here to the violent death of a young man, his life apparently blighted by passion for the Southern belle in whose memory he still has a picturesque existence. This idea becomes more potent in *A Streetcar Named Desire*.

The father-figure in *The Glass Menagerie* is 'a telephone man who fell in love with long distances', as Tom remarks in the opening monologue, yet who once had an innocent look that fooled everybody, even Amanda's father. He is conspicuous by his absence. This was a situation familiar to Williams as a child for his father was then out on the road, selling shoes. When he was promoted to a desk-job as sales manager, the rest of his family huddled together, it seems, away from his rages and his drinking and his angry disappointment in his wife and his eldest son – a Stanley Kowalski in middle age, with all the shared sexual passion in his marriage spent. When in middle age himself, Tennessee Williams was able to view his father more objectively:

> His was not a nature that would comply with the accepted social moulds and patterns without a restlessness that would have driven him mad without the release of liquor and poker and wild weekends. (*Remember Me to Tom*, 202)

In a letter written from Rome in 1955 to Kenneth Tynan, Williams saw his relationship with his father even more distinctly as simply one element in his own emotional development:

> I used to have a terrific crush on the female members of my family, mother, sister, grandmother, and hated my father, a typical pattern for homosexuals. I've stopped hating my father. [. . .] He was not a man capable of examining his behaviour toward his family, or not capable of changing it. [. . .] I find him a tragic figure now, not one that I dislike any longer. (*Letters to Donald Windham*, 301)

Not only do Tennessee Williams's mother, sister and father appear recognisably in the plays, but Williams was also acutely aware of the effect on his own nature and creativity of his inheritance and upbringing. His capacity for deep depression, for example:

> I have plunged into one of my period neuroses, I call them 'blue-devils', and it is like having wild-cats under my skin. They are a Williams family trait I suppose. Destroyed my sister's mind and made my father a raging drunkard. In me they take the form of interior storms that show remarkably little from the outside but which create a deep chasm between myself and all other people, even deeper than the relatively ordinary ones of homosexuality and being an artist. (*Letters to Donald Windham*, 91)

Williams's homosexuality figures large in his letters and *Memoirs*, although – perhaps not surprisingly – his mother's account of him makes no reference to it, recalling instead Tennessee Williams's childhood affection for a local girl called Hazel, a relationship apparently wrecked by his father. Miss Edwina explains her son's lack of a wife:

> Tom has said to me he never intends to many. [. . .] 'I have no idea of ever marrying. I couldn't bear to make some woman unhappy. I'd be writing and forget all about her.' (*Remember Me to Tom*, 240)

Williams's letters to Donald Windham sometimes conjure up an absurd caricature of himself as affectedly promiscuous and flighty, particularly those letters written from Key West in Florida where there was a bohemian colony and where homosexuality, although still illegal under state law, was tolerated by the authorities so long as it did not make itself widely conspicuous or troublesome. In the 'Vieux Carré' of New Orleans, too, he found an appealingly freewheeling way of life among artists, writers and jazz musicians in bars and brothels. He is reported to have said:

> If I can be said to have a home, it is in New Orleans where I've
> lived on and off since 1938 and which has provided me with
> more material than any other part of the country. I live near
> the main street of the Quarter which is named Royal. Down
> this street, running on the same tracks, are two streetcars,
> one named DESIRE and the other named CEMETERY. Their
> indiscourageable progress up and down Royal struck me as having
> some symbolic bearing of a broad nature on the life in the 'Vieux
> Carré' – and everywhere else for that matter.[2]

He was somewhat defensive about this lifestyle on occasion, understandably so in view of Miss Edwina's carefully cultivated respectability.

> As the world grows worse, it seems more necessary to grasp what
> pleasure you can, to be selfish and blind, except in your work,
> and live just as much as you have a chance to. (*Letters to Donald
> Windham*, 22)

The urge to seek refuge from unhappiness in the pursuit of pleasure, however destructive to self and others, is an aspect of Blanche DuBois's fall from grace. Her horror at the discovery of her young husband's homosexuality perhaps reflects the kind of response Williams himself had encountered or feared. On the other hand, Blanche may be a 'cover' for a male character, a homosexual, given a female mask by Williams so as to avoid having to confront his own feelings about himself – an example of that ingenious self-preservation referred to by Donald Windham. In that case, Blanche's shock at finding her boy-husband in bed with another man echoes the intense jealousy and sense of betrayal which Tennessee Williams expresses in letters at the ending of a love affair. In an assessment of Williams, written after his death, Murray Kempton stressed the importance of Williams's homosexuality to his creativity.

> We cannot appreciate Tennessee Williams without putting his
> homoeroticism into full account; and that may explain why women
> thought him more lovingly than men. [. . .] At bottom those plays
> of his that live most vividly in the mind tell us about how men
> must look to women – ogres to be appeased, small boys to be put
> up with, or, if one's luck turns for the better, strangers who will
> accept you and keep you safe. (*New York Book Review*, 31.3.1983)

2 Nancy Tischler, *Tennessee Williams: Rebellious Puritan*, New York, Citadel Press, 1961, 62.

Tennessee Williams described his writing as a cathartic or purging process, a way of coming to terms with his life:

> In my case, I think my work is good in exact ratio to the degree of emotional tension which is released into it. In a sense, writing of this kind (lyric?) is a losing game, for steadily life takes away from you, bit by bit, step by step, the quality of fresh involvement, new, startling reactions to experience; the emotional reservoir is only rarely replenished, by some such crisis as I've described to you at such length and most of the time you are just 'paying out', drawing off. (*Letters to Donald Windham*, 306)

A Streetcar Named Desire grew out of the turbulence of Tennessee Williams's relationships, but also out of the crisis he refers to in the letter – the months in 1946 when he endured the terror of believing that he was suffering from incurable pancreatic cancer. A morbid, shuddering preoccupation with the physical ugliness and the inevitability of death permeates the whole play.

The strong connection between the experiences and relationships of Tennessee Williams's life and the events and characters of his plays explains the intensity and vividness of his writing, but it has also been seen as a limitation, not least by Williams himself:

> Frankly there must be some limitations in me as a dramatist. I can't handle people in routine situations. I must find characters who correspond to my own tensions. If these people are excessively melodramatic [. . .] well, a play must concentrate the events of a lifetime in the short span of a three-act play. Of necessity these events must be more violent than in life. (*Tennessee Williams: Rebellious Puritan*, 246)

An American Context

The early plays of Tennessee Williams were successful in the 1940s and 1950s perhaps because they offered violence, morality, spectacle and romance in American settings, played out by characters that often managed to be both highly individual and representative of particular aspects of American life and tradition. *Streetcar* draws upon at least three of these American traditions, which had been projected effectively for twenty years by the cinema. There was a nostalgic interest in America's past, particularly in the romance of the years before and during the Civil War. Mid-twentieth-century urban Americans were intrigued and charmed by the idea of the South, by the picturesque elegance of a landed élite who flaunted their inherited wealth and their studied gentility. Morality was satisfied by the knowledge that this privileged brilliance was doomed to defeat in the Civil War and would then present an image of decorative decay. Blanche DuBois and Belle Reve belong to that tradition, crystallised for a mass audience by the highly successful film of *Gone with the Wind*, starring an English actress, Vivien Leigh, who later played Blanche in the film of *Streetcar*.

Another aspect of America's past given a wide appeal through the cinema was the folklore of the Wild West. Westerns showed home-grown heroes proving their worth in combat against savages and bandits and sticking to their friends through thick and thin – just as Stanley feels bound to protect Mitch after their time together in the army. These films also reinforced an idea of women either as child-bearers and home-makers or as whores, golden-hearted or otherwise. Stella is a home-maker and child-bearer; Blanche is neither, so might then be expected to be one of the other kind and 'no good'.

If Blanche belongs to the crumbling grandeur of the Southern plantations, Stanley is a new American, an immigrant, a man of the city. He is the one amongst his group most likely to make his mark in a world of industry and commerce, a world full of machinery like cars and locomotives. He asserts his maleness and lack of refinement; where he cannot dominate sexually he uses force. He shows, perhaps, the more acceptable face of that macho urban jungle pictured in the Hollywood gangster movies of the 1930s.

Popular entertainment, principally the cinema, offered Americans certain images of what it meant to be American. This was an idea equally important to the first or second generation immigrants from Europe as to those who thought of themselves as 'real' Americans with a pedigree reaching back to the Pilgrim Fathers or the Huguenots. Tennessee Williams's early plays dealt in familiar concepts so that even when aspects of his plots or the ideas expressed were shocking, they nonetheless were accessible to a wide audience, not only on Broadway but also, later, as successful films.

Theatre, during the 1920s, 1930s and 1940s, changed under the impact of new techniques and forms from Europe. These influences were brought to America by touring companies, by refugees from political oppression in Europe, by the influx of avant-garde films and by Americans returning from the Continent, excited by what they had seen. In the 1920s two important theatrical groups were formed: the semi-professional Washington Square Players in New York, and the amateur

Provincetown Players, who were associated with the early works of the dramatist Eugene O'Neill. The Washington Square Players developed into the wholly professional Theatre Guild which became one of the most influential organisations in the New York theatre world. The 1920s also saw the birth of various political groups; for example, those brought together in the Workers' Dramatic Council. The Federal Theatre was set up as part of Roosevelt's New Deal to encourage playwrights to use the theatre to celebrate or at least dramatise contemporary life. In 1931 Lee Strasberg, with Cheryl Crawford and Harold Clurman, founded the Group Theatre, which trained a new generation of actors and directors, Elia Kazan, for example, who later directed *Streetcar* for stage and screen. It also encouraged young dramatists with a serious social or political message, men like Clifford Odets, whose play *Waiting for Lefty* (1935) called for organised action against workers to fight against their fall in living standards. It sought 'an alliance of the men of mind, of vision, the artists, with the People, consciously working towards this creative end'.[3] It was the Group Theatre that gave the young Tennessee Williams significant encouragement in 1938 by giving him a special award for his collection of one-act plays, *American Blues*. A number of American dramatists were experimenting with a lyrical, heightened style of dialogue and extended speeches full of vivid imagery or highly rhythmic phrases, sometimes approaching the intensity and musicality of verse drama. This rhetorical style was complemented by non-naturalistic staging – as in Thornton Wilder's *Our Town* (1938) and *The Skin of Our Teeth* (1942), or many of Eugene O'Neill's experiments in style, of which *The Hairy Ape* (1922) will stand as an example. Here is the opening stage direction:

> The treatment of this scene, or of any other scene in the play, should by no means be naturalistic. The effect sought after is a cramped space in the bowels of a ship, imprisoned by white steel. The lines of bunks, the uprights supporting them, cross each other like the steel framework of a cage.

Thus Tennessee Williams's early plays were borne in on a swelling tide of new American drama now able to take possession of major theatres in the big cities, especially New York, and to become recognisably distinct from the European imports, while still benefiting from the new technology and the versatility demonstrated by European theatre. The need for a national identity had been sharpened by America's involvement in the two World Wars, as was the need to re-appraise the values and demands

3 Harold Clurman, *The Fervent Years*, London, Dennis Dobson, 1946, 79.

of American society. According to the critic Travis Bogard, through the 1920s, 1930s and 1940s many plays were concerned:

> with an aspect of the national past that gives them a strong
> emotional lever against the depressing present and the failure of
> the American dream. [. . .] The characters cling to their dreams
> tenaciously. [. . .] Their dreams are never fulfilled except in
> the fantasies of nostalgic romances and operettas. The sterner
> statements insist that the thrust of American materialism has
> destroyed all such dreams and left man destitute in a soulless
> world, a wasteland.[4]

A selection of drama reviews from the *New York Times* for the years 1945 to 1947 gives an impression of what New York audiences were being offered at the point when Tennessee Williams emerged as a significant writer. In 1945, along with *The Glass Menagerie*, there was a Rodgers and Hammerstein musical about a fairground roustabout's doomed romance with a nice all-American girl in a small fishing community. This was playing across the street from another Rodgers and Hammerstein show, *Oklahoma*, a lyrical celebration of America's mid-West where farmers and cowboys learned to live and love in energetically choreographed harmony. At the same time, Elia Kazan – first director of *A Streetcar Named Desire* – was directing *Deep Are the Roots* by Arnaud D'Usseau, a play dealing with the position of negroes in the American South. Also in production was *Home of the Brave* by Arthur Laurents about the experiences of a young Jewish soldier in the Pacific campaign of the Second World War. During 1946 New York saw translations of Anouilh's *Antigone*, Rostand's *Cyrano de Bergerac* and Satre's *Huis Clos*. An English company led by Laurence Olivier brought over a version by W. B. Yeats of Sophocles' *Oedipus*, as well as Sheridan's *The Critic*. There was a production of Oscar Wilde's *Lady Windermere's Fan* (described by the critic Brooks Atkinson as 'a trifle seedy') and of Shakespeare's *Henry VIII*. The most conspicuously American production was another musical – this time combining showground glamour with Wild West nostalgia – *Annie Get Your Gun* by Irving Berlin.

1947, similarly, offered home-grown musicals, such as the rather fey *Brigadoon* and *Finian's Rainbow* as well as the more serious *Street Scene*, based on a play by Elmer Rice, with music by Kurt Weill. *Street Scene* was praised by Brooks Atkinson as 'a musical play of magnificence and glory [. . .] it finds the song of humanity under the argot of the New York streets'. As in 1946, there were several imports from Europe, but there was also the successful debut of the young American writer, Arthur Miller, whose *All My Sons*, directed by Elia Kazan, dealt with the conflict for Americans

4 *The Revels History of Drama in English*, London, Methuen, 1977, Vol. VIII, 62–3.

between private and public loyalties in the context of the recent war. Its characters and setting were immediately identifiable by the American audience of 1947; its action was tragic. At moments the dialogue moved from the recognisably naturalistic to a more highly charged kind of rhetoric through which the questions of morality confronting the characters were imbued with a wider significance. It was enthusiastically received:

> The theatre has acquired a genuine new talent [. . .] [The play] is a pitiless analysis of character that gathers momentum all evening and concludes with both logic and dramatic impact. (Brooks Atkinson, *New York Times*, 30.1.1947)

In December 1947 came *A Streetcar Named Desire*, another Kazan production. The play was both a commercial and a critical success:

> It reveals Mr Williams as a genuinely poetic playwright whose knowledge of people is honest and thorough and whose sympathy is profoundly human. [. . .] Out of poetic imagination and ordinary compassion he has spun a poignant and luminous story. (Brooks Atkinson, *New York Times*, 4.12.1947)

Southern Roots and European Influences

Tennessee Williams was not only carried in on a twentieth-century tide of American drama dealing with the contemporary American situation, but also buoyed up by a strong current of specifically Southern writing, which had become powerful in the nineteenth century and was still significant. Some of this literature from the South celebrated with nostalgia the chivalry and romance associated with the landowners of the Southern States prior to the Civil War (1861–65) and the doomed gallantry which became part of the folklore of the war itself. Other plays and novels, however, saw flaws in the pre-war and post-war South, while still fascinated by the South's charisma. There was, for example, William Faulkner (1897–1962), with his series of novels set in North Mississippi (thinly disguised as Yoknapatawpha County), including *The Sound and the Fury* (1929) and *Go Down Moses* (1942). Lillian Hellman in her novels *The Little Foxes* (1939) and *Another Part of the Forest* (1946) showed treachery, greed and ambition in an Alabama family, the Hubbards, using melodrama as a vehicle for morality – it was an indictment of that materialism which she felt was corroding the once bright metal of American society.

Colouring this writing was the influence – still strong in the South – of the Scottish writer Sir Walter Scott (1771–1832), whose historical romances such as *Kenilworth*, *The Talisman* and *Ivanhoe* drew upon a picturesque notion of medieval and sixteenth-century courtliness, the chivalric clash between good and evil amidst castellated towers or the pavilions of crusading knights. Nineteenth-century European Gothic fiction (supernatural melodramas in feudal locations) found an echo in the macabre tales of the American writer Edgar Allan Poe (1809–49), such as *Fall of the House of Usher* (1839), and in Nathaniel Hawthorne's *Twice-Told Tales* (1857) and *The Scarlet Letter* (1859). Both men were still much in vogue in the twentieth century with Poe in particular being seized on by the cinema as well. The quivering horror of Tennessee Williams's Blanche DuBois in the face of the city's squalid vitality and her accounts of the sickness eating away at the splendour that had once been Belle Reve recall Poe's story of the decline of the Ushers, whose painfully acute sensibility, both physical and emotional, rendered them unfit for life outside their decaying mansion in which they too decayed with a diseased beauty.

Tennessee Williams's work grew not only out of this courtly-Gothic Southern heritage, but also out of a European culture that offered writers as attractive to him yet as diverse as the Russian playwright and story-writer, Chekhov (1860–1904), the Swedish dramatist Strindberg (1849–1912), the Norwegian playwright Ibsen (1828–1906) and the English novelist D. H. Lawrence (1885–1930). Ibsen's influence on American drama can be seen also in the early plays of Arthur Miller: tragedy moved out of the courts of princes and the heroic past, into a recognisably contemporary setting, concerning itself with the middle classes or with semi-skilled workers living in the crowded city suburbs of a money-making nation. In many of Ibsen's dramas, such as *Rosmersholm* or *Ghosts*, the action shows the eruption of some guilt, thought to be safely buried in the past, into the carefully constructed respectability of middle-class family life. The dramatic tension becomes more powerful as the audience grows more aware of the degree of pretence involved in the characters' image of themselves and senses the gradual but relentless revelation of a once-submerged horror. The climax comes when the central characters suffer the confrontation of past and present: the thing they have fled from corners them. Then they either acknowledge the justness of this and endure retribution for past guilt with the dignity traditionally associated with a tragic protagonist, or they may try to retreat even further into pretence, perhaps into madness. This tragic model was well suited to Tennessee Williams for it offered a means of dramatising through vividly characterised and recognisable individuals his sense of the South's past being still active and often destructive in modern America.

> *A Streetcar Named Desire* makes it clear that for Williams the
> act of fleeing always becomes the act of reliving the past. Flight
> forces the presence of the past on his characters as the presence of

what they attempted to flee. (Donald Pease in *Tennessee Williams: A Tribute*, 840)

A Streetcar Named Desire shows the conflict between traditional values: an old-world graciousness and beauty running decoratively to seed versus the thrusting, rough-edged, physically aggressive materialism of the new world. The presentation of a way of life is closely bound up with the evocation of a particular place; this 'place' both defines and explains those characters who are identified with it, and so the chopping down of a long-prized orchard or the gradual dissipation of an ancient estate gives expression to the decline of those characters themselves and of their sort of world. In this, Tennessee Williams harks back to images and emotions present in the plays of Anton Chekhov. Blanche DuBois is of the same breed as Chekhov's charming, elegantly selfish, admiration-seeking, ageing women, such as Madame Arkadina in *The Seagull* (1895) and Madame Ranevsky in *The Cherry Orchard* (1903). Interestingly Blanche explains that her name means 'White woods' (30), 'Like an orchard in spring!' But whereas Chekhov's women are still vivaciously staving off despair and the admission of defeat, Blanche is seen in her final struggles.

In *A Streetcar Named Desire* the conflict between two ways of life is concentrated within the battle between Blanche and Stanley. The old civilisation vested in Blanche is demonstrably decadent; her only means of survival in the modern world is to batten onto someone else and live off their emotional, physical and material resources, like a decorative fungus. Stanley is full of aggressive, virile energy, both contemptuous of and intrigued by the once privileged gentility of the Belle Reve world. The dramatisation of such a clash in sexual terms – the old world associated with febrile femininity, the new with a charismatic but brutal masculinity – had been tried earlier by August Strindberg. There are some interesting parallels between *Streetcar* and Strindberg's *Miss Julie* (1888). In his preface to *Miss Julie* Strindberg outlined his objectives and analysed the response he anticipated for his characters. He justified his choice of subject:

> It is still tragic to see one on whom fortune has smiled go under, much more to see a line die out. [. . .] The fact that the heroine arouses our sympathy is merely due to our weakness in not being able to resist a feeling of fear lest the same fate should befall us. [. . .] I have suggested many possible motivations for Miss Julie's unhappy fate. The passionate character of her mother; the upbringing misguidedly inflicted on her by her father; her own character; and the suggestive effect of her fiancé upon her weak and degenerate brain.

Strindberg referred to

> that innate or acquired sense of honour which the upper-classes
> inherit. [. . .] It is very beautiful, but nowadays it is fatal to the
> continuation of the species. [. . .] The servant Jean is the type who
> founds a species, we trace the process of differentiation.

Strindberg saw Jean's survival and strength as arising less from his class
origins than from his masculinity.

> Sexually he is an aristocrat by virtue of his masculine strength, his
> more finely developed senses and his ability to seize the initiative.
> His sense of inferiority arises chiefly from the social *milieu* in
> which he temporarily finds himself.[5]

Strindberg emphasises a deliberate naturalism both in the setting of the
play – the large kitchen of a Swedish manor house, on a midsummer's
eve – and in its references to the routines of life. However, both Miss
Julie and Jean can speak in heightened prose, using imagery and thought-
associations which give the play a poetic, more universal quality. In this,
too, *Streetcar* is reminiscent of *Miss Julie:*

> **MISS JULIE:**   I have a dream which recurs from time to time, and
> I'm reminded of it now. I've climbed to the top of a pillar, am sitting
> there, and I can see no way to descend. When I look down, I become
> dizzy, but I must come down – but I haven't the courage to jump. [. . .]
>
> **JEAN:**   No. I dream I'm lying under a high tree in a dark wood.
> I want to climb, up, up to the top, and look round over the bright
> landscape where the sun is shining – plunder the bird's nest up there
> where the gold eggs lie. (*Strindberg: Plays One*, 116)

In *Streetcar* Stanley's syntax remains unrefined, but his words are
nonetheless imaginative:

> **STANLEY:**   I was common as dirt. You showed me the snapshot of
> the place with the columns. I pulled you down off them columns and
> how you loved it, having them coloured lights going! (68)

Another writer who deals with the clash of lifestyles and moralities often
in sexual terms and in heightened language is D. H. Lawrence. Tennessee
Williams's early admiration for Lawrence was noticed and lamented by
his mother, who felt that Lawrence's writing lacked delicacy.

---

5   Author's Preface to *Miss Julie: Strindberg: Plays One*, trans. Michael Meyer, London,
Methuen, 1976, 92–8.

One afternoon he walked in with a copy of *Lady Chatterley's Lover*. I picked it up for a look – Tom said I had a veritable genius for opening always to the most lurid pages of a book – and was shocked by the candour of the love scenes. [. . .] I didn't like the book or D. H. Lawrence as a person. [. . .] I didn't admire anything I heard about his character or how he treated his wife, who deserted her husband and children for him. The one play of Tom's I have not read or seen is *I Rise in Flame, Cried the Phoenix*, his poetic version of Lawrence's last few hours on earth. (*Remember Me to Tom*, 33)

It is in *Lady Chatterley's Lover* that Lawrence describes the meeting rather than the conflict between a woman of the upper class and a man of peasant stock (though educated and sensitive enough not to be a prisoner of his class). The conflict is between that virile new man and the effete aristocracy from which his mistress comes – much as Stanley challenges Stella's family origins rather than Stella herself. Like Stella, Constance Chatterley is happy to be pulled off her column and to have the coloured lights going. After the gamekeeper, Mellors, has made love to her,

in her heart the queer wonder of him was awakened. A man! The strange potency of manhood upon her. [. . .] She crept nearer to him, nearer, only to be near to the sensual wonder of him.[6]

Connie's sister Hilda, however, feels threatened and alienated by his overt sexuality:

He was looking at her with an odd, flickering smile, faintly sensual and appreciative.

'And men like you', she said, 'ought to be segregated: justifying their own vulgarity and selfish lust'. (256)

One justification that even Connie herself allows for the relationship is Mellor's value as a stud, to revitalise the impotent aristocratic stock. Similarly, Blanche sees Stanley as essentially animal, a stud:

BLANCHE: He's just not the sort that goes for jasmine perfume! But maybe he's what we need to mix with our blood now that we've lost Belle Reve and have to go on without Belle Reve to protect us. (23)

And later:

BLANCHE: What such a man has to offer is animal force and he gave a wonderful exhibition of that! But the only way to live with such a man is to – go to bed with him! (39)

6 D. H. Lawrence, *Lady Chatterley's Lover*, New York, Penguin, 1994, p. 174.

In fathering Stella's child Stanley has completed his function in Blanche's eyes, so now she feels that she and Stella can leave him behind with the brutes and go forward to a life enriched by 'such things as art – as poetry and music' (41).

The conflict between innate sexuality and a consciously acquired civilisation, present in *A Streetcar Named Desire*, is also a recurring theme in Lawrence's work, often expressed in a very stylised prose full of images drawn from nature or the elements, darkness and light, earth and fire. Lawrence's kind of lyricism and this striving for the power of myth through imagery infused with a sense of ritual are features observed also in Tennessee Williams's work. For instance:

> In its sympathetic portrayal of our yearnings for transcendence,
> its realistic depiction of our inherent limitations, and its utter
> insistence on the necessity of imbuing with religious significance
> the rare and transient communion of man with his fellow,
> Williams's drama is a myth for our time. (Judith J. Thompson in
> *Tennessee Williams: A Tribute*, 684)

Such a response from a serious critic indicates the potency of these images and allusions. There are many such examples of Williams's reaching for 'religious significance':

> **BLANCHE:**   And then the searchlight which had been turned
> on the world was turned off again and never for one moment
> since has there been any light that's stronger than this – kitchen –
> candle . . .
>
> **MITCH:**   You need somebody. And I need somebody, too. Could it
> be – you and me, Blanche? [. . .]
>
> **BLANCHE:**   Sometimes – there's God – so quickly! (57)

One final instance of techniques which Lawrence and Williams share concerns the use of 'symbolic' names. The opening passage of Lawrence's autobiographical novel *Sons and Lovers* (1913) works on two levels: it describes the Nottinghamshire mining community in which the Morel family lives, but the names imbue the scene with the aura of myth or religious allegory:

> 'The Bottoms' succeeded to 'Hell Row'. Hell Row was a block of
> thatched, bulging cottages that stood by the brookside on Greenhill
> Lane. There lived the colliers who worked in the little gin-pits two
> fields away. [. . .] Mrs Morel was not anxious to move into the
> Bottoms, which was already twelve years old and on the downward

path, when she descended to it from Bestwood. (*Sons and Lovers*, Penguin, 7–9)

Tennessee Williams employs a similar device at the beginning of *Streetcar* when Blanche describes her journey to Stella's apartment:

> **BLANCHE:**   They told me to take a streetcar named Desire, and then transfer to one called Cemeteries and ride six blocks and get off at – Elysian Fields!
>
> **EUNICE:**   That's where you are now.
>
> **BLANCHE:**   At Elysian Fields?
>
> **EUNICE:**   This here is Elysian Fields. (5)

Structure: Eleven One-Act Plays United by a Purpose?

> The plot is simple. It moves from hope and frustration to destruction and despair. The characters themselves provide probability for every action. [. . .] Each scene is constructed like a one-act play, Williams's forte. (Tischler, 140–3)

> Plot in the normal sense there is not too much of, for it is men and women in their moods of hope, despair, pretence, terror and uncertainty with whom he is concerned. Yet the play is purposeful. (Elinor Hughes, *The Boston Herald*, 4.11.1947)

> It has no plot, at least in the familiar usage of that word. It is almost unbearably tragic. (Brooks Atkinson, *New York Times*, 14.11.1947)

Plot 'in the familiar usage' implies a sequence of actions or events so organised as to give them a sense of logical progression from a beginning, through a middle, to an end that seems 'right'. What is the significance of the description of *A Streetcar Named Desire* as a collection of one-act plays? It suggests that each scene describes one situation or deals with one event fully enough for it to stand alone: with an exposition, a crisis and some kind of resolution. It is possible to approach any of the scenes in this way. Scene One, for instance, introduces us to an environment, precipitates an action through the disruptive arrival into the Kowalski home of Blanche, and seems to offer a resolution in Stanley's acceptance of her. Or Scene Six: a man and a woman (in fact, Mitch and Blanche) return from an unsuccessful date. The audience is told why there is tension between them: he desires her, but is clumsy; she wishes to encourage him, but is anxious to preserve his respect for her. He reveals his vanities and insecurities, and gives an insight into the relationship with his mother which underpins his character. She reveals a tragedy in her past, giving an acceptably complete account of her marriage and widowing. The scene ends with them coming together – apparently a happy resolution. What welds these potentially self-sufficient segments into a cohesive play is not only the continuity of the characters, but also a clear relationship between the scenes which does give a sense of progress towards the final solution and achieves a unity of subject, theme and action.

The fact that each scene contains enough information to make its action comprehensible means that certain elements recur throughout the play – the story of Blanche's past, for instance – but since their relationship to the immediate situation changes from scene to scene this does not appear merely repetitive. In the first scene, the outline of Blanche's marriage is quickly drawn as part of the initial exposition, and her extreme sensitivity to its memory demonstrated – with the symbolic sound of the polka merely a faint suggestion, having little obvious significance beyond nostalgia at that point. In Scene Two, the reference to Blanche's dead husband is part of her skirmishing with Stanley; it introduces the idea of her guilt but offers no further explanation. In Scene Six, her description of the boy she married and then destroyed, the account heightened by the now ominous strains of the polka, becomes part of the action, drawing Blanche and Mitch together for mutual support. In Scene Nine, Blanche offers the death of her young husband as the reason for her subsequent fall from grace, as a mitigating circumstance to lesson her guilt rather than a cause for the guilt itself. This time Mitch does not comfort her but condemns her, so her last hope of redemption by love and of future happiness – or, at least, future security – is destroyed. Each reference to the short-lived marriage strips away a layer of Blanche's protective pretence, until she is forced to stand exposed in the harsh glare of the unshaded light. When what she *really is* is then rejected, there is no other possibility left for her except retreat into an enclosed world of her dreams. The play's tension and energy come from the audience's growing awareness of the past rising inexorably to the surface where it will erupt explosively into the present; it is this which gives *Streetcar* its sense of being 'purposeful'.

The structure of the play departs from well-established theatrical practice in having no act divisions. The eleven scenes follow upon each other without any formalised arrangement into three, four or five phrases. This is appropriate to a sense of the relentless movement towards Blanche's final catastrophe. It is also, perhaps, a product of Tennessee Williams's experiences as a screen writer in Hollywood: writing for the cinema rather than the theatre most often requires the dramatist to think in terms of a sustained sequence of relatively short episodes, capitalising on the effects made possible by crisp cutting from one image or event to the next. It is worth noting that many of his plays have transferred to the screen with considerable success.

Although the play is also concerned with the relationship between Stella and Stanley, Blanche is the organising factor: the action begins with her arrival and ends as she is led away to the mental hospital. It is significant, however, that the action is confined within the Kowalski apartment and its immediate surroundings; we do not, for instance, travel with Blanche from Laurel or on to the state institution. By maintaining this 'unity of place' Williams is doing more than merely following the 'rules' laid down by Aristotle for classic drama. He is also drawing attention to the fact that *Streetcar* explores the continuing human need to secure a territory, a home, and defend it against intruders. This is a basic animal drive, well described by Konrad Lorenz in *On Aggression* (London, Methuen, 1966). Professor Lorenz progresses from a study of aggression and appeasement patterns in animals, linked to the demands of territorial possession, sexual effectiveness and self-preservation, to a view of human behaviour as displaying essentially the same patterns, although sometimes in a more oblique or sophisticated form. The rituals of threat, appeasement, sexual display, defence and retreat have the power to involve an audience because they appeal to deeply rooted responses which are universal and vigorous. The plot of *A Streetcar Named Desire* is, in part, Stanley's recognition of Blanche as a potentially dangerous invader of his territory; he cannot, as some animals might, accept her as part of his herd of brood mares, or, in human terms, as an addition to his harem. The impossibility of such an arrangement is demonstrated when he rapes her; Blanche is not shown accepting this as an initiation into a new role within Stanley's household, and Stella is prepared to cast her sister out rather than allow her to remain as a rival for Stanley's favours. Earlier on, Blanche makes a bid for possession of Stella when she tries to persuade her sister to leave Stanley and set up a new home with her. In both phases of the struggle, Blanche is defeated.

It has been suggested that what might be regarded primarily as a plot decision – a basis for the selection and organisation of events – is more importantly the key to the playwright's intended 'message' and moral attitude. By setting the play in the Kowalskis' territory, Tennessee Williams is possibly indicating that Stella and Stanley are rightly the survivors in their world of vitality and birth, whereas Blanche's world is Belle Reve, a place of decayed gentility, of death, which must be rejected if life is to go on.

From *The Poker Night* to *Streetcar*: Approaches to Character

Tennessee Williams arrived at *A Streetcar Named Desire* through a series of stages, called variously *The Poker Night, The Primary Colors* and *The Moth*, gradually building up the plot and characters from a basic situation involving an unmarried teacher meeting a prospective husband while on a visit to her younger sister and brother-in-law. At first the action was set in Chicago, then Atlanta in Georgia, then in New Orleans. Originally the central family was Italian, then the brother-in-law became Irish while the sisters changed into Southern belles. Finally Williams settled on the Polish-American and Southern combination. Throughout all the phases, he had a fixed idea about the style of the setting:

> A symbolic link is forged between Stanley and the powerful modern engines of the railroad, and Williams once considered ending the play with Blanche throwing herself in front of the train in the freight-yards. (Vivienne Dickson in *Tennessee Williams: A Tribute*, 159)

Stanley's development is interesting. He begins, in the first draft, as

> 'a weakly good-looking young man. He has a playful tenderness and vivacity which would amount to effeminacy if he were not Italian'. (Quoted by Vivienne Dickson, 163)

In his Irish phase, in *The Primary Colors*, the Stanley character – here called Ralph – becomes more assertive. Williams adds in associations with hunting and death – the character is a salesman of 'mortuary goods'. At this stage, too, Williams suggests both the character's latent femininity and his attraction to Blanche. She rejects him:

> I think you have a very wide streak of the feminine in your nature. You think you'll obscure it by acting with the greatest possible vulgarity. But what you sometimes really remind me of is a vicious little fourteen year old girl that I've had in my class for two years.

If one remembers that view of Blanche as a disguised male, Stanley's initial effeminacy is significant in the light of Williams's homosexuality. Williams agreed in an interview that Blanche was in some ways a projection of his sense of himself; the relationship between Blanche and Stanley then becomes fraught with danger, with complications and social taboos underlying the surface conflict.

In his mature form, in *A Streetcar Named Desire*, Stanley has a force of character which has been interpreted as excitingly life-giving on the one hand, and brutally destructive on the other:

> The child of immigrants, he is the new, untamed pioneer,
> who brings to the South, Williams seems to be saying, a
> power more exuberant than destructive, a sort of power the
> South may have lost. (J. H. Adler, in *Tennessee Williams:*
> *A Tribute*, 41)

But:

> Stanley, in his ignorance and insensitivity, destroys both
> Blanche's hope and her illusion. He sees through her pose
> without understanding why she needs one. He thinks merely
> that she feels superior to him and he wishes to destroy her
> composure to make her recognise that she is the same as
> he, a sexual animal. (J. M. McGlinn in *Tennessee Williams:*
> *A Tribute*, 514)

Or:

> The conflict between Blanche and Stanley allegorizes the struggle
> between effeminate culture and masculine libido.[7]

Stanley has also been described as a twentieth-century Pan-Dionysus – that is, a modern embodiment of the ancient spirits of anarchic sexuality and the pursuit of pleasure, capable of impulsive cruelty to those who try to censor or confine them. Tennessee Williams's stage directions stress certain qualities in Stanley: his strength, his vitality, and his virility:

> *Animal joy in his being is implicit in all his movements and*
> *attitudes. Since earliest manhood the centre of his life has been*
> *pleasure with women, the giving and taking of it, not with weak*
> *indulgence, dependently, but with the power and pride of a richly*
> *feathered male bird among his hens.* (13)

It would be interesting to know whether Tennessee Williams's reference to the brilliant cockerel amongst his hens contains any of the conscious irony there would be if he had in mind the old fable of Chanticleer, the subject of Chaucer's *Nun's Priest's Tale*. Chanticleer is a farmyard cock, a richly feathered male bird among his hens, whose sexuality is so rampant that it becomes absurd. For example, he longs to mate with his favourite hen,

---

7 Robert Brustein, "America's New Culture Hero: Feelings Without Words",
   Commentary. Vol. 25 (1958), 124.

Pertelote, on their perch at night, but the beam is so narrow they would fall off. Then:

Real he was, he was namore aferd;	He was majestic, no longer afraid;
He fethered Pertelote twenty tyme,	He fondled Pertelote twenty times,
And trad as ofte, er that it was pryme.	And mated with her as often, before nine in the morning.
He looketh as it were a grym leoun	He looked like a merciless lion
An on his toos he rometh up and doun;	And roamed up and down on tiptoe;
Him deigned nat to sette his foot to ground.	Because he was too haughty to let his feet touch the ground.

The absurdity of the farmyard rooster as a sexual creature is also stressed in *A Streetcar Named Desire* by the story that Steve tells in Scene Three (25). Tennessee Williams's decision to have Capricorn as Stanley's astronomical birth sign is similarly ambivalent: it carries pagan associations with the god-goat Pan, but the goat is also traditionally associated with low sexuality, animal lust (consider how Shakespeare's Iago uses it to denigrate Othello). Williams describes Stanley as 'the gaudy seed-bearer' and the images of his mind as 'crude' – both adjectives suggesting vulgarity and lack of refinement. On the other hand, Stanley's sexual pleasure is the 'complete and satisfying centre' of his character. Is there irony here? Does the phrase *expose* rather than simply *describe* Stanley's chief quality and indicate the limitations of his life? It is important to notice that Stanley is not wholly selfish in his sexuality; he gives as well as takes pleasure. Certainly he gives Stella enough to sustain their relationship, at least at this stage of their marriage. When he is shown as the unapologetic sexual male, Stanley often appears formidable; however, there are moments when his affectation of worldly wisdom can make him seem foolish – even to Stella:

STANLEY: I got an acquaintance that deals in this sort of merchandise. I'll have him in here to appraise it. I'm willing to bet you there's thousands of dollars invested in this stuff here!

STELLA: Don't be such an idiot, Stanley!

STANLEY: And what have we here? [. . .] A crown for an empress.

STELLA: A rhinestone tiara she wore to a costume ball.

STANLEY: What's rhinestone?

STELLA: Next door to glass. (18)

He is like a bull in a china shop, massively inept, in his ramsacking of Blanche's papers (21–2), whereas she here emerges with some dignity and humour. She succeeds in making him look 'somewhat sheepish', but he regains status by revealing himself as the father of Stella's expected child.

Stanley's code of morality is clear-cut and simple, ruthlessly so. He defends his territory, his wife and his friends against invasion or imposition:

STANLEY: Mitch is a buddy of mine. We were in the same outfit together – Two-forty-first Engineers. We work in the same plant and now on the same bowling team. [. . .] I'd have that on my conscience the rest of my life if I knew all that stuff and let my best friend get caught. (62)

There are areas of his self-esteem which he protects forcefully:

STANLEY: I am not a Polack. People from Poland are Poles, not Polacks. But what I am is a one hundred per cent American, born and raised in the greatest country on earth and proud as hell of it, so don't ever call me a Polack. (67)

Yet he is able to rape his wife's sister while his wife is in hospital giving birth to his child. He justifies it to himself by seeing the event as pre-determined, as if by mutual consent, like the inevitable and proper mating of animals. Blanche's terrified defiance of him with a broken bottle shatters the last fragile social taboos and, calling her 'Tiger – tiger', Stanley responds to her gesture as part of a wild mating ritual. Even at this moment there is a possible irony, a mockery beneath the dramatic intensity, in the picture of Stanley, inflated with that 'animal joy in his being', picking up Blanche's inert form and carrying it off. It offers an image familiar to any cinema-goer who has seen Hollywood classics such as the 1932 *King Kong* in which the massive ape with the sentimental heart carries Fay Wray's limp body off to his lair. When Stanley says, 'We've had this date from the beginning' (81), it is as if twentieth-century conventions and moralities fade away in the face of the primeval sexual drive of male to female.

It is, nonetheless, important to believe that Stanley *loves* Stella, not merely with animal desire but with deep-seated feeling which sometimes expresses itself with tenderness, sometimes with anguished need. When she retreats upstairs after he has hit her, he is racked by shuddering sobs and falls on his knees before her as she returns to him, before carrying her back into their dark apartment. After Blanche's departure at the end of the play, Stella sits sobbing on the steps, holding her new baby; Stanley leaves his card game to seek reassurance that she is still bound to him body and heart:

> **STANLEY**   (*voluptuously, soothingly*). Now, honey. Now, love. Now, now love. (*He kneels beside her and his fingers find the opening of her blouse.*) Now, now, love. Now, love . . . (89–90)

Elia Kazan's *Notebook for 'A Streetcar Named Desire'* traces his approach to the play as a director. Here he discusses Stanley's inner conflicts and dominant traits:

> He wants to knock no-one down. He only doesn't want to be taken advantage of. His code is simple and simple-minded. He is adjusted *now* . . . later, as his sexual powers die so will he; the trouble will come later, the 'problems'. [. . .] Why does he want to bring Blanche and, before her, Stella *down to his level?* . . . It's the hoodlum aristocrat. He's deeply dissatisfied, deeply hopeless, deeply cynical. [. . .] But Blanche he can't seem to do anything with. She can't come down to his level so he levels her with his sex. [. . .] Stanley is supremely indifferent to everything except his own pleasure and comfort. He is marvellously selfish, a miracle of sensuous self-centredness.[8]

Stella, according to Kazan, is driven by her determination to hold onto Stanley, so that even her sister becomes a possible enemy. In her marriage to Stanley her womanhood has flowered; she is about to move into a further stage of her life-cycle – to become a mother as well as a mate. Blanche not only appears as a rival for Stanley's favours, but tries to force Stella back into a childhood rôle, calling her 'Precious lamb!' and 'Blessed baby!' and ordering her about:

> **BLANCHE:**   You hear me? I said stand up! (STELLA *complies reluctantly.*) You messy child, you, you've spilt something on that pretty white lace collar! (9)

Blanche also tries to undermine Stella's belief in the worth and rightness of her marriage to Stanley:

> **BLANCHE:**   I take it for granted that you still have sufficient memory of Belle Reve to find this place and these poker players impossible to live with. (39)

---

8 Included in *Twentieth Century Interpretations of 'A Streetcar Named Desire'*, New Jersey, Prentice-Hall, 1971, 26–7.

Her challenge forces Stella to define the nature and value of her relationship with Stanley. She stands by her love for him, which, it is true, has its centre in 'things that happen between a man and a woman in the dark – that sort of make everything else seem unimportant' (39–40). Blanche attempts to dismiss this as 'brutal desire', which will drag Stella back with the animals in a primitive life without beauty. Her failure is demonstrated as Stella turns to embrace Stanley 'fiercely and in full view of Blanche' (41) while Stanley smiles in triumph over his wife's shoulder. Kazan suggests that Stella's commitment to her marriage costs her dear:

> Stella is a refined girl who has found a kind of salvation or realization, *but at a terrific price*. She keeps her eyes closed, even stays in bed as much as possible so that she won't realise, won't *feel* the pain of this terrific price. [. . .] She's waiting for the dark where Stanley makes her feel *only him* and she has no reminder of the price she is paying. She wants no intrusion from the other world. (*Twentieth Century Interpretations*, 25)

It is possible to see Stella as the crucial battleground over which Blanche and Stanley fight, possession of which ensures final victory. She is then a key figure; her changing attitudes signal the movement of the action. When she allows Blanche to lead her out of the apartment after Stanley's drunken violence, the balance of power shifts towards Blanche. When Stella chooses to return to Stanley, Blanche is left in defeat. At the end of the play it is suggested that her loyalty is now to her child, as she sits with the baby on the steps *outside* the apartment, weeping for the sister she has allowed to be taken into a kind of captivity, and neither responding to nor rejecting Stanley's advances. There are problems in accepting Stanley's and Stella's marriage, as described by Blanche in Scene Four. From a woman's viewpoint especially, there may be disconcerting implications:

> How did Stella ever get over those critical hurdles – Stanley's table manners, Stanley's preference in dress? [. . .] Did Stanley rape Stella, too, just by way of a how-do-you-do? Do all women burn to be raped? Is this the locker room fantasy that is Williams's version of animal purity?
>
> It is hard to know what is more unpleasant in this image: the overt sentimentality it expresses, or the latent brutality it masks: a fascination with the image of the helpless creature under the physical domination of another, accepting his favours with tears of gratitude. (Marion Magid in *Twentieth Century Interpretations*, 78)

The rhetoric here is extravagant; however, it raises an important issue. In the play, it is suggested (only to be quickly denied) that during their courtship Stanley's lack of refinement and his forcefulness were disguised or, perhaps, made seem acceptable by his Master Sergeant's uniform. Stella perhaps was wise to recognise in him the best available alternative to the decadence of Belle Reve:

> **STELLA:**   The best I could do was make my own living, Blanche. (11)

This is Stella's self-justification for what might otherwise seem a betrayal of her family and heritage; she asserts herself at the expense of all that Belle Reve has stood for and Blanche has tried to cling to. To some, it is Stella's selfishness rather than her submissiveness that characterises her:

> Stella ignores the needs of others and eventually adopts her own illusion. Life with Stanley – sex with Stanley – is her highest value. Her refusal to accept Blanche's story of the rape is a commitment to self-preservation rather than love, and thus Stella contributes to Blanche's disintegration. (J. M. McGlinn in *Tennessee Williams: A Tribute*, 514)

Her marriage gives her a purpose. Her new motherhood ensures a continuing rôle even if Stanley's desire for her should fade. Blanche offers her nothing except a return to childish dependence and both emotional and material insecurity. The final image of the play, however, suggests that Blanche's intrusion and expulsion have irrevocably changed the nature of Stella's relationship with her husband and her chosen way of life.

Blanche's outstanding characteristic, according to Kazan, is desperation; her chief motivation is the urgent need to find protection: 'The tradition of the old South says it must be through another person.' Her problem arises from this Southern tradition,

> her notion of what a woman should be. [. . .] Because this image of herself cannot be accomplished in reality, certainly not in the South of our day and time, it is her effort and practice to *accomplish it in fantasy*. Everything she does in *reality* too is coloured by this necessity, this compulsion to be *special*.

Kazan reminds any actress attempting the rôle that it requires considerable emotional versatility – ranging from imperious self-assertion to fluttering helplessness, from feverish gaiety to pathetic terror. She must alternately alienate and engage the sympathy of the audience.

> The audience at the beginning should see her bad effect on Stella, want Stanley to tell her off. He does. He exposes

her and then gradually, as they see how genuinely in pain, how actually desperate she is, how warm, tender and loving she can be (the Mitch story), how freighted with need she is – then they begin to go with her. They begin to realize that they are sitting in at the death of something extraordinary [. . .] and then they feel the tragedy. (*Twentieth Century Interpretations*, 22)

The tragic flaw that undermines her heroic and admirable qualities is, then, her need to be special, which isolates her from others. Allied to this is her refusal to accept what is innate in her – part, that is, of her *common* rather than her unique humanity – her sexuality. She denigrates it as mere 'brutal desire', thinking of it as 'a rattle-trap streetcar, that bangs through the Quarter, up one old narrow street and down another' (40) while she yearns for a 'Cadillac convertible, must have been a block long' (37) or 'a cruise of the Caribbean' (76). She harbours dreams of a happy-ever-after ending to her story in which she as 'a woman of intelligence and breeding, can enrich a man's life – immeasurably!' (78). She longs to be protected against the dangers of fading physical beauty and old age:

> **BLANCHE:**   Physical beauty is passing. A transitory possession. But beauty of the mind and richness of the spirit and tenderness of the heart – and I have all of those things – aren't taken away, but grow! Increase with the years! How strange that I should be called a destitute woman! When I have all of these treasures locked in my heart. (*A choked sob comes from her.*) (78)

Kazan sees *Streetcar* as resembling a classical tragedy, with Blanche like Medea or some doomed Greek heroine, pursued to madness by the Harpies within her own nature, with Nemesis (the spirit of retribution) dogging her heels and baying for vengeance against her for the death of her boy-husband and for her sinning. She is capable of exciting pity and terror in the audience – the responses described by Aristotle as the hallmarks of tragedy.

'Pity' implies a compassionate concern; the audience must be able to believe in and care about the character. She must have, at least, a dramatic reality. How is this created? She is given a past that makes sense of her present and that makes her future fate both consistent and 'right'. Stella refers to Blanche's upbringing and her sensitivity, in defence of her behaviour (58). She also speaks of Blanche's traumatic marriage and widowing, 'an experience that – killed her illusions' (61). Blanche herself explains and justifies her desperate search for protection from poverty and physical decline when she describes the squalid horror of

> All of those deaths! The long parade to the graveyard! Father, mother! Margaret, that dreadful way! So big with it, it couldn't be put in a coffin! But had to be burned like rubbish! [. . .] Which of them left us a fortune? Which of them left a cent of insurance even? Only poor Jessie – one hundred to pay for her coffin. That was all, Stella! And I with my pitiful salary at the school. (12)

Blanche's early lessons have been bleak: gentility brought no lasting earthly rewards; marriage brought pain and horror; material possessions seeped away; the body swelled or shrivelled in death. As she says to Mitch (who cannot understand her), *desire* seemed to be the opposite of all that death, a possible antidote to the dying and the despair, so she caught the habit, became addicted. In her final fantasies (85), she yearns for the hygienic expansiveness of the sea, for a picturesque death without pain or disfigurement or loneliness ('my hand in the hand of some nice-looking ship's doctor'), for a clean, bright funeral which will be like a return to youthful romance, and the hope of eternal happiness in heaven.

The Aristotelian 'terror' comes from the audience's recognition that Blanche's destruction is inevitable, that she cannot free herself from the contradictions of her own nature nor shake off the burden of guilt she has carried ever since her husband's death. It is a tragic irony of her situation that the only way she can attract the special attention she craves, the protection she seems unable to survive without, is by exploiting the sexuality she feels debases her and which ultimately debars her from the hoped-for haven of a second marriage. She describes her dilemma defensively, but with clarity:

> **BLANCHE:**   I was never hard or self-sufficient enough. When people are soft – soft people have got to court the favour of hard ones, Stella. Have got to be seductive – put on soft colours, the colours of butterfly wings, and glow – make a little temporary magic just in order to pay for – one night's shelter. That's why I've been – not so awf'ly good lately. I've run for protection, Stella . . . protection. (45)

To Mitch she admits without coquetry that her youth has suddenly vanished, that all she wants is a peaceful hiding place that is more than simply a grave, that she has lied: 'I don't tell the truth. I tell what *ought* to be the truth. And if that is sinful, then let me be damned for it!' (72). The 'if' is important; it leaves the moral issues unresolved. Blanche's morality is that of the aesthete, the dedicated seeker after beauty before all else. Like Oscar Wilde (the Anglo-Irish playwright whose life and works were designed to celebrate beauty and wit rather than more conventional moral standards), Blanche holds to the belief that 'Lying, the telling of beautiful untrue things, is the proper aim of Art'.[9] For her, too, it is important that her life should resemble a work of art, and that art, poetry and music should be the flag she carries 'in this dark march toward whatever it is we're approaching' (41). It is fitting that she should be a teacher of English. Not only does this make credible her often rather literary and poetic language, but it also fits her search for magical beauty at the expense of common-or-garden reality. It is her business 'to instil a bunch of bobby-soxers and drug-store Romeos with reverence for Hawthorne and Whitman and Poe' (31). The images associated with Blanche generally imply fragile beauty, transience: an orchard in spring, its blossom bound to fall at the short season's end; a softly tinted butterfly or a moth, driven to seek warmth and brilliance from a flame that will sear its beauty then consume it.

As well as making sense in human terms, the character of Blanche has been seen as embodying a number of concepts or themes: the Soul subjected to physical existence and thus to 'the apishness and brutality of matter' (Leonard Quirino in *Tennessee Williams: A Tribute*, 85); a Jungian Great Mother Figure, a kind of white witch ('A Gallery of Witches' N. M. Tischler); the representation 'in her frail spirit [of] the decline and fall of a long line of decadent Southern aristocrats' (*New York Daily News*, 4.12.1947); 'beauty shipwrecked on the rock of the world's vulgarity' (*The New Republic*, 22.12.1947); 'the symbol of art and beauty, this poor flimsy creature to whom truth is mortal' (Mary McCarthy in *Twentieth Century Interpretations*, 99). Elia Kazan sees her, on the one hand, as a doomed dinosaur approaching extinction, and, on the other (with a male arrogance worthy of Stanley Kowalski), as:

> a heightened version, an artistic intensification of all women. That is what makes the play universal. Blanche's special relation to all women *is that she is at that critical point where the one thing above all else that she is dependent on – her attraction for men – is beginning to go.* Blanche is like all women, dependent on a man, looking for one to hang on to: only *more so!* (*Twentieth Century Interpretations*, 24)

Equally one might say that Blanche is 'an artistic intensification' of a common male conception of 'all women', and her dependency on a man is the expression of their commonly cherished hope – hence the play's universality.

Mitch is important to the plot of *Streetcar* as he represents the possibility – however pallid – of future happiness or security for Blanche,

9 Oscar Wilde, *Impressions*, 1891.

that hope which makes her ultimate catastrophe all the more poignant. He also serves to emphasise the strengths and vividness of both Stanley and Blanche by offering the contrast of his own weakness and insipidity. One feels that Blanche would have had to stoop to marry him, to confine her nature within his soft-centred mediocrity. Mitch sometimes emerges as a comic foil for Stanley; for example, his overscrupulous concern about the way he perspires seems funny after Stanley's easy: 'My clothes're stickin' to me. Do you mind if I make myself comfortable? (*He starts to remove his shirt.*)' (14). When Stanley charges after the pregnant Stella in drunken fury, Mitch's response sounds positively spinsterish: 'This is terrible' (31). The way he is routed by Blanche's cries of 'Fire!' is absurd and makes Stanley's subsequent domination of her seem all the more powerful.

In the early drafts of the play, the key struggle is between Blanche and the prospective suitor, rather than between Blanche and her brother-in-law. Subsequently the character becomes weaker, but in the final stage of *A Streetcar Named Desire* Williams adds two important elements to make Mitch's rejection of Blanche more credible, since one might otherwise expect her to mould his weakness to answer her own needs. Williams emphasises Mitch's reverence for and dependence on his invalid mother, who will be outraged by Blanche's lifestyle. Also, before confronting Blanche, Mitch has tried to nerve himself by drinking more than he is accustomed to. It is difficult to be sure how sympathetic a character he is meant to be: Stanley treats him with tolerant superiority, yet feels a loyalty to him; his own gentleness and hesitancy come as a relief after Stanley's blustering towards Blanche; his concern for Stella's well-being and his courtesy towards Blanche are appealing and believable. Yet his gentleness comes out of weakness rather than strength: his advances to Blanche are hesitant because he is doubtful of his power to please; his capacity for affection and tenderness has long been absorbed by a sickly mother and a dead girl; he appears childish to his friends (28); he is embarrassed by his body functions (52); he lacks the experience or the insight to see through Blanche's affected demureness, and then lacks the wisdom to recognise her worth once his first illusions have been shattered. He responds to Blanche's cry for help with injured self-esteem; then his attempt to take sexual advantage of her is a fiasco; even the words of his rejection of her are weak – he doesn't *think* he wants to marry her anymore. Williams describes him as clattering awkwardly down the steps and out of sight. His inadequacy highlights the desperation that drives Blanche to say (47): 'I want his respect. [. . .] I want to *rest*! I want to breathe quietly again! Yes – I *want*

Mitch . . . *very badly*! Just think! If it happens! I can leave here and not be anyone's problem . . .' (47). There is a truth behind the account she gives Stanley of her final encounter with Mitch:

BLANCHE: But some things are not forgivable. Deliberate cruelty is not forgivable. It is the one unforgivable thing in my opinion and it is one thing of which I have never, never been guilty. And so I told him, I said to him, Thank you, but it was foolish of me to think we could ever adapt ourselves to each other. Our ways of life are too different. We have to be realistic about such things. (78)

Is Mitch guilty of 'deliberate cruelty' in that rejection of Blanche, either in its meaning or its manner? Or, like Blanche when feeling betrayed by her boy-husband, is he simply unable to cope with this new reality, so hits out like a child then runs away?

When he reappears in the final scene, he is evidently dogged by shame and an impotent fury. He splutters with incoherent rage against Stanley, using the language of their card-playing: 'You . . . you . . . you . . . Brag . . . brag . . . bull . . . bull' (82). When he hears Blanche's voice, his arm becomes nerveless and '*his gaze is dissolved into space*' (83). He ducks his head, as if to hide from her, and remains hunched over the table, sullen and ashamed, when the others stand to let her pass. He cannot bear to look at her; undignified and cowardly evasion is all that is left to him. Only when Blanche is fighting for survival against the grim nurse is he stung into movement, but he is blocked by Stanley and his wild accusation merely ridiculed:

MITCH (*wildly*):   You! You done this, all o' your God damn interfering with things you –

STANLEY: Quit the blubber! (*He pushes him aside.*)

MITCH: I'll kill you! (*He lunges and strikes at* STANLEY.)

STANLEY: Hold this bone-headed cry-baby! (88)

Mitch collapses, sobbing helplessly over the table. He, like Blanche, will have to find some way of trying to escape from the guilt and the sense of personal failure, or he will be finished. Perhaps he will translate the whole experience into a wistful memory to keep alongside his silver cigarette case from the strange, sweet, dead girl, with its significant inscription:

And if God choose,

I shall but love thee better – after death! (29)

Poet of the Theatre/Successful Showman?

In the letter to Tynan already referred to, Tennessee Williams describes his writing as 'lyric'. This implies two important characteristics: first, that the writing has a musical quality rather than being prosaic or naturalistic, and, secondly, that it is an expression of the writer's personal experience or, more significantly, of his thoughts and feelings about that experience. The 'truth' or 'reality' is, therefore, highly subjective and the play's success is dependent on the dramatist's ability to present his personal perspective on life so persuasively that, for the duration of the play at least, the audience can understand and sympathise with that personal vision. Williams was, by his own admission, engrossed by his own biography, using the colourful facts of his life to create the patterns of his work and, at the same time, using that process of translation from life to literature as a means of freeing himself from emotions and memories which otherwise haunted him.

In *A Streetcar Named Desire* there are recurring themes and terrors: death, for instance. His mother recalls Tennessee Williams saying:

> We are all desperately afraid of death, much more than we dare admit even to ourselves. (*Remember Me to Tom*, 252)

This terror was but one element, according to Miss Edwina, in her son's general anxiety:

> Tom is so mild in looks and manner you would never suspect
> a violent feeling stirs in him. Yet violence is the way we
> fight fear and Tom has said he always had to contend with
> the 'adversary of fear' which gave him 'a certain tendency
> toward an atmosphere of hysteria and violence in my writing,
> an atmosphere that has existed in it from the beginning'.
> (*Remember Me to Tom*, 253)

A sense of the inexorable decay of beauty accelerated by the brutality of much of modern, urban life linked his fear of personal disintegration with his nostalgia for the tattered romance of the Old South – a nostalgia he could hardly escape, being Miss Edwina's son. She approvingly records this:

> Another time he declared, 'I write out of love for the South. [. . .]
> But I can't expect Southerners to realize that my writing about
> them is an expression of love. It is out of regret for a South that
> no longer exists that I write of the forces that have destroyed it'.
> (*Remember Me to Tom*, 213)

The third theme dominant in much of his work, and certainly in *Streetcar*, is the nature and effects of human sexuality: its voracious energy, its disguises, the attempts made to control or domesticate it by self-consciously civilised sections of society, the subsequent conflicts, the relationship between love and lust, between emotional and physical needs.

Any poet of the theatre, rather than of the study, has a vocabulary beyond words – the three-dimensional images of the stage itself. The first production of *Streetcar* was designed by Jo Mielziner, a man who had come under the influence of German Expressionist stagecraft while working in Berlin. The wish to communicate the *feeling* of the play through its set was reflected in the sloping telegraph poles and lurid neon lights surrounding the ornate but crumbling façade of the pale old apartment house in Elysian Fields. Tennessee Williams's stage directions are emotionally coloured. At the opening of the play,

> *the sky that shows round the dim white building is a peculiarly tender blue, almost turquoise, which invests the scene with a kind of lyricism and gracefully attenuates the atmosphere of decay.* (3)

For Scene Three, *The Poker Night*, his directions are very specific, indicating the visual tradition he is drawing on:

> *There is a picture of Van Gogh's of a billiard-parlour at night. The kitchen now suggests that sort of lurid nocturnal brilliance, the raw colours of childhood's spectrum.* (24)

He stresses the relationship between the image of the set and the nature of the characters framed within it; the card players are '*as coarse and direct and powerful as the primary colours*', with a childlike – or childish – lack of delicacy and sophistication, having no subtle shading or nuances. At the end of the play, when Blanche feels like a hunted animal finally at bay, Williams calls for her state of mind to be expressed visually in a wholly unnaturalistic but perhaps poetic – or theatrically shocking – way:

> *She rushes past him into the bedroom. Lurid reflections appear on the walls in odd, sinuous shapes.* (86)

These horrid reflections of her panic fade when she is soothed by the doctor's courteous gesture. As she is led out, like someone blind, the lyricism of the surrounding turquoise sky becomes grimly ironic.

This visual projection of Blanche's inner life is complemented by the pattern of sound Williams calls for – primarily the use of music and chanted street-cries – creating a ritualistic or dreamlike feeling. The lyricism of the opening picture (3) is given voice by the 'blue piano' which, Williams explains, '*expresses the spirit of the life which goes on here*'. It is eloquent of the '*infatuated fluency*' of the Old Quarter's picturesquely self-consuming culture. Later the strains of a polka become more and more insistent as the truth of Blanche's past moves closer and closer to her present refuge. At first it is faint in the distance (15), then, as she speaks to Mitch of her widowing, the polka sounds more strongly, in a minor key, shifting into a major key as Mitch moves towards her with awkward compassion. When Blanche is discovered alone at the beginning of Scene Nine, the polka is rapid and feverish. She sits tense and hunched, no longer dressed in a near-virginal white but in a scarlet robe:

> *The music is in her mind; she is drinking to escape it and the sense of disaster closing in on her and she seems to whisper the words of the song.* (69)

It is important to remember when *reading* the play that the music in Blanche's mind is also heard by the audience in the theatre. Tennessee Williams uses a theatrical device to draw the audience into Blanche's nightmare; she and they share the same experience at this moment and so the audience may be persuaded to believe in the truth of this vision. This may be felt as the power of poetry in the theatre, or it may be seen as successful showmanship.

It is not only Blanche's passions and qualities that are expressed through emotive sounds. Stanley, for example, is associated with the powerful note of a locomotive engine – modern, brutally impressive machine-muscle. In Scene Four (40), his invasion of the sisters' conspiracy is covered by the sound of an approaching train; so, too, is his feigned withdrawal before his victorious reclamation of Stella. It is, therefore, significant that when Blanche is telling Mitch of her marriage, the most harrowing memory is signalled by the roar of an oncoming locomotive:

> *She claps her hands to her ears and crouches over. The headlight of the locomotive glares into the room as it thunders past.* (56)

Similarly, the beginning of the last phase of the movement towards Stanley's rape of Blanche in Scene Ten is marked by the roar of an approaching locomotive which forces Blanche to crouch and press her fists to her ears while Stanley, grinning, waits between her and her means of escape.

Stanley has his music, too. When he is full of anguished rage at Stella's retreat upstairs, his violent gesture of hurling the telephone to the floor is accompanied by '*dissonant brass and piano sounds*' (33). The transition from his howl of 'STELLAHHHHH!' to the intense sensuality of their reunion is achieved by the moaning of a low-tone clarinet. His sexual domination of Blanche in Scene Ten is blared out by '*the hot trumpet and drums from the Four Deuces*'.

This deliberate orchestration of the play's emotional movement is 'lyricism' in its most literal sense. When the script is read, the lyric device can be appraised intellectually as one of the several formal elements of the play as a whole. The *idea* of it is interesting. In the theatre, however, the power of these sounds is not intellectual but makes a direct appeal to or an assault upon the audience's feelings.

The language of the play is shaped by two needs: character-identification and thematic development. On a naturalistic level, the characters are placed socially and individually by the words they use and the structure of their sentences. Stanley's sentences are generally short, with a simple syntax: challenging questions are followed by single-statement answers, with key words hammered home:

STANLEY: You know what luck is? Luck is believing you're lucky. Take at Salerno. I believed I was lucky. I figured that 4 out of 5 would not come through but I would . . . and I did. I put that down as a rule. To hold front position in this rat-race you've got to believe you are lucky. (82)

His vocabulary is drawn from his day-to-day interests: card-playing and betting (20), the popular culture of films and songs (20), slang (88), lively but hackneyed over-statement (18). Nonetheless, there is a patterning of imagery, a kind of poetic rhetoric (i.e. language used deliberately to create a desired effect or to make a specific point – here, this 'point' about those values and forces that Stanley embodies). The language of games-playing has not only an obvious naturalistic reference, but also expresses a gambler's fatalism and his faith in his strength as someone favoured by Fortune (82). It is a male-oriented philosophy: 'seven card *stud*' (25), 'One-eyed *jacks* are wild' (24), 'What do you two think you are? A pair of *queens*?' (65). It supposes a way of life played by a set of rules which might seem arbitrary, even unfair, to an outsider and which must take into account the action of forces beyond human control, where the urge to compete and conquer is celebrated and losers may be called upon to surrender all they have. The poker games that Stanley is seen playing are aggressive, individualistic. Initially he is seen losing to Mitch, Blanche's most promising ally, but by the last scene he is winning every hand (82).

Depending as it does on the skilful manipulation of the hands that chance deals out, the card game is used by Williams throughout *Streetcar* as a symbol of fate and of the skilful player's ability to make its decrees perform in his own favour at the expense of his opponent's misfortune, incompetence, and horror of the game itself. (L. Quirino in *Tennessee Williams: A Tribute*, 78)

Stanley also echoes or answers images used by Blanche. Her fear of bright light is in opposition to Stanley's delight in 'them coloured lights' that he 'gets going' with Stella. The effect of the imagery is emphasised by a strong gesture in the final scene when Stanley speaks dismissively of Blanche's impact on his life, then tears her paper lantern off the light:

STANLEY: You left nothing here but spilt talcum and old empty perfume bottles – unless it's the paper lantern you want to take with you. You want the lantern? (*He crosses to dressing-table and seizes the paper lantern, tearing it off the light bulb, and extends it towards her. She cries out as if the lantern was herself . . .*) (87)

Blanche's language, too, works both naturalistically and symbolically. With her, however, the symbolism is a more conscious part of the character's style. It is consistent with what the audience learns of her life and of her early character that she should move from breathless flirtation to deliberate rhetoric (22) and scatter literary allusions through her conversation (Shakespeare, Hawthorne, Whitman and Poe). But the insistence of the motifs, like the strains of the polka, gains momentum and demands attention: there is the image of Desire as a streetcar banging (a word with sexual connotations) through the narrow thoroughfares of the Old Quarter, taking Blanche first to Cemeteries then, if she is lucky, to Elysian Fields – that area of the classical underworld reserved for the blessed. There is a bitter irony that she who seeks happiness so fervently should be driven out of Elysium as a sinner for whom there is no apparent redemption. Like a moth, to which Williams compares her, she is a creature of the night, shrinking from strong light yet fatally drawn to the flame of passion. The songs she sings, although recognisably of the period in which the play is set, comment figuratively on her situation and make her seem not so much an individual as part of that romantic tradition of 'captive maids' brought from 'the land of the sky blue water' (16) into 'a Barnum and Bailey world. Just as phony as it can be [. . .] a honky-tonk parade' (60), whose promise of happiness *could* be fulfilled only 'If you believed in me!' In the final scene she seems to belong to another recognisable tradition, that of Shakespeare's Orphelia – the delicate, loving maid driven to madness by the betrayals and brutality of the world she has been unluckily born into. Unlike Ophelia, Blanche does not sing in her final defeat, but she echoes Ophelia's pathos and poignant lyricism in her dreams of a beautiful death on the water and in the refrain-like repetition of key words ('sea', 'death') and the ironic purity of the cathedral chimes. So much so, that Laertes's heart-wrung response to his sister Ophelia's madness is, perhaps, the kind of response Tennessee Williams aspires to as Blanche is led away:

Thoughts and affliction, passion, hell itself

She turns to favour and to prettiness.

(Hamlet, IV, vi)

Production History of A Streetcar Named Desire

The premiere

Directed by Elia Kazan, the premiere of *A Streetcar Named Desire* was on Broadway at the Barrymore Theatre. Opening on 3 December 1947, after tryouts in Boston, New Haven and Philadelphia, it ran for an impressive 855 performances and won Tennessee Williams the Pulitzer, Donaldson and New York Drama Critics' Circle awards. Kazan, who went on to direct the 1951 film version and four other works by Tennessee Williams, was already a well-established theatre and film director when Williams's agent, Audrey Wood, and the play's producer, Irene Selznick, persuaded him to take on the project. He became a great driving force behind the play, instigating many changes to the original script (over a hundred), as he would with *Cat on a Hot Tin Roof,* and keeping detailed notes on the play's characters and themes that would later be published.

Working closely with Kazan, the Broadway production's designer, Jo Mielziner, carefully balanced the play's realism and its expressionism. Thus the set suggested both the spartan apartment in its rundown neighbourhood and the dreamy romanticism of Blanche. The latter was partly achieved through the complex series of lighting effects and the insubstantial walls of the tenement building. The production's music, composed by Alex North, followed Williams's careful layering effect – the music of the Varsouviana on top of the blue piano, for example – and included miscellaneous sound effects to capture the vibrant French Quarter.

Blanche DuBois was played by Jessica Tandy who, following Kazan's interpretation of the play, suggested that the character had already become mentally unstable at the outset. The other three principal characters were played by lesser known actors: a young, and largely unknown, Marlon Brando played Stanley Kowalski; Mitch was played by Karl Malden who had been with Brando at The Actors Studio; and Kim Hunter took the role of Stella, a character who, in Kazan's view, had to be both passionate with her husband and reflect the considerable sacrifices she has made to be with him. These last three actors would all go on to appear in the 1951 film adaptation.

The huge success of the premiere led to the play going on tour across the United States. Two companies were established, the more successful of which being the one that cast Uta Hagen as Blanche and Anthony Quinn as Stanley. Hagen, also involved with the Broadway production, was a far more physical Blanche who, contrary to Tandy, suggested that the character's madness was induced by Stanley. Quinn studied Brando's interpretation of the role closely, but, despite bringing a greater brutishness to the character through his larger frame, he was not able to match the complexity of Brando's characterisation.

Other American productions

Streetcar was revived in New York at the City Center Theater in Manhattan in February 1956. It proved to be a controversial production, Tallulah Bankhead's bold interpretation of Blanche attracting much negative criticism, even from Williams himself (he later retracted this in the *New York Times*). Bankhead's Blanche was both funny and aggressive – markedly different to Tandy and Hagen's portrayals – and, for the critic Brooks Atkinson, the comedy was out of keeping with the character. Writing in the *New York Times* on 16 February 1956, he argued that Bankhead's personality was 'worldly and sophisticated, decisive and self-sufficient: it is fundamentally comic' (cited in *The Selected Letters of Tennessee Williams, vol. II*, 603). In her defence, Bankhead's Southern background meant that she could bring greater realism to the role.

Four more New York productions of note were those at the Vivian Beaumont Theater in 1973, the Circle in the Square Theater in 1988, the Barrymore in 1992 and Studio 54 in 2005. The first of these, a twenty-fifth anniversary revival, was directed by Ellis Rabb and featured Rosemary Harris as Blanche and James Farentino as Stanley. Although Brendan Gill found it 'not merely a worthy successor to the original but an illuminating companion to it' (cited in Kolin, 2000, 93), the majority of reviewers judged it unnecessarily nostalgic and overblown: Rabb filled a large stage with noisy extras, thus detracting from the play's essential claustrophobia. There were also problems with the acting. Harris's Blanche was, paradoxically, too strong (certainly for Farentino's Stanley) and too emotional. Farentino, appearing naked at one point, sublimated some of Stanley's strength in a strong sense of being wronged.

The Circle in the Square production was directed by Nikos Psacharopoulos and starred Blythe Danner as Blanche. Psacharopoulos had already developed a reputation for directing *Streetcar* in Williamstown (Massachusetts) two years before, but, apart from Danner, the principal parts were changed for New York. Aidan Quinn took the role of Stanley and, although criticised for his lack of physical presence, he brought slyness and verbal dexterity to the part. Psacharopoulos was able to give the play greater relevance to his audience by emphasising both the importance of truth in a post-Watergate era and the role of women after the rise of feminism. The production was also notable for its staging: eschewing the proscenium, the theatre's artistic director, Theodore Mann, defended the positioning of the audience on three sides in a horseshoe effect by stating that it was easier to become part of the play.

In contrast, the highly publicised 1992 production at the Ethel Barrymore Theater attempted to recreate Kazan's more conventional set. However, the director, Gregory Mosher, was ultimately unable to capture much of the play's poetry, and Jessica Lange as Blanche failed to transfer her considerable skills as a screen actress to the stage. She was overshadowed by another film actor, Alec Baldwin, who played up Stanley's vulgarity, acknowledging the influence of Brando.

The English actress, Natasha Richardson, took the role of Blanche at Studio 54 in Manhattan in 2005. This Roundabout Theatre Company production was directed by Edward Hall and was much talked about for the casting of John C. Reilly as Stanley. To many, he was the antithesis of Brando's creation, being neither menacing nor erotic (he had previously played Mitch in Chicago, a role to which he seemed much more suited). Indeed, though Richardson was more than able to suggest the sexual experience of Blanche, there was little chemistry between the two adversaries. Amy Ryan's Stella, also unable to connect with Reilly's Stanley, was, according to Ben Brantley of the *New York Times*, the production's 'anchor of authenticity'.

Two established film stars, Faye Dunaway and John Voight, took the roles of Blanche and Stanley for another twenty-fifth anniversary production of the play at the Ahmanson Theater in Los Angeles in 1973. The director, James Bridges, tried to break with tradition, but, like Mosher, ended up draining the play of much of its poetic strength. Faye Dunaway received mixed reviews: for some, she rose above the rest of the production; however, despite being chosen by Williams, it was felt she was too young and tried to bring too much comedy to the part. Voight consciously underplayed Stanley with the result that the character lost much of his force. He was even overshadowed by Mitch, played by the very good Earl Holliman.

In 1976, Jack Gerber directed the husband and wife team of Geraldine Page and Rip Torn at the Academy Festival Theatre in Lake Forest, Illinois. This production was gritty and violent, the uncompromising set, complete with strewn rubbish and a continually burning light, being complemented by Page's robust Blanche and Torn's (overly) menacing and vulgar Stanley.

London productions

The first London *Streetcar* opened at the Aldwych Theatre in October 1949. The sold-out run lasted for 326 performances until August 1950 and was a success, despite considerable moral condemnation from members of the clergy and politicians alike. Vivien Leigh (Blanche) was directed by her husband, Laurence Olivier, and the part of Stanley was taken by Bonar Colleano; Renee Asherson was Stella and Bernard Braden was Mitch. The production drew heavily on the Broadway premiere, using the same sets and music, and Olivier even studied Kazan's notes assiduously. However, Leigh interpreted the role of Blanche differently to her American predecessors and this was underlined by a greater fidelity to Williams's notes about costume. Her role was compromised somewhat by cuts enforced by the Lord Chamberlain: for example, there was to be no reference to Allan Grey's homosexuality, a crucial aspect of her past that determines much of her subsequent behaviour. Leigh won praise for her interpretation and Colleano, intentionally more subtle than Brando, was a worthy Stanley.

The 1974 London production at the Piccadilly Theatre encountered no censorship issues. Directed by Edwin Sherin, it starred Claire Bloom, Martin Shaw and Joss Ackland (Mitch). Arguably, Bloom's turbulent personal life prepared her well for the part of Blanche, allowing her to realise that the character's 'neediness only brings suffering' (from *Leaving a Doll's House*, cited in Kolin, 2000, 100). She was widely praised for a moving performance that captured both the vulnerability of the character and her determination to ensnare Mitch, and she won awards from both the *Evening Standard* and *Variety*. Shaw was an intelligent and proud Stanley, whereas Ackland offered an older Mitch, sensitive but lumbering.

The 2002 production of *A Streetcar Named Desire* at the National Theatre was directed by Trevor Nunn and starred Glenn Close as Blanche and Iain Glen as Stanley. Close's involvement was criticised by the actors' union, Equity, as depriving British talent of a chance to take the role, but she gave a consummate performance. Michael Billington, writing in the *Guardian*, said that she 'oozes fluttery condescension and coy gentility' and John Peter for the *Sunday Times* lauded the interpretation as 'thrillingly theatrical but unostentatious, and as powerful, intelligent and moving as anything I have seen on this stage'. Glen was elegant and graceful, but, for Peter, he was also 'like a matador: ruthless, confident, provocative, alert'.

Other premieres around the world

Curiously, the short Mexican premiere of *A Streetcar Named Desire* (*Un Tranvía Llamado Deseo*) in December 1948 and the follow-up run in May 1949 were the work of a Japanese director, Seki Sano. Influenced by Stanislavski, Sano had a semi-professional acting company called the Teatro de la Reforma, and it was this troupe that gave nine performances at the Palacio de Bellas Artes and then a hundred performances at the Teatro Esperanza Iris in Mexico City. Also one of the translators, Sano helped to make Williams's play both popular and respected in Mexico. María Douglas, though young and inexperienced, gave a powerful performance as Blanche, capturing, on the one hand, her arrogance and flirtatiousness and, on the other, her victimisation. Playing opposite her was an ex-boxer, Wolf Ruvinskis, who, perhaps unsurprisingly, emphasised Stanley's physical and verbal aggression.

The Italian premiere of *Streetcar* was at the Eliseo Theatre in Rome on 21 January 1949. Directed by Luchino Visconti, who would come to be known outside Italy for films like *The Leopard* (1963), the production highlighted the play's class struggle against a fussily realistic backdrop. Visconti was aided in this by his young set designer, Franco Zefferelli, the future director of the film of *Romeo and Juliet*. Zefferelli created a messy and drab apartment – simultaneously realistic and romantic – and a cacophony of sounds that reproduced both the noisy vitality of the Quarter and Blanche's breakdown. Rina Morelli played Blanche simply but effectively, concentrating on her tragic decline in a hostile world. Vittorio Gassman's Stanley was a mixture of spontaneous violence and great tenderness, while Marcello Mastroianni (also destined to be successful in the world of film) was a young and sexy Mitch, very different to Karl Malden in the Broadway premiere. Williams attended the opening night and strongly approved of the production; it ran for just over a month.

The Swedish premiere took place at the Gothenburg City Theatre on 1 March 1949, where Ingmar Bergman was the resident director. Able to benefit from a revolving stage, complete with inner and outer sections, Bergman's production added an extra building in the form of a movie theatre called Desire or the Pleasure Garden. Constantly playing *A Night in Paradise*, this cinema immediately suggested the play's main theme, while the film's title could apply to both Stanley's wedding night and his rape of Blanche; there were also echoes of the Paradise Dance Hall in *The Glass Menagerie*. An apple tree stood near the cinema – perhaps a reference to Blanche's explanation of her name as 'an orchard in spring' – visibly dropping its leaves as the play progressed. Blanche was played by Karin Kavli, an actress who impressed critics with her range of emotions; Anders Ek was a primitive but innocent Stanley.

Consistent with the Italian and Swedish premieres, the French production of *Streetcar* also involved a celebrated filmmaker: Jean Cocteau. His adaptation of the play began on 19 October 1949 and ran for 233 performances at the Théâtre Edouard VII in Paris. Cocteau's translation was rather loose in places, and his adaptation included many black extras, male and female, to help capture the spirit of New Orleans – memorably dancing in the background during the rape scene, for example. The play's set was notable for a series of transparent backdrops illuminated by important symbols or miniature scenes. Blanche was played by a comedienne, Arletty, who, at the age of forty, managed to capture all of the character's aristocratic grandeur; Yves Vincent's simian Stanley was no match for her.

The Bungakuza Dramatic Company mounted the first Asian production of *Streetcar* in Tokyo in 1953, at a time when American culture, including the already released film version of the play, was starting to have an influence. The director, Ichiro Kawaguchi, like Seki Sano in Mexico, was influenced by Stanislavski, and he made every attempt to recreate the world of the play faithfully. Blanche was played by Haruko Sugimura, a highly respected actress who went on to become identified with the role, even reviving it in 1987. Though she was prone to exaggeration in her performance, and though Japanese critics found it hard to sympathise with Blanche's character, there was considerable praise for Sugimura's interpretation, in which she captured much of the character's stature. Kazuo Kitamura (Stanley) was less successful: his inexperience was evident and he mistakenly tried to copy Brando.

Alternative productions

As well as the many international variations of *Streetcar*, there have been several productions which have foregrounded black actors or black interpretations of the play. In some cases – Jefferson City, Missouri (1953), Los Angeles (1955 and 1956), New Orleans (1984), Chicago (1987),

Washington DC (1988) – the cast was all black; in other productions –
West Berlin (1974) and Berkeley (1983) – only one of the parts was played
by a black actor: that of Stanley. While these alternative productions have
opened up the text, freeing it from conventional interpretations that may
have taken the Broadway premiere as a point of departure, they have, in
some cases, involved necessary amendments to the script – for example,
omitting references to Stanley's Polish ancestry in the Berkeley production,
or changing the number of his regiment during the war so that it faithfully
denoted a black one in the New Orleans production. The Washington
production at Howard University offered a different racial dimension
still: Blanche was supposed to be descended from light-skinned Creoles,
whereas Stanley was from the Sea Islands off the coast of South Carolina
and, therefore, noticeably darker. This interpretation sought to highlight
the racism that can be assimilated within gradations of colour, not just
between white and black.

    Gender has also proved to be an area for reinterpretation of the play.
Here the collaboration of two companies, Split Britches and Bloolips,
produced the parodically titled *Belle Reprieve* in 1991, a show that drew
on many different styles and only really used *Streetcar* as its inspiration.
Blanche was transformed into a drag queen, played by Bette Bourne,
and Stanley became a butch lesbian, played by Peggy Shaw. Offering
versions of some of the scenes in the original play, *Belle Reprieve* also
incorporated songs, dance and a humorous script that parodied some of
the serious lines of *Streetcar*. The rape, out of tune with the comic tenor
of the production, was omitted. In short, the creators of *Belle Reprieve*
aimed to deconstruct and question sexual roles generally, and more
specifically in traditional versions of Williams's play. *Belle Reprieve*
premiered at Drill Hall in London before moving to La MaMa and One
Dream, two venues in New York.

Film and television adaptations

The 1951 Warner Brothers film version, directed by Elia Kazan and
filmed in New Orleans, is justly famous. R. Barton Palmer explains
that 'its startling differences from the standard Hollywood movie in the
representation of sexual themes eminently suited Williams's play to be the
source of the first Hollywood production in a new genre: the adult art film'
('Hollywood in Crisis: Tennessee Williams and the evolution of the adult
film', in Roudané, 2001, 216). Starring three of the four main actors from
the Broadway premiere (Vivien Leigh, judged to have more box-office
appeal following her success with *Gone with the Wind*, replaced Jessica

Tandy as Blanche), the film also used the same costume designer, Lucinda Ballard, and musical director, Alex North. Amid much critical acclaim, Leigh, Kim Hunter (Stella) and Karl Malden (Mitch) all won Oscars, but the project initially encountered significant problems with the censors, the Production Code Administration headed by Joseph Breen. Kazan and Williams were ordered to make sixty-eight cuts from the Broadway version. These included removing all reference to homosexuality and, most crucially, changing the outcome of the rape. In theatrical productions, Stanley could escape punishment; however, the film's family audience would find that this was morally unacceptable. Nevertheless, determined attempts were made to retain the spirit of the original play. The rape, for example, was suggested by showing the viewer Stanley gathering up Blanche's defeated body in a cracked mirror; the film then cuts to a cleaner hosing down a street, a crude but effective way of indicating what has happened. However, Williams could never reconcile himself to the enforced ending where Stella, clutching her baby, vows she is never going to return to Stanley.

There have been two television adaptations of *Streetcar*, both of which were made quite some time after the film. The first, broadcast on ABC on 4 March 1984, was directed by John Erman and starred Ann-Margaret as Blanche, Treat Williams as Stanley and Randy Quaid as Mitch. Without the restrictions imposed on the film, this adaptation could play up Blanche's flirtatiousness and depict the rape far more directly. Ann-Margaret was tougher than previous Blanches and did not suggest the character's madness until the rape scene. Treat Williams recreated the muscular build of Brando's Stanley, but his interpretation of the character was too one-dimensional. Beverly D'Angelo's Stella forgave her husband easily and passionately.

The second television adaptation reunited Jessica Lange and Alec Baldwin (they had appeared in the 1992 Broadway revival) and was broadcast on 29 October 1995. It was directed by Glenn Jordan and featured the comic actor, John Goodman, as Mitch. Lange's screen Blanche was considered an improvement on her stage creation, while Alec Baldwin continued to impress as Stanley.

Opera and ballet versions

Given its musical content, it is perhaps not altogether surprising that *A Streetcar Named Desire* became the inspiration for an opera performed by the San Francisco Opera Company in 1998. The score was written by André Previn, who conducted the first four performances at the War

Memorial Opera House, and the libretto was written by Philip Littell. Previn steered away from the jazz that characterised Alex North's score for both the Broadway premiere and the film, choosing instead to create a modern European sound. The three acts focused strongly on Blanche, Previn firmly believing that her fate was irredeemably tragic. Consequently, Littell gave the character several arias, though the rest of the libretto had to follow Williams's play fairly closely. The set, too, reflected Blanche's centrality: with its transparent walls and the faint tilt of the apartment, it was easy to suggest the character's state of mind, particularly in the wordless rape scene where the stage split in two. Renee Fleming (Blanche) was a soprano who came to the production with an impressive reputation, and, for most, she did not disappoint, conveying the character's power and vulnerability. Rodney Gilfrey (Stanley, baritone) was imposing but subordinate to Blanche, and Elizabeth Furtel (Stella, coloratura soprano) was an effective contrast to Fleming, appropriately cast as her sister and combining well with Gilfrey.

Blanche was also intended to be the focus of a ballet based on *Streetcar* choreographed by Valerie Betis. Premiering in Montreal at Her Majesty's Theatre on 9 October 1952, before moving on to Boston, Chicago, Cleveland, St Louis and Broadway, the *Streetcar* ballet was performed by the Slavenska-Franklin troupe. Lasting a mere forty minutes, Betis' production bravely combined different dance styles, both classical and modern, culminating in a chase through several doorways (symbolising the rape) and Blanche's being led off by Death.

Betis's choreography was used again by the Dance Theatre of Harlem, an African American company, in 1981 (Montreal), 1982 (New York) and 1986 (filmed in Denmark). This ballet, initially celebrating Tennessee Williams's seventieth birthday, incorporated flashbacks in a vibrant and unconventional rendering of the original story.

Production History since 2005 (by Michael Hooper)

Interest in *A Streetcar Named Desire* since 2005 has shown little abatement and the play has continued to be attractive to both large commercial theatres and more modest acting companies working on college campuses. Its worldwide appeal also persists.

A 2008 production in New Zealand, at the Fortune Theatre in Dunedin, created something of a stir by using a Maori actor, Jarod Rawiri, as Stanley Kowalski. It was, though, Jude Gibson, the actress playing Blanche DuBois, who earned most of the critical enthusiasm. One reviewer, Terry MacTavish, raved that 'the heart bleeds for her [Blanche]' and that, as Williams intended, the character was given genuine valour. Rawiri brought the necessary machismo to his role but MacTavish felt that his ethnicity created a mismatch, a clash with Southern culture that was 'jarring rather than illuminating'. Directed by an American, Jef Hall-Flavin, this production was revived at the Provincetown Tennessee Williams Festival the following year.

In 2009, a Sydney Theatre Company production, directed by Liv Ullmann, proved successful both in Australia and on tour in America. The then co-artistic director of the company, Cate Blanchett, was widely celebrated for her role as Blanche. A stunning mix of power and defencelessness, Blanchett, better known as a film actress, made the Southern belle glide and flutter, according to Helen Barry, a reviewer for *Australian Stage*; and, just as impressively, she managed to bring out the character's humour, too. Barry also praised Joel Edgerton as Stanley – for the way he combined muscularity with a deftness of movement, and for his psychological strength. The production successfully alternated moments of theatricality with naturalism.

In 2009, another screen star who impressed reviewers and audiences was Rachel Weisz when she took on the role of Blanche for London's Donmar Theatre production. Michael Billington, reviewing the production for the *Guardian*, likened her to a young Hedy Lamarr and felt she brought to the role 'a quality of desperate solitude touched with grace'. Henry Hitchings of the *London Evening Standard* found her mesmerising and more than capable of capturing the many different sides to Blanche's character. Not all reviewers were quite so convinced, though. Michael Coveney, writing for he *Independent*, felt that Weisz's portrayal overlooked Blanche's 'cutting cruelty and sheer drag queen bitchiness'. Still worse, the physically impressive Elliott Cowan as Stanley was deemed too English and, like others in the cast, he lacked a convincing accent. Most critics agreed that Ruth Wilson admirably captured Stella Kowalski's conflicting emotions: the loyalty and passion she has for her husband and her sympathy for her fragile elder sister. There was consensus, too, on designer Christopher Oram's set which, with its spiral staircase and balconies, transformed the Donmar's relatively small acting space. In addition, this production was notable for bringing Blanche's dead husband, Allan Grey, onto the stage – a directorial decision that, not altogether successfully, attempted to simplify Blanche's incipient schizophrenia.

The success of an African-American production of *Cat on a Hot Tin Roof* in 2008 almost certainly paved the way for the first multiracial *Streetcar* on Broadway, at the Broadhurst Theatre in 2012. Its director, American playwright Emily Mann, justified the reworking of the play in an interview for the *Los Angeles Times* by claiming it was always Tennessee Williams's wish to have African Americans playing the principal roles. However, while the production promised to bring 'a whole new rhythm' to the play, the actors cast in these parts – Nicole Ari Parker as Blanche and Blair Underwood as Stanley – failed to capture crucial aspects of their characters. According to Ben Brantley of the *New York Times*, Parker was one-dimensional – manipulative and not in the least vulnerable, so much so that Stella (Daphne Rubin-Vega) had little sympathy for her; and Underwood was an irascible husband who carried little sexual threat. Overall, Brantley found the production 'torpid', characterised by flat dialogue and only briefly enlivened by part of the Poker Night scene.

Notes

The notes below explain words and phrases from the play, with page numbers referencing the Student Editions published by Bloomsbury Methuen Drama.

1   Hart Crane (1899–1932) was an American poet Tennessee Williams particularly admired. This epigraph appropriately sums up the world of the play (broken) and Blanche DuBois's elusive search for love.

3   Williams's stage directions are extremely detailed, almost cinematic in scope. The French Quarter of New Orleans where the play is set is poor and run down, yet Williams manages to invest it with considerable beauty and poetry. His sensory exploration takes in strong colours like the blue/turquoise of the sky, appropriate for spring/early summer, and the dirty brown river; the smell of coffee and bananas from the warehouses; and the atmospheric jazz piano, a strong leitmotif in the play. The river and the railroad tracks (Louisiana and Nashville) suggest transportation, an important idea, and commerce, a world only briefly glimpsed in what is primarily a domestic play. Elysian Fields is an appropriate name for the street, Elysium being the resting place for the blessed in Greek mythology. It is an ironic heaven that Blanche DuBois will be denied when she comes to stay with the Kowalskis; death is a prominent theme in the play. Williams's comment that New Orleans is racially tolerant might appear to jar with his own labelling of the 'Negro Woman', but she is a minor figure who does not need to be individualised. The term 'negro' would not have been considered pejorative when the play was written.

3   *White frame:* a French colonial style of building: wood-frame houses in-filled with stucco or plaster, with large windows and wooden verandahs.

3   *She says St Barnabas would send out his dog to lick her and when he did she'd feel an icy cold wave all up an' down her:* we enter the play midway through a conversation between the negro woman and Eunice Hubbel, the Kowalskis' neighbour. Williams immediately establishes the licentious atmosphere of this section of the city with a reference to physical pleasure.

St Barnabas (originally Joseph) was born in Cyprus to Jewish parents. He converted to Christianity and is mentioned in the New Testament. Williams's image is, therefore, an irreverent coupling of sex and religion.

3   *Red hot!*: a spicy tamale (Mexican dish of meat, crushed maize and seasonings steamed or baked in maize husks) that adds to the steamy atmosphere.

3   *Don't waste your money in that clip joint!*: this refers to the already mentioned Four Deuces, a bar that doubles up as a brothel. It is the type of disreputable establishment that might be found in the Quarter.

3   *Don't let them sell you a Blue Moon cocktail or you won't go out on your own feet!*: matching the sky and the tonal colour of the piano, this potent cocktail is a combination of blue curaçao and vodka or gin.

4   *They are about twenty-eight or thirty years old, roughly dressed in blue denim work clothes*: Stanley and Mitch are immediately identified as working-class men.

4   STELLA *comes out on the first-floor landing, a gentle young woman, about twenty-five, and of a background quite different from her husband's*: Stella's gentleness contrasts with her husband's obvious brutality. Her very different social background preoccupies Blanche later when she criticises her sister's marriage.

4   *He heaves the package at her. She cries out in protest but manages to catch it: then she laughs breathlessly*: Stanley is primitive, a caveman bringing home the kill for his woman to cook. Stella's objection to his crude behaviour is soon replaced by a sense of exhilaration.

4   *Tell Steve to get him a poor boy's sandwich 'cause nothing's left here*: a large sandwich filled with simple ingredients; a further indication of the plain lives these characters lead.

4–5   The stage direction here indicates that Blanche has come with the intention of staying (she is carrying a small suitcase) but that she cannot believe her sister has moved into such a poor neighbourhood. Blanche is comically out of place, ridiculously over-dressed as if she is attending a party in the affluent Garden District of New Orleans. She is about thirty but will claim she is younger than her sister, reflecting a deep and ongoing anxiety about ageing. Dressed in white, she suggests innocence and vulnerability, two qualities she tries to cultivate. The mention of light and the similarity to a moth returns us to her age: she is attracted to brightness, to bold characters, but a naked light cruelly exposes her age. One of the working titles for the play was *The Moth*.

5   *They told me to take a streetcar named Desire, and then one called Cemeteries*: the two streetcars embody the play's interlinked themes of desire and death and, therefore, have a symbolic value. Real streetcars with these names were running in New Orleans when Williams was working on the play.

5   *I'm looking for my sister, Stella DuBois. I mean – Mrs. Stanley Kowalski*: Blanche is unwilling to accept the fact that her sister is now a Kowalski and betrays herself here. The difficulty of the adjustment is compounded by her horror at the tenement building.

6   *Por nada*: a variant on the Spanish 'de nada', meaning 'think nothing of it / you're welcome'. The Mexican influence in the play is strong – there are the tamale vendor, the Mexican flower seller and Pablo, one of Stanley's poker players.

6   *Belle Reve?*: the DuBois family home is an impressive plantation house architecturally defined by its columns. It will remain a picture or idea throughout the play, a symbol of a privileged existence that has been forcibly relinquished, a way of life that has been superseded. It seems almost certain that Williams wrongly assumed 'rêve' (dream) to be feminine and so his intended meaning of 'beautiful dream' should have been 'beau rêve' (the French word 'rive', meaning 'shore', is feminine). The house is a fantasy, a version of the Old South that was never quite true.

6–7   The stage direction indicates Blanche's defensiveness and her nervousness. She is easily startled by the cat's screech and then instinctively looks for the bottle of alcohol. The way that Blanche very deliberately washes up the glass implies that she is well practised in deceiving people about her drinking. Alcohol steadies her nerves and is a form of escapism.

7   *Stella for Star!*: her name literally means 'star' in Latin and, though Blanche's younger sister, she is the guiding light that has brought Blanche to New Orleans. This is another example of the light imagery in the play.

8   *Only Mr Edgar Allan Poe! – could do it justice! Out there I suppose is the ghoul-haunted woodland of Weir*: we later discover that Blanche was an English teacher and so her literary reference is appropriate, if rather hurtful. The comparison with Poe's Gothicism brings out her sense of horror at the working-

class neighbourhood and underlines her poetic imagination. The 'ghoul-haunted woodland of Weir' appears in Poe's poem of 1847, 'Ulalumé'.

9   *The wire*: the telegram.

9   *But you – you've put on some weight, yes, you're just as plump as a little partridge!*: the first indication that Stella is pregnant. She says nothing about it for fear of her sister's reaction and, because Blanche is speaking so manically, there is no clear opportunity. Desperately seeking reassurance about her own looks, Blanche tells Stella that she has not put on any weight since Stella left Belle Reve, simultaneously trying to make her sister feel guilty about leaving when their father died.

10   *Polacks?*: Stanley's Polish ancestry is repeatedly attacked by Blanche in the confrontation between the aristocratic Old South (French influenced, agrarian) and the modern working-class experience (immigrant, urban). She has earlier shown her ignorance when suggesting that Poles are 'something like Irish'.

10   *A different species*: Stella knows that Blanche will compare Stanley unfavourably with the men they used to go out with at home; Blanche will later refer to Stanley as an ape, picking up on this notion of a 'different species'.

11   *He's on the road a good deal*: Stanley's job is never specified. He works at a plant with Mitch but he also travels. Williams's father, Cornelius Coffin Williams, was a travelling salesman with the International Shoe Company before taking up a management position which took the family to St Louis.

12   *Why, the Grim Reaper had put up his tent on our doorstep!*: Blanche claims to have suffered a whole series of deaths at first hand as the family has gradually been decimated. This image of death, the Grim Reaper, mounting a military campaign against the family will be replaced by desire in the form of army officers calling up to Blanche for sexual favours.

13   *Is Mass out yet?*: the joke depends on 'Mass' being said with such a drawl that it sounds like 'my arse'.

13   *Jax beer!*: produced at the Jax Brewing Company in Jacksonville. Interestingly, the company closed in 1956 after selling the Jax Beer copyright to the Jackson Brewing Company in New Orleans.

13–14   *Animal joy in his being . . . :* Stanley is animalistic and sexual, a Lawrentian figure (Williams was greatly influenced by the English writer, D. H. Lawrence, and wrote the one-act *I Rise in Flame, Cried the Phoenix* about the last days of his life). He seeks to control women, regarding them as objects to satisfy and impregnate.

14   *Why, I – live in Laurel:* a town in Mississippi. Williams may wish to suggest some notion of moral victory through the name.

14   *Do you mind if I make myself comfortable?*: Stanley is happy to remove his shirt in front of a woman he has just met. Though Blanche does not object, it is not the behaviour of a Southern gentleman. In the 1951 film version directed by Elia Kazan, Vivien Leigh as Blanche permits herself a lingering look at Marlon Brando's Stanley.

15   *The music of the polka rises up, faint in the distance*: another musical motif, the polka is inextricably linked with the death of Blanche's husband, Allan Grey.

15   *The boy – the boy died*: Blanche's husband is defined by the youth Blanche craves. The memory of his death triggers feelings of guilt so extreme that she is physically sick.

15   *Galatoire's*: a restaurant in the Quarter. Stanley is resentful of Stella and Blanche's meal at a swanky restaurant, even though his poker night requires them to leave the apartment.

16   *She's soaking in a hot tub to quiet her nerves*: Blanche makes the bathroom her domain, a place of retreat where she can escape from Stanley and cleanse her soul.

16   *'From the land of the sky blue water, / They brought a captive maid!'*: Blanche's song was composed by Charles Wakefield Cadman (music) and Nelle Richmond Eberhart (lyrics) in 1909. Appropriately, Blanche is already 'a captive maid', a prisoner in the apartment.

17   *Napoleonic code*: New Orleans is in Louisiana, a state originally settled by the French. Stanley likes to appear well-informed about his rights, but, in reality, the code, which would give him ownership of everything belonging to his wife, was probably unenforceable.

18   *He hurls the furs to the daybed. Then he jerks open small drawer in the trunk and pulls up a fist-full of costume jewellery*: in his attempts to get at the truth, Stanley is effectively unpacking Blanche's life. Blanche is a consummate actress, always playing a role, and this is the actress's wardrobe.

20   *Lay . . . her cards on the table*: as the poker party is imminent, this is an appropriate metaphor. Though poker is a game of bluff, Stanley likes transparency in life; he cannot bear Blanche's evasions.

20   *I like an artist who paints in strong, bold colours, primary colours*: colour imagery is important throughout the play. Blanche claims to be attracted to simple, dynamic, uncompromising people, but she is also repelled by them.

20   *Now let's cut the re-bop*: Stanley is a man of action. He wants to get back to what he sees as the central point because Blanche's words frustrate and unsettle him. He bullies her with the volume of his voice, knowing that her nerves are affected by any sudden sound.

21   *Atomizer*: perfume spray.

21   *If I didn't know that you was my wife's sister I'd get ideas about you*: though women are 'the centre of his life' (13), Stanley here observes the taboo about relations with his wife's sister; he reminds Blanche that she should not be flirting with him.

22   *Our improvident grandfathers and father and uncles and brothers exchanged the land for their epic fornications – to put it plainly!*: Blanche explains that the family's property and wealth were gradually lost through paying for sex. Such a history of debauchery helps us, in part, to understand Blanche's behaviour after the death of her husband.

23   *But maybe he's what we need to mix with our blood now that we've lost Belle Reve*: survival means adapting, inter-breeding; Blanche, though appalled by Stanley's materialism and lack of refinement, understands their evolutionary priority.

24   *The blind are – leading the blind!*: Blanche realises that her bid to find sanctuary is under threat from Stanley. She is confused, directionless and throws herself on her younger sister.

24   *The Poker Night*: another working title for the play. The stage directions call for bold colours – the green baize of the Van Gogh painting, the primary colours of the men's shirts, the red and green of the watermelon, for example. The kitchen may be illuminated by *'the raw colours of childhood's spectrum'* but this is to be a game for men *'at the peak of their physical manhood'*.

24   *Portières*: curtains hung over a doorway.

24   *Anything wild this deal?*: the language of the game frequently applies to the players, particularly Stanley who, at this point, is bad-tempered because he is losing. In the game, 'wild' means the players can decide the value of the card.

24   *One-eyed jacks*: the knaves of spades and hearts in a pack of cards, which, unlike the knaves of diamonds and clubs, are seen in half-profile.

24	*Ante up*: raise the sum of money originally staked as a bet.
24	*Chips*: betting money, sometimes replaced by tokens of some sort.
25	*Spade flush*: high-scoring hand, made up entirely of spades.
25	*Hurry back and we'll fix you a sugar-tit*: a sugar-tit is a baby's teat flavoured with sugar or syrup. Though he is his friend, Stanley mocks Mitch's close, somewhat Freudian relationship with his sick mother. Williams took the character's full name, Harold Mitchell, from a roommate at the fraternity house he was living in while attending the University of Missouri.
25	*Seven card stud*: mentioned again in the last line of the play, this is a form of poker, but it also refers to the sexual attraction and potency of Stanley.
26	*Could I kibitz*: Blanche feels excluded by the men's game. With no end in sight, she asks if she can look over the shoulder of another player. Stanley rejects this idea out of hand, showing no consideration for the women who have allowed the men to continue their party all evening.
26	*It makes me so mad when he does that in front of people*: understandably, Stella does not wish to be humiliated, but there is also the insinuation that she does not mind violence in the lively sexual relationship they share.
26	*That one seems – superior to the others*: Mitch clumsily holds on to the towel as he exits the bathroom, but Blanche quickly notices a courtesy and refinement in him that makes him closer to her notion of a gentleman than any of the other poker players.
27	*Is he a wolf?*: Is he a sexual predator? Blanche ignores Mitch's closeness to his sick mother and wonders why he can be single. He will turn into a sexual predator under the influence of drink in Scene Nine.
27	*One time [laughing] the plaster – [laughing] cracked*: Stella jokes about the vigorous sex lives of the men and their large wives. We are reminded of the closeness of the apartments, the lack of privacy and the inhibiting presence of Blanche on Stanley and Stella's own sex life.
28	*Sounds like Xavier Cugat*: the Latin American music on the radio breaks the concentration required for the game and is a challenge to Stanley's selfishness. Xavier Cugat was a Catalan-Cuban-American bandleader who helped popularise Latin music in America.

28   *She returns his look without flinching*: at this point in the play,
      Blanche is strong enough to stand up to Stanley's physical
      presence.

28   *Get ants*: get ants in your pants, become restless.

28   *I'm going to the 'head'. Deal me out*: Mitch is going to the toilet
      but he appears to have lost all interest in the game, distracted as
      he is by Blanche's presence.

28   *Sure he's got ants now. Seven five-dollar bills in his pants pocket
      folded up tight as spitballs*: Mitch's restlessness is attributed to
      the fact that he has been winning by the other men. The folded
      notes suggest his excessive care with money, and this becomes
      another jibe about his immaturity when Stanley says that the
      money will eventually be deposited in a piggy bank given to
      him by his mother. 'Spitballs' – wads of paper chewed into
      small balls or pellets – also seems to anticipate the name of their
      next game, 'Spit in the Ocean'.

28   *Quarters*: 25-cent coins.

29   *'And if God choose, / I shall but love thee better – after –
      death!'*: *Sonnets from the Portuguese* (no. 43) by Elizabeth
      Barrett Browning. It is not surprising that Blanche recognises
      the quotation, but, more importantly, it establishes a shared
      sense of loss with Mitch and the way in which the dead still
      haunt the play. Though nebulous, Mitch's relationship with the
      'strange' and 'sweet' girl proves that he has been able to break
      free from his mother.

30   *It's a French name. It means woods and Blanche means white,
      so the two together mean white woods. Like an orchard in
      spring!*: like the plantation house, Blanche's name reveals
      her French ancestry: she is descended from the Huguenots –
      French Calvinists. She is innocent and lost (in the woods). The
      orchard in spring also conveys youthful fertility, obviously more
      applicable to Stella.

30   *I can't stand a naked light bulb, any more than I can a rude
      remark or a vulgar action*: the paper lantern is one way that
      Blanche shields herself from the truth (light). It is particularly
      important for Blanche to continue the deception about her age
      (there are two references to it on this page) and to establish
      standards of genteel behaviour.

30   *Grade school or high school*: the American system of education
      is divided into grade school, an intermediate level, and high
      school, the final stage, possibly leading to college or university
      education.

31   *Bobby-soxers and drug-store Romeos*: bobby-soxers were
adolescent girls who wore the contemporary fashion for ankle
socks, while drug-store Romeos were the love-sick boys who
hung around shops where they could buy soft drinks.

31   *Hawthorne and Whitman and Poe*: the poet and short-
story writer Edgar Allan Poe has already been mentioned in
connection with the apartment and the neighbourhood; Walt
Whitman (1819–92) was an American poet, best known for
his collection *Leaves of Grass*, and Nathaniel Hawthorne
(1804–64) was a nineteenth-century prose writer, probably most
remembered for his novel *The Scarlet Letter*.

31   *She turns the knobs on the radio and it begins to play 'Wien,
Wien, nur du allein.'* BLANCHE *waltzes to the music with romantic
gestures.* MITCH *is delighted and moves in awkward imitation
like a dancing bear*: the lively rhumba has been replaced by a
formal Viennese waltz (Rudolf Sieczynski's 1913 composition
'Vienna, City of My Dreams' or, as written here, 'Vienna,
Vienna, only you alone'). This is a comic moment before
Stanley explodes and throws the radio out of the window. Mitch
is a buffoon, obviously incompatible with Blanche.

32   *Poker should not be played in a house with women*: Mitch
repeats this line to emphasise the discrete world of the men;
invading their territory leads to violence.

33   *The Negro entertainers in the bar around the corner play
'Paper Doll' slow and blue*: this was a hit song for the Mills
Brothers in 1943. It anticipates Stanley fondly calling Stella
his 'baby doll' and serves to create a tenderer mood in which
he seeks forgiveness from his wife. *Baby Doll* was the title of
a later screenplay by Williams, turned into a notorious film by
Elia Kazan in 1956.

33   *You whelp of a Polack, you! I hope they do haul you in and
turn the fire hose on you, same as the last time!*: Eunice resorts
to insulting Stanley's Polish background. She wants him to be
punished while realising that this behaviour characterises the
Kowalskis' marriage; it will happen again.

33   *They come together with low animal groans:* Stella and
Stanley's reconciliation will be primarily sexual, animalistic,
though there is tenderness and a recognition of Stella's role as a
mother – both to the baby and Stanley.

34   *All quiet on the Potomac now?*: the Potomac is a river that
runs into the Chesapeake Bay. On one side it borders Maryland
and Washington DC; on the other, Virginia and West Virginia.

Mitch's question, asked in the knowledge that these violent
scenes are commonplace but short-lived, echoes the opening
line of the sixth stanza of a poem, 'The Picket Guard' (1861),
by Ethel Lynn Beers (1827–79): 'All quiet along the Potomac
to-night'. The poem draws on telegrams sent by Major-General
George B. McClellan during the American Civil War when
Union and Confederate armies occupied opposite sides of
the river. The line may have influenced the English title of
the famous novel about the First World War, *All Quiet on the
Western Front*, by Erich Maria Remarque.

34   *There is a confusion of street cries like a choral chant*: another
musical variation. This conveys the busy activity of the area and
suggests the chorus of Greek drama.

35   *Her eyes and lips have that almost narcotized tranquillity that
is in the faces of Eastern idols*: the book of comics Stella is
reading suggests her childish simplicity; an image of being
drugged captures her state of post-coital bliss. Elia Kazan
regarded this drugged state as the spine of Stella's character: she
is under Stanley's influence.

36   *Why, on our wedding night – soon as we came in here – he
snatched off one of my slippers and rushed about smashing
the light bulbs with it*: another reference to light and its source.
While Blanche is wary of the truth light exposes, Stanley and
Stella seek darkness to enjoy their physical, sado-masochistic
relationship fully.

37   *Of course you remember Shep Huntleigh. I went out with
him at college and wore his pin for a while*: in her increasing
desperation, Blanche clings to figures from her past. Shep is
remembered as an honourable man, and the wearing of the pin
as a pledge to each other recalls knights displaying their ladies'
favours. Even though Blanche claims to have met him recently
and to know that he is an oil tycoon, he remains an illusory
saviour. His name suggests the desperate pursuit of something.

39   *Sometime today I've got to get hold of a bromo!*: a bromide
tablet used to calm the nerves. Blanche's dependence on alcohol
and drugs to sedate her and offer a means of escape anticipates
Williams's own dependency in the sixties.

40   *What you are talking about is brutal desire – just – Desire! –
the name of that rattle-trap street-car that bangs through
the Quarter, up one old narrow street and down another*: the
metaphorical meaning of the title is made explicit here. Stella
has admitted that sex is the foundation of her relationship

with Stanley and that it almost makes everything else appear irrelevant. However, she also says that she loves her husband. The noisy journey of the streetcar complements the violent passion of the couple. The sexual slang of 'bangs' will become more obvious when it is repeated.

40   *It brought me here. – Where I'm not wanted and where I'm ashamed to be*: another hint that Blanche is not as innocent as she would like people to believe. Sex with various men has characterised her recent past. However, she quickly juxtaposes her own desire with a plea for sympathy at her present circumstances.

40   *Then don't you think your superior attitude is a bit out of place?*: it is literally out of place because Blanche has been applying the standards of the Old South, those of Belle Reve. For all Blanche's misfortune, we sympathise with Stella here: her husband and whole way of life are under attack; Blanche is about to launch her most damning attack yet on Stanley's primitivism.

40   *Under cover of the train's noise STANLEY enters from outside. He stands unseen by the women, holding some packages in his arms, and overhears their following conversation. He wears an undershirt and grease-stained seersucker pants*: Williams skilfully uses the sound of the train to hide Stanley's entrance and permit his eavesdropping, so building up tension. Stanley will discover what Blanche really thinks of him and this will intensify his attempts to expose her. The packages remind us of his first entrance with the meat; and his dirty appearance will offer a further visual confirmation of Blanche's words. Stanley's trousers are made of a light fabric that puckers easily; they are probably striped.

40–1   *There's even something – sub-human [. . .]*: Blanche's long speech juxtaposes a world of primitive lust and violence with gauges of civilisation – poetry and music. Stanley reverses the evolutionary order and Blanche urges her sister not to get caught up in this atavism.

40   *In some kinds of people some tenderer feelings have had some little beginning! . . . In this dark march toward whatever it is we're approaching*: Blanche has already referred to the difficult task of nurturing an interest in literary culture among the young. Here she states the fight against ignorance rather melodramatically.

41   *STANLEY hesitates, licking his lips*: Stanley is relishing the fight to
     come. Appropriately, he is like a beast sizing up its prey.

41   *Them darn mechanics at Fritz's don't know their can from third
     base!*: Stanley's grubbiness can be explained by the fact that
     he had to help the mechanics at the garage. He is practical, not
     conventionally educated or sensitive. The baseball metaphor,
     'third base', points to another sphere of male interest that might
     exclude women: professional sport. 'Can' has several slang
     meanings: a toilet; someone's backside; a car, especially adapted
     to get greater acceleration; and a storage battery.

41   *STELLA has embraced him with both arms, fiercely, and full in
     the view of BLANCHE. He laughs and clasps her head to him.
     Over her head he grins through the curtains at BLANCHE*: the
     Kowalskis present a united front. Stella may have allowed
     Blanche to speak at length, but she will defend what she has got
     '*fiercely*'. Stanley's smile is smug and threatening. Vivien Leigh,
     playing Blanche in the 1951 film, has a moment of panic as she
     realises that Stanley might have heard her tirade. Whether or not
     Williams intended this, the blue piano and trumpet that follow
     capture the high tension at the end of this scene.

42   '*Most of my sister's friends go north in the summer but some
     have homes on the Gulf and there has been a continued round
     of entertainments, teas, cocktails, and luncheons –*': the life
     of the affluent Southerner, a social routine that Blanche might
     have enjoyed in the past but which is now just a fantasy. The
     palm leaf that she fans herself with further symbolises this
     world, but Blanche is highly conscious of her lies as she writes
     them.

42   *I wouldn't mind if you'd stay down at the Four Deuces, but
     you always going up*: the disagreements of Steve and Eunice
     seem intended to echo those of Stanley and Stella, though they
     often appear more comic by comparison. Eunice is objecting to
     Steve's visits to one of the prostitutes working upstairs above
     the bar area of the Four Deuces.

43   *Daemonic*: as if possessed by an evil spirit.

43   *I'm compiling a notebook of quaint little words and phrases
     I've picked up here*: Blanche's feigned ignorance of American
     slang is immediately seized upon by Stanley who is keen to strip
     away her prejudices. The battle between them will be fought on
     linguistic grounds: Blanche's poetic imagery versus Stanley's
     vivid colloquialisms.

44   *Capricorn – the Goat!*: Blanche realises that the sexually active goat is an appropriate star sign for Stanley.

44   *The Hotel Flamingo is not the sort of establishment I would dare to be seen in*: probably a brothel, the hotel adds to the colour imagery. Blanche gives telling physical reactions when both Shaw's name and the hotel are mentioned.

45   *Not in front of your sister*: Stanley makes clear just how much of a problem is Blanche's presence; he cannot be himself with his wife.

45   *I never was hard or self-sufficient enough*: now that Blanche is alone with Stella, she can hint at her recent past, a past that she fears has become common gossip. This speech really sets out Blanche's philosophy, drawing on the play's imagery of light and frailty. Soft people, like her, have got to seek protection from the likes of Stanley. They have to create the magic of illusion by glowing attractively. In stating that she had to obtain whatever shelter she could and that men only notice women when they are making love to them, Blanche gives a strong hint that she has resorted to a form of prostitution. Her comment that she does not know how much longer she can 'turn the trick' confirms this: 'trick' can mean both illusion and a prostitute's client.

46   *STELLA pours the coke into the glass. It foams over and spills. BLANCHE gives a piercing cry*: a crude image of ejaculation. The staining of Blanche's white skirt emphasises how sex has corrupted her. Her cry is probably a mixture of pleasure and pain.

47   *I want to deceive him enough to make him – want me*: Blanche considers Mitch crucial to her future, hence her continuing plan of deception. She is pretending to be a Southern belle with very strong morals. Her worry is that he will become frustrated, deterred by her not 'putting out' – making herself sexually available.

47   *Ah, me, ah, me, ah, me . . .*: in the 1951 film, Blanche touches herself quite suggestively as she says these words. Her dreamy mood is reinforced by the gathering dusk and the music from the Four Deuces.

48   *The YOUNG MAN shakes his head violently and edges hastily up the steps*: the young man immediately establishes his innocence by rejecting the advances of the negro woman.

48   *A dime*: a 10-cent coin.

48   *It's temperamental?*: in Blanche's flirtatious mood, the lighter
       becomes a phallic symbol.

48   *Fifteen of seven*: a quarter to seven.

48   *Don't you just love those long rainy afternoons in New
       Orleans when an hour isn't just an hour – but a little bit of
       Eternity dropped in your hands – and who knows what to do
       with it?*: Blanche dignifies her lust with this image of unending
       time. The answer to the question is clearly that they should
       make love.

49   *Has anyone ever told you that you look like a young prince
       out of the Arabian Nights?*: carried away with the overriding
       impression of his youth, Blanche transforms the young man
       into an exotic figure from literature, when the vivid detail of
       his drinking cherry soda has made him an archetypal American
       teenager.

49   *It would be nice to keep you, but I've got to be good and keep
       my hands off children*: an allusion to the real reason why
       Blanche is no longer teaching. To her (and the audience),
       he must seem like a child who cannot comprehend her
       suggestiveness, who *'stands like a bashful kid'*.

49   *My Rosenkavalier!*: Mitch's sudden entrance reminds us of
       Blanche's real target. He is almost as bemused but is playing
       the role that is expected of him: that of the romantic hero
       respectfully bowing before his lady. *Der Rosenkavalier* is a
       comic opera by Richard Strauss. The title translates as 'The
       Knight of the Rose'.

49   *Merciiii*: *merci* is French for 'thank you'.

50   *The utter exhaustion which only a neurasthenic personality can
       know is evident in BLANCHE's voice and manner*: this seems to
       mark a deterioration in Blanche's state. Her nervous disposition,
       reflected in her constant drinking and quick-fire conversation,
       has taken over and she is no longer able to conceal her gradual
       breakdown.

50   *MITCH is stolid but depressed*: it should be evident that Mitch is
       making the best of what has been a disappointing evening.

50   *They have probably been out to the amusement park on Lake
       Pontchartrain, for MITCH is bearing, upside down, a plaster
       statuette of Mae West, the sort of prize won at shooting-
       galleries and carnival games of chance*: Williams's 'probably'
       suggests that precisely where they have been is not as important
       as the mood of the evening. Located in Louisiana, Lake

Pontchartrain's south shore forms the northern boundary of New Orleans. Mae West (1893–1980) was a famous American actress, a sex symbol known for her irreverent *double entendres*. The 1951 film substituted a less tacky rag doll for the statuette. The fact that the statuette is held upside down suggests that something is wrong; and the '*carnival games of chance*' are a comment on the faltering relationship between Mitch and Blanche.

50   *I'll walk over to Bourbon and catch an owl-car*: Bourbon Street, in the French Quarter, is well known for its bars and entertainment. The owl-car is a streetcar running through the night.

50   *The one that says the lady must entertain the gentleman – or no dice!*: as a lady, Blanche expects to be taken out and for everything to be paid for by the man. She realises that, in return, it is her duty to entertain him in order to make the evening and their relationship a success. The reference to dice continues the game of chance/gambling theme.

50   *No, honey, that's the key to my trunk which I must soon be packing*: Blanche's trunk contains the secrets of her past that Stanley has tried to unpack and the costumes for her role playing. She realises that her stay can only be a brief one, that she will not be able to defeat Stanley.

51   *Eureka!*: Success. The cry supposedly uttered by Archimedes when he discovered the principle of water displacement while in his bath.

51   *I'm looking for the Pleiades, the Seven Sisters, but these girls are not out tonight*: another reference to stars as guiding lights. Blanche needs direction and it is interesting to note that she makes her source of help female.

52   *Joie de vivre*: happiness, joy in living.

52   *We are going to be very Bohemian. We are going to pretend that we are sitting in a little artists' café on the Left Bank in Paris!*: another example of Blanche's ability and willingness to create a fantasy world. Mitch is entirely unsuited to an unconventional or Bohemian existence.

52   *Je suis la Dame aux Camellias! Vous êtes – Armand! Understand French?*: 'I am the Lady of the Camellias! You are – Armand!' Even if Mitch could understand French, he would be unlikely to recognise this reference to the characters from a romantic novel by Alexandre Dumas Fils (1824–95).

52 *Voulez-vous couchez avec moi ce soir? Vous ne comprenez pas? Ah, quel dommage!*: 'Do you want to sleep with me? Don't you understand? Ah, what a shame!' Blanche flirts with Mitch in the full knowledge that he will not understand. She sends out conflicting messages: they are alone in the apartment together and she wants him to relax, but she is still setting boundaries over which he must not step.

52 *I am ashamed of the way I perspire. My shirt is sticking to me*: Williams parodies romantic dialogue throughout this scene. Mitch unwisely draws attention to his physical inadequacies, and we are reminded of his clumsiness when dancing with Blanche in Scene Three.

52 *It's very light weight alpaca*: Mitch chooses to wear a coat made of light weight wool to avoid the embarrassment of perspiration stains in summer. He does not realise that this is not something you disclose to a lady.

52 *A wash-coat*: jacket of light, washable material.

53 *I was given a membership to the New Orleans Athletic Club*: Williams used this club at 222 North Rampart Street. He was a particularly keen swimmer.

52 *Samson!*: an Old Testament character whose strength lay in his hair until Delilah cut it off. Again, Mitch is unaware of romantic conventions when he asks Blanche about her weight.

54 *She rolls her eyes, knowing that he cannot see her face*: Blanche is all too aware of her hypocrisy in claiming she still has 'old-fashioned ideals'; she is giving another performance.

54 *A midnight prevue at Loew's State*: Stanley and Stella have gone to a preview showing of a film at the local cinema on Canal Street.

54 *We was together in the Two-forty-first*: Mitch refers back to the Second World War and the fact that he served with Stanley in the same regiment. This provides an important bond between the two men, one that Blanche will find hard to sever.

55 *Of course there is such a thing as the hostility of – perhaps in some perverse kind of way he – No! To think of it makes me . . . .*: Blanche cannot quite bring herself to say – or pretends not to be able to bring herself to say – that Stanley's antipathy for her masks a desire that cannot be admitted. Mitch is not sharp enough to pick up on this.

55 *Why did your mother want to know my age?*: as we have seen, Blanche is sensitive about her age. She appears to sidestep the question before bringing Mitch back to it, although, tellingly,

she never answers him. Mitch's closeness to his mother is both
a problem for Blanche and an opportunity for mutual sympathy:
her terminal illness will return Blanche to the subject of her
dead husband.

56   *It was like you suddenly turned a blinding light on something
that had always been half in shadow, that's how it struck the
world for me*: love was a process of illumination. In Blanche's
youth, intense light was associated with passion, not unwanted
truth.

56   *There was something different about the boy, a nervousness, a
softness and tenderness which wasn't the least bit effeminate
looking – still – that thing was there. . . . He came to me for
help*: Williams has to use a form of code here because he was
living and writing in homophobic times. Blanche's husband
was a homosexual, something more noticeable in his gentle
mannerisms than his appearance. Like many homosexuals of
the time, he chose to carry on a secret life while outwardly
having a conventional marriage. Feeling rejected, Blanche
betrayed him.

56   *By coming suddenly into a room that I thought was empty –
which wasn't empty, but had two people in it . . . :* these lines
were regarded as too explicit for the first London production
of the play by the Lord Chamberlain; he ordered them to be
cut.

56   *A locomotive is heard approaching outside. She claps her
hands to her ears and crouches over.*: another important sound
effect that contributes to the psychological realism of the play.
We have already been told about the proximity of the L and N
tracks, so the train is not unexpected. However, its approach and
impact at this key moment suggest a huge internal scar left by
Blanche's treatment of her husband.

56   *Yes, the three of us drove out to Moon Lake Casino*: at this
point, Blanche did not want to contemplate the reason for the
presence of her husband's companion. Moon Lake Casino, now
a restaurant and inn called Uncle Henry's Place near Clarksdale,
Mississippi, continues the theme of gambling. Williams used
Moon Lake often in his plays, especially in a sad or violent
context (e.g. the destruction of Papa Romano's wine garden in
Orpheus Descending).

57   *We danced the Varsouviana!*: this happy, lively polka tune
jars with the sudden suicide of Allan Grey. It has become
inseparable from the memory.

57   *And then the searchlight which had been turned on the world
       was turned off again and never for one moment since has
       there been any light that's stronger than this – kitchen –
       candle . . . :* Blanche experienced a sort of death too. She has
       not been able to put this experience behind her and find love
       again, so racked with guilt as she still is.

57   *Sometimes – there's God – so quickly!:* given the rest of the
       scene, Mitch appears a highly ironic God, but, at this moment of
       emotional vulnerability, Blanche is desperate for comfort from
       anyone.

58   *It is late afternoon in mid-September:* having started in early
       May, we are now in the autumn of Blanche's life. The play will
       end some weeks later, possibly in November.

58   *The portieres are open and a table is set for a birthday supper,
       with cake and flowers:* the attempts at celebration create further
       tension and expectation. Will Stanley join in? Given Blanche's
       sensitivity about her age, will she want to celebrate?

58   *Temperature 100 on the nose, and she soaks herself in a hot
       tub:* in drawing attention to the temperature, Stanley indirectly
       reminds us that Blanche is not just washing but attempting to
       purify her soul; we also get a sense of the stifling atmosphere in
       the apartment.

59   *BLANCHE is singing in the bathroom a saccharine popular
       ballad which is used contrapuntally with STANLEY'S speech:*
       Williams cleverly uses the song to punctuate (contrapuntally
       means in counterpoint) Stanley's comments. It is sentimental but
       the words are appropriate for Blanche and her situation.

59   *Sister Blanche is no lily:* Stanley's tone is sarcastic. Blanche
       is Stella's sister but also, ironically, a nun. Stanley is attacking
       her claims to a virtuous life, the white lily being a symbol of
       innocence.

59   *'Say it's only a paper moon, Sailing over a cardboard seal – But
       it wouldn't be make-believe If you believed in me!':* the song is
       entitled 'It's Only a Paper Moon', the music was composed by
       Harold Arlen and the lyrics were written by E. Y. Harburg and
       Billy Rose in 1933. The song was performed by Ella Fitzgerald
       in 1938. The 'make-believe' world is the one that Blanche has
       created as a defence mechanism; it might not be necessary if
       someone truly loved and believed in her.

59   *In fact they were so impressed by Dame Blanche that they
       requested her to turn in her room-key – for permanently!:*
       'Dame' is American slang for a woman but is also a title in the

United Kingdom; Stanley is attacking Blanche's superior airs,
showing how she was even banned from an establishment with
such a poor reputation as the Flamingo.

59   '*It's a Barnum and Bailey world, Just as phony as it can
be – But it wouldn't be make-believe If you believed in me!*':
P. T. Barnum and James Anthony Bailey were famous circus
proprietors in the nineteenth century. Again, the world of
performance and illusion is alluded to.

60   *It's a honky-tonk parade!*: in this context, 'honky-tonk' means
squalid or disreputable.

60   *Regarded as not just different but downright loco – nuts*:
'loco' means crazy. Stanley wants to prove that Blanche is not
eccentric so much as insane, and therefore needs to be locked up
for everyone's good.

60   *Which brings us to Lie Number Two*: Stanley is also giving a
performance, presenting evidence systematically in the role
of a prosecuting lawyer. Blanche has already commented
sarcastically on his 'impressive judicial air' (21) when
explaining the Napoleonic code.

60   *No, siree, Bob!*: a colloquial American expression meaning 'No,
definitely not'. Warming to his task, Stanley's language becomes
increasingly more colloquial and colourful.

60   *A seventeen-year-old boy – she'd gotten mixed up with!*:
Blanche's absence from work is explained, as is her comment
about keeping her 'hands off children' (49). The meaning of
Stanley's euphemism is made all too clear by the exclamation
mark.

60   *In the bathroom the water goes on loud; little breathless cries
and peels of laughter are heard as if a child were frolicking in
the tub*: can Blanche hear the argument outside the bathroom? Is
she trying to block it out by running more water? As Stella was
with the comics, she appears childlike and vulnerable, not, at
this point, the insane and promiscuous woman Stanley has tried
to portray.

61   *But they had her on the hook good and proper that time and
she knew that the jig was all up!*: an unpleasant image, not just
of Blanche being trapped but skewered like a fish or a piece of
meat. Perhaps we think of Stanley's bloody package when he
first enters the play. Interestingly, 'jig' can mean a lively dance
(another performance) or, in fishing, an artificial bait jerked up
and down in the water; the expression 'jig is up' means that her
act of deception is finally over.

61   *Yep, it was practickly a town ordinance passed against her!*:
      exaggerating for effect, Stanley claims that Blanche's behaviour
      was so grave that legislation was very nearly passed to ensure
      that she could not return.

61   *Possess your soul in patience!*: a commonly used line from
      Shakespeare's *Hamlet*. Blanche objects to the rude way in which
      Stanley asks her how much longer she is going to be in the
      bathroom.

61   *She was always – flighty!*: Stella is defending her sister
      but concedes that some of Blanche's behaviour has been
      reprehensible. Here she is searching around for the right word to
      describe her. 'Flighty' implies fickle and irresponsible.

62   *This beautiful and talented young man was a degenerate*:
      she means that he was a homosexual but the stating of this
      in anything other than a euphemism would not be tolerated
      at the time. Williams often used the word 'degenerate' with
      its negative connotations of immorality and corruption; it is
      another example of encoding homosexuality. Stanley is not very
      interested in Blanche's marriage to a gay man because, as he
      says, it is not 'recent history', and because her behaviour with
      heterosexual men provides him with more ammunition.

62   *Mitch is a buddy of mine*: 'buddy' implies more than simply
      friend. The men have bonded through their service in the army,
      their work and their leisure pursuits. They have a loyalty to each
      other which is almost more sacrosanct than any relationship
      with a woman. Hence, Stanley has warned Mitch off Blanche
      and he will not be coming to the birthday party.

63   *Maybe he was, but he's not going to jump in a tank with a
      school of sharks – now!*: it seems that Mitch might have
      considered the possibility of marrying Blanche before Stanley's
      revelations. This second reference to fish suggests that Blanche
      is very dangerous – not just one shark but a whole school of
      them.

63   *Her future is mapped out for her*: it is 'mapped out' in the
      short-term because Stanley has bought Blanche a ticket for
      the Greyhound bus back to Laurel, a town from which she has
      already been ejected. It is unclear whether he also means here
      that she will be committed to a mental asylum in the future.

63   *She tinkles her highball glass*: in addition to the bath, Blanche
      has used alcohol to calm her nerves (whisky and soda with ice).

63   *The distant piano goes into a hectic breakdown*: the piano music
      suddenly becomes very discordant to emphasise Blanche's

increased anxiety and confusion. Williams's music again helps
to create psychological realism.

64   *A torch of sunlight blazes on the side of a big water-tank or
oil-drum across the empty lot toward the business district which
is now pierced by pin-points of lighted windows reflecting
the sunset*: the sun is setting on Blanche as Stanley closes in
for the kill. The warmth suggested here contrasts with the
emotional coldness of Blanche's birthday celebration, a dismal
occasion. The empty lot corresponds to the vacant fourth place
at the table, itself a strong visual image of Mitch's rejection
of Blanche. Williams permits us another glimpse of the larger
world outside the domestic environs of the play.

64   *I don't know any refined enough for your taste*: the play
contains several jokes or stories. Appropriately, those told by
the men are somewhat bawdy and Blanche tries to offset this
with more innocent material. Her parrot joke, which barely
raises a smile, mocks their situation: Stanley is the parrot who
is excessively rude in the daytime and better suited to darkness;
Blanche is the easily offended 'old maid' who is trying to
silence him.

65   *What do you two think you are? A pair of queens? Remember
what Huey Long said – 'Every Man is a King!' And I am the
king around here, so don't forget it!*: Stanley's somewhat
uncouth behaviour at the table has borne out Blanche's
criticisms of him. He spears the chop with his fork and then
eats it with his fingers, covering his face in grease in the
process. However, he rightly feels under attack and is stung
by the persistent slur on his ethnic origins (Polack) and the
suggestion that he has the manners of a pig. He believes that,
as the breadwinner, he should be respected, and he cites Huey
Pierce Long (1893–1935), a famous lawyer and politician (he
was governor of Louisiana), in his defence. Stanley resents any
challenges to his sovereignty, particularly when he sees Blanche
successfully influencing his wife.

65   *My place is cleared! You want me to clear your places?*: a
flamboyant gesture that, once again, highlights Stanley's
physical threat. In the film, Marlon Brando cuts a slightly comic
figure, with a napkin tucked into his shirt, before making a
sudden and impressive outburst.

66   *God, honey, it's gonna be sweet when we can make noise in the
night the way that we used to and get the coloured lights going
with nobody's sister behind the curtains to hear us!*: Stanley is

trying to get Stella back on side and the only way he knows how to do this is with a promise of energetic sex. Interestingly, the coloured lights symbolise this wild passion, but, on his wedding night, Stanley smashed an artificial source of light. His sexual frustration is all too clear.

66   *Oh, I hope candles are going to glow in his life and I hope that his eyes are going to be like candles, like two blue candles lighted in a white cake!*: Stella's baby, here assumed to be a boy, is the future, the promise of new life the play offers. Unsurprisingly, Blanche wants him to be soft and tender like candle light and the delicate colours she refers to. The contrast with Stanley's brash coloured lights is very marked.

67   *But what I am is a one hundred per cent. American, born and raised in the greatest country on earth and proud as hell of it, so don't ever call me a Polack*: Stanley's staunchest defence of his American identity. He is determined not to be labelled an outsider or an immigrant of uncertain status.

68   *The Varsouviana music steals in softly and continues playing*: previously associated with the death of Allan Grey and the guilt that produced, the polka tune is more closely linked with rejection here. As Allan Grey's homosexuality was a rejection of Blanche the young wife, so Stanley's 'birthday remembrance' signifies the rejection the desperate sister has long been expecting (even though she tells Stanley she was not anticipating a present). The connection is confirmed with a repeat of Blanche's convulsions.

68   *You didn't know Blanche as a girl. Nobody, nobody, was tender and trusting as she was. But people like you abused her, and forced her to change*: Stella reinforces the sympathy she (and the audience) feels for Blanche. Her sister is more sinned against than sinning, and here she seems to be a bygone culture rather than just an individual. The Old South, the epitome of civilisation and gentility, has been lost, assaulted as it has been by a ruthless modern America.

68   *I was common as dirt. You showed me the snapshot of the place with the columns. I pulled you down off them columns and how you loved it, having them coloured lights going!*: Stanley is proud of his working-class background and of his role as Stella's liberator. He sees the columns (significantly, he has only ever encountered them in a photograph) as a symbol of aristocratic privilege; they represent not only the plantation but also the Old South. The only way he could entice Stella away

from this world was through sex, metaphorically taking her
down from columns that provide safety and shelter.

68   *I done nothing to no one. Let go of my shirt. You've torn it*:
Stanley feels wronged and, as if to confirm the attack on his
character, one of the badges of his manhood, the '*brilliant silk
bowling shirt*', is ripped.

69   *Hoity-toity, describing me as an ape*: Stanley blames their
problems on Blanche's snobbery and belittling of him as part of
a lower evolutionary order. The use of the pronouns 'we' and
'she' before this shows Stanley trying to establish some distance
between them. Again, he is seeking to divide and rule.

69   *The 'Varsouviana' is heard, its music rising with sinister
rapidity as the bathroom door opens slightly*: another rejection
as Blanche is left 'twisting a washcloth' while Stanley tenderly
comes to his wife's aid.

69   *El pain de mais, el pain de mais, / El pain de mais sin sal*:
literally 'maize bread, maize bread, maize bread without salt'.
There is a strong Mexican influence throughout the play and this
folk song draws our attention to a staple of existence. There is
also a Maya creation myth in which man is said to have been
formed from '*masa*' or corn dough. Maize is, consequently,
regarded as a gift from the gods by the Maya people. Blanche
may be thinking of her own lonely life – plain and unseasoned,
especially now that she is being refused any further shelter; she
may be commenting on the imminent birth of Stella's child and
the nourishment it will need in a difficult world.

69   *BLANCHE is seated in a tense hunched position in a bedroom
chair that she has re-covered with diagonal green and white
stripes. She has on her scarlet satin robe*: the contrast between
Blanche's defensive foetal position and the bold colours she is
now surrounding herself with is very noticeable. It is almost as
if she has accepted that she is the scarlet woman or whore that
Stanley has accused her of being.

69   *The music is in her mind; she is drinking to escape it and the
sense of disaster closing in on her, and she seems to whisper
the words of the song*: for the first time, Williams makes it clear
that this is an interior soundtrack, that he is attempting to make
the audience experience what Blanche is thinking. Alcohol is no
longer just a relaxant but a means of banishing nightmares, of
seeking oblivion.

69   *Mitch comes around the corner in work clothes: blue denim
shirt and pants. He is unshaven*: Mitch's scruffy appearance

is an immediate indication that he does not have romantic intentions. Blanche expects her men to be smart and well-groomed and we suspect that Mitch has complied with this on their dates.

70   *She looks fearfully after him as he stalks into the bedroom*: Stanley's influence can even be detected in Mitch's movements; there are several references to Stanley stalking aggressively in the play like an animal.

70   *No, of course you haven't, you dumb angel-puss, you'd never get anything awful caught in your head!*: Blanche mocks Mitch's lack of intelligence. She is speaking quickly and he appears not to register what she is saying, partly because he has been drinking.

70   *I won't cross-examine the witness*: Blanche desperately hopes that Mitch's presence will make the Varsouviana tune disappear. Questioning Mitch is only likely to antagonise him and, anyway, she does not want to adopt Stanley's pseudo-legal methods.

71   *A distant revolver shot is heard, BLANCHE seems relieved*: more evidence of Blanche being haunted by her treatment of her young husband. The gunshot (Allan Grey's suicide) temporarily halts the painful memory.

71   *Are you boxed out of your mind?*: Are you so drunk you cannot think or speak intelligibly? We might also think of Blanche being boxed in by both her mental condition and her physical situation.

71   *I've done so much with this place since I've been here*: Blanche prides herself on her home improvements in an attempt to show that she is a good homemaker. We remember her appalled looks and superior manner when she first arrived. Of course, Blanche's legacy will be so much more than the soft furnishings with which she seems to have bedecked the apartment.

72   *He tears the paper lantern off the light bulb. She utters a frightened gasp*: a shocking action for both Blanche and the audience. She is suddenly stripped bare and left defenceless. This clearly anticipates Scene Ten.

72   *I don't want realism*; a comment on Williams's dramatic technique, which is not straightforwardly realistic but a combination of realism and expressionism, and Blanche's inability to live with the truth.

72   *I misrepresent things to them. I don't tell truth, I tell what ought to be truth. And if that is sinful, then let me be damned for it!*: Blanche talks again about the magic of invention, owning up

to the deliberate deception that is symbolised by the paper
lantern covering the light of truth. Here she introduces a note of
judgement from a Christian perspective.

72   *That pitch about your ideals being so old-fashioned and all*
the malarkey that you've dished out all summer. Oh, I knew
you weren't sixteen any more. But I was a fool enough to
believe you was straight: by using the word 'pitch', Mitch
implies that Blanche has been selling herself and that he was
taken in by her patter. He may have realised that she was not
in the prime of her youth, but the secrecy about her age has
troubled him, if only because his mother has asked about it.
John M. Clum notes (*Acting Gay: Male Homosexuality in*
Modern Drama, 152) that 'straight' is part of the language of
homosexuality, a subtext, because it defines a heterosexual
as well as meaning honest or straightforward. Clum implies
that Blanche represents the homosexual (i.e. not straight)
sensibility. Though Clum does not go this far, there is a long
critical tradition of viewing Blanche as Tennessee Williams in
drag.

73   *The Tarantula Arms!*: Blanche mocks Mitch's comments,
exaggerating her ability to control men and bring about their
downfall. Mitch does not seem to understand what a tarantula
is; he certainly does not pick up on her sarcasm about the way in
which men try to stigmatise her.

73   *I was played out*: she was drained of her youthful energy.
Perhaps there is also a suggestion of being out of a game of
cards here.

73   *I thanked God for you . . . The poor man's Paradise – is a little*
peace . . . : Blanche's language is increasingly taking on a
Christian tone. These biblical echoes convey the modest hope of
protection she had after meeting Mitch.

74   *Never inside, I didn't lie in my heart . . . .* : Blanche can
seemingly divorce her creation of magic from an inner integrity.
The fact that she presents herself as essentially truthful is likely
to make her more sympathetic.

74   *She is a blind MEXICAN WOMAN in a dark shawl, carrying*
bunches of those gaudy tin flowers that lower class Mexicans
display at funerals and other festive occasions: the appearance
of this vendor is timely. Blanche's spiritual death is approaching
and the woman is the symbol of this, a harbinger of doom. The
fact that she is blind recalls Tiresias, the sightless prophet of
Greek legend.

74   *Flores para los muertos*: flowers for the dead. The Mexican
      Spanish chant is haunting because of the subject matter but also
      because of its somewhat alien quality. It sets Blanche thinking
      about the deaths at Belle Reve again.

74   *Corones para los muertos*: crowns for the dead. We might
      think of the crown of thorns placed on Christ's head before the
      crucifixion.

74   *And other things such as blood-stained pillow-slips*: oblivious
      to Mitch at this point, Blanche has been transported back to
      Belle Reve and the painful deaths of her relatives. The blood
      represents the sin of the 'epic fornications' (22), a dynasty
      collapsing in upon itself, as well as death. Blanche's fragmented
      conversations with the dead indicate a schizophrenic state.

74   *The opposite is desire*: the relationship between death
      (Thanatos) and desire (Eros) is one that has preoccupied
      Western writers. Desire is the life-force staving off death, but
      the insatiability of desire can only be ended with death. Blanche
      can no longer court desire – it was what transported her to this
      point – and must accept death. Williams suggests the connection
      between the two themes when he has Blanche talk about the two
      streetcars (5).

74   *Later the paddy-wagon would gather them up like
      daisies . . .* : the drunken soldiers looking for sexual favours
      from Blanche would eventually collapse and be arrested for
      causing a public disturbance by police in a van. Stanley's
      information about Blanche creating a scandal is accurate.

75   *What I been missing all summer*: namely, sex. Now that he
      knows the stories about Blanche are true, Mitch can vent his
      sexual frustration.

75   *You're not clean enough to bring in the house with my mother*:
      Mitch measures women by his mother and so exhibits Freud's
      Oedipus complex: he secretly desires his mother but this is
      taboo. Of course, his mother is nearing death, another conflation
      of desire and death. Mitch implies that he wants to enjoy
      Blanche as a prostitute, rather than a girlfriend respectable
      enough to be presented to his family. Given that he was
      previously in awe of Blanche, we can see that Mitch uses a
      typical classification of woman as Madonna/whore.

75   *Get out of here before I start screaming fire*: to cry rape might
      be too sensational. A cry of 'Fire!' could refer to the force of
      Mitch's lust, as well as being a sure way to create an alarm and
      so scare Mitch off.

75   *Blanche staggers back from the window and falls to her knees.*
        The distant piano is slow and blue: reeling from the attack,
        Blanche almost falls into an attitude of prayer. The music
        appropriately captures this sombre mood.

75   *She has decked herself out in a somewhat soiled and crumpled*
        white satin evening gown and a pair of scuffed silver slippers
        with brilliants set in their heels: her trunk or wardrobe out in
        front of her, Blanche is trying to return to a world of faded
        glamour. The words 'soiled', 'crumpled' and 'scuffed' indicate
        how she has been abused, how broken and imperfect her world
        has been rendered.

75   *Now she is placing the rhinestone tiara on her head before the*
        mirror of the dressing-table and murmuring excitedly as if to
        a group of spectral admirers: just costume jewellery, the tiara
        is a symbol of the fraud Blanche has been perpetuating. She is
        increasingly unable to distinguish between fantasy and reality,
        and is haunted by the ghost of her past.

75–6   *She catches her breath and slams the mirror face down*
        with such violence that the glass cracks: unhappy with her
        appearance, probably the signs of ageing, Blanche smashes the
        mirror and, according to superstition, ensures seven years' bad
        luck.

76   *He still has on the vivid green silk bowling shirt. As he rounds*
        the corner the honky-tonk music is heard. It continues softly
        throughout the scene: the last time we saw the shirt it had
        been ripped by Stella. Now it again symbolises Stanley's
        boldness, just as the silk pyjamas will later in the scene. The
        music is coming from a tinny piano and helps to create a sleazy
        atmosphere.

76   *Does that mean we are to be alone in here?*: Blanche spells out
        her danger; this is ominous.

76   *What've you got on those fine feathers for?*: more bird imagery.
        Feathers might be a means of escape were Blanche not already
        trapped by Stanley.

76   *A fireman's ball?*: appropriate after the way the previous scene
        ended. Of course, Stanley is poking fun at Blanche's invented
        social invitations.

76   *ATO*: Auxiliary Territorial Officer.

76   *Gosh. I thought it was Tiffany diamonds*: Tiffany is an expensive
        jeweller in New York. Stanley is being sarcastic but earlier, in
        Scene Two, he had to be told that these were rhinestones and
        worth nothing.

77   *The bottle cap pops off and a geyser of foam shoots up.*
      STANLEY laughs happily, holding up the bottle over his head:
      the phallic bottle was significant before when Blanche's dress
      became stained. Here it anticipates the sexual explosiveness at
      the end of this scene. As Stanley pours the bottle over his head,
      we might also be reminded of the shower being turned on over
      him in the aftermath of the poker party (Scene Three).

77   *Shall we bury the hatchet and make it a loving cup?*: Shall we
      make peace and have a celebratory drink? It is difficult to tell
      how sincere Stanley is being here.

77   *Well, it's a red letter night for us both*: we have both received
      good news. Blanche was wearing a red satin robe when Mitch
      visited her in Scene Nine. Of course, red is a sign of danger, a
      warning.

77   *The silk pyjamas I wore on my wedding night!*: we have already
      heard of Stanley's violence on his wedding night (the smashing
      of light bulbs in the apartment). The silk pyjamas are a luxury,
      a symbol of passion. Here their connection with marriage will
      extend to infidelity and rape.

78   *But I have been foolish – casting my pearls before swine!*: a
      biblical reference (Matthew 7:6): 'Give not that which is holy
      unto the dogs, neither cast ye your pearls before swine, lest
      they trample them under their feet, and turn again and rend
      you.' It is Blanche unwisely drawing once more on the image of
      Stanley as a pig that causes him to snap. Her 'pearls', Blanche's
      misplaced superiority, as Stanley sees it, and the fake jewels she
      wears, upset him to the point where he has to bring her fantasy
      crashing down. The insult is compounded by the reference to
      Stanley's 'buddy', Mitch.

78   *Deliberate cruelty is not forgivable*: almost Tennessee
      Williams's mantra. However we judge Blanche's behaviour, she
      does not deserve what happens to her.

79   *There isn't a goddam thing but imagination!*: Stanley has little
      imagination and so all that he despises is contained within
      this one word. Stanley's lines in this section are like a boxer's
      punches; Blanche is reeling on the ropes and all she can respond
      with each time is a shocked 'Oh!'.

79   *That worn-out Mardi Gras outfit, rented for fifty cents from some
      rag-picker! . . . What queen do you think you are!*: Blanche
      looks like something out of a carnival, possibly a freak show.
      Mardi Gras is on Fat Tuesday in New Orleans, a day of feasting
      before Lent officially begins. A rag-picker is a person who

collects and sells rags, so Blanche's costume is the cheapest and tackiest that could be found. Stanley has referred to Blanche's imitation of royalty before (Scene Eight, 65), but 'queen' can also denote a homosexual and has been construed as coded language (see note 72 on p. 158).

79   *You are the Queen of the Nile!*: Stanley characterises Blanche as the Egyptian queen, Cleopatra. In Shakespeare's *Antony and Cleopatra*, she is seen by the Romans as a decadent whore who has lured Antony to his doom; her world is unashamedly hedonistic.

79   *The shadows are of a grotesque and menacing form*: Blanche's worst fears and nightmares are projected onto the wall. Again, Williams is exposing the workings of her vulnerable mind.

79   *The night is filled with inhuman voices like cries in a jungle*: auditory fears are added to visual ones. Blanche is not lost in a wood but a jungle and survival looks improbable.

79   *A prostitute has rolled a drunkard*: robbed a drunkard while he was asleep. A brief glimpse is afforded of the outside world. The prostitute takes advantage of the drunken man, just as Stanley is going to take advantage of Blanche's weakness.

80   *Some moments later the NEGRO WOMAN appears around the corner with a sequined bag which the prostitute had dropped on the walk. She is rooting excitedly through it*: a chain of theft is established. Because the characters have little, they greedily take from others. Stanley's materialism was obvious when he talked of the Napoleonic code in Scene Two.

80   *He grins at her as he knots the tasselled sash about his waist*: a smile of power and the ability to exact revenge. It recalls Stanley's grin at the end of Scene Four after listening to Blanche's speech about his primitivism.

80   *Then a clicking becomes audible from the telephone, steady and rasping*: a moment of high dramatic tension. The sound of the clicking phone is very insistent. It represents broken communication – both between Blanche and Stanley and Blanche and the outside world.

80   *The barely audible 'blue piano' begins to drum up louder. The sound of it turns into the roar of an approaching locomotive. BLANCHE crouches, pressing her fists to her ears until it has gone by*: Williams uses the lugubrious piano more intensely here to build into the crashing train sound; it is ear-splitting for Blanche.

80   *Come to think of it – maybe you wouldn't be bad to – interfere
      with . . .* : as Stanley reaches for the right word, we are left
      to wonder whether this is the first time he has thought about
      assaulting her, whether he has always desired her but has
      channelled this into hostility.

81   *What are you putting on now?*: What game of deception are you
      trying to play now? The way this is phrased makes it sound like
      another costume or performance.

81   *She smashes a bottle on the table and faces him, clutching
      the broken top*: the loving cup has been turned into a weapon.
      Blanche hopes to use it to penetrate Stanley's face, but she will
      be overpowered and he will penetrate her violently.

81   *So you want some rough-house!*: Stanley relishes the prospect of
      a violent sexual encounter; he wants Blanche to offer some sort
      of resistance in order to make conquering her that much more
      satisfying.

81   *Tiger – tiger! Drop the bottle-top! Drop it! We've had this date
      with each other from the beginning!*: Stanley makes Blanche
      out to be a highly dangerous beast of the jungle, again so that
      he has an opponent to subdue. Interestingly, Stella portrayed
      Stanley as a lamb (depicting, in his remorse, the gentleness
      of Christ) in Scene Four after the poker night: 'He was as
      good as a lamb when I came back and he's really very, very
      ashamed of himself' (36). Stanley implies an inevitability about
      what happens which might seem to contradict his apparent
      spontaneity earlier. Like two inexorable forces, Blanche and
      Stanley, old and new America, have been brought to this final
      battle of wills.

81   *He picks up her inert figure and carries her to the bed. The
      hot trumpet and drums from the Four Deuces sound loudly*:
      all resistance has been broken. The music builds to a climax,
      capturing the carnality of the scene. Inevitably, the film's
      director, Elia Kazan, encountered difficulties with the censor
      over this. His solution was to have Stanley's act of picking up
      Blanche seen through a mirror that then smashes before the shot
      dissolves into the next scene, so diminishing the expected rape.

81   *The atmosphere of the kitchen is now the same raw, lurid one of
      the disastrous poker night*: Williams revisits the world of male
      camaraderie and competition. By repeating the poker party,
      he encourages us to see both what has changed and what has
      remained constant.

81   *The building is framed by the sky of turquoise. STELLA has been
        crying as she arranges the flowery dresses in the open trunk*:
        the colour of the sky invites another comparison, this time with
        the opening scene of the play: How far has Blanche travelled
        metaphorically? There is the first sign of a response from
        Stella, though we cannot yet judge what she knows. The trunk,
        now being packed, is a reminder of Stanley's hostile questions
        and Blanche's shock at discovering him going through her
        belongings ('It looks like my trunk has exploded', 19). The
        flowery dresses suggest a softer, more innocent Blanche than the
        fake furs.

82   *Drew to an inside straight and made it, by God*: Stanley
        combines the idea of a race, possibly a horserace, with winning
        a hand of cards. His mood is far happier than when he was
        losing in Scene Three.

82   *Maldita sea tu suerto!*: literally 'Curse your good luck!'

82   *Put it in English, greaseball!*: Stanley, victimised as a 'Polack',
        does not worry about insulting his friend with this racist remark.

82   *Luck is believing you're lucky. Take at Salerno*: Stanley believes
        in making his own luck and, therefore, in controlling fate.
        Applying this to Blanche, he knew he could defeat her; he had
        the ultimate means of doing so. Salerno was the site of the
        Allied invasion of mainland Italy in the Second World War. The
        American forces were the Fifth Army.

82   *You . . . you . . . you . . . Brag . . . brag . . . bull . . . bull*: Mitch's
        lack of sophistication is all too clear in his conversations with
        Blanche. Here his anger at Stanley's insensitivity makes him
        particularly inarticulate.

82   *If it's not too crushed I'll wear it and on the lapel that silver
        and turquoise pin in the shape of a seahorse*: one of several
        references to the sea. Crushed herself, Blanche has to find some
        way through this difficult scene.

83   *I couldn't believe her story and go on living with Stanley*:
        Stella's moral dilemma. What Stanley has done is too appalling
        to contemplate; it is easier for Stella to accept that her sister is
        insane.

83   *She has a tragic radiance in her red satin robe following the
        sculptural lines of her body*: the bold colour captures Blanche's
        pain. Strong sympathy surrounds her at this point and she has
        the beauty of a work of art.

83   *At the sound of BLANCHE's voice MITCH's arm supporting his
        cards has sagged and his gaze is dissolved into space*: the first

sign of Mitch's feelings of guilt. Whereas in Scene Three he could not concentrate because of Blanche's presence, here he slumps at the table with the regret that is triggered by her voice.

83   *BLANCHE stands quite still for some moments – the silverbacked mirror in her hand and a look of sorrowful perplexity as though all human experience shows on her face*: confused and shocked by the sound of Mitch's name, Blanche transcends her own situation and becomes a figure of universal suffering. Williams is gradually increasing her tragic significance. The mirror takes us back to the one that shattered at the start of Scene Ten.

84   *MITCH ducks his head lower but STANLEY shoves back his chair as if to rise*: the contrast between the two men is effectively illustrated here. Mitch is ashamed and wants to avoid a scene; Stanley is pursuing victory to the bitter end.

84   *It's Della Robbia blue. The blue of the robe in the old Madonna pictures. Are these grapes washed?*: Blanche is anxious to establish her purity and continues the reference to her being a work of art. She has been trying to wash her soul clean and now she wants assurances that everything she touches is free from dirt and sin.

84   *Those cathedral bells – they're the only clean thing in the Quarter. Well, I'm going now. I'm ready to go*: heard for the first time, the cathedral bells signify the start of Blanche's spiritual journey.

85   *'Poor lady', they'll say, 'the quinine did her no good. That unwashed grape has transported her soul to heaven'*: typically, Blanche dreams of dying in a young man's arms. Having resisted the onset of time so assiduously, she almost seems to welcome death here. Quinine is a bitter crystalline compound found in cinchona bark and used as a tonic and to reduce fever.

85   *And I'll be buried at sea sewn up in a clean white sack and dropped overboard – at noon – in the blaze of summer – and into an ocean as blue as [chimes again] my first lover's eyes!*: Williams wanted to be buried at sea like Hart Crane, but his body was taken to St Louis for burial in the Mt Calvary Cemetery. This vignette suggests the warmth and passion of first love, not the coldness of death.

85   *The gravity of their profession is exaggerated – the unmistakable aura of the state institution with its cynical detachment*: Williams's experience of the institutions his sister

Rose stayed in is evident in the thumbnail sketches we get of the doctor and the matron. They appear coldly professional until Blanche transforms the doctor into a gentleman caller. Diagnosed as schizophrenic, Rose was given a frontal lobotomy in 1943 and spent the rest of her life in institutions. Images of madness are common in Williams's plays, and Catherine Holly, a character in *Suddenly Last Summer*, is even threatened with a lobotomy.

85   *STELLA presses her fist to her lips*: an obvious sign of tension.

86   *Please don't get up. I'm only passing through*: Blanche's life has latterly involved journeys; she has not been able to find a permanent shelter.

86   *There is a moment of silence – no sound but that of STANLEY steadily shuffling the cards*: a moment of tension that, together with the distant Varsouviana, suggests the threat to Blanche who still has to negotiate Stanley and the other card players.

87   *Lurid reflections appear on the walls in odd, sinuous shapes. The 'Varsouviana' is filtered into weird distortion, accompanied by the cries and noises of the jungle. BLANCHE seizes the back of a chair as if to defend herself*: the distorted Varsouviana represents Blanche's most recent nightmare: the rape. The scene is re-enacted in her mind and she adopts a defensive position, this time with a chair rather than a broken bottle.

87   *The greeting is echoed and re-echoed by other mysterious voices behind the walls, as if reverberated through a canyon of rock*: Williams continues to expose the workings of Blanche's mind: she hears only a jumble of confusing voices. The canyon also represents the world falling away beneath her.

87   *She cries out as if the lantern was herself*: Stanley repeats Mitch's action of Scene Nine – essentially a figurative rape.

88   *What have I done to my sister?*: Stella understands her own involvement in the betrayal of Blanche; she knows that she has helped to destroy her.

88   *Madre de Dios! Cosa mala, muy, muy mala!*: Mother of God! This is a bad thing, a very, very bad thing! Pablo is the first of the poker players to voice his concern. By stating it here in Spanish, it seems more heartfelt.

88   *You done this, all o' your God damn interfering with things you –*: guilt-ridden as he has been throughout this scene, Mitch finally turns on Stanley. He will need to be restrained as Stanley was in Scene Three.

88   *BLANCHE turns wildly and scratches at the MATRON*: Blanche is
       like a feral cat or the tiger that Stanley labelled her just before
       the rape in Scene Ten; she does not want to be caged.

88   *Jacket*: straitjacket.

89   *He takes off his hat and now becomes personalized*: Blanche
       is now able to see him as a gentleman caller, though not Shep
       Huntleigh.

89   *Whoever you are – I have always depended on the kindness
       of strangers*: Blanche is in the unfortunate position of having
       to accept help from anyone, though she implies that she has
       never really known people intimately. We are reminded of her
       comment to Mitch at the end of Scene Three: 'I need kindness
       now' (34).

89   *It is wrapped in a pale blue blanket*: the colour links the child
       with Blanche. In her delicate state, Blanche has needed to be
       handled like a child in this last scene.

89   *She sobs with inhuman abandon. There is something luxurious
       in her complete surrender to crying now that her sister is gone*:
       'inhuman' echoes the jungle cries Blanche has been hearing.
       Only now that Blanche has left can Stella give in to the fullness
       of her emotions. These are self-indulgently 'luxurious', as if
       partly for her benefit, to foreground her own remorse rather than
       just what has happened to Blanche.

90   *[He kneels beside her and his fingers find the opening of her
       blouse.] Now, now, love. Now, love . . .* : a crude sexual gesture
       on Stanley's part. The repetition of 'now' emphasises his
       conviction that their life can return to normality. For Stanley,
       this means a resumption of sexual relations, even though it
       is only 'some weeks' after the birth of the child. The stage
       direction before this is '*voluptuously, soothingly*', combining
       Stanley's sexual passion with his genuine love for Stella.
       Kazan's film version could not be seen to endorse any kind of
       acceptance of rape, so the ending sees Stella taking her baby and
       running off, promising never to return.

90   *The luxurious sobbing, the sensual murmur fade away under the
       swelling music of the 'blue piano' and the muted trumpet*: the
       music and sound effects combine here in a heady mix which is
       both 'swelling' and 'muted'. Williams effectively smothers the
       emotional crescendo of the play with the music that has helped
       to define both the Quarter and the specific events of the play.

90   *This game is seven-card stud*: this matter-of-fact statement
       indicates three things: the poker players are starting a fresh

game, one that they played before in Scene Three; life will continue in much the same way; Stanley, the 'stud', is triumphant, the luck that he believes in fashioning for himself signified by the number seven. At precisely what cost Stanley's victory has been achieved is a point that the audience is left to ponder.

Questions for Further Study

1 To what extent is Blanche the controlling force in the play?
2 Compare and contrast the attitudes of Blanche and Stella to the story of their past selves at Belle Reve.
3 How far do the audience agree with Blanche's assessment of Stanley as an 'ape'?
4 Discuss the dramatic devices which Williams uses in the play to suggest that Blanche is doomed.
5 Stanley ripping away the paper lantern represents his destruction of lies, deceit and fantasy. Explore aspects of truth and fantasy in the play.
6 'A play must concentrate the events of a lifetime into the short span of a three-act play. Of necessity these events must be more violent than in life' (Tennessee Williams). Examine the creation of tension as it is developed through the eleven scenes of the play.
7 In his directorial notes on the play Elia Kazan suggests that through watching the decline of Blanche '[the audience] begin to realise that they are sitting in at the death of something extraordinary [. . .] and then they feel the tragedy'. Discuss the fall of Blanche in the play.
8 Explore Williams's use of colour as it impacts upon the changing atmosphere of the play.
9 The 'visual projection of Blanche's inner life' is a key aspect of Williams's dramatic technique. How is it used?
10 The 'infusion' of lyricism in the atmosphere of Elysian Fields is created using a range of visual and aural devices. Examine Williams's creation of environment within the play.
11 'If Blanche belongs to the crumbling grandeur of the Southern plantations, Stanley is a new American, an immigrant man of the city.' How does the play express the conflict between traditional values and the new world?
12 'The blind are leading the blind' (Blanche, Scene Two). Examine the twinned themes of sight and blindness as they are expressed through character and dramatic incidents.
13 'Don't hang back with the brutes' (Blanche, Scene Four). Discuss the development of the character of Stanley as it is revealed, both through his own words and actions, and the perceptions of others.
14 'The relationship between Stanley and Stella is based on his need for domination and her need for protection.' Discuss.
15 The relationship between Blanche and Mitch offers an interesting perspective on the nature of gender relations in the play. Focusing on

clear examples of at least two of the relationships, explore the issues which arise.

16 'He acts like an animal, has an animal's habits' (Blanche, Scene Four). Explore the conflicts between gentility and animal brutality in the play.

17 'I lived in a house where dying old women remembered their dead men [. . .] Death . . . [. . .] the opposite is desire' (Blanche, Scene Nine). Examine Williams's use of this theme to affect the audience.

18 The lurid reflections which fall across the walls in the final scene are a potential manifestation of Blanche's terrors and fears. Discuss the dramatic devices used by Williams in the final scene.

19 'The language of the play is shaped by two needs: character-identification and thematic development.' Explore this statement.

20 Stella's apparent betrayal of Blanche offers the audience a clear insight into her character. Discuss the complexities of the relationship between the sisters in the light of Stella's final act.

21 *A Streetcar Named Desire* appears to be a hybrid drama: naturalistic, symbolic and poetic. Do you agree?

22 Blanche's response to the figure of the doctor in the final scene of the play is characteristic of her deep-rooted perception of the role of men in her life. Explore the range of Blanche's attitudes towards the men in the play.

23 'To hold front position in this rat-race you've got to believe you are lucky' (Stanley, Scene Eleven). To what extent does Williams emphasise the role of luck in dictating the course of the lives of his characters?

24 Is *A Streetcar Named Desire* a moral play?

Cat on a Hot Tin Roof

commentary and notes by
PHILIP C. KOLIN

Plot

Act One

Cat opens with the physical symbols Williams uses to develop his characters. Coming out of the bathroom, after freshening up from a disgustingly messy dinner with Gooper's 'no-neck' children, Maggie stands in front of a mirror and a dressing table. Showering and powdering are part of her repertoire to entice Brick back to bed and continue to be alluring to Big Daddy. The mirror reflects her identity, and Brick's too. 'Who are you?' she says in front of it (30). She is worried that Brick's older brother Gooper and his obnoxious wife Mae will cut Brick and her out of Big Daddy's inheritance. They never let Big Daddy and Big Mama forget that Maggie is childless and that Brick is a drunkard. Branding Mae's repulsive children as 'no-neck monsters', she tries to thwart Gooper and Mae's plot to disinherit Brick and her.

Brick is symbolised throughout the play by his crutch, his liquor cabinet, and his pyjamas. He needs the crutch because of a broken ankle he suffered jumping hurdles on the athletic field at his old high school at 3 a.m. In every act, he hobbles and falls on stage. Dressed in silk pyjamas, he is a patient in his own isolated world/ward. When Maggie informs him that 'Now we know that Big Daddy's dyin' of *cancer*', all he can say is, 'Do we?' His terse replies to her – 'Did you *say* something', or 'How about that' (9–10) – show that he is disconnected, emotionally and physically, from his wife as well as from his father. Refusing to communicate or sleep with Maggie, and drowning himself in liquor, Brick wants to escape the pain and the obligation of self-disclosure. He drinks until he hears the 'click', the silence that brings him peace. The empty bed in the middle of the room, another key prop, is an accusing reminder of Maggie and Brick's childless, loveless marriage. Wanting no part of family life, Brick refuses to even sign a card or play a part in giving Big Daddy the birthday present Maggie has bought. The white silk pyjamas Maggie asks Brick to wear parallel the soft cashmere robe she buys for Big Daddy. In the midst of Maggie's litany of hurts, Sister Woman, Mae, barges in, berating Brick and Maggie. Attempting to convince her meddling sister-in-law that Brick is a loyal husband, Maggie talks about a hunting trip that she and Brick plan to make very soon to Moon Lake. When Big Mama bursts in, overjoyed by the news that Big Daddy does not have cancer, she also attacks Maggie for not having children and for having a husband who drinks. Disgusted, Big Mama leaves the room.

Quick-witted and tenacious, Maggie quickly recovers from Big Mama's inquisitorial intrusion to return to her attempted conversation with Brick. Hoping to coax him into bed, she informs him that other men find her attractive, including Big Daddy whom she likes and admires, and reveals that a man tried to pick her up recently. Even though the mirror in the bedroom reflects a beautiful, desirable wife, Brick refuses to see Maggie or himself clearly in it. Wanting her out of his life, he encourages Maggie to 'take a lover', but she refuses because it would lead to a divorce. She vows to take care of Brick, but he rejects everyone's help, especially hers. Maggie is determined that they will not lose Brick's inheritance; after an impoverished childhood she could not bear to be poor again. Standing in front of the mirror, she sighs folornly, 'I'm dressed, all dressed, nothing else for me to do' (35), while Brick whistles 'vaguely' at her, another sign of his cool estrangement.

But Brick's apathy turns to anger when she mentions his relationship with his deceased friend Skipper. When Maggie declares that love-making with Brick 'didn't just peter out in the usual ways, it was cut off short long before the natural time for it to' (30), she summarises what has happened and forecasts confrontations to come. Nothing thus far has brought Brick's emotions to the surface as much as Maggie's reference to 'the truth about that thing with Skipper' (35). *Cat* gives us several accounts of 'that thing'. In Act Two, we will hear Brick's and Big Daddy's side, but, according to Maggie in Act One, she made love to Skipper to be closer to Brick and to put Skipper on notice that Brick was her husband. But Brick accuses her of smearing that relationship as 'dirty', and blames her for destroying his friendship with Skipper. Maggie protests that she saw their friendship as 'pure'. Confessing that she tried to get Skipper to stop loving her husband, she went to his room one night, but after he was unable to make love, Skipper drank himself to death, for which Brick will never forgive Maggie. At the end of Act One, Dixie, one of Gooper's unmannerly brood, barges into the bedroom, taunting Brick and Maggie once more. Linking birth and death, Act One ends with the family gathering in Brick's room to celebrate Big Daddy's sixty-fifth birthday.

Act Two

Act Two, with Big Daddy's long-awaited entrance, might be divided into three parts. In the first part, Big Daddy responds to the uninvited guests in Brick's bedroom. Like his son, he has little tolerance for his family and only contempt for his wife Ida, who brings in '*an enormous birthday cake ablaze with candles*' (44). Given Big Daddy's real medical condition, ordering Ida to blow out the candles is painfully ironic. As in Act One,

Brick evades contact and conversation by leaving the room, going back and forth to the bar, and refusing to answer direct questions with direct answers. Big Daddy's interrogations begin with wanting to know why Brick is crippled, which triggers talk about his son's sexual identity. Brick's character has been besmirched by Gooper and Mae because of their disgusting eavesdropping, and an angry Big Daddy orders them out of Brick's bedroom, another in a series of evictions in *Cat*.

In the second part of Act Two, Big Daddy demands to know why Brick does not sleep with Maggie. Big Daddy asserts that 'the human animal is a beast' because he tries to win immortality through accumulating possessions. He then describes his trips to Europe where Big Mama tried to purchase everything in sight and to Africa where a woman made her young daughter solicit him. Just as Brick repulses Maggie's lovemaking, Big Daddy rejects his wife's. But for all of Big Daddy's power he cannot communicate with his son, who blames his father for talking in circles. Brick finally confesses that he drinks because of 'disgust', a response which sparks a father–son confrontation over lies and corruption. Brick complains, though, that he never lied to his father, and Big Daddy likewise responds, 'Then there is at least two people that never lied to each other' (75). Sadly, Brick is the only one to tell his father the truth. Yet Brick's disgust translates into mendacity, a subject Big Daddy knows well, having lived in an abhorrent marriage and dealing with the rest of his contentious family. But having received a good bill of health, he orders Brick to straighten up.

In the third part of Act Two, pressuring Brick further, Big Daddy wants to know how and why Skipper died. At the turning point of the play, Big Daddy declares that Brick's relationship with Skipper was 'not exactly normal' (76). Vindictively, Brick intimates that his father was also in a compromised (homosexual) relationship with Jack Straw and Peter Ochello, the old 'bachelors' who many years ago hired Daddy as an overseer on their plantation. But Big Daddy discusses the Straw–Ochello relationship without ever directly answering Brick's charge. Through a fiery volley of words, Brick resents his father's accusation that the relationship with Skipper was 'unnatural', and assures him that he would have spurned Skipper if he were gay. Inquiring, then, why Skipper cracked up, Big Daddy learns that Brick blames Maggie for Skipper's death. But when Big Daddy insists that something has been left out of his son's story, Brick confesses that one night Skipper called to make 'a drunken confession' (84) but that he hung up on him. Because of Brick's cowardice and self-deception, Big Daddy accuses him of mendacity, translated into 'disgust' with himself for not facing the truth. Amid fireworks celebrating Big Daddy's birthday, Brick inadvertently reveals what everyone but Big Daddy knows – this is his last birthday. He quickly regrets the disclosure and accuses himself of being 'less alive'. The act ends with Big Daddy's harrowing cry condemning all liars.

Act Three

Serving as a bridge between acts, Big Daddy's condemning voice cascades into Act Three as he exits. Unlike the intimately charged conversations in Acts One and Two, the exchanges in Act Three occur when the Pollitt clan/ensemble gather to discuss Big Daddy's medical condition and to break the bad news to Big Mama. Reassured that Big Daddy is all right, judging by the huge meal he has just eaten, Big Mama is nevertheless concerned about this 'mysterious family conference' (138). When the time comes to reveal the truth about this 'black thing' that has invaded the Pollitt house, Dr Baugh vindicates himself by telling Big Mama that Big Daddy's condition has 'gone past the knife' (97). As he has done throughout *Cat*, Brick leaves the room, and even sings a song, sealed in his own pain-proof world. Unscrupulously, Gooper produces a briefcase (a symbol of his mercenary world) containing trustee papers and medical reports and asserts that as a corporation lawyer he can continue to run the estate. Incensed, Big Mama demands that Gooper put the documents away and implores Brick and Maggie to have an heir.

But, as Williams was keen to emphasise, Big Daddy is not dead yet, and coming back briefly on stage, he vows to keep control of his land. Symbolising the turmoil inside the Pollitt family, a storm blows in, Williams's use of what is known as 'pathetic fallacy': nature reflecting human emotions. Big Daddy then tells his famous crude joke about an elephant's erection and how small it was in comparison to a husband's whose wife and children accompany him at the zoo. The joke reaffirms Big Daddy's manhood while his family paints him as dying. To everyone's shock, Maggie announces she is pregnant. Elated, Big Daddy declares she has 'life in her body' (112), then retreats to where he can look at his plantation, leaving Mae and Gooper in Brick's bedroom where they angrily accuse Maggie of lying before leaving outraged. Confronting Brick, Maggie claims she is now the stronger one, hides his liquor, and insists that he sleeps with her 'to make the lie true' if he wants it back. Echoing a line from Big Daddy in Act Two (52), Brick's words, 'Wouldn't it be funny if that was true?' provocatively refer to Maggie's love for him and her hoped-for conception.

Commentary

Like many of Williams's plays, *Cat on a Hot Tin Roof* takes place in a highly symbolic setting, one that is steeped in the history and myths of the South. In fact, *Cat* excavates two levels of history – the long tradition of ante- and post-bellum (Southern) customs and their literary expression and the more recent history of the 1950s in American political life, the time when *Cat* was written and first performed.

Cat and the Plantation Mythos

Cat is inseparable from its Southern plantation setting. The South, especially the Mississippi Delta, exerted a strong influence on Williams's life and work. Stretching from Memphis to Yazoo City, the Mississippi Delta comprises an area of 6,250 square miles of flat land enriched by the alluvial deposits of the Mississippi River which was frequently impoverished by floods, insects, and drought. Growing up in Clarksdale in the Mississippi Delta, just seventy miles south of Memphis, Williams was familiar with the Delta towns and people because he visited them with his maternal grandfather, the Reverend Mr Dakin, whose Episcopal church, St George's, was one of Clarksdale's cultural centres. *Cat* is filled with references to Williams's boyhood South: Big Daddy's sprawling plantation of 28,000 acres is located near Clarksdale; Brick's accident at the high school running track is reported in the *Clarksdale Register*; and Big Daddy eats huge quantities of Delta food, such as 'hoppin' John', 'candied yams', and all ingredients for 'a real country dinner' (90). His most important cash crop is cotton, and to celebrate King Cotton, the Delta held festivals with a cotton queen, also alluded to in *Cat*. Although Clarksdale was known for the blues, there are, unfortunately, no references to this musical form (as in *Baby Doll* or *Orpheus Descending*), but a saxophonist played a Louis Armstrong score before each act in the production of *Cat* in 2008 with an all-black cast.

With its large cotton plantations and the wealthy families that owned them, the Delta was enshrined in the mythos of the nostalgic, antebellum South, the land of valiant courtiers and fair ladies in the spirit of *Gone with the Wind*. Plantation life was often idealised as idyllic and heroic, the aristocratic world of the Wilkes and O'Haras who controlled huge estates such as Twin Oaks and Tara. Planters were portrayed as cultured gentlemen, educated, refined. Their columned houses – such as Longwood – were modelled on classical architecture. The plantation economy was rooted in cotton and harvested by field hands, chattel slaves, whose labour sustained the fictions created about a genteel way of life. Masters and their male heirs adhered to a strict code of chivalry where women were idealised, and business deals were transacted with honour. Plantation life also was noted for its hospitality and romance. Many nineteenth- and twentieth-century plantation novels centred on love affairs amid the magnolias and azaleas. It is this world that *Cat*'s setting evokes.

Yet, despite his Southern roots, Williams replaced the nostalgia of the Old South and its sophisticated planters and elegant rituals with a crass, menacing new South. Big Daddy, the master, is a 'Mississippi redneck' (33) who rode 'a yellow dog freight car' and lived in 'hobo jungles' (78). His daughters-in-law, Maggie and Mae, also come from dirt-poor backgrounds. As Maggie confesses: 'Always had to suck up to people I couldn't stand because they had money and I was poor as Job's turkey' (34). But Mae still pretends she descends from the gentry. Debunking the beauty queen ethos of the South, Maggie satirises the ritual of the cotton queen who would 'sit on a brass throne on a tacky float an' ride down Main Street, smilin', bowin', and blowin' kisses to all the trash on the street' (13). She further recounts how one cotton queen, Susie McPheeter, was riding in a parade when 'some old drunk' in front of the Gayoso Hotel 'shot out a squirt of tobacco juice right in [her] face' (13). Disdaining the world of debutantes, Maggie wore a 'hand-me-down from a snotty rich cousin' (34). Hardly attractive or ladylike, Big Mama looks like a 'Japanese wrestler' (25). And Brick is no dashing, romantic cavalier protecting his lady's honour; twice he tries to hit Maggie with his crutch, once even hurling it at her (39).

Yet Big Daddy's South contains all the comfortable conventions – the setting, quaint, bizarre characters, black servants, and sensational events – that Broadway audiences expected to see and could approve of. The Pollitt plantation with its colourful and crude patriarch, his life-threatening sickness and wealthy estate, the bitter family feud over the inheritance, Brick's alcoholism, secrets from the past, and a steamy, oppressive climate – these were all part of the literary heritage of the South. But, as Albert J. Devlin convincingly argues, Williams 'cunningly' exploited the conventions of the plantation South to 'obscure' his own scepticism about the Broadway commercial theatre (and its values) as he actually sought its approval to secure his fame. Within the historical/economic context of the plantation South, Williams could express the tensions and anxieties of his own troubled sexual identity through Brick, 'a mirror of [his] artistic identity and his besetting career' (Devlin, 105). Adhering to the nationally acceptable conventions of 'genre, race, class, [and] economy' associated with the South, Williams inserted Brick's (and his own) 'aberrant silence' (Devlin, 104), the 'speechless voice' of a dissident homosexual/playwright who could not openly reveal his 'deepest secrets', his 'mystery'. Williams had thus sown his own failures (the recent commercial disaster of *Camino Real* on Broadway, 1953) into his character besieged with disappointments. According to Devlin, Brick's dilemma reflected, as it disguised, Williams's own 'problematic . . . relations with the Broadway theatre' (107).

Williams also used this symbolic setting to raise questions about and express anxieties over patriarchal control and the rites of inheritance. Traditionally, the economy and hierarchies of plantation life were created and sustained through the power of a patriarch whose legacies exerted control over the land and those who lived on it. A history of the Old South – with its famous plantations – is a history of big daddies, strong-willed men who shaped the world around them. Plantations were passed down from one generation to another through patrilinear succession, fathers to sons, the heirs of heterosexual unions. But, as Michael Bibler argues, *Cat* undermines, even as it sustains, conventional patriarchal control and heterosexuality. For example, Jack Straw and Peter Ochello, the homosexual couple who owned the plantation before Big Daddy, dispel the plantation laws of inheritance through their love affair and their relationship to Big Daddy. In a key speech, he declares:

> I made this place! I was overseer . . . on the old Straw and Ochello
> plantation. I quit school at ten! I quit school at ten years old and
> went to work like a nigger in the fields. And I rose to be overseer
> of the Straw and Ochello plantation. And old Straw died and I was
> Ochello's partner. (51)

Sexually tolerant, Big Daddy had no qualms about being Ochello's partner and inheriting the plantation. But by admitting that he received the plantation from this gay couple, Big Daddy subverts a heterosexual, patrilinear line of inheritance. Interestingly, no one ever inquires why or how Big Daddy inherited the plantation from Ochello.

Brick also destabilised the plantation mythos. While Blanche loses her ancestral plantation Belle Reve ('Beautiful Dream') in *A Streetcar Named Desire* because of her male ancestor's 'epic fornications', ironically, it is the son, Brick, who risks losing his inheritance by refusing to have an heir with Maggie and because of his ambiguous friendship with Skipper. The conflicts and tensions over Brick's relationship with his wife and with Skipper are more clearly understood in the light of the imperatives of a plantation culture. Like Big Daddy, Brick and Maggie are under the influence of Ochello and Straw. They stay in a '*room that hasn't changed much since it was occupied by the original owners of the place, Jack Straw and Peter Ochello*'. The entire plantation is thus shrunk to this sexually symbolic room. As Bibler again asserts, the shared bedroom 'establishes homosexuality not only as the physical origin of the plantation but also as its metaphysical origin in the loving relationship that "haunts" the room' (384). To Big Daddy, 'it doesn't matter if Brick is homosexual' since 'homosexuality does not destabilize his social position or his masculinity because homosexual desire operates well within plantation hierarchies and codes'. After all, Big Daddy regarded Straw and Ochello as 'double patriarchs' whose lifestyle was not inconsistent with a plantation ethos (395).

Cat and America in the 1950s

America in the 1950s could be termed the age of repression, a time of conformity, insisting that citizens adhere to intensely conservative values. The country was ruled by a staunchly conservative Republican President/General Dwight D. 'Ike' Eisenhower, America's Big Daddy, and his Vice-President, Richard Nixon, whose later presidency (1968–74) scandalised the world by the mendacity of Watergate. In his *Memoirs* (1975), Williams lampooned Nixon for his 'total lack of honesty and . . . moral sense' (95). Big Daddy, too, decries the deceptive language of elected officials: 'Mendacity is one of them five dollar words that cheap politicians throw back and forth' (71). Ike's America was patriotic, heterosexual, and paranoid. America in the 1950s waged a Cold War against Communism, which was demonised as a threat, both from within and outside the country. It was popular, even mandatory, in America to be anti-Communist. A 'Red scare' terrified the country. Fearing a nuclear attack from Russia, America routinely held air-raid drills during which millions of citizens fled to bomb shelters, usually built in their basements, to survive an inevitable nuclear Armageddon.

America's strategy for national defence also lay in vigilantly finding, repelling, and punishing Communists at home. During the 1950s, as never before, the US House and Senate justified taking extraordinary, and sometimes illegal, measures to contain the Communist attack against American family values and national security. To battle the 'Reds' and their 'Pinko' sympathisers, the House on Un-American Activities Committee (HUAC), founded in 1938, and chaired by Senator Joseph McCarthy (Republican, Wisconsin) in the early 1950s, embarked on a notorious witch hunt looking for Communists, especially in entertainment and in the arts. Described as McCarthyism, the HUAC's policy was to search out witnesses to name names and, rather than insisting on hard evidence, accepted and validated lies, innuendo, hearsay, guilt by association, biased informers, and unregulated government eavesdropping. Ten years before *Cat* premiered, Williams had warned America about the dangers of McCarthyism:

> Today we are living in a world which is threatened by
> totalitarianism. The Fascist and the Communist states have thrown
> us into a panic of reaction. Reactionary opinion descends like
> a ton of bricks on the head of any artist who speaks out against
> the current of prescribed ideas. We are all under wraps of one
> kind or another, trembling before the spectre of investigation
> committees . . . ('Something Wild', 46).

Cat satirises and scourges McCarthyism through Gooper's and Mae's despicable, covert actions to gather information about Brick and Maggie to ruin their reputations. Sharing the room next to Brick and Maggie's, they listen through the walls to the couple's conversations, all of which infuriates Big Daddy:

> I hate eavesdroppers, I don't like any kind of sneakin an'
> spyin'. . . . You listen at night like a couple of rutten peekhole spies
> and go and give a report on what you hear to Big Mama an' she
> comes to me and says they say such and such and so and so about
> what they heard goin' on between Brick an' Maggie. (55)

Their reports include information such as 'You won't sleep with her, that you sleep on the sofa' (50). Illustrating their spying, Big Mama and Mae whisper in collusion behind Big Daddy's back (49). Whisper campaigns, eavesdropping, and spying were tactics associated with the HUAC. 'The walls have ears in this place', warns Big Daddy. Earlier, Maggie asks, 'Hush! Who is out there? Is somebody out there?' (21). Just as Brick's and Maggie's names were sullied in the Pollitt family (allegorised into America, circa 1955), many actors, writers, directors, singers, artists, and musicians were accused of Communist sympathies and affiliations and blacklisted from working in Hollywood.

Gays in particular were targeted by policing agencies such as the HUAC, the FBI, and the military for their supposed Communist leanings. In 1950, the Republican National Chairman, Guy Gabrielson, informed his constituents that 'Sexual perverts . . . have infiltrated our Government in recent years . . . [and they were] perhaps as dangerous as the actual Communists' (quoted in Paller, 54). It was an easy leap of (bad) faith to make gays into Communists. According to John S. Bak, a 'communist suspicion . . . inextricably accompanied the effete male' (232), branded for being a non-conformist, a seditious foe of family values, and a threat to national security. Gays were forced to go underground, stay in the closet, thus masking their sexual identity. In homophobic America in the 1950s, they were harassed by the police who arrested or institutionalised them for deviant sexual behaviour. (The Stonewall Riots, igniting the gay liberation movement in the summer of 1969, were more than a decade off.) If found out, gays in the 1950s were fired from their jobs or discharged from the military. The FBI, led by J. Edgar Hoover, who history records was himself a closeted gay, conducted intensive surveillance of gay bars, clubs, and bathhouses to crack down on this suspicious population. Williams himself was the subject of FBI and the Department of Navy surveillance for his sexual contact with sailors during the Second World War (Mitgang, 122). Being labelled gay was a political crime in 1955.

In such a context, Brick's fear of being branded a homosexual symbolised a crisis in national identity politics. In the 1950s, America saw itself as staunchly heteromasculine. Coming out gay ran the risk of being persecuted as a Communist, a misfit, the Other, a threat to democracy and decency. But, as John Bak, Michael Paller, David Savran, and others have argued, America's identity crisis in the 1950s was in part triggered by the Kinsey report – *Sexual Behavior in the Human Male* (1948) – which documented two very troubling facts: many American men had at least one homosexual experience and that the enforced dichotomy between gay and straight was not always clear cut. The destabilisation of gay and straight identities led to this national anxiety. Brick's anguish over his sexual identity thus brings this controversy to the surface by illustrating the homophobia of the times. His refusal to sleep with Maggie became a tell-tale sign of his homosexuality for Gooper and Mae. After all, Skipper, who confessed his love for Brick, could not perform the sexual act with Maggie. Moreover, Brick's vitriolic homophobic denials do little to deter the smear campaign against him.

Making sure that they represented an acceptable and conservative national identity, movies were also policed in 1950s America. Hollywood films were strictly censored by the PCA (the Production Code Administration), 'the industry's moral guardian' (Palmer and Bray, 62). To ensure that films adhered to unsullied, conservative standards, the PCA could insist that offensive material be omitted, a script be shortened, or even that a scene be reshot from a different, less sexualising angle. The PCA fought liberal politics, suggestive sexuality, indecent language, and any scandal of homosexuality. As we shall see, the film version of *Cat* (1958) differed significantly from Williams's script. Williams's 'play explores the discontent of desire – and its polymorphous perversity as well. No previous production, however, had dealt at such length and in such depth with sexual questions' (Palmer and Bray, 8). The *Cat* film was, however, heavily censored. Together with the PCA, the Legion of Decency, the rating board of the Roman Catholic Church, censored films by classifying them as 'A' (Acceptable), 'B' (objectionable in parts), or 'C' (objectionable). Receiving a rating of 'C' crippled a film's chances of making money because theatres would not dare to show it or, if they did, audiences, guided by the Legion's assessment, would be likely to stay away.

Seen as a latent or repressed homosexual, Brick was far removed from the strong male leads that dominated the popular films of the decade, such as Charlton Heston's Moses in *The Ten Commandments* (1955), the quintessential Cold War film of the decade, or Gregory Peck's Captain Ahab in *Moby Dick* (1956). Strong, hypermasculine images – such as John Wayne, the warrior cowboy – were the norm because they espoused family values, the hallowed foundation of democracy. Because of its homosexuality, alcoholism, adultery, Skipper's impotence, and Maggie's sexual aggressiveness, *Cat* hardly fostered the wholesome virtues espoused by the PCA and the Legion of Decency. The Pollitts were not the models of the happy 1950s American family that the PCA and the Legion wanted to see portrayed on screen. Thus, Williams's play, but not Brooks's 1958 screenplay, fomented a 'rebellion against social order' (Palmer and Bray, 163), challenging the creed of the conservative 1950s. For instance, by casting Brick as an ex-football player and a hunter, Williams shattered the stereotype that all gay men were effeminate.

Versions of *Cat on a Hot Tin Roof*

Like many of Williams's plays, the source for *Cat on a Hot Tin Roof* is one of his short stories, 'Three Players of a Summer Game' (1952), including the trio of Brick, Margaret, and Mary Louise Grey, the young widow of a doctor. In the story Margaret vanishes early and does not appear until the end; there is no Skipper or Big Daddy; and Brick's problem is ambiguous. The croquet game alluded to in Act One of *Cat* (7) is not fully developed in the story. In 1953, Williams also worked on the draft of a play, *A Place of Stone*, which became the intermediary script between 'Three Players' and *Cat*. In 1954, he showed a draft of *Cat* to the director Elia Kazan who insisted on three major changes: (1) have Big Daddy return in Act Three because he was 'too vivid and important a character to disappear from the play except as an offstage cry after the second act'; (2) make Maggie more sympathetic to audiences; and (3) show Brick experiencing a transformation as a result of his confrontation with Big Daddy and thereby reconciling with Maggie to end his 'moral paralysis'.

To ensure that the highly influential Kazan would direct *Cat* and to make his play commercially profitable, Williams agreed to the revisions but feared he would become 'a sort of ventriloquist's dummy for ideas which are not his own' ('Author and Director', 118). But when *Cat* was published in 1955, he included the two endings – his original one and the revised, Broadway version. Endlessly revising his plays, even after they were performed and printed, Williams created a new hybrid third act for the American Shakespeare production in 1974, incorporating some of Kazan's changes (e.g. Big Daddy returns in the third act and Maggie is more sympathetic) as well as others in his original draft, but the Brick–Maggie relationship still remained problematic. Williams's final version of *Cat* (1975) is used in this volume.

There has been a continuing debate about which version of *Cat* a director should choose to stage, although the Broadway version, which bears Kazan's heavy emendations, is usually not favoured. Even so, Kazan's decision to bring Big Daddy back on stage in Act Three has major implications for how the play is structured and staged.

Structure

Cat on a Hot Tin Roof, one of Tennessee Williams's most tightly crafted plays, runs about three hours. Divided into three acts, it has no scenes but includes two intermissions. Act Two, the turning point of the play, is rightfully the longest part and is flanked by two shorter acts, each approximately the same length. *Cat* is structurally a well-made play with a rising opening, complete with exposition giving us background information in Act One about Brick, Maggie, Big Daddy, and so on, a turning point at the end of Act Two, and a climax in Act Three. Even though it follows the model of a well-made and seemingly realistic drama, Tennessee Williams still introduces non-realistic elements into the script, such as his highly expressionistic stage directions at the start of the play, those dealing with lighting, colour, and atmosphere.

Like a Greek tragedy, *Cat* follows the classical unities of action, time, and place. All events happen on a 'late and fair summer afternoon' and into that evening. The action revolves around Brick's relationships – with Maggie, Big Daddy, the Pollitt family, his friend Skipper, and himself. Big Daddy's health, fortune, and past sexual experiences also form a major part of the dramatic action. In fact, the fates of Big Daddy and Brick unfold like a classical tragedy adopted for modern times, with Southern landscapes, allusions, and dialects. Reflecting the play's continuous action, '*There is no lapse of time'* between Acts Two and Three. All the action in *Cat* also occurs in one place – in Brick and Maggie's bedroom – with a door to the adjoining bathroom and others leading to the gallery outside. For Brick, the bedroom is his sanctuary; for Maggie, it's her prison. For the other characters, it becomes the place where Big Daddy's sixty-fifth birthday party is celebrated or lamented. Symbolising barriers to communication, a constant flow of interruptions disrupt conversations in Brick's bedroom (Kolin, 'Obstacles'). Even with these interruptions *Cat* moves seamlessly, straightforwardly from one act to another.

Structurally, and poetically, *Cat* might also be compared to a musical composition. In many ways, the play is operatic, a score written for many different voices. Maggie's *'voice has range and music'* (9), and at times she sounds like a *'priest delivering a liturgical chant'* (40); offstage, Big Daddy's *'long drawn cry of agony and rage fills the house'* at the end of Act Three; birthday and children's songs, black work songs, music from a hi-fi, scat music, Wagner, and Beethoven also play during *Cat*. In his 'Notes for the Designer', Williams himself characterised the stage for *Cat* in musical terms: he wanted it to be roomy enough for a 'ballet'. Commenting on the 'musical structure' of the play, Brian Palmer claimed that Act One, where Maggie dominates, 'is practically an aria. Act Two focuses on a duet between Brick and Big Daddy; and Act Three is finally an ensemble' ('Swinging a Cat', 177).

Language

Cat on a Hot Tin Roof is poetic, compelling, explosive. Reviewing the 1955 premiere, Richard Watts characterised Williams's language as 'insistently vulgar, neurotic and ugly [yet it] still maintains a quality of exotic lyricism'. The blend of the lyrical and the ugly (cruel, lustful, distorted) nicely defines Williams's Southern grotesque. When *Cat* debuted on Broadway in 1955 Williams had to use such quaint words as 'rutten' (Mae and Gooper act like 'a couple of rutten peekhole spies' [55]), 'duckin', and 'frig' (as in Brick's imperative 'frig all dirty lies and liars!' [81]) in place of the four-letter taboo word and its participial variants. Soon after *Cat* opened, a New York City licence commissioner demanded that Big Daddy's elephant joke and other offensive language be cut. As Donald Spoto observed, 'the salty language, an off-color joke, and the psycho-sexual turmoil sent shock waves through audiences' (*Kindness*, 200). When Williams revised *Cat* in 1974–5, he updated and increased the profanities. Even today, productions of *Cat* have been labelled 'shocking' because of explicit language, and thus are often rated 'R' or 'restricted' (individuals of seventeen and younger are not admitted unless accompanied by an adult). In the 2008 *Cat*, James Earl Jones's Big Daddy shocked audiences 'with [his] unrestrained ribaldry' (Robertson).

Beyond doubt, Big Daddy's speech is expletive driven. It is poetic and filthy, sometimes simultaneously. In his *Memoirs*, Williams glowed: 'Big Daddy has a kind of crude eloquence of expression . . . that I have managed to give to no other character of my creation' (168). His speeches are peppered with four-letter words ranging from the mild 'damn', 'hell', and his favourite 'crap' to taboo words and blasphemies against the Deity. Listening to his colourful assortment of curse words, Big Mama admonishes him not to 'talk that way', but he bellows: 'I'll talk like I want . . . and anybody here that don't like it knows what they can do' (50). Big Daddy's speeches pulsate with obsessive repetitions that 'imitate the very mood and rhythms of . . . sexual intercourse', according to Dan Isaac (273) – 'All that stuff is bull, bull, bull!' (62) or 'I was Ochello's partner and the place got bigger and bigger and bigger and bigger' (51). Relishing sexual metaphors, Daddy Pollitt asks if Brick's injury in the middle of the night was the result of 'jumping or humping' in search of 'a piece o' poon-tang' (49); speaking of his own sex life with Big Mama, he brags that he 'laid her, regular as a piston' (72). But now dreading sex with her, he vows to find a 'choice one', 'strip her', and 'hump her from hell to breakfast'. Like his father, Brick digs into the lexicon of vulgarity. In denying homoerotic feelings on his part, Brick damns all 'fairies' and 'fuckin' sissies . . . [and] Queers' (79).

Given *Cat*'s intense sexuality, the human body is a frequent topic of conversation as well as a powerful visual symbol. Though 'crippled', Brick has lost none of his good looks. 'I actually believe you've gotten better looking since you've gone on the bottle' (16), claims Maggie. Muscular, tanned, and youthful, Paul Newman's body in the 1958 film was foregrounded with close-up shots of his chest. Less age-proof, Maggie retains her looks but declares, 'My face looks strained, sometimes, but [. . .] men admire it [her figure] . . . and last week . . . everywhere that I went men's eyes burned holes in my clothes' (30). James Earl Jones's Big Daddy was guilty of 'ogling Maggie from eyebrows to toenails' (Teachout). Exuding sexuality, Lindsay Duncan's Maggie (London, 1988) had 'carnivorous lips' and a 'debutante's sway' (Ratcliffe, 140). But beneath these external references to Brick's and Maggie's bodies lie sexual anxieties/confusions. Unable to discuss homosexual desire, a taboo subject, directly on stage in 1955 America, Williams projected the psychological torments and transformations gays experienced by showing their bodies realigned, torn apart, reconfigured, or deconstructed in a homophobic America.

According to David Savran, Williams used the language of fragmentation and marginalisation to 'characterise the inhabitants of the [homosexual] closet'. From his gay perspective he 'configure[ed] the female body constantly in danger of disintegrating' and in the process, 'throughout Act One Williams's stage directions teem with Maggie's body parts, arms, hands, throat'. By doing this, Savran contends, Williams was able to dramatise the homoerotic. Disengaged from a heterosexual, binary anatomy, 'the absent phallus [Skipper] becomes reinscribed in Maggie's body and allows her to be produced as the object of [male] desire'. As a result, Brick turns into 'the castrated male and Maggie the phallic woman'.

Animal imagery, another of Williams's staples, further helps to explain his characters. If the cat is Maggie's totem animal, capturing her wily tenacity, her nervous energy, and her fears, the elephant is Big Daddy's emblem of virility. More commonly, though, animal images evoke the cruelty or foolishness that transform human beings into grotesque creatures. Mae is cast as the 'monster of fertility' (10–11), and her five children as 'no-neck monsters' (7), who bear names (Dixie, Trixie, Buster, Sonny, Polly) that 'sound like four dogs and a parrot' (22). Big Daddy castigates the lot as 'little monkies'. Because of their beast-like behaviour, Gooper's brood descends down the great chain of being. His own name suggests a deformed creature with bulging body parts. Like a snake, Mae is heard 'hissing' at Maggie (114). Big Mama is comically likened to a charging rhino, 'an old bulldog' (25), or a pig when she grunts. In her patterned chiffon, she has 'the markings of some massive animal' (43). When the Pollitt clan gathers, 'the room sounds like a great aviary' (42). Big Daddy 'grins . . . wolfishly' about his future sex life.

Characteristic of Williams's plays, sickness symbolises greed, mendacity, and/or betrayals. Though the least mendacious character in *Cat*, Big Daddy nonetheless has an unquenchable desire for power and land. His inoperable intestinal cancer may possibly symbolise his aggressiveness and his own past homosexual relationships. A sick patriarch, a sick Big Daddy, suggests the entire family is ill. His sickness is both literal and symbolic: 'it's spread all through him and it's attacked all his vital organs, including the kidneys and right now he is sinking into uremia . . . poisoning of the whole system due to the failure of the body to eliminate its poisons', says Gooper (104). Brick is 'crippled' because of a jumping accident, but his physical malady suggests a deeper psychological and spiritual malaise – he is sick from guilt and cover-ups. (Maggie opens 'the sore of his friendship with Skipper'.) But his broken ankle is only the current manifestation of a lingering illness. As Big Mama recounts, Skipper's sickness affected Brick's crippling:

> That boy is just broken up over Skipper's death. You know how poor Skipper died. They gave him a big, big dose of that sodium amytal stuff . . . give him another big, big dose of it at the hospital and that and all of the alcohol in his system . . . just proved too much for his heart . . . I'm scared of needles! I'm more scared of a needle than the knife . . . I think more people have been needled out of this world than – (93).

Considering Big Mama's fear of injections (and Williams's, as in *Memoirs*, 232), it is frightening to think that 'Mae took a course in nursing during the war' (99). Everyone in *Cat* is in danger of being injected – Big Daddy will need a hypo and Maggie acts like a '*child about to be stabbed with a vaccination needle*' after dealing with Big Mama (29). Big Mama herself is in danger of having a stroke because of her excitability. When the family breaks the news to her about Big Daddy's cancer, she thinks they are looking at her 'as if big drops of blood had broken out on m'face' (95); her high blood pressure is 'riskin' a stroke' (70). Later, Big Daddy warns her 'you better watch that, Big Mama. A stroke is a bad way to go' (111). The fireworks display in honour of Big Daddy's fatal birthday party makes her 'feel a little bit sick at my stomach' (89), possibly her sympathy pains for Big Daddy's gastro-intestinal ravages. Given his alcoholism, Brick might be heading for similar medical problems. Countering all these dire medical reports, Maggie claims she is pregnant after consulting 'one of the best gynecologists in the South' (113).

Fire imagery also spreads through *Cat*. Helping to visualise the dangers that engulf the characters, Maggie describes Brick's desire for Skipper and its devastating effect on their marriage as a house fire: 'When something is festering in your memory or your imagination . . . it's just like shutting a door and locking it on a house on fire in hope of forgetting that the house is burning. But not facing a fire doesn't put it out' (18). Brick mockingly copies his wife's fire imagery: 'Lately, your voice always sounds like you'd been running upstairs to warn somebody that the house was on fire' (23). Big Daddy similarly characterises Big Mama's European passions as 'just a big fire sale, the whole fuckin' thing' (57–8). Ironically, his own house, crammed full of Big Mama's European purchases, is ripe for a fire sale. Bursts of fireworks, an omen of Big Daddy's last birthday, suggest that the Pollitts are being consumed by the flames of mendacity and hate. Yet fire both punishes and cleans a house. The fireworks tolling Big Daddy's death might be interpreted as a birth announcement, thanks to Maggie's 'lie'.

Through its imagery, *Cat* shows how characters are trapped claustrophobically because of guilt, hate, and estrangement. Big Daddy and Brick, for example, 'talk, in circles' (68) and behind 'closed doors' (55). Without love, Brick and Maggie are 'caught in the same cage'. Ironically, Big Daddy's infamous final joke is about elephants in 'adjoinin' cages' (109). Maggie tells Brick that 'death was the only icebox' that could hold his epic love for Skipper, and Big Daddy warns his son that he'll hear 'a lot . . . of unbroken quiet . . . in the grave' (60). Brick sees himself as trapped, having to sit 'in a glass box watching games' he could not play (76). Entrapment becomes cosmic alienation as well. Thinking he is cancer-free, Big Daddy claims he has 'come back' from 'the other side of the moon, death's country' (80). That's the place where light is shut out, and darkness is sealed in. Unfortunately, Mae cannot escape this dark prison either; she stands 'on the wrong side of the moon' (55), according to Big Daddy.

Characters

Creating memorable characters was Williams's trademark. 'My characters make my plays' ('Critic Says', 77), he declared. In *Cat* he used psychological realism to develop characters who act out of strong emotions and deep conflicts. Williams wanted his characters to tell their life stories; in fact, *Cat* is made up of the characters' confessional monologues. But Brick, Maggie, and Big Daddy also reveal various sides of Williams's own personality, his inner life. He seems torn between the melancholy Brick and the sexually frustrated Maggie.

Brick

Charles May rightly identifies Brick as 'the ambiguous center for all the characters' because he functions as 'the catalyst for the dramatic action'. We often see things from Brick's perspective. He is a central player in the confrontations with Maggie in Act One and with Big Daddy in Act Two. Much of *Cat* explores Brick's demons and how he battles with them. Cool, depressed, and detached – adjectives that describe him and how he communicates (or fails to do so). Leading a dissipated life, Brick is a drunk who refuses to go to bed with his wife and denies complicity in Skipper's death. He fights being vulnerable, but his behaviour says otherwise. 'Give me my crutch', he orders Maggie. The crutch is Brick's signifier. Frequently losing his balance and crawling along the floor, Brick is a broken man – emotionally, physically, sexually, and spiritually. He uses his crutch as an escape, a weapon, and an emblem of his sexual/ psychic wounds. It speaks for him when he strikes out at Maggie.

Like Blanche in *Streetcar* and Tom in *The Glass Menagerie*, Brick mirrors Williams's own sexual/psychic struggles. He suffers from the same 'blue devils', fits of depression, that plagued Williams. Moreover, as Margaret Bradham Thornton observes, 'Williams was a part of a private world of gay men who lived an existence secret from their families. In [*Cat*] he creates men who have had unusually close relationships with other men, who marry, and then have conflicts over the two relationships' (9). Just like Williams's friends, Brick is the estranged husband who protects his sexual identity in a repressive society that would condemn him if he dared to reveal his secret. Brick thus fulfilled a key role for Williams as his creator. He allowed Williams to express his gay subjectivity without 'coming out' as a gay playwright', according to Dean Shackelford (106–7). Following the 1974 revival, Clive Barnes thought that *Cat* was Williams's 'most honest play'. Williams admitted it was his favourite. In order to write any play, Williams claimed he had to fall in love with one of the characters. In *Cat*, Brick is the object of masculine beauty for Williams; 'a gay playwright [thus] places himself and his own gaze at the center' of *Cat*, according to Shackleford. In the 1988 London *Cat*, Ian Charleson's Brick had 'the sort of charismatic male divinity Williams must have had in mind when writing the part' (Edwards, 136). Furthermore, as George Crandell maintains, Brick becomes the spokesperson for Williams the artist, crying out for attention and connection (438).

Brick plays other key roles. He is the prodigal son (eight years younger than Gooper) who throws his father's inheritance away. Once a conquering hero, Brick is the fallen, failed athlete reduced to announcing games rather than starring in them, and he forsakes even this job. (Ironically, he may be named after Jack 'Bud' Pollitt, a football star and acquaintance of Williams at the University of Missouri in 1931–2 [Hale].) An alcoholic, he chases the click that will bring him into oblivion. The large console on stage contains his liquor, television, radio, and a hi-fi, all the 'comforts and illusions' (Williams, 'Notes for the Designer', 6) protecting him from self and the truth. The 1958 film of *Cat* included so much drinking that it is listed in the top 100 booziest movies ever made. Once a charming, confident lover, Brick is now a used-up stud gone dry. As we saw, Mae and Gooper label him a sexual deviate. Several classical myths further illuminate Brick's role. Achilles' legendary friendship with Patroclus may be a prototype for his affection for Skipper (Hurd); and Brick is certainly a broken Apollo (Thompson, 70). Drinking '*Echo Spring*' (Southern Bourbon) associates him with another classical figure, Narcissus, the beautiful young man who, seeing his reflection in a pool, jumped in and drowned. As Crandell argues, Brick's behaviour is 'fairly typical of the Narcissistic personality' (434) – self-love, rage, lack of empathy for others, need for constant attention. More favourably, Brick has been seen as the Sartrean existential hero trying to determine his own identity (Bak). But his sense of truthfulness is, at best, highly controversial.

Unquestionably, Brick is one of Williams's most complex and conflicted characters who raises key questions about mendacity – with others and with himself, including: (1) Is he gay? (2) What was his relationship with Skipper?

(1) *Cat* is problematic about Brick's sexual identity. Williams's own views on the subject are ambiguous, even contradictory. In the most famous stage direction in the play, Williams confessed, '*The bird that I hope to catch in the net of this play is not the solution of one man's psychological problem . . .* [but the] *interplay of live human beings in the thundercloud of a common crisis. Some mystery should be left in the revelation of character in a play*' (77). Rebutting the *New York Herald Tribune* critic Walter Kerr who attacked him for writing about a homosexual, Williams declared: 'Frankly, I don't want people to leave the Morosco Theatre knowing everything about all the characters they witnessed that night in violent interplay' ('Critic Says', 78). Three years after *Cat* opened, Williams again waffled in an interview with Arthur Walters: 'Brick is definitely not a homosexual. Brick's self pity and recourse to the bottle are not the result of a guilty conscience in that regard. . . . He feels that the collapse and premature death of . . . Skipper . . . have been caused by unjust attacks against his moral character made by outsiders, including Maggie. . . . It is his bitterness at Skipper's tragedy that has caused Brick to turn against his wife . . . although I do suggest that . . . there might have been unrealized abnormal tendencies' (Walters, 73).

The 'mystery' of Brick's sexual identity is at the heart of *Cat*. On the one hand, he never admits physical desire for Skipper and demonises homosexuals. Yet he describes intimate moments he shared with Skipper. Brick might not know or understand what homosexuality really is, dissociating his homosocial relationship with Skipper from a homosexual one. Or perhaps, though, he might be lying to himself. In that case, Brick's homophobia might be the mendacious façade for his true feelings about Skipper; he might be experiencing 'homosexual panic', the fear that he does in fact desire Skipper. This panic unsettles his self-image as the strong, heterosexual athlete hero (Arrell, 60–72). He is furious at Maggie for even suggesting to Skipper that he was gay. Or, more damningly, he might 'fail ethically because, finally, he seems willing to deny his nature and a lover before forfeiting his comfortable position in the world' (Paller, 112).

Each of these interpretations speaks to Williams's precarious position of couching Brick's sexual problems as 'mysteries'. In a 'Note of Explanation' (1955), he declared, 'I don't believe that a conversation, however revelatory, ever effects so immediate a change in heart or even conduct of a person in Brick's state of spiritual disrepair.' As we saw, Williams could not offend conservative Broadway audiences who supported his work. But by presenting Brick as 'conflicted', Williams was able to keep his character's sexual identity a mystery, leaving audiences wondering, asking probing questions. The problematic ending that has disturbed so many critics, therefore, may be Williams's way of drawing audiences into Brick's moral paralysis, the world of his mendacity and that of others. Ultimately, though, directors and actors have great leeway in how they represent Brick.

(2) There seems to be little doubt that Skipper was gay and that he desired Brick's love. But Brick, like Blanche DuBois in *Streetcar*, rejects a homosexual who then commits suicide. This surely is a sign of Brick's deliberate cruelty, the worst sin for Williams. Moreover, Brick does not accept his responsibility for Skipper's death. It leaves him depressed and brings into question his maturity, his narcissism. By idealising Skipper's friendship, Brick lessens every other relationship, for example his marriage to Maggie and his obligations to Big Daddy. He refuses to enter the adult world with its responsibilities to father children and to run his father's estate. Instead, he prefers to 'foster the illusion that [he and Skipper] are still boys' (Winchell, 704). In such a world, Brick can be as close to Skipper as he wishes. Their friendship is 'purged from any allusion to homosexuality' since they live in a world of 'prolonged adolescence' where 'homosocial discourse and activities are acceptable and free from any stain of sexual transgression' (Winchell, 705). In sum, Brick does not want to grow up; he still wants to run the football field with his best friend to the cheers of a fawning crowd – to be 'teammates forever' (38).

Maggie

Williams named the play in her honour. 'I am Maggie the Cat', she declares. In a letter to Lady Maria St Just, who inspired the role of Maggie (*Five O'Clock Angel*, 167) and to whom the play is dedicated, Williams insisted that Maggie was the central character. 'The story [in *Cat*] must be and remained the story of a strong determined creature

(Life! Maggie!) taking hold and gaining supremacy over and converting to her own purposes a broken, irresolute man' (*Five O'Clock Angel*, 110). Her final lines sum up her determination – 'Oh, you weak people, you weak, beautiful people! who give up with such grace. What you want is someone to – take hold of you. – Gently, gently with love hand your life back to you, like somethin' gold you let go of' (115). Dominating the stage in Act One, essentially a monologue lasting about an hour, Maggie battles fiercely throughout *Cat*, and is responsible for its startling revelation in Act Three.

She seems far removed from Williams's doomed Southern belles – Amanda, Blanche, or Alma. Instead, Maggie prowls with his more feisty heroines such as Serafina in *The Rose Tattoo*, the Princess in *Sweet Bird of Youth*, or even Myrtle in *Kingdom of Earth*. Like her namesake, Maggie is sleek, agile, tenacious, clever, and seductive; she can manoeuvre in tight places and claw her way to the top. She is both a sex-starved kitten and an alley fighter. She has the predatory instincts of an animal yet she is also the spirit of life and love in *Cat*. Even so, like many of Williams's women, Maggie fears losing her dreams. In *Cat* they include: (1) regaining Brick's love; (2) satisfying her sexual needs; and (3) receiving Big Daddy's inheritance by having a child with Brick. As Maggie strives to achieve these goals, we witness a woman who is lyrical, sexy, determined, and inherently decent.

Like Brick and Big Daddy, Maggie takes on several roles. Above all, she is a fighter/redeemer, resolved to overcome a husband's rejection, a family's scorn, and a life of poverty. While Brick is comfortable with 'the charm of the defeated', she is not. Nothing stands in her path. At one point, she grabs Brick's leg, allowing him to drag her across the stage, demonstrating that she will never let go of him, never stop loving him. She wants to save him from alcoholism; from his greedy sibling; and from consuming guilt over Skipper's death. She courageously tries to 'restore Brick's self-respect and faith in his manhood' (Adler, 19). Like Brick, she is surrounded by myths. She wins a 'Diana' trophy for archery (21) – a sign of her skill at identifying and attacking a target. In Greek legend, Diana was the huntress and protector of the woods. Evoking the classical goddess, Maggie sees herself as Brick's hunting partner and the protector of her husband's share in the Pollitt plantation. Combining her feline and mythic roles, Maggie is 'endowed with the animal sinuosity and instinctive tenacity of a cat [and] the athletic aggressiveness of the Roman Diana' (Thompson, 68), but, ironically, she is also linked to Artemis, the Greek counterpart of Diana, famous for chastity. Nevertheless, Maggie is determined to end the enforced chastity imposed on her by Brick.

As Williams emphasised, Maggie is the life-force in *Cat*. 'I am alive', she declares. She is a sexual dynamo, crying out for satisfaction. The empty bed, the centrepiece of the play, is her symbol of loneliness, sexual unfulfilment. She wants to reclaim it, make it her territory. A Southern Aphrodite, Maggie uses her beauty and charm to save her husband and dissuade Big Daddy from leaving the estate to Gooper. Portraying a woman in heat in 1955 was a daring move on Williams's part. Maggie's 'slip of ivory satin and lace' (7), her garter belt, her bracelets, her make-up rituals before the mirror, and her smoking, are signifiers of her sexual being. Her sexual identity points to how successful she could be as wife and mother. Moreover, she claims to bring 'life to this place that death has come in to' (115) by declaring she is going to produce a Pollitt heir. Maggie is thereby associated with renewal and redemption. A birth was associated with good fortune in the American South.

But only by dislodging Skipper's ghost from a place of prominence in Brick's heart and psyche can she give her husband a new identity/life. *Cat* is a play of triads, and the most significant is that of Brick, Maggie, and Skipper. Yet Maggie is a one-man woman. Brick's relationship with Skipper ostracises her as wife and woman; he has usurped her role as Brick's partner, turning her into the Other. When she and Brick 'double-dated at college' (37), she tells him 'it was more like a date between you and Skipper. Gladys and I were just sort of tagging along as if it was necessary to chaperone you!' (37). She uses her sex to counter Skipper's claims to Brick and so she can get her husband back to bed. Clearly, Maggie wanted to prove that Skipper was a homosexual to protect her marriage – 'Leave my husband alone.' But her breaking up Skipper's relationship with Brick has often elicited hostile responses. Robert F. Gross, for instance, insists that Maggie 'gives male bonding a guilty conscience' (21). Seeing her victory really as a defeat, Mark Winchell claims Williams is 'using a symbolic code to tell others in the audience that Brick is vicariously making love to Skipper when he "humps" Maggie in Straw and Ochello's bed' (712). Similarly, queer readings of the play by David Savran and Dean Shackleford conclude that Maggie's body becomes the site where Brick and Skipper can finally meet, thus restoring Skipper's place as Brick's partner. Ironically, in trying to make love to Skipper, Maggie allowed herself and Brick's best friend 'to dream it was you, both of us!' (35).

Undeniably, the most problematic issue in *Cat* is whether Maggie will be successful in getting Brick back to bed. Kazan pushed for such an ending to demonstrate that Maggie 'was sympathetic, but she was strong. This revision resulted from exactly the kind of dialectic process that had occurred in all of Williams's work with Kazan' (Murphy, 101).

Like Kazan, it was the way Hollywood wanted Williams's play to end in the 1958 film version. Resisting Kazan, Williams did not believe that Brick could undergo a complete transformation, which included an eager return to the marriage bed. Though Williams wrote a problematic, ambiguous conclusion, he nonetheless saw (and wanted) Maggie 'gaining supremacy'. Williams maintained that Brick 'will go back to Maggie for the sheer animal comfort of sexual release' and become 'her dependent' ('Critic Says', 78). And, to the very end of *Cat*, Williams portrays an invincible Maggie. She tells Brick, 'I am stronger than you . . . I can love you more truly.' Preparing for her long-postponed sexual conquest, she orders: 'Don't touch that pillow', and declares 'I know what to do.' In one of the most telling lines in the play, she insists, 'We're going to make the lie true' (115). 'Lie' is a loaded word in *Cat*, a play filled with dirty secrets, mendacity, scandals, misrepresentations, and false accusations/reports. Big Daddy himself attests to Maggie's redemptive fertility: 'Uh-huh, this girl has life in her body, that's no lie' (112). Yet by making a 'lie' (a child) into truth (reality), she hopes Brick will love her again, and that Skipper will be laid to rest in Brick's conscience. In the end, Maggie wants Brick to find the intimacy with her that he never did with Skipper or Big Daddy. Clearing this major hurdle, she will have 'convert[ed] a broken, irresolute man'.

But all Brick does is '*smil*[e] *with charming sadness*' (115). Is this the charm of the defeated that Maggie earlier attacked (i.e. that Brick has resolutely refused to accept a new identity as husband and father)? Williams's final stage direction, however, might translate into Brick's surrender to his wife's pleas. In response to Maggie's 'What do you say?' Brick answers, 'I don't say anything. I guess there's nothing to say.' What does Brick's 'nothing' signal – his capitulation and Maggie's triumph or her defeat and his victory in their concession to mutuality? Significantly, *Cat* ends with a question mark – 'Wouldn't it be funny if that was true?' – echoing Big Daddy's words about Big Mama's love (52), which do prove unshakably true. But controversy has swirled around any resolution – Brick's, Maggie's, Kazan's, or Williams's. For over five decades, critics have complained that Williams leaves us in a muddle. Some have assaulted him for being 'cowardly' and compromising his integrity as an artist. Others have, as we saw, supplied their version of a satisfactory closure, applauding Maggie's confidence or recuperating Brick's ideal lost teammate through a rebirth of Skipper in sex with Maggie. Yet, as productions of *Cat* over many decades and several continents have established, if anyone can make lies on the Pollitt plantation come true, it is Maggie, the agile cat.

Big Daddy

'I'm the boss here now', shouts Big Daddy thinking he has been spared from cancer. Bigger than life, Big Daddy is an epic figure, an icon of masculinity, vitality, and power. Williams claimed he bestowed 'a kingly magnitude' on him (*Memoirs*, 234), an image reinforced by Big Daddy in his belvedere like a god overseeing his empire in Act Three. The sheer strength of his will, even when he is in pain, drives *Cat*. The award-winning Broadway playwright Neil Simon exclaimed that '*Cat on a Hot Tin Roof* is a beautiful play, but it's got size to it, and there is no one around who does that anymore' (Bryer, 77). Big Daddy contributes immensely to the breadth and depth of Williams's play. Dressed in a white linen suit, smoking a huge cigar, he looks like the boss, the patriarch, a figure of authority and power. Physically large, robust actors such as Burl Ives, Charles Durning, or James Earl Jones have captured Big Daddy's dominating presence. Summarising the image Big Daddy creates, Ellen Donkin and Susan Clement point out:

> He effortlessly commands attention no matter where he goes, automatically positioning everyone around him as adjunct. His judgments are so powerful that they will resonate in everyone's head long after he is offstage. His presence is synonymous with control and power in ways that are profoundly linked to the social structures of marginalization and erasure. (3)

Everything about him is large. Big Daddy's possessions are big; he owns 'twenty-eight thousand acres of the richest land this side of the valley Nile' (74); his net worth comes 'close on ten million in cash an' blue-chip stocks'. (In the 2008 production, with a black cast, that sum had been increased to 80 million.) He is a force of nature. 'All of my life I been like a doubled-up fist . . . Poundin', smashin', drivin'!' (62). When he learns that his condition is not fatal, he declares, 'I want you to know that I breathed a sigh of relief almost as powerful as the Vicksburg tornado' (68). His commanding presence led Eric Bentley, in his review of the *Cat* premiere, to proclaim that 'Big Daddy is Williams's best male character' (29). Fortunately, director Elia Kazan prevailed over Williams to bring Big Daddy back in Act Three. According to Brenda Murphy, 'The most striking pictorial and kinetic statement Kazan encoded with the performance [of *Cat*] involved Big Daddy. He brought Big Daddy down front to address the audience four times' (116).

There were several Big Daddies in Williams's life. He grew up with a father, Cornelius Coffin (C.C.) Williams, who matched Big Daddy in size and intimidation. In fact, Williams admitted that *Cat* was about his relationship with his own father. The victim of Cornelius's frequent and sharp criticism, Williams tried to escape his father's harrowing questions and rages. Only later in his life did Williams turn towards his father with a kinder eye, evidenced in his late short story, 'The Man in the Overstuffed Chair'. Colby H. Kullman indentifies other big daddies in Williams's life – especially Kazan, who through his 'strong influence and constant expression of restraint and correction . . . cast and directed many of Williams's plays but also defined his characters, called for new lines, and changed endings' (668). The prototype for Big Daddy, though, was the father of one of Williams's close friends, Jordan Massee Senior, whom Williams had met in 1941 on St Simon's Island, off the coast of Georgia. According to Williams's biographer Lyle Leverich, Massee Senior was 'an imposing southern gentleman whose granddaughter had dubbed him "Big Daddy", [and] was a true raconteur and used expressions such as "nervous as a cat on a hot tin roof". . . . He was also endowed with an inexhaustible supply of stories about plantation life . . . Tom [Tennessee] was clearly in awe of the huge elder Massee in his white linen suit' (417).

   Big Daddy is deeply invested in the homo-/heterosexual politics of the play. He confesses that in his earlier years 'I bummed, I bummed this country till I was – ' and that he 'Slept in hobo jungles and railroad Y's and flophouses in all cities' (77). Big Daddy's 'bummed' carries overtones of sodomy. YMCAs and flophouses were also often locations of homosexual trysts. Because of his past sexual experience, Big Daddy for David Savran is a 'carrier of homosexuality' from Straw/Ochello to his son Brick. Yet Big Daddy's sexual alliances come at a price for some critics who see his intestinal cancer as a punishment for sodomy, linking him to Emiel Kroger, the old homosexual who suffers from the same malady in Williams's short story 'The Mysteries of the Joy Rio' (written in 1941; published in 1954). Despite Big Daddy's homoerotic past, he brims over with heterosexual hedonism. A keen observer of women's bodies, he regrets wasting his seed on Big Mama. 'They say you got just so many and each one is numbered' (65). Sounding like an older Stanley Kowalski, whose '*life has been pleasure with women, the giving and taking of it*' (*Streetcar*, Scene One), Big Daddy exults, 'I'm going to pick me a choice one . . . I'll strip her naked and smother her in minks and choke her with diamonds! Ha ha!' His joke about the elephant also advertises Big Daddy's libido; it is no coincidence that the creature has a large proboscis (phallic signifier), and that the husband bests the pachyderm in size and vigour.

   As patriarch, Big Daddy presides over one of the most dysfunctional families in American drama. Williams chose a symbolic time to stage *Cat*, Big Daddy's sixty-fifth birthday party. As in his other plays (*Glass Menagerie*, *Streetcar*, *Baby Doll*, etc.), a celebratory event turns into a ruined occasion. Rivalry, jealousy, greed, anger and backbiting eat up the mendacious Pollitt family. Gooper and his social-climbing wife scheme to gain control of the plantation even before Big Daddy dies. There is no fraternal love between Brick and Gooper. Sisters-in-law Mae and Maggie cat-fight throughout the play. Even though Big Daddy has not made a will, he has made up his mind. 'Who said I was "leaving the place" to Gooper or anybody. This is my sixty-fifth birthday! I got fifteen years or twenty years left in me! I'll outlive *you*! I'll bury you an' have to pay for your coffin', he shouts at Brick. He bluntly tells him, 'But why in hell . . . should I subsidize a fool on the bottle?' (74). Moreover, Big Daddy finds his grandchildren, sired by Gooper and breeder-wife Mae, obnoxious, intrusive, animal-like. He cannot even remember their names. Without necks, the children are unnatural, unlovable, unconnected to their patriarch. 'Their heads are directly connected to their stomachs, symbolizing their greed/appetite for food, attention, control' (Dukore, 97). Given Big Daddy's strong personality, however, it is no wonder that the Pollitts inherited his boisterous ways.

But they have not received his heart. That sensitive side of Big Daddy is revealed only in conversations with his favoured son Brick. Their confrontation is one of the most powerful father/son scenes in modern American drama, alongside those in Arthur Miller's *Death of a Salesman* and *All My Sons*, and Eugene O'Neill's *Long Day's Journey into Night*. Uncovering psychic wounds after years of 'talking in circles', Brick and Big Daddy at last bare their souls. Determined to save his son from self-destruction, Big Daddy declares, 'I am going to straighten you out' and probes Brick's façade with dagger-like accuracy. Trying to rouse Brick out of guilt and spiritual lethargy, Big Daddy gives him no opportunity to evade or downplay his questions. He refuses to allow Brick to use Maggie as an excuse for the way his relationship ended with Skipper and accuses Brick of the mendacity that will ruin his life. He wants Brick to grow up and accept the responsibility for Skipper's death. 'This disgust with mendacity is disgust with yourself' (84). His confrontation with Brick is fast-paced, throbbing, and, at times, physical. He pushes him down and takes his crutch. But when Brick '*loses his balance* [and] . . . *grabs the bed and drags himself up*', Big Daddy offers him his hand, which at first Brick rejects, but then a domineering father becomes the tender loving parent, declaring, '"Well I want yours. Git up!" *He draws him up, keeps an arm about him with concern and affection*' (80). Wanting to ease Brick's pain, physical and mental, Big Daddy welcomes the prodigal home to his arms.

Exploring how large issues such as love, life, and death are sewn into Big Daddy's character, *Cat* merits being seen as a tragedy of universal importance. Like a tragic protagonist, Big Daddy is proud, valiant; he is Williams's King Lear. Like Lear, he rages against his fate and the mortality it imposes on him. He battles death itself. His words to Brick, 'Life is important. There's nothing else to hold onto' (56), segue into the Dylan Thomas epigraph to *Cat*, 'father . . . Rage, rage against the dying of the light'. Ironically, the old man wants life, while his son Brick wants death (Dukore, 96). Big Daddy's imprecation, leaving his voice '*hoarse*' at the end of Act Two, can be likened to Lear's rage against injustice on the moor (Act Three, Scene One). In one of his most impassioned speeches, Big Daddy tragically comments on man's existential strength in the face of death:

> Ignorance – of mortality – is a comfort. A man don't have that comfort, he's the only living thing that conceives of death, that knows what it is. The others go without knowing which is the way that anything living should go, go without knowing, without any knowledge of it, and yet a pig squeals, but a man sometimes, he can keep a tight mouth about it. Sometimes he – (61)

Like King Lear, Big Daddy is surrounded by a family who betray him and by retainers (Reverend Tooker and Dr Baugh) who lie to him. Like Lear's eldest daughters, his rapacious children (Gooper, Mae, and their hoard) seek to rob him of his kingdom. As in *King Lear*, too, Williams included a raging storm in Act Three symbolising the larger cosmic forces that threaten Big Daddy's hold on the plantation, family, self, and life. But like Lear or Agamemnon, Big Daddy has a tragic flaw – his overweening pride, his defiant egotism. Believing he is cured, he struts across the stage thinking he is still boss. Speaking of Maggie and Mae, he declares: 'I got a surprise for those women. I'm not gonna let go for a long time yet if that's what *they're* waiting for' (53). But learning the truth about his medical condition, Big Daddy, like great tragic heroes, experiences the terror of a *peripetia*, a reversal of fortune. He leaves *Cat*, though, not as a defeated victim but as a force that death will have to reckon with.

Big Mama

Compared with her husband, Big Mama is a secondary character who seems easy to stereotype as clownish, a garrulous, hysterical woman, a coarse harridan. Yet she manifests a much more noble self and serves an important structural function in *Cat*. Like Maggie, she is married to a man who has rejected her, leaving her sexually starved. It has been four long years since Big Daddy has made love to her yet she remains loyal and caring. According to Nancy Tischler, Big Mama is a 'beautiful, strong study in unfilled love' (201). Even the thought of Big Daddy's having cancer evokes a painful gesture of love from her – '*Big Mama's chest heaves and she presses a fat fist to her mouth*' (50). Yet critics have seen her actions as a 'distorted manifestation' of Maggie's plight (Mayberry, 361). Obviously, she does not have Maggie's voice and spirit. In the hands of such veteran actresses as Judith Anderson, Kim Stanley, or Kate Reid, all of whom have tackled the role, Big Mama aspires to greater heights. Though she lacks her husband's overwhelming drive, she comes forward as his staunch supporter when, at the end of the play, she adopts his voice (including his swear words) to thwart Gooper and Mae's coup. She is a mix of laughter (often at her expense) and tears. Like so many women of her generation, she has sublimated her desires for the welfare of the family. Only a grandmother like Big Mama could think Gooper's brood was adorable. At the end of the play, when she asks if she can accompany Big Daddy to the belvedere and he allows her to, she reaches the apex of her life – to be valued as his caring wife.

Jack Straw, Peter Ochello and Skipper

The ghosts of these gay men haunt *Cat on a Hot Tin Roof*. Though they never appear on stage, these characters embody many of the sexual anxieties in *Cat* and express Williams's own problematic attitudes toward homosexuality. Straw, Ochello, and Skipper join the company of other absent, dead, gay characters in Williams whose claims on their respective plays long survive the grave – Allan Grey in *Streetcar*, Sebastian Veneble in *Suddenly Last Summer*, or Williams's favourite poet, Hart Crane in *Steps Must be Gentle*. To accommodate a homophobic Broadway theatre, and perhaps to assuage his own psyche (Paller), Williams erased the presence of gay characters, although through them he was able to voice the cries of a gay man. In his early and late plays, Williams had no qualms about including overtly gay characters on stage. His first gay character, a transvestite, Queenie, was one of the prisoners in *Not About Nightingales* (1938) and, towards the end of his career, Williams openly portrayed his homosexuality through the writer and his own personification, August, in *Something Cloudy, Something Clear* (1981). But none of his plays feature as many gay figures, absent or present, as does *Cat*.

The play was guardedly subversive for its times. Williams describes the gay couple of Straw and Ochello as 'a pair of old bachelors who shared this room all their lives together' and whose relationship 'must have involved a tenderness which was uncommon' ('Notes for the Designer'). John Clum stresses that Williams did not stereotype the pair but presented them as shrewd and sensitive, running a 'successful enterprise' and not 'self hating' like Skipper. Unlike his son's relationship with Skipper, Big Daddy was empowered through his partnership with Straw and Ochello. Keep in mind, though, that Williams's admiration for the couple's '*uncommon tenderness*' was expressed in an authorial stage direction, not in lines spoken before an audience. According to Savran, Williams thus 'reveals his homosexuality in extremely conflicted ways, as a focus of desire and scandal'. For example, his 'naming of these two characters . . . provide[d] significant insight into [Williams's] oblique way of approaching the subject of homosexuality' (Cañadas, 60). 'Straw' implies that as a homosexual 'he is a man of straw, a man of no substance'; and Ochello 'suggests the Italian word, *occhiello*, meaning "buttonhole" or "eyelet" '. In using these names, Williams 'introduced metaphoric allusions to male homosexuality [with] specific reference to sexual penetration' (Cañadas, 58).

Skipper is *Cat*'s sexual barometer. Emerging like a dangerous, guilty secret from Brick's past, he is at the centre of Brick's sexual, marital, and filial conflicts. As Brick's team/roommate at Ole Miss, Skipper evokes the glory days of their championship football careers. Brick emphatically denies that there was anything 'dirty' or 'sissie' about his friendship with Skipper. 'Skipper and me had a clean, true thing between us! – had a clean friendship. . . . Oh, once in a while he put his hand on my shoulder or I'd put mine on his, oh, maybe even, when we were touring the country in pro-football an' shared hotel-rooms we'd reach across the space between the two beds and shake hands to say goodnight' (81). By characterising his relationship as 'clean', 'the one', and 'pure', Brick, according to Judith Thompson, is equating it with 'philosophical terms of Platonic absolutes in Ideas of the Good, the Beautiful, the true'. Yet when Maggie agrees with Brick that his relationship with Skipper was ideal, as in Greek mythology, she ironically alludes to its homosexual undercurrents, since classical myths of male friendship were often rooted in homoerotic desire.

Like the names Williams uses for the 'old bachelors', 'Skipper' onomastically underscores the sexual tensions in *Cat* and those harrowing Williams himself. Paller argues that the name alludes to Kip Kiernan, the young Canadian dancer with whom Williams fell in love in the summer of 1940 in Provincetown, Massachusetts, but who broke his heart. Through Skipper, Williams 'was venting anger, exercising a psychological revenge on Kip Kiernan who died of a brain tumor'. Skipper's name also suggests boyhood immaturity, a sign, in terms of a 1955 psychotherapy, of latent homosexuality, according to Clum. Like Skipper, Brick refuses to grow up, to become a man, but, instead, is locked into a world of college football. The name 'Skipper' also links the nautical and the sexual, a crucial connection for Williams. Sailors were among the primary agents through whom he sought to fulfil his homoerotic desires and he often stereotypes them as sexualised figures – for example, *Glass Menagerie, Streetcar,*

Rose Tattoo, Something Cloudy. Finally, the name 'Skipper' physicalises Brick's condition. Hobbling along with his crutch, Brick becomes a skipper, a halting, wounded and defeated man (Kolin, 215).

Gooper and Mae

Grasping, vicious, and jealous, Gooper and Mae are foils to Brick and Maggie in Williams's dysfunctional family drama. Gooper is a fawning, untrustworthy son who has the audacity to tell Big Mama: 'I've always loved Big Daddy in my own quiet way. I have never made a show of it, and I know that Big Daddy has always been fond of me in a quiet way, too, and he never made a show of it neither' (102). Big Daddy has never been quiet about a thing, least of all his contempt for his elder son. 'I hate Gooper and Mae an' know that they hate me' (74). Gooper likes power, and he uses an assortment of stratagems to win Big Daddy's plantation, including making his children pawns, protecting Big Mama's interests, and denouncing Maggie's 'lie'. The noisy games that his 'monsters' play with their cap pistols comically parallel their father's assaults against Big Daddy and Brick. Even the name of Gooper's law partner – Tom Bullit – suggests the combative tactics he employs to secure Big Daddy's fortune for himself and his 'screamin' tribe' of monsters.

Gooper symbolises a character type Williams loathed – the American corporate man of the 1950s, the arch-conservative hypocrite. Big Daddy is the corporation Gooper wants to take over, but the old man is too shrewd to fool. When he sees the trusteeship papers scattered about Brick's room, knowing they really spell 'nothing', Gooper and Mae hurriedly gather them up, stage business that underscores their cover-ups and trickery. Behind everyone's back, Gooper has garnered a cache of damaging papers – power of attorney to 'cut off' Brick and Maggie's credit (10), a trusteeship for the estate, reports on Big Daddy's prognosis from Oschner's, and possibly a court order sentencing his younger brother to Rainbow Hill. As Maggie warns Brick, when news breaks about Big Daddy's fatal condition, 'Brother Man and his wife . . . hustl[ed] down here. . . . And why so many allusions have been made to Rainbow Hill lately. You know what Rainbow Hill is? Place that's famous for treatin' alcoholics an' dope fiends in the movies!' (10). If Gooper gains control of Big Daddy's fortune, Brick is destined to be locked up.

Biographically, Gooper evokes the fraternal tension and rivalry between Williams and his younger brother Dakin. A football star, military hero, and successful lawyer, Dakin was Cornelius Williams's favourite, while Tennessee was attacked as the Other. Just as Gooper intended to send Brick to Rainbow Hill, Dakin was responsible for committing his brother to the psychiatric ward of Barnes Hospital in St Louis in 1969 for alcohol and drug abuse. Tennessee's greatest fear was being committed, as his sister Rose was in the 1930s for her schizophrenia. Dakin was also responsible for having his brother buried in the place Tennessee despised – St Louis (or 'St Pollution', as he called it). A further (but kindly) parallel between Dakin and Gooper surfaces in Gooper's shrewd handling of money, a talent that Tennessee later benefited from when he sought his brother's advice on finding tax shelters. Dakin referred to himself as Tennessee's 'professional brother'. What Tennessee Williams did, then, in *Cat* was to switch his younger brother's life with Brick's older brother's resulting in an overall unflattering portrait of Dakin Williams (Spoto, *Kindness*).

Mae also embodies a character type frequently satirised by Williams – the social-climbing club woman whose passion is backbiting. The gossiping women in *The Rose Tattoo*, *Spring Storm*, or *Orpheus Descending* are Mae's compatriots, as are the sarcastic matrons in Williams's other plays. The snooty socialites who visit flophouses in *Fugitive Kind* (1937) or nursing homes in *This Is the Peaceable Kingdom* (1970) can also claim kinship with Mae. Unrelentingly repugnant, Mae is a fitting consort for her crafty husband. She is condescending to Big Mama, spiteful to Maggie and Brick, and stuffed with vanity. Yet Mae's looks belie her self-image. She is a 'monster of fertility'. In recent productions, she has been portrayed as a bottle-blonde loud-mouth. Appropriately, she comes from a family of crooks. Her 'ole Papa Flynn . . . barely escaped doing time in the Federal pen for shady manipulations on th' stock market' (13). Mae's father sounds like the swindlers arrested for their Ponzi schemes during the 2009 recession in America. Like her cheating father, Mae hopes to manipulate Big Daddy with her inflated stock of monsters. She is all those things that Maggie is not and vice versa.

Production History

Broadway

Cat premiered on Broadway at the Morosco Theatre on 24 March 1955 and ran until 17 November 1956, for a total of 694 performances. In a long line of Broadway premieres (*Glass Menagerie*, 1945; *Streetcar*, 1947; *Summer and Smoke*, 1948; *Rose Tattoo*, 1951; *Suddenly Last Summer*, 1958; *Sweet Bird of Youth* 1959; *Night of the Iguana*, 1961), *Cat* won Williams his second Pulitzer Prize and the New York Drama

Critics' Circle Award. Directed by Elia Kazan, with stage designs by Jo Mielziner and costumes by Lucinda Ballard, *Cat* boasted the same artistic team that helped Williams receive his first Pulitzer for *Streetcar* in 1947. The actors in *Cat* received undiminished praise. Barbara Bel Geddes was applauded for her 'authoritative and appealing' Maggie (McClain) and for her uncapped energy. Ben Gazzara's anguished Brick was 'handsome, melancholy, sensitive' (Atkinson), and even though he had to 'hop, fall and drag himself' across the stage, he did so with 'great grace' (Hawkins). His depressed Brick set the tone for later actors who took the role. Folk-singer Burl Ives, then forty-six years old and whose appearance in *Cat* was his first professional acting role, was hailed for his 'Rabelaisian' Big Daddy (Kerr), an 'unforgettable character' who questions an 'empty existence' (Coleman). Despite Big Daddy's charisma, many critics faulted his gratuitous and disturbing vulgarity. Kudos went to Mildred Dunnock (Linda Loman in *Death of a Salesman*) for her interpretation of Big Mama who 'has unexpected strength of character' (Atkinson) and was both 'fragile and touching' (Chapman). Pat Hingle's Gooper was suitably 'shifty' and shrewd, while Madeleine Sherwood as the venal and annoying Mae, oversaw 'the South's most horrifying children' (Hawkins).

Cat itself did not fare as well. While the critics handily recognised Williams's craftsmanship, his ability to offer shocking theatre, and his powerful dialogue, they found his new play 'tormented and tormenting' (Watts), a work that left audiences torn between 'frustration and revulsion' (McClain). Reviewers sensed that Kazan's changes were very much at odds with Williams's original script. Chapman complained that 'this time Williams has out-frustrated himself by failing to remain in control of his own play'. The critics also took Williams to task for *Cat*'s confusing characterisations, its unbelievable ending, and its revolting subject matter. Zeroing in on Brick's submerged homosexuality, Kerr complained that 'truth dodges around corners' and, consequently, judged *Cat* to be 'a flawed work', telling his readers: 'You will believe every word that is unspoken; and you may still long for some that seem not to be spoken.' He further warned that Williams's 'new play' lacks the 'staggering clarity of *Streetcar*'. Kerr's point of view was echoed over the next half century. Chapman, however, had no trouble speaking the unspeakable – Brick was a 'drunkard and a queer'. Overall, the problems the critics identified in the *Cat* premiere did not go away in the four major Broadway revivals the play has had up to 2009.

Over twenty years passed between the *Cat* premiere and its first Broadway revival. Initially performed at the American Shakespeare Festival in Stratford, Connecticut, in the summer of 1974, *Cat* opened at the ANTA Theatre on 24 September and closed on 8 February 1975 for a total of 160 performances. It was the first time Williams's definitive third act was staged in the United States, which incorporated Kazan's suggestion from the Broadway script to bring Big Daddy back in Act Three as well as changes Williams made in his original draft. In the process, Williams provided a 'more sensitive handling of the Brick and Maggie relationship' (Barnes), but the couple's reconciliation was still problematic. Snyder complained that in the new version of *Cat* 'there are no winners in this stark contest'. But the play had changed with the times. Homosexuality and women's sexual hunger were no longer as shocking as they were in 1955. Consequently, the emphasis fell on the family's deceit and hate – 'They all seem to have a cancer . . . eating away at their insides' (Probst).

If *Cat* itself still worried critics, this production nevertheless justified the high praise it earned. Deftly directed by Michael Kahn, it starred Elizabeth Ashley as Maggie; Keir Dullea as Brick; Fred Gwyne as Big Daddy; Kate Reid as Big Mama; Charles Siebert as Gooper and Joan Pape as Mae. Hands down, Ashley's Maggie was the star, a performance that received Williams's enthusiastic endorsement. Her Maggie was 'sensuous, wily, febrile, gallant, scorchingly Southern' (Kalem); she was the 'calculating bitch' as well as the 'ingenious' wife pleading for love (Wilson). Ashley's Maggie had displaced Brick as 'Williams's mouthpiece' (Sharp). On the other hand, Keir Dullea's Brick was disappointing. Playing a brooding Brick in the tradition of Gazzara and Newman, Dullea was no match for Ashley; he was underwhelmed. Injecting humour into Brick's role was a fresh interpretation, although Dullea's 'boyish laughter undercut' the play (Wilson). Gwyne's (Herman in the *Munsters*) Big Daddy was lanky, too young, and resembled Abraham Lincoln. Looking more like 'Tall Daddy' than Big Daddy, he lacked Burl Ives's 'roguish animal magnetism' (Kalem).

Thirty-five years after *Cat* premiered, the second Broadway revival made history, too. Howard Davies, who two years earlier had directed the play in London, brought *Cat* to the Eugene O'Neill Theatre in March 1990 using Williams's original script (1955), unedited by Kazan, for the first time on Broadway. The only changes Davies made were to keep the storm that Kazan inserted and to create a naturalistic set. Edwin Wilson glowingly wrote: 'This present version suggests Williams's first instincts about the play have been right after all.' William Henry agreed, claiming that there was now 'an altogether redemptive final scene'. Yet Jack Kroll insisted that the third act remained the 'weak limb' of the play.

There was nothing weak about their production; in fact Kathleen Turner and Charles Durning were credited for even mounting a second revival. With her 'throaty molasses voice' (Barnes), Turner's Maggie was the star of this *Cat*, a position Williams's original script intended. Flirtatious, determined, funny, and in love with her own sexuality, she 'prowls the stage in a second-skin slip, brushing her electric blond mane, tugging her nylons up her long legs, rigging her garter belt, applying mascara with spit and polish' (Kroll). Though Turner's cat was red hot, critics begged her to 'expose her emotions a shade more' (Wilson), especially in expressing her love for Brick. Durning's Big Daddy in his rumpled white suit, and vaudeville-sized cigar, was a 'hybrid of red-neck cut-up and aristocratic tragedian . . . a cracker barrel Lear and Falstaff in one' (Rich). Though he did not appear in Act Three, Durning's overwhelming presence as Big Daddy still dominated. Brick, played by Daniel Hugh Kelly, who paraded on stage in his bath towel, could have been more forceful, his anger more intense. Yet when he defended his relationship with Skipper, Kelly gave 'an impassioned hint of the noble figure who inspired worship from all who knew him' (Rich). According to Barnes, though, he never captured 'the complexity of a man who betrayed the thing he so loved and [also] possibly his own sexuality'. WABC TV's Joel Siegel bluntly announced: 'We realize he [Brick] is a homosexual even if he doesn't.' However brilliant the acting, this *Cat* also was dated for many critics: 'The 50s sexual tension now seems overripe; its hush-hush attitude toward cancer and scandal over childlessness seems almost quaint' (Winer, 358).

Like the second revival, the third revival of *Cat* came to Broadway, at the Music Box Theatre, on 3 November 2003, via London where the play had been directed by Anthony Page two years earlier, but with a different cast. Despite Page's superlative craft and an all-star cast, this revival was possibly the least successful of the four thus far. Under Page's direction, *Cat* manifested a tragic-comic spirit, mixing the hilarious with the mendacious, an apt combination for Williams's Southern grotesque. Yet Howard Kissel smarted from the 'sardonic, angry humor' in the play. Ned Beatty's Big Daddy was the driving force behind this *Cat* rather than Ashley Judd's Maggie. Despite having a smaller frame than Burt Ives or Charles Durning, Beatty was 'emotionally towering' (Murray); 'his prickly spirit catches all the cunning and cruelty of Big Daddy's vulgar energy' (Lahr). Ben Brantley exulted in Durning's performance, calling him a 'jig dancing bantam, a Napoleonic figure who has lulled himself into power'. Beatty's Big Daddy was likeable and feared at the same time. Though ravishingly beautiful, comic, and steely, Judd's Maggie 'showed little spontaneity' (Brantley); 'we don't see her suffocating under the threat of mendacity' (Murray). As Elyse Sommer put it, her Maggie 'was more fidgety and cool than fiercely hungry'. Maggie must show spite as well as sensitivity. Jason Patric's representation of Brick had a limited 'emotional range' – from amusement to annoyance (Murray). He 'compacts Brick into cement' for Lisa Schwarzbaum. In his confrontation with Beatty, Patric could not muster up the tension, hurt, and rage inside Brick. Even more disappointingly, he did not show 'the sexual ambiguity' that crippled Brick (Kissel). Assessing Judd and Patric's chemistry, Schwarzbaum bristled: 'She's unsure and he's unreceptive'. Surprisingly, Margo Martindale's Big Mama, a 'large woman whose charm bracelet jiggles along with the wattles under her chin', lifted the Pollitt matriarch above the bovine stereotype that has stamped the role (Lahr).

The fourth Broadway revival (6 March to 22 June 2008) was a landmark production. It was the first time a professional all-black cast staged *Cat* on Broadway and featured James Earl Jones (*Great White Hope*) as Big Daddy, Phylicia Rashad (television's *Bill Cosby Show*) as Big Mama, Terrence Howard (*Hustle and Flow*) as Brick, and Anika Noni Rose (*Dreamgirls*) as Maggie. Though the director Debbie Allen 'wisely pushes past the issue of race' (Brantley), her *Cat* should be seen in terms of contemporary racial issues. During the spring and summer of 2008, Barack Obama electrified the world in his bid to be the first African American president. Change had come to the American theatre too, as Broadway attracted more black audiences than ever before, eager to see their favourite black stars on stage. In fact, seventy to eighty per cent of the audiences for Allen's black *Cat* were African Americans (Fisher). Critics asked if indeed Broadway had gone black. There was no question that Williams's 'tale of dirty politics among a filthy right, white family in the Mississippi Delta in 1955 [was] universal enough to withstand color-blind treatment' (Portantiere). While she strove not to change Williams's language, Allen omitted the elephant joke and shifted the time-frame closer to 1990 when Ole Miss was no longer segregated (as it was in 1955). But she was faulted for the changes she made in Williams's dramaturgy – that is, for having a saxophonist play a bluesy score before each act and for placing the major characters in a confessional spotlight which 'carr[ies] us out of the naturalistic world of the play' (Denton). Even more seriously, though, she was accused of sentimentalising Williams's script, taking *Cat* down to the level of black sit-com and lowering its 'emotional intensity, bringing it down to a simmer' (Dziemianowicz).

That charge could not be levelled at James Earl Jones's Big Daddy. With his resounding baritone voice and impressive stature, Jones's Big Daddy made history. As Clive Barnes proclaimed, his 'portrayal [of Big Daddy] with bluster and subtlety . . . will surely leave a permanent mark on a role he both inhabits and embodies'. Terry Teachout declared, 'Jones gets Big Daddy – the pride, the contempt, the half-concealed terror.' 'I always wanted to play that cracker', Jones laughingly told ABC News

(Fisher). His intensity contrasted with Terrence Howard's soft spoken and, even more inebriated and detached, Brick. In sum, Howard's performance received mixed reviews. Portantiere hailed his Brick as one of the 'most complex, fully realized . . . human portrayals' which escaped 'the two note trap of playing him as "taciturn and angry" throughout . . . he is often smiling and even laughing over the absurdities' on the Pollitt estate. But Martin Denton complained that Howard 'plays up the detachment to a point where he's almost not there sometimes'. For Brantley, Howard 'is wearing his character's pain all too palpably, mopping his eyes and tearfully bleating his lines . . . [turning] Brick into a wounded boy instead of the willfully numbed creature he must be to challenge Big Daddy'.

Rose's Maggie more than compensated for Howard's anaesthetised performance. Dressed in a slinky slip and falling backwards onto a sumptuous bed to adjust her garter belt, Rose exuded a steamy sexuality, yet she possessed an incredible shrewdness, anticipating how to act and react to Brick's and his family's attacks. Brantley affirmed that Rose's Maggie 'pretty much owns the show when she is on stage'. However, Rose may have paid a price for Maggie's intensity. Dziemianowicz found that she 'shows us Maggie's sexual claims but not the vulnerability that would snare us as allies'. Williams's script asks a great deal from any actor playing Maggie; she has to be sexual, shrewd and honest, yet also reveal a hurting, vulnerable side. Rashad's Big Mama undeniably showed her character's pain. For Clive Barnes, she was 'broken and defiant', but she also provided 'tragic-comic relief as the shrill, underappreciated Big Mama'. Arrindell Anderson's Mae was 'too smart, too well put together' and too good-looking (Denton).

British productions

Two and a half years after the US debut, *Cat* premiered in Britain on 30 January 1958. Produced and directed by Peter Hall, this *Cat* starred the American actress Kim Stanley as Maggie, Paul Masse as Brick, and Leo McKern, wearing shoulder pads, as Big Daddy. Williams's play (with his original third act intact) had to be staged as a club performance – at the Comedy Theatre in London – because the Lord Chamberlain banned it from public theatres for its objectionable subject matter. Brick's latent homosexuality, as well as the sexual excesses of the other characters, stirred up a controversy in the United Kingdom. The reviewer for the *News Chronicle* hailed *Cat* as 'Williams's most enthralling play', while the *Daily Mail* critic found it Williams's 'cruellest but at times most dramatic' work (quoted in 'London Sees'). An unsigned reviewer for the *Times*, however, attacked *Cat* not so much for its homosexuality as for the 'animal ferocity' of its characters – 'they cease to resemble human beings'. According to the reviewer, Williams wrongly 'injected . . . into his leading characters . . . a special serum of greed, sexual frustration, sexual longing, and sexual uncertainty' that was lethal. Unfortunately, Stanley's 'touchingly shameless' Maggie lacked the 'wiry defiance' the character needed and McKern's Big Daddy was 'not ideally suited' to the part, 'playing it a little outside of the character'. Masse's Brick existed in 'a kind of gentle haze'. Though Kenneth Tynan recognised that *Cat* was 'a magnificent play', he faulted Hall for his 'lethargic pace; he stresses everything except what needs stressing' (203), and thought Masse was 'callow and absurdly unprepared for a searching test like Brick', while Stanley was a 'gifted' Maggie, though she lacked the tension the role demanded.

When Howard Davies's production of *Cat* opened in London on 17 February 1988 on the National Theatre's Lyttelton stage, it made British theatre history for several reasons. It was the first production of Williams's play in the United Kingdom for thirty years and the first time *Cat* was staged at a public theatre there. Ironically, as Davies's *Cat* was playing, the House of Lords was debating the so-called 'notorious' Clause 28, banning the funding of any art project that promoted homosexuality. Davies used Williams's restored original third act which presented a less sympathetic Maggie. Nonetheless, Lindsay Duncan's Maggie successfully competed with Eric Porter's Big Daddy. It would appear that Williams's *Cat* had improved with age. The critics lavished praise on him for his 'masterpiece', which 'demonstrates that poetry in the theatre does not necessarily consist of heightened language and blank verse' (King). The actors spoke Williams's poetry with an accurate Southern accent, though at times it was hard to understand for London audiences. For the most part, the acting was judged superlative. Looking 'even Burlier than Ives', Portman did not simply replicate his American counterpart but brought a new perspective to the role of Big Daddy – subtlety and 'an intelligence and worldliness that begin to look wise' (Ratcliffe). His grey locks and beard, powerful voice, and compassion made Porter stand out. With her golden hair and smooth white shoulders, Duncan represented a Maggie that looked a little too Hollywood – 'somewhere between Marilyn Monroe and Elizabeth Taylor' (Radin). Still, she was a 'triumphant mixture of sexual hunger, venomous wit, and smouldering defiance, not least in the way she angles her head when she announces her pregnancy as if to defy her husband or anyone else to say her nay' (Billington). Succumbing to Maggie's power, Ian Charleson (star of *Chariots of Fire*) played a brooding, even catatonic at times, Brick who, dressed in symbolic white silk pyjamas (Edwards), was lost in the illusory world Skipper represented but sprang to life at the very mention of his name (Kemp). The set with bamboo furniture, marble pillars, and swaying chandelier suggested a Delta awash in 'sweaty carnality' (Kemp). Davies's tragi-comic *Cat* ranks as possibly the most powerful production of Williams's play in the United Kingdom to date.

A well-received London revival of *Cat* was directed by Arthur Page at the Lyric Theatre in Shaftsbury Avenue, London, on 19 September 2001, and, as we saw, was taken to the United States in 2003. Unlike some earlier American revivals where humour was not a part of Williams's Delta tragedy, Page's stressed the 'Gothic comedy' and the 'supple sinuous nature of [Williams's] prose' (Billington). That 'barbed comedy' came out in exchanges between Brendan Fraser's Brick and Frances O'Connor's Maggie as well as in their caustic attacks on Mae, the children, and Gooper. As Maggie, O'Connor was sexual, witty, but also exhibited the 'frantic restlessness' of a frustrated wife and poverty-fearing daughter-in-law. Taylor found O'Connor 'pent up and wiry . . . a terrific performance'. Even though Fraser's Brick was in his cups, he never lost sight of the mendacity around him, even if at times he was 'bland' (Taylor). His wit, however, was searing, especially in his confrontation with Big Daddy. The 'paradox' of Brick's role for Taylor was that his anger at a 'corrupt society' was 'less a matter of principle than a frightened flight from his own rigid values'. Compared with earlier Big Daddys, the American actor Ned Beatty might not have been as 'earth-laden', but he nonetheless delivered a resonating performance as both boss and caring father.

Australia

The first Australian production of *Cat* was at Union Theatre in Melbourne on 21 October 1957. Union Theatre was run by the University of Melbourne at the time and became the precursor of the current Melbourne Theatre Company. Like premieres in New York and London, *Cat* stirred up controversy in Australia over its strong sexual content and language.

Productions of Cat *on non-English-speaking stages*

Along with *Streetcar* and *Glass Menagerie*, *Cat on a Hot Tin Roof* remains one of Williams's most popular plays worldwide. Within a few months of its American premiere in March 1955, the Swedish director Ake Falck mounted the first European production of *Cat* on 2 September at the City Theatre in Gothenburg. Starring Gunnel Brostrom as Maggie, Herman Ahlsell as Brick, Karen Kavli as Big Mama, and Kolbjorn Knudsen as Big Daddy, the play erupted into explosive confrontations that made it a box-office hit. Later that season, film and theatre director Ingmar Bergman also staged *Cat*, with a blond, muscular Max von Sydow as

Brick and a portly Benkt-Ake Benkstsson as Big Daddy. Though he admitted it was a 'huge success' (*Five O'Clock Angel*, 127), Williams was still not pleased with the production. Unfortunately, Bergman's *Cat* did not equal his Swedish premiere of *A Streetcar Named Desire* six years earlier in Gothenburg (Kolin, *Streetcar*).

The German premiere of *Cat* at Düsseldorf's Schauspielhaus on 26 November 1955 was heavily cut and bowdlerised (the elephant joke was omitted as well as numerous stage directions suggesting sexualised behaviour). Even though the translation considerably toned down Williams's script, there was 'enough sexual explicitness left to make the play sensational'. Reviewers could still stress, though, that 'voyeurs need not go because they would not be gratified'. So heavy was Brick's drinking that Alfons Neukirchen told his readers that after going to *Cat*, they would not touch a drink for three days'. Contextualising *Cat*, some critics diminished the play as a 'cheap dramatization of the Kinsey report' (Wolter, 17) countering the German view of America as wholesome and heroic. Even so, the play remained popular in Germany and Austria. As Sonja Luther points out, *Cat* saw an unparalleled revival through eight major productions in Vienna, Hanover, Wiesbaden, Dusseldorf, Salzburg, and so on during the 2004–5 season. The increased German interest in *Cat* reflected contemporary political concern, that is, discontent with America over the Iraq war as well as dissatisfaction with German politics (Luther, 60). In Andrea Breth's production in Vienna, for instance, an American flag was burned on top of Big Daddy's birthday cake. That is not to say that the sexual elements in *Cat* were censored or omitted. Burkhard C. Kosminski directed a risqué *Cat* on 24 September 2004 at the Düsseldorf Schauspielhaus, where Maggie 'walk[ed] around in her panties, bra, and high heels'.

The French premiere of *Cat* on 16 December 1957 at the Théâtre Antoine, directed by Peter Brook, elicited extremely angry reviews that faulted Williams for his subject matter and especially the conclusion of his play (Falb). As their American counterparts did, French critics found Brick's sexual identity troubling. Like the Swedish press, too, the French reviewers found *Cat* far less satisfactory than *Streetcar*. Yet despite such negative press, *Cat* had a run of 192 performances in Paris.

Not surprisingly, *Cat* did not come to Communist countries until many years after its New York premiere. *Cat* was not staged in the USSR until December 1981, twelve years after the Soviets had seen *Streetcar* and *Glass Menagerie*. No doubt the Soviet censors, like their American counterparts three decades earlier, were troubled by the play's strong sexual content, particularly its references to homosexuality. When *Cat* did open at the Mayakovsky Theatre in Moscow, the Soviet director in all likelihood received permission to stage the play 'to expose the degradation and decadence of the bourgeoise world' (Schmemann). Nonetheless, Soviet audiences responded positively to Williams's play and saw numerous comparisons between his work and Chekhov's – in tone, characterisation, and plot (the fragmentation of the family and the questions over inheritance). The Russian translator proclaimed that Williams was 'the biggest success since Chekhov' (quoted in Schmemann). This reaction is not surprising given Williams's life-long indebtedness to Chekhov, even adapting *The Seagull* (1896) in his *The Notebook of Trigorin* in 1981.

In May 1987, the Shanghai University Drama Institute staged a stirring *Cat on a Hot Tin Roof* (rendered *Cat on a Hot Iron Roof*), which may have been the earliest professional production of Williams's play in Communist China (Kolin and Shao, 19).

Adaptations of *Cat* for Film and television

The film adaptation (1958)

Three years after the Broadway premiere, MGM released the film adaptation of *Cat* in 1958. A huge box-office hit grossing ten million dollars in the United States alone, *Cat* was the most commercially successful film of any Williams play. Using the Kazan-influenced Broadway script, the director Richard Brooks (who in 1962 directed the film version of *Sweet Bird of Youth*) and James Poe co-wrote the MGM screenplay (108 minutes). The film featured two sky-rocketing stars – Paul Newman as the arrogant, sullen, non-conformist Brick, a character type he would develop more fully in *Cool Hand Luke* and *The Hustler*, and a sensual, kittenish, yet aggressive twenty-six-year-old Elizabeth Taylor as Maggie who later played the seductive and wily queen in *Cleopatra* (1964). Together they carried audiences into the steamy world of passion that the trailers promised. Posters in the United Kingdom and America showed Taylor lying, longingly, on a big brass bed or peering, like a prisoner, between the bars of the headboard, begging for sexual satisfaction. Reprising his Broadway role as Big Daddy, Burl Ives again won raves for his boisterous interpretation, but he got much closer to his estranged son Brick in the film than he did in Williams's play. The film was nominated for six Oscars but, unfortunately, did not win any.

The MGM *Cat* was a provocative film in 1958, and even today retains sensational qualities. The reviewer for *Harrison's Report* observed, 'Some slight and necessary changes have been made in the story to clean it up for the film version, but the considerable talk about sex is as frank and forthright as anything ever heard in a motion picture' (quoted in Palmer and Bray, 174–5). Brooks was faced with the thorny problem of sanitising Williams's script while still being faithful to his intentions. To accommodate Hollywood censors, and pass the Production Code, Brooks severely muted or veiled any references to homosexuality. Brick's major problem in the film was not his sexual identity but his estrangement from Big Daddy (Spoto, 'Commentary'). Family problems became the leading theme in the film version of *Cat*.

While Skipper does not appear in Brooks's film, he was nevertheless transformed from the closet gay into the unrepentant stud. Audiences are led to believe that Maggie tried to seduce or was nearly seduced by Brick's best friend. Going to Skipper's hotel room, she reports to Brick: 'He kissed me. That was the first time he'd ever touched me. And then I knew what I was gonna do. I'd get rid of Skipper. I'd show Brick that their deep true friendship was a big lie. I'd provide it by showin' that Skipper would make love to the wife of his best friend. He didn't need any coaxin'. He was more than willin'. He even seemed to have the same idea.' Maggie then tells Brick that 'Skipper was no good' and that 'Without you Skipper was nothing'. Celebrating heterosexual marriage, the film supplied a conventional Hollywood happy ending. Brick hobbles upstairs to the bedroom, and insists that Maggie join him. To which Taylor's Maggie confidently, and loudly, sounds off, 'Yes, sir.' The film closes with Taylor at the bedroom door as Brick declares, 'Maggie, we are through with lies and liars in this house. Lock the door.' Brooks left no doubt that Maggie's 'lie' will come true. While Brooks created a box-office sensation, Williams claimed that the film was not faithful to his characterisation of Brick and Maggie.

Although Brooks made substantial changes to Williams's play, he nevertheless built upon its formidable cinematic qualities. Consistent with MGM's action-packed films, he opened *Cat* up by including several new sets where we hear Hollywood dialogue and witness additional action. A pre-opening scene shows a drunken Brick jumping hurdles in the dark at his high school athletic field to the sound of cheering crowds, but when he stumbles and breaks his ankle, the camera pans to an empty, silent stadium. From Brick's midnight run, *Cat* moves to the airfield where Big Daddy returns home from the Oschner clinic and is driven by Maggie to his mansion via his horse farm. His birthday dinner is outside on the lawn, complete with the caterwauling of Gooper's no-neck offspring. After telling Big Daddy the truth in Act Two, Brick tries to leave the estate, but his car gets stuck in the mud on a stormy night; he sits in an open convertible, rain pelting him until Maggie comes to the rescue. In Act Three, Brooks moves to the basement of the mansion where, amid cobwebs hanging over the Pollitt's possessions, an emotional conversation occurs between father and son. Retreating there to kill his pain with booze, but refusing the injection that Brick wants to administer, Big Daddy bonds with his son, asking, 'Why didn't you come to me . . . and not Skipper?' To which Newman's Brick confesses, 'All I wanted was a father, not a boss.' Brooks makes a powerful statement about Brick's destructive self-image and his failed relationship with Big Daddy when Newman tears apart a large poster of him in his college football uniform hanging on the basement wall.

Television adaptations

A trendy made-for-television *Cat on a Hot Tin Roof*, produced by Laurence Olivier, appeared on NBC television, 6 December 1976. Although Olivier attempted to restore Williams's original script, his *Cat* had to be trimmed into six short scenes (100 minutes) to accommodate commercials, lessening the emotional effect of the play. According to Hal Erickson, Olivier's production was 'more sexually explicit than the censor-driven 1958 Hollywood version, but [it] wasn't quite as strong dramatically despite its powerhouse cast'. Olivier's Big Daddy was very different from Burl Ives's interpretation of the role. Dressed in a tailored white linen suit and with his coiffed white hair and moustache, Olivier looked more like a stately elder Mark Twain or slimmer Colonel Sanders projecting an aristocratic Big Daddy, not the self-made, coarse man Williams imagined. According to John O'Connor, Olivier's Big Daddy 'has been artistically castrated. His language has been toned down, his off-color jokes have been eliminated, his incorrigible lustfulness has been diluted' (D: 29). Big Daddy's plantation, too, underwent remodelling. In Olivier's version, it became an elegant mansion with exquisite furniture, crystal chandeliers, and white-jacketed servants evoking the lavish homes in such television epics as *Dallas* or *Dynasty*.

The husband-and-wife team of Natalie Wood and Robert Wagner were (mis)cast as Maggie and Brick. While critics praised Wood for her sensuality and sincerity; O'Connor, however, faulted her for 'wielding a cigarette, [that] seems to be offering a campy imitation of Bette Davis'. Wagner was not up to the role and was compared to a soap-opera actor. At forty-six, he was older and less passionate than Newman's thirtyish Brick. Regrettably, there were few sparks in his conversations with Maggie. Moreover, his confrontations with Olivier were tepid compared to Newman's with Ives's Big Daddy. As if symbolising his indolence, Wagner's Brick languished in a Victorian-era bath tub, a drink in his hand and his leg, in a partial cast, hanging over the side.

A second made-for-television *Cat* premiered on Showtime on 19 August 1984 and was re-broadcast on 24 June 1985 on PBS as part of the American Playhouse series. Using the uncensored text of *Cat* (1975), this televised version was classified as 'Family Drama', 'Psychological Drama', and 'Melodrama'. Directed by Jack Hofsiss (*Elephant Man*), the 1984 televised *Cat* was an improvement over Olivier's but still 'flounder[ed]' because of miscasting and misguided acting. According to O'Connor, Tommy Lee Jones (Brick) 'feels as though he is acting with a muzzle on'; his Brick was so forlorn, so removed from Maggie that there could be 'no ambiguity' about any future with her. While Jessica Lange portrayed Maggie's beauty and sensuality, she was 'curiously distant', behaving as if 'she hasn't been introduced to the rest of the cast'. A cool Brick works; a cool Maggie 'disables' the play. Lange made a better Blanche DuBois (2004) than she did a Maggie. Rip Torn's Big Daddy, however, received high marks for his intensity, and his interactions with Jones marked the highlight of the televised version, as in so many stage productions of *Cat*. But Torn's thick Southern accent was sometimes hard to understand. Kim Stanley, who played Maggie in the British premiere, brought an unexpected shrewdness to the role of Big Mama. Yet even with this star power, this televised *Cat* could not measure up to Williams's script.

Production History since 2013 (by Katherine Weiss)

Williams's Pulitzer Prize winning play, *Cat on a Hot Tin Roof*, has just had its fifth Broadway revival, but despite its excellent cast and creative team, the production was received by critics with little enthusiasm. The director Rob Ashford is best known for his Tony Award winning choreography for musicals. Hollywood star and Tony Award winning actor, Scarlett Johansson was cast as a red-headed Margaret Pollitt, and Tony Award winner Benjamin Walker was cast as the handsome but injured Brick.

Ben Brantley of the *New York Times* praised Johansson for being 'truly feline, and for a poor but well-brought-up debutante, her accent is strangely common'. He asserts that Johansson, whose 2010 Broadway debut in the role of Catherine in Arthur Miller's *A View from the Bridge* was sensational, has proved herself as a stage actor. Although admitting the production was flawed, Elisabeth Vincentelli of the *New York Post* also enjoyed the show, noting that while Johansson's 'performance often lacks nuance and starts off too shouty, the star eventually gain[ed] the confidence' she needed for the role.

Not all critics, however, agree with this assessment. Don Aucoin of the *Boston Globe* called the production a patchy, tepid revival at best, noting that there was not much 'chemistry' between Johansson and Walker. The lack of chemistry, he suggested, lies with Johansson as she was unable to create 'sufficient electricity to transfix us during the Maggie-centric first act'. Joe Dziemianowicz of the *New York Daily News* called the production a 'misguided new take', arguing that Johansson seemed 'overwhelmed' by the role. Even Brantley, who praised Johansson, admits that the acting in the production often lacked inspiration. Aucoin and Thom Geier of *Entertainment Weekly* found, too, that the set was too expansive, losing the claustrophobia the play requires.

Perhaps because of the overall weakness of the production, the ending of the play which reviewers of past productions have found so problematic was not commented on, nor was the production's interpretation dealt with. The trend to cast Hollywood stars in Williams's unforgettable female roles may be a mistake because too much weight is placed on a central character. Moreover, the depth required to play characters like Maggie, Amanda Wingfield, Blanche DuBois and Alexandra Del Lago is far beyond what the actor for the camera is accustomed to.

Notes

The notes below explain words and phrases from the play, with page numbers referencing the Student Editions published by Bloomsbury Methuen Drama.

page

10   *Great Smokies*: the Great Smokey Mountains in Tennessee were relatively cool in summer and a popular place for a holiday.

10   *Rainbow Hill*: sanitorium for alcoholics; the name suggests the popular 1940s song 'Somewhere Over the Rainbow'.

10   *AP/UP*: news wire services – Associated Press/United Press.

11   *lech*: to be sexually aroused.

12   *Books of Knowledge*: lavishly illustrated encyclopedias published by the Grolier Society in 1928 and intended for children.

13   *Spanish News*: inflated journalism associated with reporting events from the Spanish-American War, 1898; Williams's father, Cornelius Williams (C.C.), was a veteran of this war.

13   *Ward-Belmont*: a prestigious women's school in Nashville, Tennessee.

13   *Gayoso*: a fashionable, historic Memphis hotel; Williams's grandfather once resided there.

21   *Moon Lake*: a notorious resort, scene of gambling, prostitution, fights, and murders, twenty miles from Clarksdale. It is referred to in several of Williams's other plays: a cock-fighting event takes place there in *Summer and Smoke* and in *Streetcar* it is where Blanche's husband Allan Grey commits suicide.

22   *Shantung*: a type of silk imported from the Shantung Province of China and used in fine, lightweight men's and women's suits.

26   *Ochsner Clinic*: New Orleans hospital founded in 1942 and widely respected for its care of cancer and heart patients. (Williams was treated there for a heart ailment in 1954.)

27   *spastic colon*: colitis.

28   *Commercial Appeal*: Memphis newspaper.

33   *redneck*: derisive name for poor Southern white farmers, synonymous with bigot.

33   *overseer*: manager responsible for running a plantation.

34   *poor as Job's turkey*: emaciated, not fed; refers to someone with no money, after the impoverished patriarch in Scripture.

34   *Vogue*: popular women's magazine on fashion.

37   *Ole Miss*: affectionate name for the University of Mississippi, located in Oxford, Faulkner's hometown, about sixty miles south of Memphis.

38   *Blackstone*: elegant Chicago hotel facing Lake Michigan.

38   *Dixie Stars*: appropriate team name since the South was the 'Land of Dixie'.

40   s*ashays*: to strut or to glide, often stepping sideways to emphasise self-confidence and grace.

41   *St Paul's*: an Episcopal church by that name in Columbus, Mississippi, where Williams was born.

41   *Tiffany*: Louis Comfort Tiffany (1848–1933) was a famous American designer, stained-glass artist and maker of highly decorative glass objects.

42   *Gus Hamma*: a Delta resident, also mentioned in the one-act *Last of My Solid Gold Watches* (1945), plays poker with C.C. (a reference to Williams's father).

44   *Dubonnet*: a sweet liqueur/cocktail made from wine and flavoured with spices.

44   *old fox teeth*: treacherous.

44   *horsin'*: fooling, joking around.

45   *Skinamarinka-do*: children's song with this ironic stanza, given Big Daddy's inevitable voyage to the dark side of the moon: 'I love you in the morning / And in the afternoon / I love you in the evening / And underneath the moon.'

47   *Loewenstein's*: Memphis department store.

47   *Stork/Reaper*: in folklore, the stork, a gawky bird, was said to deliver babies; the Grim Reaper is a personification of death.

49   *humping*: sexual intercourse.

49   *poon-tang*: vulgar word for female genitalia; also refers to sexual intercourse.

57   *Cook's Tour*: tour of the principal places of interest. Thomas Cook founded a travel agency in the nineteenth century which arranged tours and excursions. The agency continues to this day.

58   *blue-chip stocks*: shares in solid, established companies (Standard Oil, etc.) which often cost more but were thought the safest investments.

67   *Skid Row*: poorest section of a city where transients live, often on the streets.

68   *Vicksburg tornado*: a devastating natural disaster that hit the Mississippi river town on 5 December 1953; also the basis of an

influential investigative report – *The Child and His Family in Disaster: A Study of the Vicksburg Tornado.*

69   *all balled up*: to be confused, troubled, bungled or in a mess.

73   *Elks! Masons! Rotary!*: civic and quasi-religious organisations which stress the brotherhood of the members and are involved in charitable activities.

77   *hobo jungles*: large makeshift camps (tents, lean-tos) built by shiftless itinerants (hobos) who illegally stole rides aboard railroad trains during the Great Depression.

77   *Y's*: YMCAs.

78   *yellow dog freight car*: short-lived (1897–1903) Mississippi Delta Railroad, from Clarksdale to Yazoo City, known as the Yellow Dog; William C. Handy, founder of the blues, wrote a popular turn-of-the-twentieth-century song 'The Yellow Dog Blues'.

80   *pledge*: usually a college freshman who must undergo initiations before becoming a member of a fraternity. A fraternity is a social organisation of college men bonded together by tradition and ritual. Known as Greeks because their names came from Greek letters of the alphabet, fraternities had strict rules about dress codes, social events, living accommodation, etc. At the University of Missouri, Williams was a member of Alpha Tau Omega where he met fellow fraternity brother Jack Bud Pollitt, known as 'The Bull of the Ball'.

82   *shako*: bearskin cap popular in the 1930s and 1940s.

82   *moleskin*: heavy cotton fabric sheared to create a short pile on one side, like moleskin.

83   *bursitis*: inflammation, especially of elbows and knees.

84   *passing the buck*: dodging one's responsibility; US President Harry S. Truman (1945–52) had this sign on his desk – 'The Buck Stops Here'.

89   *abolition*: the abolition of slavery in 1863 in the United States; the Thirteenth Amendment to US Constitution.

89   *War between the States*: US Civil War, 1861–5.

90   *hoppin' John*: a Southern dish of black-eye peas and rice, sometimes with bacon grease and chopped onions; it is a Southern custom to eat black-eye peas on New Year's Day for good luck.

92   *Friar's Point*: community near Clarksdale, also mentioned in *Summer and Smoke.*

92   *chasuble*: garment like a poncho worn by Christian priests when celebrating the Eucharist.

Questions for Further Study

1 There are different types of mendacity in *Cat*. Identify three or four and provide examples from the play.
2 Where do we see Maggie at her most vulnerable and at her most powerful?
3 Does Brick change at the end of the play? Provide convincing reasons why or why not.
4 Where do we see Big Daddy as kind towards Brick besides giving him a helping hand in Act Two?
5 Sports play an important role in Brick's and Skipper's lives. How do sports reflect the larger issues of the play?
6 Identify other image patterns in *Cat* besides those discussed in the Introduction.
7 Where in *Cat* do we find references to the steamy, passionate South. How does the landscape reflect/symbolise the characters and conflicts in *Cat*?
8 Big Daddy comes back briefly in the third act. Should he? If yes, what impact does he have on the ending of the play?
9 Compare and contrast *Cat* as a tragedy with another Shakespearean tragedy besides *King Lear*, for example, *Macbeth*.
10 What roles do Reverend Tooker and Dr Baugh fill in the play? How and what does Williams comment on concerning religion and medicine through these characters?
11 There are several phone calls in *Cat*. How do they fit into the play – its themes, characters, symbols?
12 Williams was accused of introducing melodrama into *Cat* – the storms, the family feud, etc. How does the play still use these dramatic techniques but transcend them at the same time?
13 Find examples of Williams's use of the Southern Gothic in *Cat*. Explain how this Williams trademark combines the lyrical with the ugly.
14 Time as the enemy is one of Williams's most persistent themes. Discuss how this theme is foregrounded in *Cat* through the characters' narratives, props, and costumes.
15 Compare and contrast Maggie with another of William's heroines, such as Blanche in *Streetcar* or the Princess in *Sweet Bird of Youth*.
16 Assume you have been asked to cast the roles of Brick, Maggie, and Big Daddy for a revival of *Cat*. Identify and justify your choice of actors you believe are best suited for these parts. Do not select actors who have previously appeared in the play.

17 Dean Shackelford has claimed that Skipper is 'the central figure' in
    Cat. Do you agree or disagree? Summon up evidence from the play
    to defend your decision.
18 Discuss the importance of Williams's stage directions for an
    interpretation of *Cat*.
19 Directors have used productions of *Cat* to make political statements
    (e.g. Watergate mendacity). How might the play be a reflection of
    current political events in your country or in the world?
20 How might *Cat* be (re)designed today to reflect an internet culture?
    For instance, characters using BlackBerries, Blue-rays, etc.

Sweet Bird of Youth

commentary and notes by
KATHERINE WEISS

Plot

Act One

Scene One

Chance Wayne, a twenty-nine-year-old man whose good looks are fading, has returned to his birthplace, St Cloud, Florida, with an ageing movie star, Alexandra Del Lago, on Easter Sunday. While Del Lago sleeps, a coloured waiter, Fly, delivers a bottle of vodka and Bromo-Seltzer. Fly recognises Chance as the young man who used to take out Governor Boss Finley's daughter. Uncomfortable with being recognised, Chance offers Fly a large tip if he forgets he ever saw him.

However, word has already got out that Chance has returned to this Gulf Coast town. After Fly's departure, George Scudder, St Cloud's local doctor, arrives, trying to persuade Chance to leave at once. In the process, Scudder reveals two crucial events that have occurred while Chance has been away. The first is that Chance's mother has died. Although he attempted to locate Chance, Chance never received the letters the doctor sent. The church had to take up donations to have Mrs Wayne buried. The second event involves Heavenly Finley, Chance's young love. While Scudder does not reveal what has happened to Heavenly, he impresses on Chance that ever since he has become a 'criminal degenerate', he is not welcome in St Cloud. In fact, the doctor tells Chance that Boss Finley has vowed to have Chance castrated if he was ever to return to town. Before leaving, Scudder throws one more bit of devastating news Chance's way. Scudder and Heavenly will be married in a month's time.

Stunned, Chance calls Aunt Nonnie, his former ally and Heavenly's aunt; however, she is unable to speak to him openly on the phone. At this moment, Del Lago awakens, bewildered and needing oxygen. From her interaction with Chance, we learn that while fleeing from her failed comeback on screen, travelling incognito as the Princess Kosmonopolis, she picked up Chance at a beach resort in Palm Springs, Florida. He is essentially her gigolo. Yet Chance has not offered to be her driver and male companion merely for money. He has a plan to blackmail her. To execute his plan, he attempts to trick Del Lago into confessing to a federal offence on tape. Along with recalling her failed comeback, she, unknowingly, confides that she smuggled Moroccan hashish into the United States. However, Chance is unable to beat this 'monster'. She calls his bluff, forcing him to go to bed with her if he wants her to sign over her travellers' cheques and stand by a contract, which she drew up in Palm Springs, to introduce Chance into the film industry.

Scene Two

Having obeyed Del Lago, Chance is seen dressing as Del Lago signs her travellers' cheques. As she does this, she persuades Chance to tell her his life story as a screen test of sorts. The rest of the scene consists of Chance recollecting, and perhaps fabricating, a narrative of his past. We learn that Chance first left his birthplace at the age of nineteen. Initially, he appeared to have some success in minor roles in musicals and even appeared on the cover of *Life* magazine. However, as his luck waned, Chance began to prostitute himself before going into the Navy during the Korean War. While in the Navy, Chance suffered from nightmares and began to drink. He tells Del Lago that he hated the routine and discipline required of him in the Navy, and shortly after divulges that he 'cracked up' and was discharged. He returned to St Cloud but noticed a difference in the attitudes of the people who once admired him. For Chance, St Cloud was still a haven because Heavenly, his teenage love, whose nude photo he shows to Del Lago, lives there. Chance reveals, however, that even Heavenly's attitude towards him had changed; the last time he returned to St Cloud, Heavenly urged him to go away, calling him a liar.

After telling his life story to Del Lago, Chance discloses the later part of his plan. He needs the money and Del Lago's Cadillac to impress the people of St Cloud, and most of all Heavenly, convincing them that he is a success. Moreover, he wants Del Lago to arrange a talent show celebrating youth and declare Chance and Heavenly the winners so that they can leave for the West Coast together.

Act Two

Scene One

On the terrace of the Finley home, Boss Finley and George Scudder discuss how to handle Chance's return, particularly since Boss Finley will be holding a rally for the Youth for Tom Finley clubs to state his position on desegregation and the youth group's violent tactics. This rally will be televised at the same hotel where Chance and Del Lago are staying. During this, we learn that Boss Finley's grudge against Chance stems from the nude photograph of his daughter which unbeknown to Chance was circulated by the photographic shop clerk who made extra copies of it. As if this scandal were not enough, news of Heavenly's operation to cure her of the venereal disease she contracted from Chance, which was performed badly by Scudder and left Heavenly barren, has leaked out. As a result, Boss Finley has been heckled at previous rallies.

Tom Junior, Finley's violent son and president of the Youth for Tom Finley clubs, sees Aunt Nonnie run up the drive. Chance has driven up to the house in Del Lago's Cadillac and is calling out to Aunt Nonnie. Ignoring him, she runs to the house. Boss Finley and Tom Junior taunt the old woman for being gullible and having favoured Chance over other suitors. After Aunt Nonnie leaves, Tom Junior, when berated by his father for his promiscuity, confronts his father with his own promiscuity. Tom Junior informs Boss Finley that Miss Lucy, Boss's lover, ridicules him by claiming that he is 'too old for a lover' and has written this insult for all to see on the mirror of the ladies' room at the hotel. He, we learn, is not the only person who knows about Boss Finley's promiscuity. Heavenly, who enters reluctantly, scorns her father for his affair. She scolds him for trying to marry her to rich old men rather than allowing her to marry Chance, a boy she loved. Furthermore, she blames her father for Chance's moral decay. In his attempt to compete with these wealthy, ageing men, Chance tried his luck in Hollywood. Boss Finley now bares his plan to silence all rumours of Heavenly's impurity, which are damaging him politically, by having her stand beside him, in white, at the rally.

Scene Two

In the hotel cocktail lounge, an antebellum Southern belle with her index finger bandaged accuses Stuff, the bartender, of breaking her trust by telling others what she had written on the mirror of the ladies' room. Miss Lucy explains that Boss Finley brought her a brooch in an Easter egg. As she opened the velvet box in the egg and went to take out the diamond pin, Boss Finley shut the lid on her finger. Noticing a stranger in the bar and suspecting that he is the heckler, Miss Lucy seeks out revenge on her former lover. She promises to aid the Heckler, giving him a jacket and tie so that he will be able to enter the ballroom where the televised rally will take place.

Chance enters, but shortly after getting his martini, is called out to the royal grove and beach by Aunt Nonnie who wishes to speak to him. She urges Chance to leave town and stop dreaming of a future that will not come true. Taking a pill and washing it down with a drink, Chance reminisces over his stage debut and the loss of his virginity. Aunt Nonnie reminds Chance that rather than winning first or second place, as he says he did, he only received an honourable mention. Although Aunt Nonnie has tender memories of Chance, she is no longer charmed by him; she tells him that his real flaw is that he cannot confront his failures.

Once alone, Chance takes another pill. A small group Chance once socialised with spot him. The ladies in the group leave while their husbands, Scotty and Bud, remain. Taking advantage of his weakness, Scotty and Bud heckle Chance. Perhaps as a threat, Bud tells Chance of the emasculation of a black man – a fate that Chance will face if he remains in St Cloud. Insightfully, Chance condemns the racist act, calling castration a crime of 'sex-envy'. He also doubts that Heavenly will accompany her father in such a despicable rally.

Miss Lucy, attempting to ease the tension between Chance, Bud and Scotty, reveals that Dan Hatcher, the assistant manager of the hotel, saw Chance working in Palm Beach as a beach boy. Perhaps Chance's only friend in St Cloud, Miss Lucy, afraid of what will happen to Chance if he stays, offers to drive Chance to the airport. He turns her offer down.

Del Lago enters, dishevelled and high. She has had an epiphany. Chance's return to St Cloud has made her feel something tender for him and she wants him to help her be good and kind. Although Chance has no desire to leave with Del Lago, when he sees Tom Junior and Scotty, he is affectionate and kind to the ageing star, but only to save himself from imminent harm. Boss Finley enters, sees Chance, raises his cane and nearly strikes him before letting it drop. Stunned, Chance watches Heavenly go to the platform with her vicious father. All this, the Heckler witnesses.

Still by Chance's side, Del Lago is silenced by fear when Hatcher, Bud, Scotty and Tom Junior approach. She senses danger as the men try to convince Chance to step outside. He refuses, but in the course of this Tom Junior reveals that Chance polluted his sister with a venereal disease which he contracted from one of the many women who paid his way. Again, Del Lago tries to convince Chance to flee – the only action to take, she claims, after failure is flight. He does not, however, listen to her. Instead, he calls for a wheelchair to have her taken away. Miss Lucy and Stuff turn on the television to watch the rally. The back wall of the stage projects the image of Boss Finley, speaking and being humiliated by the Heckler who is dragged out and beaten. Heavenly is escorted out, weeping.

Act Three

Past midnight in the hotel room, Del Lago speaks to the operator trying to find a driver so that she can flee St Cloud. The rally has degenerated into a riot. Chance is seen briefly by the audience; as he hears others, he ducks into the shadows. Looking for Chance, Hatcher, Tom Junior, Bud and Scotty force their way into the hotel room and threaten Alexandra Del Lago with violence if she does not leave.

After they have left, Chance, who is shaken, makes his way to the room. There, he commits one more desperate act. He phones Sally Powers, a journalist and friend of Del Lago's, and attempts to have Del Lago praise him and Heavenly as new talent. However, Chance fails again. Del Lago learns that her comeback was not a failure and, caught up by the news, keeps Chance away from the phone; she does not mention him. After the phone call, they struggle, trying to get one another to look in the mirror. Del Lago taunts Chance with his ageing, his lack of achievement in contrast to hers and his crime towards Heavenly. He moves to strike her but instead punches himself in the stomach.

Following this struggle, a change occurs in Del Lago. She is fearful, lonely and tender, knowing that her comeback will not last and that time will destroy her eventually. Out of pity for herself and Chance, she again asks him to join her. He refuses in recognition of his doom and, once Del Lago departs, Chance with a '*sort of deathbed dignity*' (96) waits for Tom Junior and the other thugs to castrate him.

Commentary

Context

Sweet Bird of Youth comes from the middle period of Tennessee Williams's career. Williams met with great success in the 1940s to mid-1950s with *The Glass Menagerie* (1944), *A Streetcar Named Desire* (1947) and *Cat on a Hot Tin Roof* (1955). After his first two successes, Williams began writing 'a varied assortment of one-act plays and sketches', which, according to Drewey Wayne Gunn, would eventually become *Sweet Bird of Youth*. He points out that 'about 450 pages of manuscripts . . . remain from this incubatory stage' (Gunn, 26–7). Moreover, with *Sweet Bird of Youth*, Williams 'began a new process of trying out a "work in progress" in a regional or off-Broadway theatre, revising it heavily both during rehearsals and after he had had the benefit of a full production' (Murphy, 135).

In 1957, Williams's success was met with the disappointing reception of *Orpheus Descending* which opened in New York City in March. In May, his father died. Although his father was a source of pain and sorrow for Williams because he taunted his son for not being interested in sports and did not understand his desire to write, the failure of *Orpheus Descending* and of the death of Cornelius Coffin Williams led to feelings of depression. Shortly after the death of his father, Williams began to see a psychoanalyst.

The following two years proved to be much more productive. With the opening of *Garden District*, comprising *Suddenly Last Summer* and *Something Unspoken*, the London premiere of *Cat on a Hot Tin Roof* and other theatre activity in 1958, Williams stopped going to psychoanalysis and travelled to Europe in June. Once back in America, Williams and Elia Kazan began preparing for the Broadway debut of *Sweet Bird of Youth*. Elia Kazan, who had attended the try-outs in Coral Gables, Florida, directed the play and aided Williams in his revisions.

Williams's work has been compared both to his contemporaries and to playwrights of the past. Philip C. Kolin draws a link between Williams and Eugene O'Neill, claiming that O'Neill's *Desire Under the Elms* 'is something of a palimpsest in the Williams canon' (23). In Williams's *A Streetcar Named Desire*, *Kingdom of the Earth* and *Sweet Bird of Youth*, O'Neill's play can be found in similarities in plot, setting and in the biblical allusions. Kolin goes on to show that the character of Boss Finley may have stemmed from O'Neill's play. Ephraim Cabot, O'Neill's tyrannical

Puritan farmer, bears a striking resemblance to Williams's Boss Finley, as both struggle to maintain their power.

In addition to drawing on O'Neill's theatrical genius, Williams learned a great deal from William Faulkner, a novelist of the Southern Gothic tradition (see 251–2). Faulkner's novel of 1940, *The Hamlet*, which was made into the award-winning film *The Long, Hot Summer*, bears striking similarities to *Sweet Bird of Youth*. Boss Finley, for instance, may be based in part on Will Varner, the domineering father and corrupt businessman, who owns most of the small Mississippi town. Moreover, like Chance Wayne whose presence threatens the political stability of St Cloud, Ben Quick, an outsider trying to make a name for himself, threatens the stability of Varner's quiet Mississippi town and home because of his dangerous reputation as a barn burner. Interestingly, Martin Ritt's film of 1958 and Williams's play both starred Paul Newman as the outsider attempting to rise above his lower socio-economic background.

While in O'Neill and Faulkner Williams may have found his literary fathers, in William Inge, author of *Come Back, Little Sheba* (1950) and *Picnic* (1953), he found a kindred spirit. His close friendship and brief love affair with the playwright Inge had an impact on *Sweet Bird of Youth*. Ralph F. Voss shows that Williams's and Inge's careers in the world of theatre were similar in many ways. Both authors had won Pulitzer prizes, both worked with the director Elia Kazan and both wrote about sexuality in daring new ways. Williams and Inge often spoke about their work and read each other's plays, and thus ultimately influenced each other.

Other playwrights sharing the stage with Williams were Arthur Miller and Edward Albee, both of whom admired Williams. After seeing *A Streetcar Named Desire*, Miller 'was inspired to work even more precisely with his language in a play he was struggling with at the time' (Roudané, 2–3); this play would later turn into Miller's masterpiece *Death of a Salesman* (1949). As well as being drawn to the poetic language of Williams's plays, Miller shared with Williams a distrust of the so-called American Dream – a dream that was thinly disguised consumer capitalism. In addition to a critique of the American Dream, a theme that Albee in *The Zoo Story* (1959) and *Who's Afraid of Virginia Woolf?* (1962) also took up, these playwrights 'produced new and radical theater that challenged and undermined the Cold War order' (Savran, ix). All three playwrights worked to upset the political climate of the 1950s and 1960s, and Miller and Albee learned from Williams, who had been pushing the limits of theatre since 1944. By challenging the nuclear family, masculinity and sexuality, Williams, Miller and Albee attempted to dismantle the patriarchal, anti-communist sentiments and politics of 1950s and 1960s America.

Themes

'The Catastrophe of Success' and Sweet Bird of Youth

After the success of *The Glass Menagerie* and just days before he was to see his second Broadway play open, Williams wrote a bitter critique of success and the Hollywood Dream. This essay, 'The Catastrophe of Success', first appeared in the *New York Times* on 30 November 1947. Though he would go on to write *Sweet Bird of Youth* among several other successful plays, the importance of this essay is felt throughout his body of work and is crucial to understanding the themes of lost youth and broken dreams in *Sweet Bird of Youth*. In the essay, Williams begins to define his experience as 'not unique. Success has often come that abruptly into the lives of Americans. The Cinderella story is our favourite national myth, the cornerstone of the film industry if not of the Democracy itself' (*Glass Menagerie*, 99). By evoking the Cinderella story, Williams does more than argue that in America it was possible to move suddenly from rags to riches. He brings an awareness of class divisions when he claims that 'Hotel service is embarrassing [. . .] Nobody', he writes, 'should have to clean up anybody else's mess in this world' (102). Williams's characters are plagued with the embarrassment that comes with belonging to the lower socio-economic classes – the classes that clean up after the rich. *Sweet Bird of Youth*'s protagonist Chance Wayne, we discover in Act Two, was once a bartender at the Royal Palms Hotel where he has returned with Alexandra Del Lago, an ageing movie star. Like so many of Williams's protagonists, Chance is in a desperate struggle to become 'Cinderella' and tries to attain his ambition through the film industry. Yet while the Cinderella story is a feasible dream (success does come abruptly to some who seek their names to appear on the Silver Screen), it is not easy to achieve as we see in his desperate struggle to be 'somebody'.

In the 'Catastrophe of Success', Williams recognises, too, that the 'happily ever after' in the Cinderella story is nothing but a myth. For those who achieve fame and wealth, the very problem of their success, a problem that Alexandra Del Lago and Boss Finley face, is that of identity:

> the public Somebody you are when you 'have a name' is a
> fiction created with mirrors and that the only somebody worth
> being is the solitary and unseen you that existed from your
> first breath and which is the sum of your actions and so is
> constantly in a state of becoming under your own volition – and
> knowing these things, you can even survive the catastrophe of
> Success! (104)

The identities both Del Lago and Boss Finley create to hold on to their public are familiar to most American audiences; they are clichés still present in American media – whether it is in the political arena or the Hollywood scene. Boss Finley has made a name for himself by evoking the rags-to-riches myth – the political leader who rose from poverty to lead the common man into better days. On the television screen broadcasting his speech nationwide, the old stag boasts, 'I got a mission that I hold sacred to perform in the Southland. When I was fifteen I came down barefooted out of the red clay hills. Why? Because the Voice of God called me to execute this mission' (84). Although Boss Finley may have been a common hillbilly, he has turned into a 'monster', a corrupt political figure who has filled his pockets with oil money and allowed innocent black men to suffer racially motivated crimes. Likewise, Alexandra Del Lago has invented herself. When Chance reveals his life story to Del Lago in Act One, Scene Two, the Princess interrupts with 'BEAUTY! Say it! Say it! What you had was beauty! I had it! I say it, with pride, no matter how sad, being gone, now' (35). In this and in her sometimes coarse expressions, she reveals that, unlike her pseudonym, she has risen from rags as well. In other words, Del Lago, like Chance and Boss Finley, comes from humble beginnings. In her flight, she has created yet another self, the Princess Kosmonopolis – a name that reveals that this royal diva is in exile. Chance, wanting badly to become famous and continually failing to do so, also has a fictional identity, apparent in his drastic shifts from fragile and lost to a false confidence.

Although Del Lago and Boss Finley have negotiated their fictional identities with that of their private selves, the mirrors have begun to show the downfall of their public selves. When telling Chance about her 'tragic' comeback in Act One, Scene One, Del Lago reveals:

> The glorious comeback, when I turned fool and came back. . . . The screen's a very clear mirror. There's a thing called a close-up. The camera advances and you stand still and your head, your face, is caught in the frame of the picture with a light blazing on it and all your terrible history screams while you smile. (25)

Del Lago explains that after she heard the audience gasp at the close-up she fled the auditorium and kept on running in a desperate flight from the public. The camera has awoken her to the ticking of the clock that whispers 'Loss, loss, loss' (*Glass Menagerie*, 105).

In *Sweet Bird of Youth* Williams again uses the mirror to create tension between characters. Tom Junior confronts his father, Boss Finley, with the fact that Miss Lucy, the Boss's mistress, has used her lipstick to write 'Boss Finley [. . .] is too old to cut the mustard' (50) on the mirror of the hotel's ladies' room. In other words, she exposes his lack of sexual virility and by extension his lack of political potency – she shatters the fiction he has been struggling to keep up.

In the final battle between Chance and the Princess, the mirror is used a last time. After Del Lago's phone conversation with Sally Powers, a conversation that has informed Del Lago that her comeback was a success after all, Chance, infuriated that Del Lago has not mentioned his own talent, forcibly turns her to the mirror: 'Look in that mirror. What do you see in that mirror?'

> **Princess**   I see – Alexandra Del Lago, artist and star! Now it's your turn, you look and what do you see?
>
> **Chance**   I see – Chance Wayne . . .
>
> **Princess**   The face of a Franz Albertzart, a face that tomorrow's sun will touch without mercy. Of course, you were crowned with laurel in the beginning, your gold hair was wreathed with laurel, but the gold is thinning and the laurel has withered. Face it – pitiful monster. (95)

Chance's inability to fill in who he is when looking in the mirror suggests that he recognises his failure to become a star and artist like Del Lago. He is not even able to convince himself that he will be one. After he falters to define himself as anyone other than a man whose chances are all spent, Del Lago parallels Chance to Franz Albertzart, a young man who, failing to make it in the movies, is fated to be the male companion of an elderly lady. Chance, like Albertzart, has two choices: to be Del Lago's gigolo (a form of castration) or to face Tom Finley and his gang of thugs. Ultimately, like the abruptness of success the fall from that success can be just as sudden.

Despite his critique of success, failure was even more bitter for Williams. In 1957, *Orpheus Descending* met with disappointing reviews and audience turn-out. The show closed only two months after it had opened on Broadway. *Sweet Bird of Youth*, although written in 1952 and receiving its try-outs in 1956, was first produced on Broadway two years after the dismal reception of *Orpheus Descending*. Despite some of the criticism the play received, particularly of its potentially confusing plot development, *Sweet Bird of Youth* was well-received by audiences and is now held in high regard among scholars and theatre buffs for its experimentation with 'plastic theatre' and Williams's even bolder attempts to stage subject matter that was deemed too sensitive for modern audiences.

Preaching hate

Tennessee Williams's concern with humanity's violence and cruelty and his ponderings about the causes of such savagery are evident in both *Sweet Bird of Youth* and his contemplations on the play. In his 'Foreword' to the play, he reveals that during the time he struggled to write *Sweet Bird of Youth* he was full of anger and envy, much like his character Chance Wayne. He wrote to a friend at this time that 'We are all civilised people, which means that we are all savages at heart but observing a few amenities of civilised behavior'. Human existence, then, for Williams, was a thinly veiled savagery, a condition that Williams had not risen above. According to Williams, we are all susceptible to releasing our savagery. Williams sets out to expose 'a good many human weaknesses and brutalities' in his plays (*Where I Live*, 109), and openly admits that he, too, embodies such weaknesses. These human failings, his scenario for the play further reveals, are the 'betrayal of people's hearts by personal and social corruption, identifying the sources of corruption as the individual will-to-power and the fierce competition in capitalist society' (Murphy, 136). The individual will-to-power, that disease that Chance is infected with, the disease Williams maps out in 'The Catastrophe of Success', is of course the desire for fame and fortune. The identification of capitalism, which is linked to the individual will-to-power, as being one of the other corrupting forces is crucial to understanding Williams's play. Like his contemporaries, Arthur Miller and William Inge, Williams is highly critical of 1940s and 1950s America – an America saturated with an ideology of individualism and capitalism, but an ideology that does not allow all Americans equal footing in the competition.

Written in 1952 but revised several times until its Broadway debut in 1959, *Sweet Bird of Youth* resonates with the troubled climate of the Eisenhower era (1952–60), McCarthyism (1947–57) and racial tension in the South – a time when communists, homosexuals and people of colour were not tolerated within mainstream America. As a Southern, gay writer, that is, an outsider in an America that was desperately trying to hold on to a unified white, heterosexual identity, Williams was conscious of the troubled times this play depicts. In his 'Foreword' to *Sweet Bird of Youth*, Williams, keenly aware of the intolerance for those who challenged white America by being left-wing, non-heterosexual, or non-white, stated profoundly, 'I think that hate is a thing, a feeling, that can only exist where there is no understanding'. As an example, Boss Finley is one of the few of Williams's characters that neither he nor the audience has sympathy for. Boss Finley and his son, Tom Junior, have no understanding of the changing world. They do, however, understand how to use rhetoric to perpetuate their race crimes.

The Eisenhower era is sometimes romanticised as a time of prosperity and consumerism. Nearly everyone was said to have a television, a car and a washing machine – luxuries which previously were not commonplace items in the average middle-class household. However, this period was also wrought with fear and hate. The Republican Senator Joe McCarthy, who won the respect of both President Dwight Eisenhower and President Harry Truman before him, succeeded in stirring up hate and fear in his attempt to rid America of political dissidents. The House on Un-American Activities Committee (HUAC) was formed in 1938, but McCarthy did not lead his anti-Red campaign until the early 1950s at which time the hearings were also televised. Among those who were questioned and silenced were playwrights, directors and actors. Elia Kazan, who directed the debut of *Sweet Bird of Youth*, was one such individual. If the committee found that the individual on trial was guilty, he/she was blacklisted from the industry. As a consequence, many in theatre and Hollywood found themselves out of work. Fear soon spread throughout the American entertainment business. In fact, these hearings had such a detrimental effect on theatre and film that one New York theatre critic, Brook Atkinson, was moved to blame McCarthyism for the lousy Broadway season in 1952.[1]

This play is deeply rooted in an era of racial segregation. The Civil Rights Act of America was not passed by Congress until 1964, five years after this play premiered on Broadway and twelve years after the play was initially conceived. Williams's childhood and much of his adult life (he was forty-one years of age when he wrote *Sweet Bird of Youth*) was spent witnessing legally sanctioned racist policies and racist acts. Along with the legally sanctioned segregation, it was not uncommon between the years of 1882 to 1968 (though occurrences became increasingly rare after 1964) for black men to be lynched by white mobs. Many of the lynchings, which sometimes involved castration, were acts of retribution; white populations took it on themselves to 'punish' black men for 'raping' white women, a violation of the Jim Crow laws (1887–1965) which made it illegal for black men to have *any* sexual relations with white women. While the accusations of 'rape' were often made when such violence took place, many black men were mutilated without evidence.[2]

1   Richard H. Rovere, *Senator Joe McCarthy*, Berkeley and Los Angeles, University of California Press, 1996, 9.
2   David Pilgrim, 'What Was Jim Crow?', Museum of Racist Memorabilia, Ferris State University, 2000 (www.ferris.edn/jimcrow).

Indeed, the fear of miscegenation is crucial to the play's political climate. While the cast is predominately white and Southern, Chance's fate is paralleled to a black man who is castrated by the Youth for Tom Finley gang to send the message that they will not allow black men to taint the purity of white women. Boss Finley makes clear his position on the desegregation debate. Speaking to his daughter, Heavenly, he explains:

> I'm relying a great deal on this campaign to bring in young voters for the crusade I'm leading. I'm all that stands between the South and the black days of Reconstruction. And you and Tom Junior are going to stand there beside me in the grand crystal ballroom, as shining examples of white Southern youth – in danger. (56)

Boss Finley repeats this racist rhetoric during his television appearance. While Chance and Miss Lucy watch and comment on the speech, the audience hears the ageing politician bark his racist propaganda:

> As you all know I had no part in a certain operation on a young black gentleman. I call that incident a deplorable thing. [. . .] However . . . I understand the emotions that lay behind it. The passion to protect by this violent emotion something that we hold sacred: our purity of our own blood! (85)

In the early sketches for the play, Boss Finely was drawn from the real-life political leader Huey Long, who served as Louisiana's governor from 1928 to 1932 and US Senator from 1932 to 1935. This right-wing politician's views on miscegenation left much to be desired (Parker, par. 1). While Elia Kazan is credited with softening the character perhaps because of Kazan's own guilt for naming names when questioned by the HUAC, Boss Finley remains a problematic character. He is 'neither Kazan's "sincere" statesman and caring father, nor the hateful political and domestic bully that Williams had come to consider him' (Parker, par. 18). Disliked by readers and audience but not despised by them, Boss Finley's wrath against Chance is in part understandable; after all, Chance did infect the lovely Heavenly with a sexually transmitted disease.

Part of the problem with the character of Boss Finley is that it is unclear whether he believes that black men are a physical threat to white womanhood or whether he uses the rhetoric of the fear of blood contamination to further his political career and protect his oil money. He does, after all, attempt to marry his daughter to oil tycoons. Heavenly confronts her father with his greedy intentions: 'you took me out of St Cloud, and tried to force me to marry a fifty-year-old money bag that you wanted something out of –' (53). Perhaps afraid that Chance would corrupt more than Heavenly's body – that is, that he would ruin her social status and thus his own status – Boss Finley employs this rhetoric in his hatred of Chance. Williams complicates the matter in that Chance has polluted Heavenly's body. Repeatedly, the disease that Heavenly contracted from Chance is referred to as 'rot' (95, 97) and something only 'whores' (45, 81) contract. Having infected Heavenly with a venereal disease which results in a badly performed hysterectomy, he will face the knife at the end of the play.

Although we understand the anger of Boss Finley and Tom Junior, their retribution does not fit the crime. Williams is able to ridicule the Boss Finleys who 'preach hate' (79–80) and see desegregation and ruptures in the class system (Chance is of a lower economic social group) as a danger to white women's sexual purity in the South.

The Korean War

Having made love to Alexandra Del Lago in Act One, Scene Two, Chance tells the Princess his life story. While much of his story appears to be exaggerated boasting (beginning with his being a twelve-pound baby), Chance's account of his stint in the Navy appears to be genuine. He recalls:

> when I came home for those visits, man oh man how that town
> buzzed with excitement. I'm telling you, it would blaze with it, and
> then that thing in Korea came along. I was about to be sucked into
> the Army so I went into the Navy, because a sailor's uniform suited
> me better, the uniform was all that suited me, though. (36)

At the first mention of the Korean War, Chance's mood shifts from one of remembering how the town 'buzzed with excitement' each time he returned from his stage and film adventures to the reality of the danger that awaited him. He, much like Tom Wingfield in *The Glass Menagerie* who has returned from the Merchant Marines to remember his regrets, is afflicted by this experience. Chance perhaps imagined that the Navy would be a glorious adventure as depicted in films, such as those starring Victor Mature (one of Chance's heroes as we discover in Act Two, Scene Two). What he discovers, however, is that he could not cope with the pressures of war. Although initially he blames his failure to complete his tour of duty on 'the goddam routine, discipline', he reveals that his medical discharge was the result of a much more serious problem:

> I started to have bad dreams. Nightmares and cold sweats at night,
> and I had palpitations, and on my leave I got drunk and woke up
> in strange places with faces on the next pillow I had never seen
> before. [. . .] I cracked up, my nerves did. I got a medical discharge

out of the service and I came home in civvies, then it was when I
noticed how different it was, the town and the people in it. (37)

Suffering from a debilitating fear that one day 'a bit of hot steel' would
end his life, Chance has a nervous breakdown. Coming home, he notices
that the people of St Cloud have changed in their reaction to him, in part,
because he has no medals or visual battle wounds. In the 1950s, military
discharges were published in newspapers; hence, the people of St Cloud
would have known the cause of Chance's early release from the service.
And, being discharged for psychological breakdown and perhaps drug and
alcohol addiction, would have been viewed with disdain by the general
public. However, what the people of St Cloud do not see, except perhaps
for Aunt Nonnie, is that Chance's failure to become the heroic soldier is
indeed one of his more endearing qualities. When he confronts Tom Junior
in Act Two, Scene Two, he draws a distinction between himself and Boss
Finley: 'He was just called down from the hills to preach hate. I was born
here to make love' (79–80). Although Chance's love-making has resulted
in pain and destruction, unlike the Tom Juniors and Boss Finleys of the
world, Chance is not fit to fight even for self-preservation. In the play's
conclusion, he cannot strike Del Lago after she verbally cuts him down
nor can he fight off Tom Junior's thugs. His fate is sealed.

Chance's naval experience is also possibly what sets his thinking apart
from that of the closed-minded folk of St Cloud. Two years before the
onset of the Korean War, the armed forces implemented a desegregation
policy. Starting in 1948, white Americans in the Navy and other branches
of the US military worked side by side with black Americans and other
soldiers of colour. When Scotty tells Chance that the Youth for Tom
Finley clan 'picked out a nigger at random and castrated the bastard to
show they mean business about white women's protection in this state',
Chance responds, 'You know what that is, don't you? Sex-envy is what
that is, and the revenge for sex-envy which is a widespread disease that
I have run into personally too often for me to doubt its existence or any
manifestation' (70–1). Chance's diagnosis may not be psychologically
or socially correct in the world outside this play, but for the audience
who has witnessed Boss Finley's sexual and political potency waning
Chance's definition appears right on the mark.

'The enemy time'

'Tennessee Williams's writing reveals a striking preoccupation with
the problem of time', as Mary Ann Carrigan rightly posits (221). Like
Carrigan, other scholars have written about the theme of the passing of
time in Williams's plays. *Sweet Bird of Youth* is no exception. Alycia

Smith-Howard and Greta Heintzelman assert that the primary theme of *Sweet Bird of Youth* is decay and claim that to attempt to flee the inevitable process of ageing, Chance Wayne returns to St Cloud 'to retrieve his youth by rekindling an innocent relationship and time in his life' (293). In his attempt to rekindle his first love, Chance devises a plan to blackmail the Princess into staging a contest which he and Heavenly will win. This contest 'to show [her] faith in YOUTH' (40) never materialises despite the empathy Del Lago feels for Chance.

Later, in Act Two, Chance's tactics to show the town of St Cloud that he is somebody change. After popping pills and drinking vodka, he brags to Scotty and Bud that Del Lago has signed a contract, giving him the lead role in a film called 'Youth' (73). Immediately, Scotty and Bud point out the ridiculousness of the title, seeing through Chance's lies. However, Chance's fantastical schemes reveal that he still buys into the Hollywood dream of glamour and youth. The movie camera, unlike the snapshots Chance took of Heavenly, capturing and immortalising her young body, threatens to frame and forever reflect back one's ageing body as Del Lago reveals to Chance in Act One. Ultimately, his efforts to regain his youth are met with devastating failure. His own fall from innocence has infected Heavenly's body. Despite Chance's desperate attempt to retrieve his youth, like that of Alexandra Del Lago's comeback and Boss Finley's rally, there is no turning back the clock. Even the act of cutting out the rot decaying Heavenly's body does not leave her unscarred. No longer a symbol of virtue, Heavenly speaks of herself as a corpse: 'The embalmers must have done a good job on me, Papa' (52). Williams, in essence, reveals that there is no way to turn back the clock, no way to wipe the slate clean, and thus there is no redemption to be had. The passing of time, as he writes in 'The Catastrophe of Success', is 'Loss, loss, loss, unless you devote your heart to its opposite' (*Glass Menagerie*, 105).

Chance's struggle to stave off time is not unique. Alexandra Del Lago and Boss Finley also fear the 'tick-tick' of time which threatens to expose the 'burnt-out pieces' (97) each character has become, and although Heavenly also is a victim of time, she, unlike the others, is resigned to its devastating cruelty. Both Chance and Boss Finley, like Del Lago, a fugitive of her last screen debut in which the camera's close-up exposed her age, are in a desperate battle against time. Boss Finley's mistress reveals that he can no longer 'cut the mustard' sexually (50), and his extreme and out-of-date politics lead him to resort to violence in the struggle to maintain his power. Chance, never having made it in Hollywood, relies on his good looks to latch on to wealthy and powerful women to pay his bills, but does so with the knowledge that his hair is thinning and that which makes him attractive to these women is fading. Heavenly, he believes, is his only way to recapture and maintain his youth. However, she, too, has become 'an old childless woman' (56) after her hysterectomy.

At the play's conclusion, the audience realises that Williams's 'sweet bird of youth' is yet another myth – a myth that according to Williams we have become infected by. Nearing the tragic end of the play, Chance and Del Lago hear '*The sound of a clock ticking . . . louder and louder*'. To this, Chance responds:

> It goes tick-tick, it's quieter than your heartbeat, but it's slow dynamite, a gradual explosion, blasting the world we lived in to burnt-out pieces . . . Time – who could beat it, who could defeat it ever? Maybe some saints and heroes, but not Chance Wayne. I lived on something, that – time? (97)

And continues after a brief affirmation from the Princess:

> Gnaws away, like a rat gnaws off its own foot caught in a trap, and then, with its foot gnawed off and the rat set free, couldn't run, couldn't go, bled and died. (98)

Chance's description of 'the enemy, time, in all of us' is grotesque and violent. Time as a gradual explosion turning all humankind into burnt-out scraps conveys images of war. Time wages a slow war on the body and mind; it turns us into nothing more than refuse eaten by flames. His second metaphor, one equally violent, relates to the way in which the characters feel trapped. Caught in this trap called life, Chance reveals that the destruction of time is an act of self-mutilation. Yet the violence we inflict on ourselves in an attempt to flee the ticking of the clock is futile. While Chance's return to St Cloud, his drug and alcohol abuse and his sexual encounters may at times allow him to ignore the passing of time, ultimately, as he reveals, his attempts to flee merely result in paralysis. Moreover, the image of the rat gnawing off its foot suggests that he has already castrated himself. Although the physical mutilation that will occur offstage will be committed by Tom Junior and his gang, Chance admits that as a result of the choices he has made he is already maimed.

Good Friday and Easter

Williams makes the setting of *Sweet Bird of Youth*, 'an Easter Sunday, from late morning to late night', explicit throughout. From the opening of the play when Fly, the room-service attendant, tells Chance that 'it's *Easter* Sunday' (8) to Boss Finley's closing political speech, Williams continually reminds the audiences of the religious holiday during which the action takes place. Although the play takes place during Easter, the significance is anything but obvious. The audience might reasonably await a resurrection and renewal of sorts. However, Williams exploits the audience's expectations, simultaneously revealing the way in which Christianity itself is exploited. Boss Finley, on numerous occasions, uses religion, particularly Good Friday and Easter Sunday, to attempt to elevate his status as well as to hurt Miss Lucy. The crucifixion and resurrection of Jesus Christ becomes a tool, and, in certain circumstances, a weapon for those attempting to maintain or seize power. Boss Finley first employs the image of Christ's crucifixion after he is attacked by Tom Junior about his relations with Miss Lucy: 'Mind your own goddam business. A man with a mission, which he holds sacred, and on the strength of which he rises to high public office – crucified in this way, publicly, by his own offspring' (51). Using the rhetoric of religious doctrine, Boss Finley sets himself up as a Christ-like figure, crucified by his son.

Having been 'crucified' by his lover as well, Boss Finley seeks revenge on Miss Lucy. When Miss Lucy first appears with her finger bandaged, she relates to Stuff the extent of Boss Finley's cruelty. Boss Finley, she explains, brought her a candy Easter egg with a jewellery box inside it. When she opened the Easter egg and the jewellery box, she found a lovely diamond pin inside, but as she was about to remove the pin, 'the old son of a bitch slam[med] the lid of the box on [her] fingers' (59). Disguising his 'weapon' in a candy Easter egg, Boss Finley masks his violent nature. While at times seemingly sweet and generous to Miss Lucy, unlike Christ he does not forgive and he is not afraid to punish those who threaten his sexual and political image.

Boss Finley again draws a parallel between himself and Christ during his television rally:

Last Friday . . . Last Friday, Good Friday. I said last Friday, Good Friday . . . Quiet, may I have your attention please. . . . Last Friday, Good Friday, I seen a horrible thing on the campus of our great State University, which I built for the state. A hideous strawstuffed effigy of myself, Tom Finley, was hung and set fire to in the main quadrangle of the college. This outrage was inspired . . . inspired by the Northern radical press. However, that was Good Friday. Today is Easter. I say that was Good Friday. Today is Easter Sunday and I am in St Cloud. (86)

In this passage, in which Boss Finley struggles to be heard by a crowd already stirred up by the Heckler's intrusion, the ageing politician grasps at Christian doctrine to appeal to his audience. Revealing that the youth of Florida have burned an effigy of him on Good Friday, Boss Finley attempts to position himself as a saviour whom the youth of his state, polluted by what is written in the Northern papers, cannot yet appreciate. Ending his speech (which also concludes Act Two) with 'Today is Easter Sunday and I am in St Cloud', Boss Finley evokes a resurrection, but this is a resurrection that never takes place perhaps because, although Boss Finley may attempt to fashion himself as a saviour, for Williams and his audience, this demagogue is more clearly aligned with the thieves crucified alongside Christ. Thomas Adler adds that '*Sweet Bird of Youth* ends, significantly, not on Easter morning – which is the moment of complete belief and hope – but on Easter evening, biblically a moment of absolute doubt and challenge to faith that can be alloyed only by dependence on experimental proof of a resurrection' (148), but it is a resurrection that Williams never allows for.

Williams also cheats his audience into believing that Alexandra Del Lago and Chance Wayne might possibly be resurrected – he cheats us into believing that there might be a happy ending after all. Although Chance has returned to regain his lost youth and his lost girl, his desperate attempts are met with failure. He gains the Princess's sympathy for a time, and with it her financial and emotional support, but finds himself 'lost in beanstalk country, the ogre's country at the top of the beanstalk, the country of the flesh-hungry, blood-thirsty ogre' (77), as Del Lago so fittingly describes the world of St Cloud and beyond. St Cloud is, indeed, a place where 'monsters' like Tom Junior and his father seek out and commit violent acts against those perceived as trespassers. In the end, Chance, '*with a sort of deathbed dignity and honesty*', resigns himself to his fate. He allows Tom Junior, Scotty and Bud to enter the room, and as these brutal youths surround him, he rises up to approach the audience with his last words: 'I don't ask for your pity, but just for your understanding – not even that – no. Just for your recognition of me in you, and the enemy, time, in us all' (98). By having the last lines before the curtain falls spoken to the audience, Williams positions Chance as the audience's messenger. Yet, rather than have this messenger rise up triumphantly, as would be fitting for Easter, he has Chance face his doom, his crucifixion of sorts. However, before his castration, Chance asks his audience to recognise that a part of him resides within us. We desire success, youth, happiness and love, but the 'monsters' in this play (the Finley clan and time) keep us from succeeding.

Del Lago, one of the few characters who sympathises with Chance, knows very well how hard it is to succeed in this monstrous world. In the last act, it is tempting to associate the Easter resurrection with Del Lago's comeback, especially after she discovers that her last film has 'broken box-office records' and been called 'the greatest comeback in the history of the industry' (94). Yet, even Del Lago does not believe that her rebirth as a film star will last. While nothing in Del Lago's dialogue gives her doubts away, Williams reveals that the Princess, even after her bitter argument with Chance, again tries to convince him to leave with her because she knows her fame will be short-lived:

> *The report from Sally Powers may be and probably is a factually accurate report; but to indicate she is going on to further triumph would be to falsify her future. She makes this instinctive admission to herself when she sits down by* **Chance** *on the bed, facing the audience. Both are faced with castration, and in her heart she knows it.* (97)

This knowledge of the castration she too faces is difficult for an actress to convey. Without dialogue that designates her doubt and lack of faith in her future, Del Lago must express through her gestures that she is fated, as is Chance. Her journey, Williams reveals, is one that will result in future disappointment, flight from failure and ultimately crucifixion without resurrection.

Cut: Film and television

When Chance recalls for Del Lago and later for Aunt Nonnie his past, the audience learns that his first attempt to make a name for himself was on stage. His plan, like the dreams of many actors of the 1950s, was to land roles on Broadway (at which he is in part successful) before heading out to Hollywood. This Hollywood dream, the dream of seeing one's name on a screen shown across the country, is for many a bitter nightmare. The film industry, for Williams, has the ability to offer instant success as well as instant failure. Del Lago testifies to this when she bitterly says:

> Ha . . . Ha. . . . The glorious comeback, when I turned fool and came back. . . . The screen's a very clear mirror. There's a thing called a close-up. The camera advances and you stand still and your head, your face, is caught in the frame of the picture with a light blazing on it and all your terrible history screams while you smile . . . (25)

Once a star with her own fan club, Del Lago, having agreed to come back to the movies, takes desperate flight after hearing the audience gasp at her close-up at the film's premiere. Oddly, her description of the close-up resembles that of a torture sequence – a light blazing in her face as her 'terrible history screams' out. Her 'history', while in part a reference to having aged, also reflects how she has passed the years. There is a sense in her recollection of the premiere that Del Lago's initial disappearance from the Silver Screen was the result of some undesirable past behaviour; she was, according to her own accounts of Franz Albertzart, a diva. What she then sees and perceives others witnessing is her past, those years she hid from the camera. This camera, like 'a very clear mirror', reflects not only her physical flaws but also her ethical and moral blemishes.

When Del Lago asks Chance to tell his life story as an 'audition, a sort of screen test' (35), she symbolically places a mirror in front of him. He begins boasting about his popularity in St Cloud and his minor successes on Broadway, but Chance's 'screen test' begins to reflect a troubled youth. Williams 'proposed to use the screen as the metaphor for consciousness, a consciousness both lyrical and philosophical – personal and public – in nature' (Jackson, 196). While no camera or screen is present in this scene, Chance's monologue is directed on the forestage; he is speaking out to the audience while Del Lago, staring into a mirror, applies her make-up. Speaking to an imaginary camera, Chance's mood shifts as he recollects his Navy service, his drinking, his sexual promiscuity and his other failures, including Heavenly's attempt to push him away, with a tragic aura. It is when he becomes sincere that he captures the Princess's attention. 'Chance', Del Lago tenderly says moving away from the mirror, 'you're a lost little boy that I really would like to help find himself' (41). At this point, Chance awakens from the trance of the imaginary mirror reflecting his sad life, and states confidently, 'I passed the screen test!' For Williams, acting is not pretending to be someone one is not; it is not just play. He worked with method actors – actors working with techniques of tapping into one's own past experiences to convey the emotional depth of the characters they are embodying. In acting and perhaps in writing for the screen or stage, one inadvertently expresses one's own tragedy. This is not to be mistaken with biographical interpretations of plays, that is, Williams is not staging his life over and over again in his plays. He understands, however, that an actor and a writer brings his history with him, and ultimately this is also what makes the industry so cruel. Those who cannot face the mirror that will expose their ugliness as well as beauty fail.

Williams additionally takes his pen(knife) to the television industry. Not only does the camera threaten Del Lago, exposing more than she wishes others to see, but also television allows Boss Finley, and politicians like Joe McCarthy, to stage, perform and ultimately to try to 'cut' his way to the top. Williams's technique to represent the television screen on stage warrants some note. While Stuff, Miss Lucy and Chance initially look out towards the fourth wall, where a beam of light flickers indicating the television screen, a sudden shift takes place. When Chance walks downstage, '*the whole back wall of the stage*' becomes a giant television screen. Boss Finley is seen, larger than life, with his '*arm around*

Heavenly' (84). Despite Boss Finley's attempt to use national television coverage to boost his voting public, the screen, which has the potential to manipulate time, place and circumstances (Jackson, 195–6), ultimately reveals his personal ugliness when he has the Heckler removed from the rally. Captured on screen is not just the apparently pure image of Heavenly and her proud brother and father, but also Boss Finley's inability to face his 'terrible history' – the family tragedy and his failing political pull is captured on the public screen/mirror. If, as Roland Barthes argues, what politicians attempt to create when they appear in front of a camera is an image that their public recognises within themselves,[3] then here the public sees its own racism and sexism. Williams asks his audience to see the stage as a mirror of an America polluted by narrow-minded Boss Finleys. However, Williams incites his audience with an urge to rid America of such ugliness – the ugliness of the HUAC, of a segregated South and of a homophobic nation.

Structure, Language and Style

Structure

While the structure of *Sweet Bird of Youth* often has been criticised as clumsy and disjointed, it pulls together private and public anxieties concerning age, the loss of power and the fear of the 'other' through spacial arenas. The play is set in two main spaces – the hotel (the bedroom and lounge) and the terrace of the Finely home. These spaces interestingly blur the distinction between the private and public, as does Boss Finley who uses his children to further his political means. Jo Mielziner's original set design in which the hotel bedroom was present in each act realises this breakdown of the personal and political tragedies in *Sweet Bird of Youth*. The structure and the set design ultimately bring together the stories of Chance and Del Lago, Chance and Heavenly, and the political turmoil of the South.

Sweet Bird of Youth takes a great deal from Greek tragedy. Despite the various locations, the play, like those of the Greeks, takes place in one day 'from late morning till late night'. As the play continues, the dramatic urgency intensifies until the tragic end. The tragedy, in *Sweet Bird of Youth* as in Greek drama, lies in the downfall of a larger-than-life character. Williams interestingly depicts the downfall of three demigods – Alexandra Del Lago who is in exile after her fall, Chance Wayne whose

3 *Mythologies*, trans. Annette Lavers, New York, Hill and Wang, 1972, 91.

boasting elevates his status to a monumental gigolo and Boss Finley whose bellowing at rallies cannot stop his political power from coming to an end. Both Boss Finley and Chance are sacrificed within the action of the play. Chance's castration (though never enacted on stage) is more than brutality; it is a ritualistic cutting to send a warning to those who threaten the social structure of St Cloud. Boss Finley's rally is disrupted in the same manner as it had been before; the repetition in method and of questions transforms the event into a ritualistic roasting.

Language

Williams's writing is often described as poetic. His use of metaphors, symbols, repetition, dialect and slang help to construct the vivid worlds he stages. Embodying his central characters, Chance and Del Lago, with a language rich in images borrowed from children's fairytales, images of insects, rats and other animals gnawing at abstractions such as time, and endowing them with lengthy personal histories, Williams elevates their status. Chance and Del Lago are not only given the most lines but their use of language also reveals that these two figures are dreamers, rich in imaginative power and longing to create personas on the Silver Screen. They, like Boss Finley, are hyper-aware of the audience, speaking always as if they are performing. Along with the rich images that Chance conjures up, he turns to the auditorium, speaking to the audience in Act One, Scene Two, when he recalls the life he has led, and in Act Three when he is about to face castration. Unlike Boss Finley whose speeches are disrupted, Chance's are observed in silence, much like those of a Shakespearean hero.

The use of slang and dialect in *Sweet Bird of Youth* is often associated with the antagonists. Tom Junior and his father speak with strong southern accents, often leaving off the endings to words. Although they know how to use language to perpetuate their racist ideologies, ultimately for an educated audience, their dialect and slang signal their barbarism. Tom Junior, for example, uses profanity such as 'ruttin' and shows little respect to his elders. Williams aligns the way in which a character speaks with his temperament.

Plastic theatre

In his production notes for *The Glass Menagerie*, Williams wrote of a form of theatre that he hoped would take hold on the American stage. Plastic theatre, as he called this form, was an attempt to create theatre in which 'truth, life, or reality is an organic thinking which poetic imagination can represent or suggest, in essence, only through changing into other forms than those which were merely present in appearance'. Leaving behind realist conventions which had all too much dominated the American stage, Williams created a dramatic form which merged a poetic, lyric quality with popular appeal. His revolutionary concept of plastic theatre merged non-verbal expressions to illuminate the dialogue and textual version of the play. In *Sweet Bird of Youth*, Williams achieves this new dramatic form through his use of symbols, as seen in the gulls, the recurring musical composition called the 'Lament' and the use of a cyclorama on which 'nonrealistic projections' 'should give a poetic unity of mood to the several specific settings' (5).

Before any word is uttered on stage, the audience hears '*the soft, urgent cries of birds, [and] the sound of their wings*' (7). Immediately, Williams signals to the audience that this play is about an urgency to soar above one's status and to flee one's failures. After this, Fly, the black man who provides room-service at the Royal Palms Hotel, appears with vodka, another form of escape. This minor character, only seen briefly, reminds the audience that, like Chance, he is stuck in a dead-end job in a racist Southern town which will viciously cut him if he is caught on the street after midnight.

The gulls appear again immediately after Chance learns of his mother's death: '**Chance** *slowly turns his back on the man and crosses to the window. Shadows of birds sweep the blind. He lowers it a little before he turns back to* **Scudder**' (10). They reappear only a few pages later, after Scudder has left and once Alexandra Del Lago has woken from her drunken sleep. While Del Lago attempts to figure out where she is and with whom she shares her bed, the audience sees '*Gulls fly past window, shadows sweeping the blind: they cry out with soft urgency*' (21). These birds are not 'birds of youth', frolicking and singing in the sun without cares. In both instances, the shadows of their wings signal a desire to flee, yet an inability to escape. The gulls stay near the sea, as Chance does, because the ocean is their home; however, it is a home that is bound up with uncertainty and danger. What lies beneath the water is unknown. The cries of these gulls, moreover, are not sweet, like the cooing of pigeons. Del Lago remarks that they sound like 'pigeons with laryngitis' (21). Their hoarse cries are filled with a panic-stricken urgency which is mirrored in Chance and the Princess.

Although Williams's positioning of the gulls is not as specific later in the play, the terrifying cries of these birds are ever-present in Act Two, Scene One. '*The Gulf*', he writes, '*is suggested by the brightness and the gulls crying as in Act One*' (43). Here the gulls heighten the audience's awareness of Boss Finley's desperate attempt to maintain his political power and to re-establish the respect he once held in his family. When told that his mistress, Miss Lucy, has exposed his ageing and no longer virile body, Boss Finley is '*wounded, baffled*' (51). Indeed, the description 'baffled' is used in conjunction with Boss Finley again when he watches his daughter shortly after.

The ever-present cries of the gulls, moreover, reflect Heavenly's tragedy. Rendered barren by her hysterectomy, she has become a corpse. When asked where Heavenly is, her brother, Tom Junior says, 'She's lyin' out on the beach like a dead body washed up on it' (46). Williams asks us to imagine the beauty, washed up on the shore, as gulls frantically swoop down and devour her much like Boss Finley who insists that she escort him in his television appearance in a 'stainless white' dress 'to scotch these rumors about your corruption' (56). But by putting Heavenly in the public eye, Boss Finley exposes her to the Heckler's and by extension the viewing public's vicious pecking.

Apart from the '*Mozartian music, suggesting a court dance*' (52), which was cut from the production of the play and the popular tunes sung in the bar during Act Two, Scene Two, the only music in *Sweet Bird of Youth* is the 'Lament', or 'Lamentation' as it is sometimes called. Although this piece of music was composed specifically for the play by Williams's old friend Paul Bowles, author of *The Sheltering Sky*, the 'Lament' has a long tradition in the arts. It is one of the oldest poetic expressions of grief, regret and sorrow in Western music. In Baroque opera, the Lament is often an aria sung by the leading lady. Williams's 'Lament', heard seven times during the play, serves a similar purpose. When this composition is heard, Chance is hopeless. Towards the end of Act One, Scene One, as Chance's situation becomes increasingly desperate, the Lament makes its first appearance. From this moment, we understand Chance's attempt to blackmail the Princess Kosmonopolis is an act of desperation – not an act of greed but a struggle to regain his lost youth by winning over the girl he loved. The Lament, however, also signals that his plan will backfire. Despite his attempt to make the ageing actress submit to him, he will have to submit to Alexandra Del Lago before the end of Act One. After the Lament begins again, Del Lago softly tells Chance that she needs

> that distraction. It's time for me to find out if you're able to give it to me. You mustn't hang onto your silly little idea that you can increase your value by turning away and looking out a window when somebody wants you . . . I want you . . . I say now and I mean now, then and not until then will I call downstairs and tell the hotel cashier that I'm sending a young man down with some travelers' checks to cash for me . . . (33)

Attempting to shame the Princess into signing her cheques, he in turn is shamed as he becomes her gigolo. The Lament arises early on in Scene Two of the First Act. Full of regret and sorrow for his shameful sexual act, Chance now reveals more than his current desperation. He reveals his entire lamentable history.

The Lament is not heard again until Act Two, Scene Two, after Tom Junior confronts Chance with Heavenly's tragedy. In response to Tom Junior's charge that Chance passed on a venereal disease which he contracted after sleeping with 'Minnie, that slept with any goddam gigolo bastard she could pick up on Bourbon Street or the docks', Chance says, 'I left town before I found out I –' (81). Here, the Lament signals Chance's sorrow at discovering he has infected Heavenly, and that, as a result, Heavenly was operated on. The Lament may also signal his regret for not contacting her once he knew of his own diseased body. If Heavenly had known and if the disease had been diagnosed early on, she would have been spared being 'spayed like a dawg by Dr George Scudder's knife'. The Lament, here, works to draw out sympathy for Chance. While his actions are not commendable, he does feel sorrow and regret.

As Chance returns to the Princess, who has since ventured downstairs in a dishevelled and drugged state, '*"The Lament" is in the air. It blends with the wind-blown sound of the palms.*' It is at this moment that the Lament is clearly defined. Del Lago describes it as a feeling of loss:

> All day I've kept hearing a sort of lament that drifts through the air of this place. It says, 'Lost, lost, never to be found again.' Palm gardens by the sea and olive groves on Mediterranean islands all have that lament drifting through them. 'Lost, lost'. . . . The isle of Cyprus, Monte Carlo, San Remo, Torremolenas, Tangiers. They're all places of exile from whatever we loved. Dark glasses, wide-brimmed hats and whispers, 'Is that her?' Shocked whispers. . . . Oh, Chance, believe me, after failure comes flight. Nothing ever comes after failure but flight. Face it. Call the car, have them bring down the luggage and let's go on along the Old Spanish Trail. (*She tries to hold him.*) (82)

While St Cloud is initially a place of exile for the Princess, the whispers begin to haunt her, revealing that she must flee again. But more importantly, she recognises before Chance does that his comeback has been a failure. His only chance of escaping bodily harm, she knows, is flight. For Chance, St Cloud was once an exile from his failure to become a film star but now it is his doom.

During the play's last moments in Act Three, the Lament returns signalling Chance's doom. After the frightening visit Tom Junior and his clan pay to Del Lago, she reminds Chance that he was the one who 'put such rot in [Heavenly's] body she had to be gutted and hung on a butcher's hook, like a chicken dressed for Sunday'. Hearing this, initially aiming at the Princess, he '*strikes down at his own belly and he bends double with a sick cry. Palm Garden wind: whisper of "The Lament"*' (95). And only a few moments later when Chance is resolved to face his castration, the Lament fades in and continues for the remainder of the play (97). The echo of 'lost, lost, lost' is crucial here. Not only is Chance about to lose his virility, but also recognises that he has lost his youthfulness, his hope and his will to go on. His acceptance of his fate is almost honourable.

The sets, Williams urges, 'should be treated as freely and sparingly as the sets for *Cat on a Hot Tin Roof* or *Summer and Smoke*' (3). Murphy confirms that the Broadway premiere of *Sweet Bird of Youth* did indeed resemble *Cat on a Hot Tin Roof*, with a bed occupying a large part of the playing field. Furthermore, no walls or doors were constructed on stage; all the doors and windows were mimed. The spaces were non-realistic as they ran into one another. Even during the bar-room scene, for example, the bedroom was partly visible. To suggest this non-realistic, fluid space, the cyclorama at the rear of the stage was essential as it conveyed 'shutters in the first scene and palms, sea, and sky when the "shutters" were "opened"' (Murphy, 145). In his 'Setting and Special Effects', Williams stressed that 'During the daytime scenes the cyclorama projection is a poetic abstraction of semitropical sea and sky in fair spring weather. At night it is the Palm Garden with its branches among the stars' (3). The focus on the non-realistic, the abstract, moves this play away from realist conventions in which the setting or projections would reflect the current turmoil of the characters. Instead, Williams uses the cyclorama to create a contrast between the lives of Chance and the Princess, and the seemingly peaceful outside world. The beauty of the palm garden and the sea remind the viewers just how artificial such hotel settings are. In other words, the world Chance and Del Lago live in is brutal; it only appears to be calm and beautiful. Moreover, the image of the palm branches among the stars is symbolic. While never reaching the stars, the night shadows give the illusion of reaching for the unobtainable. Chance's attempt to reach for Heaven(ly) – is an impossibility.

Southern Gothic

Sweet Bird of Youth is an example of Southern Gothic, which draws on the Gothic tradition of nineteenth-century England that, among other traits, questions whether monstrous outcasts are truly monstrous – as seen in Mary Shelley's *Frankenstein* (1839). A key feature of Southern Gothic is the plight of ostracised and oppressed individuals, such as blacks, homosexuals, women and Northerners, who were deemed dangerous to the fragile antebellum South. In *Sweet Bird of Youth*, while all the characters are damaged and delusional (another feature of Southern Gothic), Williams succeeds in stirring up panic and sympathy for Chance whose fate parallels the story of a black man castrated by Tom Junior and his Youth for Tom Finley clan. Chance is the ostracised Other who threatens the stability of St Cloud because his presence is a constant reminder of the corruption and pollution eating away at the community.

Characters

Despite his previous successes with creating vivid characters such as Tom and Amanda Wingfield in *The Glass Menagerie*, Blanche and Stanley in *A Streetcar Named Desire*, Maggie and Brick in *Cat on a Hot Tin Roof*, among other notable characters, Tennessee Williams was never quite satisfied with the characters of *Sweet Bird of Youth*. Although he 'was deeply interested in the two main characters [Chance and Del Lago]', he told *Manchester Guardian Weekly*'s W. J. Weatherby in 1959, 'the other characters did not have the same interest for me' (quoted in Devlin, 60). He felt particularly dissatisfied with Boss Finley. The power of *Sweet Bird of Youth* rests in the two main characters' struggle against a world of hateful and cruel monsters.

Chance Wayne

Although Williams was interested in the development of Chance Wayne, more than a decade after the play opened on Broadway he was still unsatisfied with this 'hustler hero of *Sweet Bird of Youth*' (Clum, 128). In a 1971 interview with Jeanne Fayard, Williams expressed that he never felt that Chance was an effective character. He went on to explain that Chance

> is used in a symbolic manner. It [his castration] is a ritualistic
> death, a metaphor. He had to be real to be important. You cannot
> use a character as a dramatic symbol if he is important. You cannot
> use a character as a dramatic symbol if he is not first real to you. I
> didn't discover his real value until the end. (Quoted in Devlin, 211)

For his audiences, however, Chance is much more than a symbol. The play's intrigue is partly a result of the empathy that characters like Chance evoke in viewers. We see ourselves, or at least our dreams, in his struggle to be famous and his failure to achieve that success. This particular myth, rooted in the American consciousness, commonly referred to as 'the American Dream', recalls a tradition depicted in American Realist novels such as Theodore Dreiser's *An American Tragedy* (1925). Like Clyde, the protagonist of Dreiser's novel, Chance strives to rise above his poverty and in doing so compromises ethical and moral codes. In *Sweet Bird of Youth*, however, the gigolo's failure does not leave the audience with a moral lesson. For Williams, those who succeed and those who do not are no more or less virtuous than the other characters struggling to make a name for themselves.

Furthermore, Williams reveals that the American dream, or the Cinderella story, turns individuals into monsters. This is clearly seen when Chance, struggling to capture the attention and trust of the bar-room crowd in Act Two, is suddenly faced with Del Lago. High on drugs and alcohol, the Princess, having felt something for Chance when he confessed his failures to her in Act One, Scene Two, ventures to find him so that they can escape the doom she feels approaching in St Cloud. Alone and seeking comfort from him in the flight she wishes for them both, she pleads, 'Don't leave me. If you do I'll turn into the monster again. I'll be the first lady of the Beanstalk Country' (82). Chance, however, does not soften to her desperate appeal. Instead, '*in [his own] desperation*', he calls out, 'Wheel chair! . . . Wheel chair! Stuff, get the lady a wheel chair! She's having another attack!' While Chance's inability to care for Del Lago in her moment of despair is undoubtedly cruel, it is important to note that at this very moment he is desperate to regain his reputation and his youth. He is consumed with a dream which has infected him like the disease he has put into Heavenly's body, rotting away his moral and ethical responses and transforming him into a monster – cruel and selfish, ready to destroy those in his way.

Chance is much more complicated than Williams realised. While he displays cruelty when desperate, he is quite tender and lovable when he remembers his failures. When reminiscing with Aunt Nonnie about his first stage appearance at 'a lousy national contest', he finally lets his guard down after trying to convince himself that they won a prize:

> We would have won it, but I blew my lines. Yes, I that put on and produced the damn thing, couldn't even hear the damn lines being hissed at me by that fat girl with the book in the wings. (*He buries his face in his hands.*) (63)

Aunt Nonnie here speaks for the audience: 'I loved you for that, son, and so did Heavenly, too.' These moments of weakness, vulnerability and honesty set Chance apart from the cruel inhabitants of St Cloud.

Williams's genius as a playwright lies in his ability to stir sympathy for Chance, to transform this tainted man who lacks moral fibre into a hero of sorts. Despite his bad choices, selfishness and bravado, among other vices, Chance is wronged; the audience does not want this faded golden boy to be castrated.

Alexandra Del Lago

Alexandra Del Lago is notably one of Williams's complex and memorable female characters. This ageing, washed-up movie star is at times a self-proclaimed 'monster'. In her heyday, she was a diva, breaking the careers of young men like Franz Albertzart: 'I had to fire him. He held me too tight in the waltz scene, his anxious fingers left bruises once so violent, they, they dislocated a disc in my spine' (90). Even after her return to the screen, a return she believes has been a failure, she asserts her power over young men. In her flight, she uses beach boys like Chance to distract her from the harsh reality that '*she is equally doomed. She can't turn back the clock any more than can* **Chance**, *and the clock is equally relentless to them both*' (96–7). Her ability to devour and destroy men is, according to Chance, an act of emasculation. When Del Lago tries to convince Chance to leave with her in the final act, reminding him that if he stays he will be castrated, Chance says, 'You did that to me this morning, here on this bed, where I had the honor, where I had the great honor . . .' (95). However, her acts of emasculating men are not out of 'sex-envy', bigotry or hate. Rather, her acts are tied to her vanity – her longing for youth. Like Chance, she seeks to blind herself to the ticking of the clock through sexual unions with the young.

Del Lago is not simply a frustrated monster, seeking the admiring gaze of her fans and the 'hairless, silky-smooth gold' (18) bodies of young men. She is, as Williams's agent asserted about all Williams's female characters, an ordinary woman. Recalling an encounter with a group of angry women after the premiere of *Summer and Smoke*, Williams writes that they asked, 'Why do you always write about frustrated women?' (*Where I Live*, 26). His agent, Margo Jones, rescued him from the confrontation. Williams recalls that Jones told these women, 'Tennessee does not write about abnormal characters!' He writes about 'People!' Alexandra Del Lago is very real, complete with grand neuroses and the means temporarily to forget them. At times monstrous, the Princess is also a vulnerable, frightened animal. She does not stick around to fight her battles, but runs until all is clear. While we often see the Princess bossing Chance around, calling his bluff and ridiculing his pathetic attempt to blackmail her, Del Lago also displays moments of vulnerability. In Act One, Scene Two, she is touched by Chance's life story (perhaps because it is similar to her own). In the following act, she stumbles into the bar, drunk and high, but ready to admit that Chance has made her feel something for someone other than herself. And in Act Three, after her encouraging phone call with Sally Powers, Del Lago, revealing her own vulnerability, again identifies with Chance:

> *In both* **Chance** *and the* **Princess**, *we should return to the huddling together of the lost, but not with sentiment, which is false, but with whatever is truthful in the moments when people share doom, face firing squads together.* (96)

Regardless of the positive reviews of her comeback, Del Lago knows her success will not last.

Her alias, the Princess Kosmonopolis, likewise points to the complexity of Del Lago's character. Not merely a diva, struggling to survive in the movie industry that turned her into a monster, her alias leads back to Williams's discussion of the 'Cinderella story' as well as suggesting that before being consumed by this Hollywood dream, she was capable of kindness, generosity and grace – traits that in fairytales lead the princess to winning her prince. However, in the modern age, even when this princess displays kindness and generosity, she is ultimately unable to transform or for that matter save Chance. The pseudonym, furthermore, reflects her past. Like Chance (and Cinderella who cleaned and toiled for her step-sisters), Del Lago was not always rich and famous. She began, like them, with only beauty to boast of. The power struggle between Chance and Del Lago is, in part, fuelled by their recognition of their similarities. Chance could easily have reaped the benefits of fame as Del Lago does and she could easily have remained paralysed in her poverty.

Boss Finley

Tennessee Williams revealed that for him it was important to like his characters, but to like Boss Finley was impossible (Gunn, 27). Never quite satisfied, Williams allowed Elia Kazan to develop the Boss Finley sections for the 1959 Broadway debut of *Sweet Bird of Youth*. Kazan softened the tyrant considerably, transforming him into a sincere politician and loving father (Parker, par. 18). However, when Williams revised the play for publication in 1960–1, he omitted many of Kazan's additions (Parker, par. 1), leaving contemporary readers and viewers with a portrait of a 'hateful political and domestic bully' (Parker, par. 18).

Nevertheless, Boss Finley's desperate struggle to survive the changes occurring in the modern world, a struggle against time, makes him more than just a political and domestic tyrant. Indeed, there is an unmistakable resemblance between Boss Finley and *Cat on a Hot Tin Roof*'s Big Daddy, as Brenda Murphy and other scholars point out. However, unlike Big Daddy who is an 'epic figure, an icon of masculinity, vitality, and power' (see 196), Boss Finley is not bestowed with 'a kingly magnitude', a description given to Big Daddy by the playwright in his *Memoirs*. While Big Daddy, like Boss Finley, is a domineering father who is desperately trying to maintain his patriarchal position within the family, he, unlike Boss Finley, is just and kind as is notable in his behaviour towards Maggie. Although a hateful figure, Boss Finley is much more complex than the bigoted and corrupt politician Williams thought him. A hillbilly, according to himself and Miss Lucy, he is perhaps a victim of his own environment and upbringing. He is not an educated man, although he has helped to build the state's university. Despite being one of the founders of this institution, his attitude towards education is mixed. Although he is humiliated by Tom Junior's having 'flunked out of college with grades that only a moron would have an excuse for', Boss Finley does not value the process of learning. He aids his son in being readmitted 'by fake examinations, answers provided beforehand, stuck in your fancy pockets' (50). Helping his son to cheat his way back into college, Boss Finley reveals that his corruption goes beyond pocketing oil money; it has infected every institution in Florida.

Boss Finley will go to great lengths to create the illusion of a happy and successful family. Along with attempting to create the illusion of his son's intellectual integrity, he also attempts to mask the tragedy of his daughter's venereal disease. Initially he tries to cover up her operation. Even after promoting Dr Scudder to chief surgeon and arranging a marriage between the two (a marriage that has not yet taken place), Boss Finley fails to keep Heavenly's secret. Forcing his daughter to join him at the Youth for Tom Finley televised rally to represent white purity, he believes that 'lookin' at you [Heavenly], all in white like a virgin, nobody would dare to speak or believe the ugly stories about you' (56). However, he is not really concerned about his daughter's reputation or feelings nor is he concerned about Tom Junior's obscene behaviour. He ultimately uses his children: his concern is his own reputation and the winning of the next election. He is afraid that the scandals surrounding his children will 'defeat the mission' to eradicate 'all of them that want to adulterate the pure white blood of the South' (57).

These extreme attempts to hide his family's failures reflect Boss Finley's awareness of his loss of power, both in the home and in the political arena. Angry and frustrated with Tom Junior, he says,

It's a curious thing, a mighty peculiar thing, how often a man that rises to high public office is drug back down by every soul he harbors under his roof. He harbors them under his roof, and they pull the roof down on him. Every last living one of them. (49)

During their family dispute, Boss Finley and his son are described as '*two stags*', prepared to buck each other. The description is one that leads back to masculinity and power. Boss Finley, being the older 'stag', is bound to lose. He can no longer maintain the alpha position, as seen when the hillbilly heckler disrupts the rally. The Heckler unsettles Boss Finley, not by attacking his politics in an objective debate, but by targeting Boss Finley's greatest wound – Heavenly's impurity.

Heavenly Finley

At the opening of the play, Fly, the bellboy, speaks of Heavenly and Chance's young love. Having been a waiter in the Grand Ballroom years ago, he tells Chance that he used to see him 'with that real pretty girl you used to dance so good with, Mr Boss Finley's daughter' (8). While this reference to Heavenly seems insignificant at first, as Act One progresses the audience discovers that Chance has returned for the young Heavenly whose photograph he carries around with him. This photograph both reveals what she once was to Chance and what she has become. A nude image of a fifteen-year-old girl with the tide 'beginning to lap over her body like it desired her like [Chance] did and still [does] and will always, always' (38), the photograph signifies youth and Chance's desire to possess that youth. The water lapping over Heavenly's body, furthermore, preps the audience for another destructive image. In Act Two, Scene One, she stops and contemplates a fern ravished by the wind. Like the delicate fern '*that the salty Gulf wind has stripped nearly bare*' (53), the salt water of the Gulf of Mexico symbolises the process of decay. Heavenly, while only fifteen in the photograph, has already been sexually involved with Chance – an involvement which is the end of her purity and innocence.

Photographs are mere traces, shadowy figments, of the individual photographed. As a reproduction of Heavenly, the photograph signifies the hollowness of this idealised image which Chance carries around with him. She, as Clum astutely describes, is 'a mirage, the shell of the girl Chance loved' (140). Not only is the photograph a false image of the Heavenly that we meet in the second act, but it is also only a trace of what she once was.

She is, indeed, washed up on the shore like a shell, or as Tom Junior more crudely puts it, 'She's lyin' out on the beach like a dead body washed up on it' (46). Several of the play's characters, including Heavenly herself, refer to her body as dead, gutted and old. Defeated, Heavenly apologises to her father for the embarrassment her hysterectomy causes him but reveals that her own pain exceeds his:

> I felt worse than embarrassed when I found out that Dr George Scudder's knife had cut the youth out of my body, made me an old childless woman. Dry, cold, empty, like an old woman. (55–6)

Acknowledging her own emptiness, she cannot be anything more to Chance than an empty, hollow dream – a mirage in desolate Beanstalk Country.

Tom Junior

While Boss Finley represents politically charged hatred and bigotry, his son, Tom Junior, is perhaps more despicable. He has been the subject of many scandals. Without the help of his father's corrupt methods, Tom Junior would not have been to college. Furthermore, he has received newspaper coverage for 'drunk drivin'' and 'once for a stag party' that cost Boss Finley a considerable amount of money to 'hush it up' (49). Despite the supposed justice he seeks for his sister, Tom Junior is not concerned with Heavenly's well-being. His actions are motivated by his own loss of pride; like his father he has been shamed by her sexual relationship with Chance, an individual whose own conduct is questionable. For Tom Junior, his sister contracted a whore's disease, and thus she has tainted the family's reputation.

The leader of a small gang of thugs, Tom Junior employs his father's name to commit acts of violence that are motivated by racism, 'sex-envy' and pride. The Youth for Tom Finley clubs, endorsed by Boss Finley, are a sadistic and immoral lot. Tom Junior and his gang are responsible for randomly picking out a black man and castrating him 'to show they mean business about white women's protection in this state' (70). Regardless of the rhetoric Tom Junior and his gang use to condone their actions, these acts are not carried out to 'protect' white women. These acts, including Tom Junior's threat to castrate Chance if he does not leave town, are tied to his own emasculation. As the Finley empire is challenged, Tom Junior and his father resort to desperate and violent deeds. He and Boss Finley are envious of those who are gaining power – both in the political arena and in the private one. Having corrupted his sister, Chance represents the encroaching threat to Tom Junior's power. He no longer has control over his little sister's behaviour. With his masculinity in jeopardy, Tom Junior resorts to lashing out at those whom he perceives as holding power over women.

Miss Lucy

An opportunist, Miss Lucy, like Alexandra Del Lago, uses men. While Del Lago uses Chance to distract her from what she believes has been a failed comeback and from the destructive forces of time, Miss Lucy in essence prostitutes herself for 'a fifty-dollar-a-day hotel suite' and other luxuries Boss Finley showers on her. Before she ever appears on stage, both Tom Junior and Heavenly tell their father that they and everyone else in St Cloud know that Miss Lucy is his mistress and has been even before the death of Mrs Finley. And, to make matters worse, Tom Junior reveals that Miss Lucy 'don't even talk good of you' (50). Exposing Boss Finley's impotency in lipstick on the ladies' room mirror of the hotel bar, she unintentionally causes him to confront his waning sexual power. Like Del Lago and others of Williams's heroines, she is 'an agent of truth forcing weak men to face reality' (Clum, 140). In doing so, she exposes herself to danger. Boss Finley retaliates with physical violence, clamping a jewellery box on her finger.

Despite his violence, Miss Lucy is a survivor. When she makes her entrance in Act Two, Scene Two, she is described as '*dressed in a ball gown elaborately ruffled and very bouffant like an antebellum Southern belle's. A single blonde curl is arranged to switch girlishly at one side of her sharp little terrier face*' (58). Like Scarlett O'Hara, to whom Chance compares her, she holds on to her dignity and pride even under attack by enemy forces and when scorned by her lover. But her gentility and girlish behaviour is, Williams suggests, a façade. Like a terrier, a dog used for hunting, she is quick and wily. Miss Lucy wastes no time in retaliating. Seeing someone new enter the bar, she immediately approaches him, asking questions until she discovers that he is a heckler 'come to hear Boss Finley talk' (59). Providing the Heckler with a jacket and tie and directing him to the ballroom where the rally will take place, she seeks a revenge which will expose Boss Finley's waning political potency.

Miss Lucy is one of the few characters who attempts to help both Del Lago and Chance. Perhaps because she prostituted herself to obtain a type of lifestyle similar to that of Del Lago's – a lifestyle that Chance seeks and Del Lago is potentially losing – Miss Lucy identifies with both of them. When Miss Lucy, who has been trying to figure out what has changed about Chance, ruffles his hair, he bristles. In response, she says, 'Is your hair thinning? Maybe that's the difference I noticed in your appearance'.

Without intending harm, she forces Chance to confront his failure when she tells him in front of the crowd in the bar that Dan Hatcher had seen him in Palm Beach working 'as a beach-boy at some big hotel' (69). Even though she exposes his failure to beat time and to be anything better than beach-boy, she tries to save Chance from the monsters of St Cloud, urging him to flee with her to New Orleans.

As the 'president of [Del Lago's] local fan club' (61), Miss Lucy reveals that like Chance she bought into the Hollywood dream, worshipping those whose names appeared on the Silver Screen. When she sees Del Lago's miserable state in Act Two, Scene Two, unlike Chance who brushes her aside, Miss Lucy shows compassion: 'Honey, let me fix that zipper for you. Hold still just a second. Honey, let me take you upstairs. You mustn't be seen down here in this condition' (76). Aware of how cruel the inhabitants of St Cloud can be, Miss Lucy attempts to preserve Del Lago's appearance, and by extension the Cinderella myth. While she may not be able to assist her in much else, she tries to make sure that Del Lago is presentable even in her desperation – a skill that Miss Lucy has perfected. She shows no signs of distress though cut off financially from her former benefactor, Boss Finley.

Stage, Film and Television Productions

Written in 1952 and first produced at the Studio M Playhouse in Coral Gables, Florida, in 1956, *Sweet Bird of Youth* underwent several revisions. The play did not make an impact on New York critics and audiences until March of 1959. The Broadway premiere took place at the Martin Beck Theatre and was directed by Elia Kazan who collaborated with Williams on *A Streetcar Named Desire, Camino Real* and *Cat on a Hot Tin Roof*. Jo Mielziner, also no stranger to Williams, designed the set and lighting. Paul Newman, who only a year before had starred in the film version of *Cat on a Hot Tin Roof*, was cast in the role of Chance Wayne and Geraldine Page was Alexandra Del Lago. *Sweet Bird of Youth* received mixed reviews from New York critics, many of whom felt Williams had gone too far. John J. O'Connor of *Audience* wrote,

> The play, a hodgepodge of familiar Williams themes,
> sensationalism, and pseudo-poetically stated truisms, might have
> been an interesting one-acter. Certainly its content and scope
> do not justify the two-and-a-half hour ordeal it now demands.
> (Quoted in Murphy, 160)

Moreover, the critic John Gassner reported that he 'was disturbed by the attempted focusing of sympathy on two self-confessed "monsters"' (123). Along with criticising Williams's sensationalism, Gassner, who overall praised the play, saw problems in the structure of *Sweet Bird of Youth*. He found the play weakened by 'the split dramatic construction that divides attention between the personal drama and an attack on racist demagoguery in the South' (123). Despite these reviews, the play is considered one of Williams's many successes. Audiences stood in long queues to see this play which ran for almost a year and a total of 375 performances. In addition to a positive audience reception, the play was nominated for four Tony Awards.

The Broadway revival of *Sweet Bird of Youth* at the Harkness Theatre in 1975 also met with mixed reviews. Gina Mallet, a reviewer for *Time* magazine, wrote, 'Today [the play] seems fatally misconceived, a sentimental melodrama instead of a savage, black comedy on southern mores'. Despite the problematic production, Irene Worth's portrayal of Alexandra Del Lago was praised. Mallet and other critics noted that Worth 'overwhelm[ed] the play, with a sexy vibrato not unlike Al Jolson's, and stalk[ed] the stage like a jaguar vacationing among field mice'. She won a Tony for Best Actress.

Not until twenty-six years after its American debut did the play reach London's West End. Directed by the Nobel Prize-winning playwright Harold Pinter, the play opened at the Haymarket Theatre on 8 July 1985. Despite the praise Lauren Bacall received for her charming and cool portrayal of Alexandra Del Lago, London critics and audiences were disappointed. Mel Gussow, in his review of the London production for the *New York Times*, argued that the play's failure to captivate English audiences stemmed in part from cultural expectations. He revealed that since its world debut, English critics such as Kenneth Tynan have dismissed Williams's work as 'operatic and hysterical'. Pinter's attempt to create a cooler version of the play, however, diffused the panic and anxiety of Chance Wayne and Alexandra Del Lago, which ultimately for Gussow diminishes the angst of *Sweet Bird of Youth*.

Nine years after the London debut of *Sweet Bird of Youth*, the play was revived at the National Theatre. Directed by Richard Eyre and starring Robert Knepper as Chance Wayne and Clare Higgins as Alexandra Del Lago, this 1994 production restored the heated tension and anxiety absent in Pinter's subdued production. According to critic Clara Hieronymus of *The Tennessean*, while 'Williams's melodrama ends up a sad spoof', London audiences 'listened attentively, absorbed in its raffishly dramatic performance and gave it a succession of curtain calls'. Indeed, most critics, while acknowledging that the play is flawed and its themes are perhaps no longer relevant, praised Eyre's production and the acting of the two leads. Michael Billington of the *Guardian* called Eyre's production 'superbly atmospheric' with a 'knock-down performance from Clare Higgins as a fading movie queen'. Knepper's performance, too, was deemed exceptional. Neil Smith, in his article for *What's On*, wrote, 'The role of Chance Wayne is an Everest for any actor, but Knepper tackles the challenge head-on'. Michael Coveney of *The Observer* called the production 'a blazing restoration' and Dale Maitland Cartwright of the *Southern Cross* decreed it 'A real stunner, make sure you see!'.

In 1962, the first film version of the play hit the big screen, directed by Richard Brooks. Newman and Page once again took on the roles of Chance and the Princess. The film veers from the text in drastic ways and a dismayed Williams complained that the happy ending to the film was 'a contradiction to the meaning of the play' (quoted in Devlin, 275). However, the performances of Newman and Page are unforgettable and Page won an Oscar for her part. Despite the softening of the racial/political tensions, the change from Heavenly Finley being infected with a venereal disease to having an abortion and the film's happy ending, which allowed Chance and Heavenly to unite after Tom Junior breaks Chance's nose, the film's aura is definitely Williams's, leaving the audience to wonder whether Heavenly and Chance can really make it.

Nearly thirty years after the play hit the stage, the American television broadcasting system NBC aired a new version of *Sweet Bird of Youth* in 1989, directed by Nicholas Roeg, starring Elizabeth Taylor as Alexandra Del Lago, Mark Harmon as Chance Wayne and Rip Torn as Boss Finley. Although in the fifties and sixties Taylor starred with great success in film adaptations of plays, including the 1958 film adaptation of *Cat on a Hot Tin Roof* and the 1959 film adaptation of *Suddenly Last Summer*, this made-for-television version of the play is deeply disappointing. Despite restoring the original ending (Chance's castration), this film is no more faithful to the playtext than the earlier film; production and acting also leave much to be desired.

Production History since 2010 (by Katherine Weiss)

Out of the four works discussed here, *Sweet Bird of Youth* has been Williams's least successful play. *The Glass Menagerie, A Streetcar Named Desire* and *Cat on a Hot Tin Roof* have been revived several times in the past two decades. The popularity with theatre professionals most likely lies in their superior structure rather than the characters; Del Lago and Chance Wayne are monumental. The frequent revivals and classroom usage of

Menagerie, Streetcar and *Cat* have made them familiar to audiences and students of drama, if not to most Americans. Even those who have not seen a staged production of any of these three plays have undoubtedly heard much buzz about them. It is uncertain if this is the case with *Sweet Bird of Youth*.

In the past three years, however, there has been considerable interest in Williams's play about time and corruption. The first of the major revivals scheduled for *Sweet Bird*, regrettably, has been indefinitely postponed. With Nicole Kidman lined up to play Alexandra Del Lago and James Franco lined up to make his Broadway debut as the gigolo Chance Wayne, the show was sure to attract crowds. In August 2011, the *New York Times* reported that Franco dropped out of the project and the play, that was to open in the fall of the same year, was on hold indefinitely. Since the disappointing news, the producer, Scott Rudin, poured his attention and money into other projects, most notably the revival of Arthur Miller's *Death of a Salesman*, directed by legendary Mike Nichols and starring Philip Seymour Hoffman as Willy Loman.

While *Sweet Bird* has not been performed on Broadway since 1975, the director hoping to bring the play back to a major New York stage, David Cromer, instead, took the play to the Goodman Theatre in Chicago. With a changed cast, the 2012 revival starred Diane Lane (known for her roles in movies such as *Perfect Storm* and *Under the Tuscan Sun*) as Del Lago and Finn Wittrock (who played Happy in Nichol's revival of *Death of a Salesman*) as Chance Wayne. The production was applauded by critics. The *New City Stage* recommended the production to its readers. The rotating stage and white and grey colour scheme of the production was viewed by Kris Vire of *Time Out Chicago* as evoking the 'eerie atmospheric' quality of Williams's play. It is the performance of Diane Lane, however, that received the most praise (with the performance of Wittrock commented on positively but with little elaboration). Jonathan Abarbanel of *Theatre Mania* wrote that Lane 'smartly underplays Del Lago without making her weak'. And, Chris Jones of the *Chicago Tribune* gave the play three and a half stars, noting that although the play is a 'meandering text filled with a plethora of furiously miserable souls', Lane's 'richly textured performance is a needed anchor for director David Cromer's passionate, arresting and unwieldy Goodman Theatre production'.

Sex and the City star, Kim Cattrall tried her hand at Alexandra Del Lago in the summer of 2013, starring alongside Seth Numrich, known for his roles in Broadway musicals. The London revival of *Sweet Bird* at the Old Vic received mixed reviews. No fan of the script (like most theatre critics), Michael Billington of the *Guardian* nevertheless applauds the director, Marianne Elliott, calling the revival 'first-rate', noting that the cast 'is as good as any you'll find in a national company'. Sarah Hemming of the *Financial Times* argues that James Graham's edited text and Elliott's direction helped the production achieve 'not just a wealth of autobiographical pain, but a searing response to the viciousness afoot in America's Deep South in the 1950s'.

Known for directing successes such as *War Horse*, it is a shame that Elliott's *Sweet Bird*, as Tim Walker from the *Telegraph* bluntly states, 'fails dismally'. Compared to Cromer's direction, Elliott missed opportunities by trying too hard to recreate Williams's 'plastic theatre'. Twice a ghostly image of a woman lingered behind the semi-transparent walls of the hotel room; the purpose of which, however, was not clear. While most likely signifying the ghost of Heavenly haunting Chance, this technique tried too hard to make the play about their young love. In his review, Walker trashes the production, noting everything from Cattrall's awful red wig to the more damaging commentary that Cattrall 'hasn't any of the fading grandeur that the part requires'. Kate Bassett of the *Independent* shares Walker's disappointment, even calling her review, 'I wouldn't get out of bed for this, Kim'. Although not much is said in these reviews about Numrich, his performance from what I witnessed on opening night, was imprecise, and more devastatingly, his 'audition' in which he tells Del Lago his life story, dragged. During his monologue, he mostly stood behind the bed, missing opportunities to use his body to express the twists and turns Chance Wayne has faced.

These recent productions reveal that the play has become a showcase for an ageing actress. Bacall in 1985, Lane in 2012 and Cattrall in 2013, for most critics, stole the show. Chance Wayne and the actors who have played him in recent years have sadly been overlooked.

Notes

The notes below explain words and phrases from the play, with page numbers referencing the Student Editions published by Bloomsbury Methuen Drama.

page

1   *Hart Crane*: (1899–1932) an American poet and novelist.

2   *Cheryl Crawford*: (1902–86) an American theatre producer and director who produced Williams's *The Rose Tattoo* in 1951 and later *Sweet Bird of Youth*. Along with Elia Kazan, Robert Lewis and Anna Sokolow, she is also known for founding The Actors' Studio, an organisation of theatre professionals who taught movement and method acting. Among the famous actors to be trained at the studio were Marlon Brando, Paul Newman and Geraldine Page.

7   *tabouret*: a small cabinet.

7   *domino*: eyeshade.

7   *Give me the Bromo first*: possibly due to excessive drinking and drug use, Chance asks for a Bromo-Seltzer, a popular effervescent antacid.

9   *ether*: an organic compound that was once used as an anaesthetic.

10   *wire*: telegram.

12   *state line*: border into the next state, out of range.

14   *A pink one*: slang for diamorphine, diacetylmorphine, acetomorphine.

20   *Palm Beach*: a tropical, beach city in Florida.

20   *I'm the Princess Kosmonopolis*: while there is no direct origin for Alexandra Del Lago's alias, kosmo/cosmo may refer to the universe or world and monopolis/monopoly is the exclusive possession of the trade in some commodity. Her alias, then, may refer to her sense of grandeur. She ruled the film universe. Moreover, calling herself 'Princess' resonates with other references and allusions to children's tales.

20   *Tallahassee*: the capital of Florida and home to Florida State University. In Southern college towns in the 1950s, the purchase of alcohol on Sundays was prohibited.

21   *package store*: an off-licence, so called because alcohol had to be sold in a sealed container and wrapped up to take away.

21   *Old Spanish Trail*: a small highway that spans 3,000 miles of
        the United States. This stretch of road, based on an historic trade
        route from the nineteenth century, was completed in 1929.

23   *neuritis*: a serious nerve disorder, one which results in weakness,
        loss of reflexes and a change in sensitivity.

31   *You wouldn't want 'Confidential' or 'Whisper' or 'Hush-Hush'*:
        all three magazines were popular gossip rags during the time.
        The bi-monthly *Confidential* ran from 1952 to 1978; the more
        blatantly and violently sexual *Whisper* ran from 1946 to 1958;
        and *Hush-Hush*, which often ran stories of interracial affairs and
        homosexuality, was popular in the 1950s and 1960s.

35   *twelve-pound baby*: 5.45 kilos.

35   *the boys belong to the Junior Chamber of Commerce*: JCCs
        or Jaycees are tax-exempt, non-profit organisations for youths
        interested in financial or business networking, like the Youth for
        Tom Finley clubs.

36   *clubs in New Orleans such as Rex and Comus*: while this is a
        reference to social clubs in New Orleans, Rex and Comus are
        a part of Louisiana folk tradition. Rex, the carnival king, and
        his wife visited the court of Comus. This meeting of the courts
        evolved into what today is Mardi Gras, the carnival celebrated
        before Lent.

36   *freshmen at Tulane or LSU or Ole Miss*: first-year students at
        Tulane University in New Orleans, Louisiana, or at Louisiana
        State University in Baton Rouge, or University of Mississippi in
        Oxford, Mississippi.

36   *Oklahoma!*: a popular musical which opened in 1943; written
        and composed by Richard Rodgers and Oscar Hammerstein II.

36   *had pictures in 'Life' in a cowboy outfit*: *Life* magazine featured
        articles on political and cultural events. The cowboy outfit may
        refer to his role in *Oklahoma!*.

36   *then that thing in Korea came along*: the Korean War, 25 June
        1950 to 27 July 1953.

37   *swabbies*: enlisted men.

42   *porch*: veranda.

43   *Georgia O'Keefe*: (1887–1986) an American artist, famous for
        her paintings of flowers and desert landscapes.

43   *Pass Christian*: Williams often uses real place-names. Pass
        Christian is a costal town in Mississippi.

44   *Discreetly, like you handled that operation you done on my
        daughter*: Dr Scudder performed a hysterectomy on Heavenly.
        In the early- to mid-twentieth century, hysterectomies were

often performed on women with advanced stages of venereal diseases.

46   *There's a pretty fair doctor that lost his license for helping a girl out of trouble, and he won't be so goddam finicky about doing this absolutely just thing*: the doctor in question has lost his licence for performing an abortion, a procedure that was illegal in America until 1973. The 'just thing' that Tom Junior refers to is castration.

50   *the Queen of Sheba*: in ancient mythology, the Queen of Sheba tested King Solomon's wisdom by questioning him. She was also known for her gold and gifts.

54   *as if you were buyin' a trousseau to marry the Prince of Monaco*: the Prince of Monaco married the American film star Grace Kelly, known for roles that exuded innocence and sweetness.

54   *backhouse*: an outside toilet.

56   *the black days of Reconstruction*: after the Civil War and the emancipation of slaves, the era of Reconstruction (1865–77) worked to restructure the power and wealth distribution among whites and blacks. Among the attempts to reform the South, blacks were given land and sometimes money, and some black men were placed in government offices. The placing of blacks in government offices was, at times, destructive because most had had no prior training, let alone a formal education. Before the Civil War and the Emancipation, black men and women were not even allowed to learn how to read.

58   *novachord*: a polyphonic synthesiser, manufactured by Hammond between 1939 and 1942. Only 1069 examples were made.

58   *Grant's twelve-year-old?*: whisky.

58   *Walgreen's*: a popular drugstore, much like Boots. In the fifties, Walgreen's would also have had a soda fountain, a counter at which customers could order soft drinks and milkshakes.

59   *He has the length and leanness and luminous pallor of a face that El Greco gave to his saints*: El Greco (1541–1614) was a late Renaissance Spanish painter, sculptor and architect.

61   *outfit Vic Mature wore in a Foreign Legion picture*: although never receiving the attention he deserved from film critics, Victor Mature (1913–99) was one of the busiest and most popular actors after the Second World War. A Southerner like Williams, he was born in Louisville, Kentucky. Mature's popularity waned in the sixties.

61   *Quiereme Mucho*: the song was published in 1931 and became
            very popular in the thirties. Its English title is 'Yours'.

62   *The Valiant*: a 1920s one-act play by Holworthy Hall and
            Robert Middlemass, turned into a successful film in 1929. It
            was nominated for two Oscars and its leading actor, Paul Muni,
            won an Oscar for his performance. The play is about a convicted
            murderer who goes to his execution without ever revealing his
            true identity.

62   *'If you like-a me, like I like-a you, / And we like-a both the
            same'*: Chance is singing part of 'Under the Bamboo Tree',
            featured in *Meet Me in Saint Louis* (1944) and sung by Judy
            Garland.

65   *The Princess Kosmonopolis's best friend is that sob sister,
            Sally Powers*: sob sister was a derogatory term used to describe
            female journalists whose reporting style was to evoke sympathy
            from her readers.

67   *'It's a Big Wonderful World'*: probably the popular Dean Martin
            song 'It's a Big, Wide Wonderful World'. Its refrain is 'It's swell
            when you're really in love'.

67   *arpeggio*: a musical term meaning 'broken chord'. The
            technique requires that instead of playing a chord the notes are
            played consecutively.

68   *Scarlett O'Hara?*: Chance refers to the infamous Southern belle
            in Margaret Mitchell's *Gone with the Wind*, an epic novel that
            was turned into the famous MGM production, starring Vivien
            Leigh and Clark Gable, in 1939. When working with MGM,
            Williams wrote a screenplay about a modern day Scarlett
            O'Hara, a woman representing 'the natural elegance in the old
            South' (Williams quoted in Leverich, 509), taking her out of the
            Civil War period and into the twentieth century. His script, *The
            Gentleman Caller*, eventually became *The Glass Menagerie*.

70   *There's been a whole lot of Northern agitation all over the
            country*: Bud refers to movements that condemned segregation
            and discrimination which continued in America until 1968.

72   *pink pill . . . goof-ball*: slang for diamorphine, diacetylmorphine,
            acetomorphine.

74   *That's a fine setup, Scotty, if you're satisfied with it but it's
            starting to give you a little pot and a can*: sitting all day at his
            job, Scotty is developing a large mid-section and large buttocks.

77   *Lost in the beanstalk country, the ogre's country at the top of
            the beanstalk*: a reference to Jack and the Beanstalk, the popular
            fairytale.

80   *Keep your ruttin' voice down*: rutting holds the same vulgar
      meaning as fucking.

82   *'Bonnie Blue Flag'*: a marching song, also known as 'We are
      a Band of Brothers', composed in 1861 and associated with
      the Confederate States of America. For an audience in tune to
      the racial unrest in America, this march would bring home the
      extreme racist politics of the Finley clan.

83   *'Liechtensteiner Polka'*: popular folk song composed by the
      German accordionist Will Glahé.

89   *'a criminal degenerate'*: this phrase was 'usually applied to
      homosexuals' (Clum, 142). To read Chance as a homosexual
      is problematic, though. Hence, the phrase takes on the broader
      meaning of referring to someone who has committed sexual
      crimes.

89   *You couldn't drive through the Palm Gardens*: Del Lago reveals
      that Chance is still under the influence of drugs and alcohol.

90   *Grand Corniche*: a winding road along the south coast of
      France, roughly 2,000 feet above sea-level.

91   *Chasen's*: a luxurious restaurant located in Beverly Hills,
      California. Chasen's has been a favourite spot for Hollywood
      stars such as Elizabeth Taylor and Frank Sinatra.

Questions for Further Study

1 Critics insist that the plays of Tennessee Williams, unlike those of his contemporaries such as Arthur Miller, are 'poetic' rather than 'realistic'. What elements of *Sweet Bird of Youth* represent a 'poetic' aesthetic?

2 The protagonist, Tom Wingfield, in *The Glass Menagerie*, says: 'I am the opposite of a stage magician. . . . I give you truth in the pleasant disguise of illusion'. How is this an equally accurate description of *Sweet Bird of Youth*?

3 In his 'Foreword' to the play, Williams claimed his use of violence is Aristotelian – that the audience reaches a catharsis (or emotional cleansing) through the watching of violence on stage. To what extent do you see the violence in *Sweet Bird of Youth* offering the audience catharsis?

4 The scholar David Savran argues that while Tennessee Williams has on many occasions spoken out against racism, calling it 'the most horrible thing', he objectifies and exoticises those that are deemed as other within the social setting of his plays, exemplifying 'a contradiction inherent within a certain liberal egalitarianism' (126–7). Assuming this contradiction is apparent in *Sweet Bird of Youth*, which characters are objectified and exoticised, and how so?

5 How does Williams's *Sweet Bird of Youth* fit into the tradition of Southern writing? What comparisons can be drawn between Williams and other Southern writers such as Carson McCullers and William Faulkner?

6 What significance can be drawn from the names of characters (Chance, Heavenly, Stuff, Fly, Boss Finley, etc.)?

7 The action of the play is set '*somewhere on the Gulf Coast*' in the '*Royal Palms Hotel*', in which '*a grove of palm trees*' is ever present on the cyclorama. How does the tranquillity of the luxurious seaside hotel inform the tragedy of the play?

8 A four-lane highway, although never seen on stage, is said to run past the Royal Palms Hotel. What does this image of encroaching modernisation suggest about the time period, place and context of the story, and the relationship between the characters?

9 Taking into account the play's title as well as the '*soft, urgent cries of birds*' and '*the sound of their wings*' that are heard throughout, what is the symbolic significance of 'birds' in *Sweet Bird of Youth*?

10 Throughout *Sweet Bird of Youth*, there are many references to age, ageing and a desire to recapture one's youth. Alexandra Del Lago

has fled from the Silver Screen after her close-up reveals her age, and Chance Wayne considers himself old at twenty-nine. What makes youth so sweet and desirable to the characters in this play?

11 From Dr Scudder, the audience learns that Chance's mother has died, and, unable to reach Chance, a collection at her church was taken up in order to bury her. What relevance does the death and burial of Chance's mother have on the play?

12 Del Lago refers to herself and to Chance as 'monsters'. What makes these two characters monstrous? What other characters in the play can be described as 'monsters'?

13 The children's tale of Jack and the Beanstalk is mentioned in Act Two, Scene Two. How does it help to define the characters in this play? How does it inform the plot? What other references to children's fairytales are there and what significance can be attached to them?

14 What is the symbolic significance of Del Lago's need for oxygen and her desire to retire to the moon, a dead planet without oxygen?

15 What is Williams suggesting about Chance and Del Lago's drug and alcohol abuse? How does this form of abuse function in the play?

16 Many of Williams's memorable female characters, such as Amanda Wingfield from *The Glass Menagerie* and Blanche DuBois from *A Streetcar Named Desire*, are described as 'antebellum Southern belles', evoking Scarlett O'Hara in *Gone with the Wind*. In what ways is Miss Lucy part of this tradition?

17 *Sweet Bird of Youth* may be said to be a play about the tension between needing illusions and being disillusioned. How are the characters of Alexandra Del Lago, Chance Wayne, Heavenly and Boss Finley defined by this tension and how do they cope with it?

18 In Act Two, Scene Two, Chance sings two songs. How does his singing inform the play?

19 Twice we hear of the nude photograph Chance took of Heavenly when she was only fifteen years of age. In the first instance, Chance shows Del Lago the photograph (Act One, Scene Two). In Act Two, Scene One, Boss Finley tells Dr Scudder that the first time he warned Chance to leave town was after he had discovered the photograph of his daughter had been taken. What significance can be drawn from the photograph?

20 How does Boss Finley, a figure of authority and wealth, use his ability to instil values of young masculine power and feminine purity to aid his racist agenda? And why is that agenda crumbling as seen in Miss Lucy's lipstick graffiti and the Heckler's ability to shake up Boss Finley?

21   The movie and television industry are both under attack in *Sweet
     Bird of Youth*. What is Williams's critique of these media? How is
     his critique of television similar and how is it different to that of his
     critique of the film industry?
22   *Sweet Bird of Youth* is set in the 1950s and displays the attitudes and
     politics of the time. Does it still have power and relevance today?
23   Imagine that you are going to direct a production of *Sweet Bird of
     Youth*. How would you stage a production of the play? What would
     the set look like? What would the Lamentation sound like? Who
     would you cast as Chance Wayne and Alexandra Del Lago?

Further Questions on Williams's Plays

1 Tennessee Williams's *The Glass Menagerie* is the best-known American 'memory play', a genre in theatre in which a central character remembers his past as it is acted out on stage. One could argue that Williams's other plays, which do not adhere to the structure of the memory play, too, are concerned with the way the past preoccupies a character and shapes his or her identity. Chart how memory haunts and transforms the characters in *The Glass Menagerie*, *A Streetcar Named Desire*, *Cat on a Hot Tin Roof* and *Sweet Bird of Youth*.

2 In *Sweet Bird of Youth*, the protagonist Chance Wayne returns to his hometown to reunite with his 'girl', Heavenly. What becomes apparent is that he still clings onto an illusion of their young love, even carrying a photograph of Heavenly with him. Chance is not the only Williams character to romanticise young love. Identify moments in *The Glass Menagerie*, *A Streetcar Named Desire*, *Cat on a Hot Tin Roof* and *Sweet Bird of Youth* when characters romanticise or idealise young love. Then discuss the effects of such illusions on the development of the characters and the events in the plays.

3 Stephen Bottoms insightfully argues that Laura Wingfield in *The Glass Menagerie* 'has created an imaginary world for herself, into which she retreats whenever she can, and especially when she is placed under pressure' (see 22). Which other characters in *The Glass Menagerie*, *A Streetcar Named Desire*, *Cat on a Hot Tin Roof* and *Sweet Bird of Youth* create imaginary worlds? For what reasons do they create these worlds? When and to what effect do their make-believe worlds crumble?

4 In addition to creating imaginary worlds, several of Williams's characters 'manufacture illusions', as Amanda Wingfield accuses her son of doing in *The Glass Menagerie* (95). Is Tom alone in escaping into illusions? Who else, on Williams's stage, does this? What is Williams's attitude towards this type of escapism?

5 Scholars have found many similarities between the events and persons in Williams's life and his plays. Where do you see biography enter into *The Glass Menagerie*, *A Streetcar Named Desire*, *Cat on a Hot Tin Roof* and *Sweet Bird of Youth*? How has Williams transformed these biographical details to serve his fiction? Is

Williams successful in transforming the personal details of his life into depersonalised fictions? Support your answers with examples from *The Glass Menagerie*, *A Streetcar Named Desire*, *Cat on a Hot Tin Roof* and *Sweet Bird of Youth*.

6   Williams strived to break from the conventions of realism. He, instead, identified his theatre as 'plastic' by which he meant a theatre of poetry and images to suggest reality and truth. Discuss the poetic and imaginative elements present in *The Glass Menagerie*, *A Streetcar Named Desire*, *Cat on a Hot Tin Roof* and *Sweet Bird of Youth*.

7   Several scholars, including Philip Kolin, Michael Hooper and Patricia Hern (whose commentaries are included here) have argued that Williams's plays are like classical tragedies. What similarities do *The Glass Menagerie*, *A Streetcar Named Desire*, *Cat on a Hot Tin Roof* and *Sweet Bird of Youth* share with classical tragedies, especially those from ancient Greece and/or by William Shakespeare? Be sure to discuss what Williams takes from the tragic tradition and how he modernises this tradition?

8   Explore Williams's representation of the South and of Southerners in *The Glass Menagerie*, *A Streetcar Named Desire*, *Cat on a Hot Tin Roof* and *Sweet Bird of Youth*.

9   Williams provides his readers with detailed set descriptions and specific location markers. How do the sets and locations inform the plays? Draw your responses from *The Glass Menagerie*, *A Streetcar Named Desire*, *Cat on a Hot Tin Roof* and *Sweet Bird of Youth*.

10   Williams often incorporated music in his plays. In what ways is music implemented in *The Glass Menagerie*, *A Streetcar Named Desire*, *Cat on a Hot Tin Roof* and *Sweet Bird of Youth*? How does the incorporation of music in these works shape the mood of the characters and, more generally, the plays?

11   *The Glass Menagerie*, *A Streetcar Named Desire*, *Cat on a Hot Tin Roof* and *Sweet Bird of Youth* all begin with an epigraph. These epigraphs are rarely included in the programmes of productions. What do they express to the reader, director or actor? How would an audience benefit from knowing the epigraphs?

12   Williams often uses animal imagery to describe his characters. Where in *The Glass Menagerie*, *A Streetcar Named Desire*, *Cat on a Hot Tin Roof* and *Sweet Bird of Youth* do we find characters compared to or referred to as animals? Explore the interpretative possibilities of such comparisons and references.

13   What role does substance abuse play in *The Glass Menagerie*, *A Streetcar Named Desire*, *Cat on a Hot Tin Roof* and *Sweet Bird of Youth*?

14 Williams recalled that the director Margo Jones told a group
    of women once that 'Tennessee does not write about abnormal
    characters'. He writes about 'People! . . . Life' (*Where I Live,* 27).
    Using examples from *The Glass Menagerie, A Streetcar Named
    Desire, Cat on a Hot Tin Roof* and *Sweet Bird of Youth*, argue Margo
    Jones's position that Williams's characters are not abnormal.

15 Williams has created some of the most powerful patriarchs on the
    American stage. Pulling your examples from *The Glass Menagerie,
    A Streetcar Named Desire, Cat on a Hot Tin Roof* and *Sweet Bird of
    Youth*, explore the image of the father-figure on Williams's stage.

16 So many of Williams's characters are concerned with 'time'. Explore
    the ways in which Williams in *The Glass Menagerie, A Streetcar
    Named Desire, Cat on a Hot Tin Roof* and *Sweet Bird of Youth*
    depicts time as a matter of concern.

17 Williams once said in an interview that 'people who are shocked
    by the truth are not deserving of the truth. The truth is something
    you need to deserve.'[1] Which of Williams's characters are shocked
    by the truth? Which have deserved the truth? Are there moments
    in Williams in which the audience is shocked by the plays'
    truthfulness? Draw your discussion from *The Glass Menagerie, A
    Streetcar Named Desire, Cat on a Hot Tin Roof* and *Sweet Bird of
    Youth*.

18 Explore the ways in which homosexuality, sexual promiscuity and
    rape are depicted in Williams's *The Glass Menagerie, A Streetcar
    Named Desire, Cat on a Hot Tin Roof* and *Sweet Bird of Youth*.

19 Imagine that you are putting on a season of Tennessee Williams at
    your university. As the artistic director of the project, you need to
    decide in what order the plays, *The Glass Menagerie, A Streetcar
    Named Desire, Cat on a Hot Tin Roof* and *Sweet Bird of Youth*, will
    appear. While you could show them in chronological order, you have
    been asked to consider other alternatives. What other options would
    you consider? What rationale do you have for your decision?

20 Imagine you are putting on a season of Tennessee Williams plays at
    your local theatre. To add some cohesion to the project, you, as the
    director, want to highlight some recurring themes and styles that run
    through *The Glass Menagerie, A Streetcar Named Desire, Cat on
    a Hot Tin Roof* and *Sweet Bird of Youth*. What themes and stylistic
    choices would you highlight and why?

---

1   This interview is available on YouTube at www.youtube.com/watch?v=FScWlr5qZUY

21   Early in his career as a writer, Williams worked for MGM, and,
     perhaps because of this experience, Williams's plays contain a
     cinematic quality to them. Several of his stage works have been
     turned into major motion pictures. Identify and discuss elements in
     The Glass Menagerie, *A Streetcar Named Desire*, *Cat on a Hot Tin
     Roof* and *Sweet Bird of Youth* that are cinematic.

Further Reading

Selected Works by Williams

American Blues: Five Short Plays. New York: Dramatist Play Service, 1948.

Baby Doll and Other Plays (Suddenly Last Summer, Something Unspoken). Harmondsworth: Penguin, 1968.

Candles to the Sun. New York: New Directions, 2004.

Cat on a Hot Tin Roof and Other Plays (The Milk Train Doesn't Stop Here Anymore, Night of the Iguana). Harmondsworth: Penguin, 1976.

Cat on a Hot Tin Roof, with commentary and notes by Philip C. Kolin. London: Methuen Drama, 2010.

The Collected Poems of Tennessee Williams, edited by David Roessel and Nicholas Moschovakis. New York: New Directions, 2002.

Collected Stories. New York: New Directions, 1994.

Dragon Country: A Book of Plays. New York: New Directions, 1970.

Five O'Clock Angel: Letters of Tennessee Williams to Maria St Just, edited by Alfred A. Knopf. New York: Knopf, 1990.

Fugitive Kind. New York: New Directions, 2001.

The Glass Menagerie (with 'The Catastrophe of Success'), with commentary and notes by Stephen J. Bottoms. London: Methuen Drama, 2000.

The Magic Tower: An Unpublished One-Act Play by Tennessee Williams, edited by Nicholas Moschovakis and David Roessel. New York: New Directions, 2011.

Memoirs. New York: Doubleday, 1975.

Mister Paradise and Other One-Act Plays, edited by Nicholas Moschovakis and David Roessel. New York: New Directions, 2005.

Moise and the World of Reason. New York: Simon and Schuster, 1975.

Not about the Nightingales. London: Methuen Drama, 1998.

Notebooks, edited by Margaret Bradham Thornton. New Haven and London: Yale University Press, 2006.

One Arm and Other Stories (revised edn). New York: New Directions, 1957.

Period of Adjustment, Summer and Smoke and *Small Craft Warnings*. Harmondsworth: Penguin, 1989.

The Roman Spring of Mrs Stone. London: Lehmann, 1952; republished by London: Vintage, 1999.

The Rose Tattoo and *Camino Real*. Harmondsworth: Penguin, 1958.

The Selected Letters of Tennessee Williams, Vol. I, 1920–1945, edited by Albert J. Devlin and Nancy M. Tischler. London: Oberon Books, 2001.

The Selected Letters of Tennessee Williams, Vol. II, 1945–1957, edited by Albert J. Devlin and Nancy M. Tischler. New York: New Directions, 2004.

Something Cloudy, Something Clear. London: Methuen Drama, 1996.

Spring Storm. New York: New Directions, 1999.

Stairs to the Roof. New York: New Directions, 2000.

Stopped Rocking and Other Screenplays. New York: New Directions, 1984.

A Streetcar Named Desire, The Glass Menagerie and *Sweet Bird of Youth*. Harmondsworth: Penguin, 1962.

A Streetcar Named Desire, with commentary and notes by Patricia Hern and Michael Hooper. London: Methuen Drama, 1984; republished in 2009.

Sweet Bird of Youth, with commentary and notes by Katherine Weiss. London: Methuen, 2010.

The Theatre of Tennessee Williams, Vol. 1: Battle of Angels, The Glass Menagerie, A Streetcar Named Desire. New York: New Directions, 1971.

The Theatre of Tennessee Williams, Vol. 2: The Eccentricities of a Nightingale, Summer and Smoke, The Rose Tattoo, Camino Real. New York: New Directions, 1976.

The Theatre of Tennessee Williams, Vol. 3: Cat on a Hot Tin Roof, Orpheus Descending, Suddenly Last Summer. New York: New Directions, 1971.

The Theatre of Tennessee Williams, Vol. 4: Sweet Bird of Youth, A Period of Adjustment, The Night of the Iguana. New York: New Directions, 1972.

The Theatre of Tennessee Williams, Vol. 5: The Milk Train Doesn't Stop Here Anymore, Kingdom of Earth. New York: New Directions, 1990.

The Theatre of Tennessee Williams, Vol. 6: Wagon Full of Cotton and Other Plays. New York: New Directions, 1992.

The Theatre of Tennessee Williams, Vol. 7: In the Bar of a Tokyo Hotel and Other Plays. New York: New Directions, 1994.

The Theatre of Tennessee Williams, Vol. 8: Vieux Carré, A Lovely Sunday for Creve Coeur, Clothes for a Summer Hotel, The Red Devil Battery Sign. New York: New Directions, 2001.

The Traveling Companion and Other Plays, edited by Annette J. Saddik. New York: New Directions, 2008.

Twenty-Seven Wagons Full of Cotton and Other Plays. New York: New Directions, 1945.

Where I Live: Selected Essays, edited by Christine Day and Bob Woods. New York: New Directions, 1978.

Books and Other Full-Length Studies

Adler, Thomas P., *Mirror and the Stage: The Pulitzer Prize Play as an Approach to American Drama*. West Lafayette: Purdue University Press, 1987.

Bak, John, *Tennessee Williams: A Literary Life*. London and New York: Palgrave Macmillan, 2013.

Bigsby, C. W. E., *A Critical Introduction to Twentieth-Century American Drama: Volume Two: Williams, Miller, Albee*. Cambridge: Cambridge University Press, 1984.

—, *Modern American Drama, 1945–1990*. Cambridge: Cambridge University Press, 1992.

Boxill, Roger, *Tennessee Williams*. London: Macmillan, 1987.

Bray, Robert, *Tennessee Williams and His Contemporaries*. Newcastle-upon-Tyne: Cambridge Scholars, 2007.

Clum, John, *Acting Gay: Male Homosexuality in American Drama*. New York: Columbia University Press, 1992.

Donahue, Francis, *The Dramatic World of Tennessee Williams*. New York: Frederick Ungar, 1964.

Donkin, Ellen, and Susan Clement (eds), *Upstaging Big Daddy: Direct Theatre as if Gender and Race Matter*. Ann Arbor: University of Michigan Press, 1993.

Falb, Lewis W., *American Drama in Paris: 1945–1970. A Study of Its Critical Reception*. Chapel Hill: University of North Carolina Press, 1973.

Falk, Signi Lenea, *Tennessee Williams*. New York: Twayne, 1961.

Griffin, Alice, *Understanding Tennessee Williams*. Columbia: University of South Carolina Press, 1995.

Hayman, Robert, *Tennessee Williams: Everyone Else Is an Audience*. New Haven: Yale University Press, 1993.

Holditch, W. Kenneth, and Richard F. Leavitt, *Tennessee Williams and the South*. Jackson: University of Mississippi, 2002.

Hooper, Michael S. D., *Sexual Politics in the Work of Tennessee Williams: Desire over Protest*. Cambridge: Cambridge University Press, 2012.

Jackson, Esther Merle, *The Broken World of Tennessee Williams*. Madison: University of Wisconsin Press, 1965.

Kolin, Philip C., *The Influence of Tennessee Williams: Essays on Fifteen American Playwrights*. Jefferson: McFarland, 2008.

—, *Tennessee Williams: A Guide to Research and Performance*. Westport: Greenwood Press, 1988.

— (ed.), *The Tennessee Williams Encyclopedia*. Westport: Greenwood Press, 2004.

—, *Williams: A Streetcar Named Desire. Plays in Production*. Cambridge: Cambridge University Press, 2000.

Leverich, Lyle, *The Unknown Tennessee Williams*. New York: Norton, 1995.

Mitgang, Herbert, *Dangerous Dossiers: Exposing the Secret War Against America's Greatest Authors*. New York: Ballantine, 1988.

Murphy, Brenda, *Tennessee Williams and Elia Kazan: A Collaboration in the Theatre*. Cambridge: Cambridge University Press, 1992.

Nelson, Benjamin, *Tennessee Williams: His Life and Work*. London: Peter Owen, 1961.

Paller, Michael, *Gentleman Callers: Tennessee Williams, Homosexuality, and Mid-Twentieth-Century Drama*. London and New York: Palgrave Macmillan, 2005.

Palmer, R. Barton, and William Robert Bray, *Hollywood's Tennessee: The Williams Films and Postwar America*. Austin: University of Texas Press, 2009.

Robinson, Marc, *The Other American Drama*. Cambridge: Cambridge University Press, 1994.

Saddik, Annette, *The Politics of Reputation: The Critical Perception of Tennessee Williams' Later Plays*. London: Associated University Press, 1998.

St Just, Maria, *Five O'Clock Angel: Letters of Tennessee Williams to Maria St Just*. New York: Penguin, 1990.

Savran, David, *Communists, Cowboys and Queers: The Politics of Masculinity in the Work of Arthur Miller and Tennessee Williams*. Minneapolis: University of Minnesota Press, 1992.

Smith, William, and Suzanne Marrs, *My Friend Tom: The Poet-Playwright Tennessee Williams*. Jackson: University of Mississippi Press, 2012.

Smith-Howard, Alycia, and Greta Heintzelman (eds), *Tennessee Williams: A Literary Reference to His Life and Work*. New York: Facts on File, 2005.

Spoto, Donald, *The Kindness of Strangers: The Life of Tennessee Williams*. New York: Da Capo Press, 1997.

Thompson, Judith, *Tennessee Williams's Plays: Memory, Myth, and Symbol*. New York: Peter Lang, 1989.

Tischler, Nancy, *Student Companion to Tennessee Williams*. Westport: Greenwood, 2000.

—, *Tennessee Williams: Rebellious Puritan*. New York: Citadel, 1961.

Vannatta, Denis, *Tennessee Williams: A Study of the Short Fiction*. Boston: Twayne Publishers, 1988.

Williams, Dakin, and Shepherd Mead, *Tennessee Williams: An Intimate Biography*. New York: Arbor House, 1983.

Williams, Edwina Dakin, as told to Lucy Freeman, *Remember Me to Tom*. New York: Putnam, 1963.

Volumes and Collections

Arnott, Catherine M. (ed.), *File on Tennessee Williams*. London: Methuen, 1985.

Bloom, Harold (ed.), *The Glass Menagerie: Modern Critical Interpretations*. New York: Chelsea House, 1988.

Devlin, Albert J. (ed.), *Conversations with Tennessee Williams*. Jackson: University of Mississippi Press, 2000.

Kolin, Philip C. (ed.), *Confronting Tennessee Williams's A Streetcar Named Desire: Essays in Critical Pluralism*. Westport: Greenwood Press, 1993.

Kolin, Philip C., and Colby H. Kullman (eds), *Speaking on Stage: Interviews with Contemporary American Playwrights*. Tuscaloosa: University of Alabama Press, 1996.

Kolin, Philip C., and Douglas B. Chambers (ed.), 'Special Issue: The Legacy of Tennessee Williams', *Southern Quarterly: A Journal of the Arts in the South*, Vol. 48, No. 4 (2011), pp. 5–138.

Martin, Robert A. (ed.), *Critical Essays on Tennessee Williams*. New York: G. K. Hall, 1997.

Roudané, Matthew (ed.), *The Cambridge Companion to Tennessee Williams*. Cambridge: Cambridge University Press, 1997.

Stanton, Stephen S. (ed.), *Tennessee Williams: A Collection of Critical Essays*. Englewood: Prentice Hall, 1977.

Tharpe, Jac (ed.), *Tennessee Williams: A Tribute*. Jackson: University Press of Mississippi, 1977.

Voss, Ralph F. (ed.), *Magical Muse: Millennial Essays on Tennessee Williams*. Tuscaloosa: University of Alabama Press, 2002.

Wilmeth, Don, and Christopher Bigsby (eds), *The Cambridge History of American Theatre: Vol. III: Post-World War II to the 1990s*. Cambridge: Cambridge University Press, 1998.

Windham, Donald (ed.), *Tennessee Williams' Letters to Donald Windham, 1940–1965*. London: Brown Thrasher, 1996.

Articles and Book Chapters

Adler, Thomas P., 'Tennessee Williams's "Personal Lyricism": Toward an Androgynous Form', in William W. Demastes (ed.), *Realism and the American Dramatic Tradition*, Tuscaloosa: University of Alabama Press, 1996, pp. 172–88.

Arrell, Douglas, 'Homosexual Panic in *Cat on a Hot Tin Roof*', *Modern Drama*, Vol. 51, No. 1 (2008), pp. 60–72.

Bak, John S., '"Sneakin' and Spyin'" from Broadway to the Beltway: Cold War Masculinity, Brick, and Homosexual Existentialism', *Theatre Journal*, Vol. 56 (2004), pp. 225–49.

—, '*A Streetcar Named Desire*: Tennessee Williams and the Semiotics of Rape', *Tennessee Williams Annual Review*, Vol. 10 (2009), pp. 41–72.

Balestrini, Nassim W., 'Shattered Rainbows in Translucent Glass: Tennessee Williams's *The Glass Menagerie* (1945)', in Jerilyn Fisher and Ellen S. Silber (eds), *Women in Literature: Reading through the Lens of Gender*, Westport: Greenwood, 2003, pp. 115–17.

Bibler, Michael P., '"A Tenderness Which Was Uncommon": Homosexuality, Narrative, and the Southern Plantation in Tennessee Williams's *Cat on a Hot Tin Roof*', *Mississippi Quarterly*, Vol. 55, No. 3 (2002), pp. 381–400.

Bray, Robert, '*A Streetcar Named Desire* Interior Panic', *Tennessee Williams Annual Review*, Vol. 9 (2007), pp. 3–5.

Brooks, Daniel, 'Williams's *A Streetcar Named Desire*', *Explicator*, Vol. 65, No. 3 (2007), pp. 177–80.

Cañadas, Ivan, 'The Naming of Jack Straw and Peter Ochello in Tennessee Williams's *Cat on a Hot Tin Roof*', *English Language Notes*, Vol. 42, No. 4 (2005), pp. 57–62.

Cobbe, Elizabeth C., 'Williams's *The Glass Menagerie*', *Explicator*, Vol. 61, No. 1 (2002), pp. 49–51.

Crandell, George, 'Echo Spring: Reflecting the Gaze of Narcissus in Tennessee Williams's *Cat on a Hot Tin Roof*', *Modern Drama*, Vol. 42, No. 3 (1999), pp. 427–41.

—, 'Misrepresentation and Miscegenation: Reading the Racialized Discourse of Tennessee Williams's *A Streetcar Named Desire*', *Modern Drama*, Vol. 40, No. 3 (1997), pp. 337–46.

Debusscher, Gilbert, 'And the Sailor Turned into a Princess: New Light on the Genesis of *Sweet Bird of Youth*', *Studies in American Drama, 1945 to the Present*, Vol. 1 (1986), pp. 25–31.

Di Giuseppe, Rita, 'Monsters: Tennessee Williams, Darwin and Freud', *Quaderni di Lingue e Letterature*, Vol. 16 (1991), pp. 163–73.

Dukore, Bernard F., 'American Abelard: A Footnote to *Sweet Bird of Youth*', *College English*, Vol. 26, No. 8 (1965), pp. 630–4.

—, 'The Cat Has Nine Lives', *Tulane Drama Review (TDR)*, Vol. 8, No. 1 (1963), pp. 95–100.

Earthman, Elise Ann, 'Riding Tennessee Williams' *A Streetcar Named Desire* (1947)', in Jerilyn Fisher, Ellen S. Silber and David Sadker (eds), *Women in Literature: Reading through the Lens of Gender*, Westport: Greenwood, 2003, pp. 274–6.

Everding, Anna Maria, 'Complements of Home: Belle Reve and Elysian Fields in Tennessee Williams's *A Streetcar Named Desire*', in Klaus Stierstorfer (ed.), *Constructions of Home: Interdisciplinary Studies in Architecture, Law, and Literature*, New York: AMS, 2010, pp. 327–37.

Fambrough, Preston, 'Williams's *The Glass Menagerie*', *Explicator*, Vol. 63, No. 2 (2005), pp. 100–2.

Freshwater, Lori, 'Hearts That Refuse to Burn: American Existentialism in the Plays of Arthur Miller and Tennessee Williams', *Arthur Miller Journal*, Vol. 5, No. 1 (2010), pp. 29–45.

Gint, Dirk, 'Torn between "Swedish Sin" and "Homosexual Freemasonry": Tennessee Williams, Sexual Morals and the Closet in 1950s Sweden', *Tennessee Williams Annual Review*, Vol. 11 (2010), n.p.

Gross, Robert F., 'The Pleasures of Brick: Eros and the Gay Spectator in *Cat on a Hot Tin Roof*', *Journal of American Drama and Theater*, Vol. 9, No. 1 (1997), pp. 11–25.

Gunn, Drewey Wayne, 'The Troubled Flight of Tennessee Williams's *Sweet Bird*: From Manuscript through Published Texts', *Modern Drama*, Vol. 24, No. 1 (1981), pp. 26–35.

Hale, Allean, 'How a Tiger Became the Cat', *Tennessee Williams Literary Journal*, Vol. 2, No. 1 (1990–1), pp. 33–6.

Hays, Peter, 'Tennessee Williams's Use of Myth in *Sweet Bird of Youth*', *Educational Theatre Journal*, Vol. 18, No. 3 (1966), pp. 255–8.

Hovis, George, '"Fifty Percent Illusion": The Mask of the Southern Belle in Tennessee Williams's *A Streetcar Named Desire*, *The Glass Menagerie*, and "Portrait of a Madonna"', *Tennessee Williams Literary Journal*, Vol. 5, No. 1 (2003), pp. 11–22.

Hurd, Myles Raymond, 'Cats and Catamites: Patroclus and Williams's *Cat on a Hot Tin Roof*', *Notes on Mississippi Writers*, Vol. 23 (1991), pp. 63–5.

Isaac, Dan, 'Big Daddy's Dramatic Word Strings', *American Speech*, Vol. 40, No. 4 (1965), pp. 272–8.

Kolin, Philip C., 'Obstacles to Communication in *Cat on a Hot Tin Roof*', *Western Speech Communication*, Vol. 39 (1975), pp. 74–80.

—, 'Parallels Between *Desire under the Elms* and *Sweet Bird of Youth*', *Eugene O'Neill Review*, Vol. 13, No. 2 (1989), pp. 23–35.

—, 'Popular Dance Music in Tennessee Williams's *The Glass Menagerie*', *Popular Culture Review*, Vol. 23, No. 1 (2012), pp. 67–74.

—, '"Red Hot" in *A Streetcar Named Desire*', *Notes on Contemporary Literature*, Vol. 19, No. 4 (September 1989), pp. 6–8.

—, '"A River Flows through it": Tennessee Williams and the Mighty Mississippi', *Big Muddy: A Journal of the Mississippi River Valley*, Vol. 12, No. 1 (2012), pp. 7–38.

—, 'The Sobbing DuBois Sisters in Tennessee Williams's *A Streetcar Named Desire*', *Notes on Contemporary Literature*, Vol. 33, No. 3 (2003), pp. 6–8.

—, 'Williams's *A Streetcar Named Desire*', *Explicator*, Vol. 66, No. 1 (2007), pp. 34–7.

—, 'Williams's *Cat on a Hot Tin Roof*', *Explicator*, Vol. 50, No. 4 (Summer 2002), pp. 214–15.

Kullman, Colby H., 'Rule by Power: "Big Daddyism" in the World of Tennessee Williams's Plays', *Mississippi Quarterly*, Vol. 48, No. 4 (1995), pp. 667–76.

McAdam, Ian, 'Remembering Ibsen in Tennessee Williams', *Notes on Contemporary Literature*, Vol. 42, No. 4 (2012), pp. 6–8.

Mayberry, Susan Neal, 'A Study of Illusion and the Grotesque in Tennessee Williams's *Cat on a Hot Tin Roof*', *Southern Studies*, Vol. 22 (1983), pp. 359–65.

Murphy, Brenda A., 'Tennessee Williams', in David Krasner and Molly Smith (eds), *Blackwell Companions to Literature and Culture*, Malden: Blackwell, 2005, pp. 175–91.

Parker, Brian, 'Problems with Boss Finley', *Tennessee Williams Annual Review*, Vol. 9 (2007), pp. 53–65.

—, 'Swinging a Cat', in *Cat on a Hot Tin Roof*, New York: New Directions, 2004, pp. 175–86.

Pawley, Thomas D., 'Where the Streetcar Doesn't Run: The Black World of Tennessee Williams', *Journal of American Drama and Theatre*, Vol. 14, No. 3 (2002), pp. 18–33.

Ribkoff, Fred, and Paul Tyndall, 'On the Dialectics of Trauma in Tennessee Williams' *A Streetcar Named Desire*', *Journal of Medical Humanities*, Vol. 32, No. 4 (2011), pp. 325–37.

Roulet, William M., '*Sweet Bird of Youth*: Williams's Redemptive Ethic', *Cithara*, Vol. 2 (1964), pp. 31–6.

Saddik, Annette J., '"You Just Forge Ahead": Image, Authenticity, and Freedom in the Plays of Tennessee Williams and Sam Shepard', *South Atlantic Review*, Vol. 70, No. 4 (2005), pp. 73–93.

Schulte-Sassa, Linda, 'Fixing a Nation's Problems: When a *Sweet Bird of Youth* Crosses the Line', *Cultural Critique*, Vol. 43 (1999), pp. 13–37.

Schvey, Henry I., 'The Tragic Poetics of Tennessee Williams', *Etudes Anglaises: Grande-Bretagne, Etats-Unis*, Vol. 64, No. 1 (2011), pp. 74–85.

Shackelford, Dean, 'The Truth That Must Be Told: Gay Subjectivity, Homophobia, and Social History in *Cat on a Hot Tin Roof*', *Tennessee Williams Annual Review*, Vol. 1 (1998), pp. 103–8.

Single, Lori Leathers, 'Flying the Jolly Roger: Images of Escape and Selfhood in Tennessee Williams's *The Glass Menagerie*', *Tennessee Williams Annual Review*, Vol. 2 (1999), pp. 69–85.

Smith, William Jay, 'My Friend Tom: The Poet-Playwright Tennessee Williams', *Hopkins Review*, Vol. 4, No. 2 (2011), pp. 162–88.

Thornton, Margaret Bradham, 'Between the Lines: Editing the *Notebooks* of Tennessee Williams', *Theatre History Studies*, Vol. 28 (2008), pp. 7–20.

Vlasopolos, Anca, 'Authorizing History: Victimization in *A Streetcar Named Desire*', *Theatre Journal*, Vol. 38, No. 3 (1986), pp. 322–38.

Voss, Ralph F., 'Tennessee Williams's *Sweet Bird of Youth* and William Inge's *Bus Riley's Back in Town*: Coincidences from a Friendship', *American Drama*, Vol. 15, No. 1 (2006), pp. 62–73.

Waters, Arthur, 'Tennessee Williams: Ten Years Later', *Theatre Arts*, Vol. 39 (1955), pp. 72–3; 96.

Waters, John, 'The Kindness of a Stranger: How a 12-Year-Old from Baltimore Searching for a Bad Influence Discovered Tennessee Williams', *New York Times Book Review*, 19 November 2006, pp. 20–1.

Winchell, Mark Royden, 'Come Back to the Locker Room Ag'in, Brick Honey!', *Mississippi Quarterly*, Vol. 48, No. 4 (1995), pp. 701–12.

Theatre Reviews of *The Glass Menagerie*

Andrews, David Brooks, 'Theater Review: Cambridge's ART illuminates "The Glass Menagerie"', *Metrowest Daily News*, 20 February 2013.

Barnidge, Mary Shen, *Windy City Times*, 19 December 2012.

Billington, Michael, *Guardian*, 14 February 2007.

—, *Guardian*, 17 November 2010.

Brantley, Ben, 'A "Menagerie" Full of Stars, Silhouettes and Weird Sounds', *New York Times*, 23 March 2005.

—, 'The Shape of Memory, Both Fragile and Fierce', *New York Times*, 14 February 2013.

Cavendish, Dominic, *Telegraph*, 24 March 2010.

Crawford, Brett Ashley, *Theatre Journal*, Vol. 57, No. 2 (2005), pp. 308–11.

Delmar, Carol Jean, 'An Innovative "Glass Menagerie" Leaves Questions Unanswered', *Opera Theater Ink*, 20 September 2010.

Fisher, Philip, *British Theatre Guide*, 2007, www.britishtheatreguide.info/reviews/leavesglass-rev

Gantz, Jeffrey, 'Heart of "Glass"', *Boston Globe*, 7 February 2013.

Gardner, Lyn, *Guardian*, 12 March 2010.

'*The Glass Menagerie* to Play at the Booth Theatre', *New York Theatre Guide*, 16 May 2013.

Gregory, Dolores W., *Curtain Up*, 2005, www.curtainup.com/glassmenageriedc. html

Hayford, Justin, '*The Glass Menagerie*, Inside Out', *Chicago Reader*, 12 December 2012.

Hemming, Sarah, *Financial Times*, 18 November 2010.

Henerson, Evan, *Examiner*, 24 September 2010.

Hodgins, Paul, 'Taper's "Glass Menagerie" Reveals New Insights', *Orange County Register*, 21 August 2010.

Isherwood, Charles, 'Gritty Polish for a Tennessee Williams Jewel', *New York Times*, 25 March 2010.

—, 'In a World of Crystal, Flashes of Steel', *New York Times*, 26 May 2009.

Jones, Chris, '"Menagerie" Is a Great Storefront Reinterpretation of a Classic', *Chicago Tribune*, 2 June 2013.

Kubicki, Paul, *Stage and Cinema*, 18 June 2012.

McNulty, Charles, *Los Angeles Times*, 13 September 2010.

Marks, Peter, '"*Glass Menagerie*": Fragile and Beautiful, in All Its Facets', *Washington Post*, 23 July 2004.

Marzullo, Joseph, 'Photo Call: Meet the Cast of Broadway's *The Glass Menagerie*, with Cherry Jones, Celia Keenan-Bolger and Zachary Quinto', *Playbill*, 20 August 2013.

Murray, Matthew, *Talkin' Broadway*, 22 March 2005, www.talkinbroadway.com/world/GlassM.html

Oleksinski, Johnny, *New City Stage*, 15 June 2012.

Reid, Kerry, 'Brother and Sister at Center of an Intimate "Glass Menagerie"', *Chicago Tribune*, 12 October 2011.

Rizzo, Frank, *Variety*, 10 February 2013.

Sava, Oliver, *Time Out Chicago*, 13 December 2012.

Sommer, Elyse, *Curtain Up*, 2005, www.curtainup.com/glassmenagerie10.html

Spencer, Charles, *Telegraph*, 18 November 2010.

Taylor, Paul, *Independent*, 19 November 2010.

Toscano, Michael, *Theater Mania*, 26 July 2004.

Vire, Kris, *Time Out Chicago*, 11 June 2012.

Weiss, Hedy, 'Words of "The Glass Menagerie" Like You've Never Heard Them Before', *Chicago Sun Times*, 2 June 2013.

Theatre Reviews of *A Streetcar Named Desire*

Barry, Helen, *Australian Stage*, 7 September 2009.

Barth, Diana, *Epoch Times*, 11 December 2009.

Billington, Michael, *Guardian*, 28 July 2009.

—, *Guardian*, 29 July 2009.

Brantley, Ben, 'Hey, Stella! You Want to Banter?', *New York Times*, 22 April 2012.

'Cate Blanchett Upstaging Marlon Brando? *A Streetcar Named Desire* Review at BAM', *Faster Times*, 2009.

Coveney, Michael, 'Weisz Struggles to Reveal the Magic in Williams Classic', *Independent*, 29 July 2009.

Dziemianowicz, Joe, *New York Daily News*, 23 April 2012.

Haagensen, Erik, *Backstage*, 22 April 2012.

Hemming, Sarah, *Financial Times*, 30 July 2009.

Hitchings, Henry, 'Rachel Weisz Mesmerizes in Magical *Streetcar Named Desire*', *London Evening Standard*, 29 July 2009.

Huntley, Dent, *Berkshire Review*, 4 August 2009.

Kellaway, Kate, *Observer*, 1 August 2009.

McNulty, Charles, *Los Angeles Times*, 2 December 2009.

MacTavish, Terry, 'Gibson a Riveting Blanche in Faithful Production', *New Zealand Performing Arts Review and Directory*, 29 May 2008.

Rich, Frank, '*A Streetcar Named Desire*: Alec Baldwin Does Battle With Ghosts', *New York Times*, 13 April 1992.

Rooney, David, *Hollywood Reporter*, 22 April 2012.

Sommer, Elyse, *Curtain Up*, 5 December 2009.

Streetcar on Broadway.com. 2012. 27 September 2013.

Wittenberg, Polly, *New York Theatre Guide*, 26 April 2005.

Yarger, Lauren, *Reflections in the Light*, 25 April 2012.

Theatre Reviews of *Cat on a Hot Tin Roof*

Atkinson, Brooks, *New York Times*, 25 March 1955, p. 18; reprinted *New York Theatre Critics' Reviews*, Vol. 16 (1955), p. 344.

Aucoin, Don, 'On Broadway, "Cat on a Hot Tin Roof" Is merely Tepid', *Boston Globe*, 18 January 2013.

Barnes, Clive, *New York Post*, 22 March 1990; reprinted *New York Theatre Critics' Reviews*, Vol. 51 (1990), pp. 353–4.

—, *New York Times*, 25 September 1974, p. 26; reprinted *New York Theatre Critics' Reviews*, Vol. 35 (1974), p. 242.

—, "Roof" Is the Cat's Meow', *New York Post*, 7 March 2008.

Bentley, Eric, *New Republic*, 11 April 1955, pp. 28–9.

Billington, Michael, *Guardian*, 4 February 1988; reprinted *London Theatre Record* (1988), p. 135.

—, *Guardian*, 19 September 2001.

Brantley, Ben, 'Big Daddy's Ego Defies Death and His Family', *New York Times*, 3 November 2003.

—, 'A Storm from the South, Brewing in a Bedroom', *New York Times*, 17 January 2013.

—, 'Yet Another Life for Maggie', *New York Times*, 7 March 2008.

'*Cat on a Hot Tin Roof*', *The Times* (London), 31 January 1958, p. 3.

Chapman, John, '*Cat on a Hot Tin Roof* Beautifully Acted, but a Frustrating Drama', *New York Daily News*, 25 March 1955, p. 65; reprinted *New York Theatre Critics' Reviews*, Vol. 16 (1955), p. 343.

Coleman, Robert, '*Cat on a Hot Tin Roof* Is Likely to Be a Hit', *New York Daily Mirror*, 25 March 1955; reprinted *New York Theatre Critics' Reviews*, Vol. 16 (1955), p. 342.

Dziemianowicz, Joe, *New York Daily News*, 16 January 2013.

—, 'Only James Earl Jones', *New York Daily News*, 7 March 2008.

Edwards, Christopher, *Spectator*, 20 February 1988; reprinted *London Theatre Record*, Vol. 8 (1988), p. 136

Fisher, Luchina, 'Is Broadway Going Black?', ABC News, 1 May 2008.

Geier, Thom, *Entertainment Weekly*, 17 January 2013.

Hawkins, William, 'Cat Yowls High on "Hot Tin Roof"', *New York World-Telegram*, 25 March 1955; reprinted *New York Theatre Critics' Reviews*, Vol. 16 (1955), p. 342.

Henry, William A., *Time*, 2 April 1990, pp. 71–2; reprinted *New York Theatre Critics' Reviews*, Vol. 51 (1990), p. 357.

Kalem, T. E., *Time*, 7 October 1974, p. 107.

Kemp, Peter B., *Independent*, 4 February 1988; reprinted *London Theatre Record* (1988), p. 134.

Kerr, Walter F., *New York Herald Tribune*, 25 March 1955, p. 12; reprinted *New York Theatre Critics' Reviews*, Vol. 16 (1955), p. 342.

King, Francis, *Sunday Telegraph*, 7 February 1988; reprinted *London Theatre Record* (1988), p. 138.

Kissel, Howard, '*Cat* – Down Home Southern Hostility', *New York Daily News*, 3 November 2003.

Kolin, Philip, and Sherry Shao, 'The First *Streetcar* in Mainland China', *Tennessee Williams Literary Journal*, Vol. 2, No. 1 (1990–1), pp. 19–32.

Kroll, Jack, *Newsweek*, 2 April 1990: 54; reprinted *New York Theatre Critics' Reviews*, Vol. 51 (1990), p. 355.

Lahr, John, 'Bitches and Witches: Ulterior Motives in *Cat on a Hot Tin Roof* and *Wicked*', *New Yorker*, 10 November 2003.

'London Sees *Cat*, Opinion Is Divided', *New York Times*, 31 January 1958, p. 21.

Loveridge, Lizzie, *Curtain Up*, 19 September 2001, www.curtainup.com/catonahottinroof.html

Lunden, Jeff, 'A Cooler Roof for a New Cat', *National Public Radio (NPR)*, 17 January 2013.

Luther, Sonja, 'German Translations and Performances of Tennessee Williams's *A Streetcar Named Desire* and *Cat on Hot Tin Roof*: 1955 until 2005'. MA thesis. University of Southern Mississippi, August 2007.

McClain, John, 'Drama Socks and Shocks', *New York Journal American*, 25 March 1955, p. 20; reprinted *New York Theatre Critics' Reviews*, Vol. 16 (1955), p. 344.

Murray, Matthew, *Talkin' Broadway*, 6 March 2008, www.talkinbroadway.com/world/CatTinRoof2008.html

Portantiere, Michael, *Theater Mania*, 21 June 2004, www.theatermania.com/washington-dc-theater/reviews/06-2004/cat-on-a-hot-tin-roof_4846.html

Probst, Leonard, NBC Radio, 25 September 1974; reprinted *New York Theatre Critics' Reviews*, Vol. 35 (1974), p. 246.

Radin, Victoria, *New Statesman*, 19 February 1988; reprinted *London Theatre Record* (1988), p. 137.

Ratcliffe, Michael, *Observer*, 7 February 1988; reprinted *London Theatre Record* (1988), pp. 139–40.

Rich, Frank, *New York Times*, 22 March 1990, p. 81; reprinted *New York Theatre Critics' Reviews*, Vol. 51 (1990), pp. 356–7.

Robertson, Campbell, 'A Black *Cat*, Catching an Elusive Audience', *New York Times*, 20 March 2008.

Schmemann, Serge, 'The Russian Theatregoers Take Tennessee Williams to Their Hearts', *New York Times*, 31 December 1981.

Schwarzbaum, Lisa, 'Meow Mix', *Variety*, 2 November 2003.

Sharp, Christopher, *Women's Wear Daily*, 25 September 1974; reprinted *New York Theatre Critics' Reviews*, Vol. 35 (1974), p. 244.

Siegel, Joel J., WABC TV, 21 March 1990; reprinted *New York Theatre Critics' Reviews*, Vol. 51 (1990), p. 359.

Snyder, Louis, *Christian Science Monitor*, 27 September 1974; reprinted in *New York Theatre Critics' Reviews*, Vol. 35 (1974), pp. 244–5.

Taylor, S., 'The Claws Are Still Sharp', *Independent*, 20 September 2001.

Teachout, Terry, '*Cat* Freshly Skinned', *Wall Street Journal*, 7 March 2008, p. W9.

Tynan, Kenneth, *Curtains*. New York: Atheneum, 1961, pp. 202–4.

Vincentelli, Elisabeth, 'ScarJo Is Red-Hot in "Cat on a Hot Tin Roof"', *New York Post*, 17 January 2013.

Watts, Richard, Jr, 'The Impact of Tennessee Williams', *New York Post*, 25 March 1955, p. 57; reprinted in *New York Theatre Critics' Reviews*, Vol. 16 (1955), pp. 343–4.

Wilson, Edwin, *Wall Street Journal*, 27 September 1974; reprinted *New York Theatre Critics' Reviews*, Vol. 35 (1974), pp. 243–4.

—, *Wall Street Journal*, 26 March 1990; reprinted *New York Theatre Critics' Reviews*, Vol. 51 (1990), p. 356.

Winer, Linda, 'In *Cat*, It's Kathleen's Show', *New York Newsday*, 22 March 1990; reprinted *New York Theatre Critics' Reviews*, Vol. 51 (1990), p. 358.

Wolter, Jürgen, 'Tennessee Williams in Germany', *Tennessee Williams Literary Journal*, Vol. 3 (1995), pp. 9–13.

Theatre Reviews of *Sweet Bird of Youth*

Abarbanel, Jonathan, *Theatre Mania*, 27 September 2012, www.theatermania.com/chicago-theater/reviews/09–2012/sweet-bird-of-youth_62953.html

Bassett, Kate, 'I Wouldn't Get out of Bed for This, Kim', *Independent*, 15 June 2013.

Bemrose, John, *MacLean's*, 2 May 1988.

Billington, Michael, *Guardian*, 12 June 2013.

Corry, John, *New York Times*, 18 June 1982.

Cropper, Martin, 'Unexpected Delights of Character and Charm', *The Times* (London), 10 July 1985.

Gassner, John, *Educational Theatre Journal*, Vol. 11, No. 2 (1959), pp. 117–26.

Gussow, Mel, 'Critic's Notebook: The English Remain Cool to Tennessee Williams', *New York Times*, 1 August 1985.

Hattersley, Roy, 'Endpiece Column', *Guardian*, 31 August 1985.

Healy, Patrick, 'Franco Looks Likely to Join Kidman in "Sweet Bird of Youth" on Broadway', *New York Times*, 2 February, 2011.

—, '"Sweet Bird" Won't Fly on Broadway This Fall; Franco No Longer Involved in Revival', *New York Times*, 30 August 2011.

Hemming, Sarah, *Financial Times*, 14 June 2013.

Jones, Chris, 'Turning the Tables on Tennessee Williams' Story of Fading Beauty', *Chicago Tribune*, 24 September 2012.

Lahr, John, 'Fugitive Mind', *New Yorker*, 18 July 1994.

Lewin, David, 'Bacall: The Need to Live Dangerously', *Courier Mail*, 20 July 1985.

Lochte, Dick, *Los Angeles Magazine*, February 1987.

Mallet, Gina, 'Petit Guignol', *Time*, 15 December 1975.

'New Plays on Broadway' *Time*, 23 March 1959.

Nightingale, Benedict, *New Statesman*, 19 July 1985.

—, 'Off Season Is High Season for Theater in London', *New York Times*, 11 August 1985.

O'Toole, Fintan, *Irish Times*, 5 September 2003.

'The Poet of Obsession', *Harper's Bazaar*, April 1985.

'Review: *Sweet Bird of Youth*/Goodman Theatre', *New City Stage*, 24 September 2012.

Selznick, Daniel, 'London Digs Deeper into Familiar Plays', *Christian Science Monitor*, 21 September 1994.

Vire, Kris, *Time Out Chicago*, 27 September 2012.

Walker, Tim, *Telegraph*, 16 June 2012.

Film and Television Reviews

Brennan, Patricia, '*Sweet Bird of Youth*: Rip Torn Putting His Accent on the Bigot Boss' (NBC production), *Washington Post*, 1 October 1989.

Carter, Alan, 'Tennessee Williams's *Sweet Bird of Youth*' (NBC production), *People Weekly*, 2 October 1989.

Erikson, Hal, *Cat. All Movie Guide*, movies.msn.com

Leonard, John, '*Sweet Bird of Youth*' (NBC production), *New York Times*, 2 October 1989.

O'Connor, John J., 'Elizabeth Taylor's Star Turn as Williams's Aging Star' (NBC production), *New York Times*, 29 September 1989.

—, 'From Cable to Air: *Cat*', *New York Times*, 24 June 1985.

—, 'The Tribute Smacks of Exploitation', *New York Times*, 5 December 1976, D29 *TV, 1984.*

Park, Jeannie, 'Playing *Sweet Bird of Youth*'s Abandoned Love, Cheryl Paris Draws on Her Own Unhappy Past' (NBC production), *People Weekly*, 2 October 1989.

'Putting on the Cat' (1962 film), *Time*, 30 March 1962.

Spoto, Donald, 'Commentary', *Cat on a Hot Tin Roof* (DVD) Warner Home Video. Burbank, CA, 2004.

'Sweet Bird of Youth' (NBC production), *Variety*, 25 October 1989.